PEACEMAKING IN
INTERNATIONAL CONFLICT
Methods & Techniques

PEACEMAKING IN INTERNATIONAL CONFLICT
METHODS & TECHNIQUES

I. William Zartman
J. Lewis Rasmussen
Editors

UNITED STATES INSTITUTE OF PEACE PRESS
Washington, D.C.

The views expressed in this book are those of the authors alone. They do not necessarily reflect views of the United States Institute of Peace.

United States Institute of Peace
1550 M Street NW
Washington, DC 20005

First published 1997

Printed in the United States of America

The paper used in this publication meets the minimum requirements of American National Standard for Information Sciences—Permanence of Paper for Printed Library Materials, ANSI Z39.48-1984.

Library of Congress Cataloging-in-Publication Data
Peacemaking in international conflict : methods and techniques / I. William
    Zartman and J. Lewis Rasmussen, editors.
        p.   cm.
    Includes bibliographical references.
    ISBN 1-878379-61-5 (hardback). — ISBN 1-878379-60-7 (paperback)
    1. Pacific settlement of international disputes. 2. Diplomatic negotiations
in international disputes. 3. Mediation, International. 4. Arbitration,
International. 5. Conflict management—Methodology. I. Zartman, I.
William. II. Rasmussen, J. Lewis, 1963–
JZ4473.P42 1996
327.1'72—DC20

Contents

FOREWORD

Peacemaking, under the best of circumstances, is a complicated and difficult endeavor. Indeed, the general notion of peacemaking now comprises a great many approaches and methods for understanding, managing, and ultimately settling conflicts. This variety of methods is a product of the increasing complexity of international conflict as well as the growing experience of the international community in interventions in support of resolving intrastate or regional conflicts. While wars in times past were largely the province of august heads of state and foreign ministers representing powerful nations and grand alliances, conflict in the twentieth century evolved to bring destruction and death to mass publics and threaten stability on a global scale.

Fortunately, we are not helpless in confronting such organized violence and social chaos. Ever since nation-states first went to war with each other, scholars in the social sciences and members of the foreign policymaking establishment have developed a vital body of knowledge about how to curb the destructiveness of state-organized aggression. Over time, as international wars became more extensive and complex, the relevant body of knowledge has become more elaborate, and approaches to peacemaking have become more diversified through their sheer number.

Making violence-prone adversaries put a halt to acts of carnage and destruction does not always rely on detailed analyses or the invocation of time-honored principles and techniques. In many cases, snap judgments and plain luck guide a peacemaker's tactics and stratagems. Nevertheless, peacemakers today can arrive at their assignments with an intellectual arsenal of knowledge, theories, and techniques that have proved successful in managing previous conflicts.

The objective of this volume, so ably assembled and edited by Professor William Zartman and Lewis Rasmussen, is to present state-of-the-art approaches to peacemaking. Some of the methods explored in this collection of essays are time-honored and well known, such as negotiation, bargaining, and third-party mediation. Some are relatively new to the peacemaking community, such as conflict transformation and peacebuilding, problem-solving workshops, and training in conflict resolution techniques. What they all share is their intent to bring together analytical and prescriptive components.

This book is not a *tour d'horizon* of peacemaking methods and techniques. Rather, the approaches assembled here were selected for their durability and effectiveness in diverse conflict settings. Fortunately, the editors were well placed to make their selections, after extensive consultation with specialists in the field and appropriate Institute staff.

I. William Zartman is well known to specialists in conflict and peace studies as director of both the African Studies and Conflict Resolution programs at Johns Hopkins University's Nitze School of Advanced International Studies and a preeminent scholar on conflict resolution. Bill brings to this project a lifetime of distinguished scholarship and writing not only on Africa's various national and subnational conflicts but on the cognitive and policymaking dimensions of peacemaking and conflict resolution. Lewis Rasmussen, program officer in the Institute's Education and Training Program, has been an invaluable link between the book's analytical themes and the practical aspects of the Institute's ongoing efforts to train officials in the foreign policymaking community in how to bring warring parties to the table in order to make peace.

We must also acknowledge the contributions to this undertaking of Hrach Gregorian, who served as one of the project's originators and who provided expert advice in the selection of approaches. A special note of thanks also goes to Rachel Barbour, program specialist in the Institute's Education and Training Program, who assisted in the research for the contributions from our in-house authors, and to Peter Pavilionis of the Publications Department, who ably shepherded this complex project through the editorial process. Thanks also to reference librarians Rebecca Caponi and James Cornelius for their expert bibliographic research.

Since the Institute's principal mission is to educate as well as to advise in matters of international conflict management and resolution, we wanted the book's chapters to reach as broad a readership as possible. Consequently, this volume reflects the editors' overriding concern that the approaches presented herein do more than provide academic investigations of the origins and dynamics of large-scale aggression; their objective has been to offer a practical repertoire of methods peacemakers typically use to understand the various dimensions of conflicts—large and small—and the methods used to bring them to an end.

Those readers interested in complementary perspectives on conflict and peacemaking might also wish to explore another volume recently published by the Institute, *Managing Global Chaos: Sources of and Responses to International Conflict*, edited by Chester Crocker and Fen Hampson with Pamela Aall.

In sum, *Peacemaking in International Conflict* represents an important addition to a growing body of analytical and practical writings on approaches to international conflict resolution. The essays in the following pages present with scholarly care, yet practical relevance, the kinds of issues that the staff and scholars at the United States Institute of Peace are preoccupied with daily in their efforts to understand and educate those professionally concerned with international peacemaking.

Richard H. Solomon, President
United States Institute of Peace

Peacemaking in International Conflict

Methods & Techniques

Toward the Resolution of International Conflicts

I. William Zartman

On the edge of the millennium, the methods of conflict have been more brutal and the methods of conflict resolution more sophisticated than ever before, leaving a tremendous gap between reality and theory that remains to be filled. Courage and commitment are most needed to use the tools required to meet the challenge—to move people away from their proclivity to violence and nations away from the temptation to war. To see virtue in these values and purposes is a matter of choice and conscience. To build an awareness of the many tools and techniques that are available to pursue this goal is the purpose of this book.

This is a book about international conflict resolution. It concerns conflict among states and nations and therefore deals with their power and their interests. It also concerns conflicts among people, who act in the name of states and nations, and therefore concerns basic human interactions and reactions. It bridges and unites these two areas of interest, as it looks for lessons that each one has for the other. It recognizes the inevitability of conflict among sovereign and nonsovereign groups speaking in the name of peoples or nations, but it presents ways in which that conflict can be first managed, moving it from violent to political manifestations, and then resolved, transforming it and removing its causes. This book presents the state of the art of the subject in descriptions, generalizations, and concepts, organized according to different methods of international conflict resolution, with the aim of emphasizing their usefulness and limitations.

THE CHALLENGES OF THE POST–COLD WAR CONTEXT

The Cold War had barely become history when it was already commonplace to note that its passing had opened an era of vicious "little" conflicts, uncontained by superpower restraints and impervious to regional ministrations. Although regional conflicts and national struggles for power had been used by the Cold War protagonists for their own purposes (or to thwart their opponent's suspected purposes), these conflicts had also been kept under careful control by the Cold War's system of world order, lest they turn into tails that wag the dogs of global war. When these constraints suddenly vanished at the end of the 1980s, conflicts of many types sprang forth again. Many of these conflicts arose over the inheritance of a former communist-supported domestic order—Angola, Mozambique, Ethiopia, Somalia, Cambodia, Yugoslavia, Armenia, Tajikistan, Afghanistan, Georgia, Moldova, and Nicaragua, among others.

Elsewhere (and in some of the same cases), conflicts arose from deep-rooted antagonisms that had lain dormant or been held in check. Such antagonisms rise and fall according to external conditions. When national systems of order break down, people fall back on ethnic or confessional identities that exclude others with whom they formerly lived in harmony. When economic conditions worsen and the national resource pie shrinks, people (again, often mobilized by a selective sense of identity) fight over the scraps. International pressures for competitive, pluralist political and economic systems can actually augment the problem, creating a new context of conflict that the societies cannot handle productively. These conditions gave rise to conflict in Algeria, Rwanda, Burundi, Somalia, Ethiopia, Liberia, Sierra Leone, Lebanon, Yugoslavia, Albania, Afghanistan, Sri Lanka, India, Guatemala, Haiti, El Salvador, Mexico, Peru, and Colombia, to name the more prominent among them. (On conflict resolution measures in some of these conflicts, see Zartman 1995b and Damrosch 1993.)

The other inheritance from the Cold War besides unsupported authoritarian systems is the sea of arms that has flowed into potential conflict areas. Africa, the former Soviet littoral from Afghanistan to Yugoslavia, Southeast Asia, and Andean and Central America are all awash with arms (Boutwell, Klare, and Reed 1995). In some places, an AK-47 is cheaper than a bucket of grain, and yard sales of ex-Soviet heavy armaments are a thriving discount business. While conflicts are pursued and atrocities committed using even the most primitive weapons, the widespread availability of modern weaponry has provided the means to make so many people mass murderers.

The one striking limitation on the conflicts of the 1990s is that, despite spillover effects and "neighborhood" involvement, they have not been the kind of classic interstate conflicts over causes such as boundaries, territory, hostile regimes, or resources. Only the second Gulf War, between Iraq and Kuwait, involved interstate aggression; as such, it was the last of the Cold War conflicts (see Zartman and Kremenyuk 1995). Indeed, neighbors tend to regard conflicts with apprehension, fearing that there too (but for the grace of God) go they; conflicts do tend to become regionalized, not by unbridled aggression but by "contamination," as in West Africa (Liberia, Sierra Leone), Central Africa (Rwanda, Burundi), the Horn of Africa (Ethiopia, Somalia, Sudan), Central Asia (Afghanistan, Tajikistan), Central America (Mexico, Guatemala, Nicaragua, El Salvador), and the Balkans. (For a good debate on the issue of contamination, see Lake and Rothchild 1997.)

Everywhere, the limits of the new situation are being tested. How much unrestrained conflict and brutality will the international community allow? How immutable are the existing states and their boundaries? How widespread is the right of self-determination, and who may claim it? How long may a rapacious ruler take his turn at the trough to enrich himself before someone replaces him, and will the replacement be domestically, regionally, or internationally imposed? Until restive populations and ambitious actors have learned the new rules of the international and national communities, and until new and effective systems of world and domestic order are recognized, conflict over values worth fighting for, such as sovereignty, liberty, self-determination, identity, and power, will continue to take place.

The conflict occurs on two levels—opposing sides fight for the specific and the general, the case and the principle, the exception and the precedent. Serbs in Yugoslavia are fighting for a Greater Serbia against Croats and Bosnians fighting for recognition of established states and boundaries. But the Serbs are also fighting to establish an ethnic (nation) state and the Bosnians a multiethnic state with a constructed national identity principle (with the Croats' putting a foot on each principle). The conflict arises because old limits, criteria, and principles were broken and new ones are being tried. Southern Sudanese wrestle with the advisability of secession, spurred not only by the increased aggressiveness of the Muslim Sudanese of the north but also by the idea that the new Eritrean precedent for secession might apply to them as well.

Sometimes, old criteria and principles applicable to the case in point are not called into question (as yet), but the fact that limits applicable to other cases have been challenged raises the possibility of new challenges in new areas. Saddam Hussein invaded Kuwait not because the restrictions against aggression had been relaxed, but because other restrictions on state behavior had been broken without attracting an international reaction—so why not neighborly annexation? Extremists in the Rwandan government wiped out a sixth of their population not because restrictions on genocide had been erased, but because international enforcement of other supposedly universal national norms in places like Burundi, Somalia, and Sudan had proved uncertain. More than anything else, it is the uncertainty following the passing of the old order that allows conflict to break out with such abandon at the end of the millennium.

THE CHALLENGE OF THE POST–COLD WAR CONTEXT—MANAGEMENT

Thus, the absence of certainty about world order and of commitment to enforce norms and limits on deviant behavior has allowed conflict to rise in the 1990s. Not only is the international response weak, its very weakness causes an increasingly stronger challenge in a vicious circle of action and inaction. With the lifting of the nuclear balance of terror and the lessening of Cold War tensions, the world's leaders have lost interest in mediation and engagement as ways to impose restraint. The basic cause is doubtless a sense of relaxation and relief that follows half a century of hot-war conflagrations and Cold War tensions, a political demobilization akin to that which characterized the latter half of the 1940s, between the world conflict orders of World War II and the Cold War.

This demobilization breaks down into many specific components. The absence of a system of world order has left leaders and their publics alike without a sense of the shape of the world, without a notion of friends and enemies, even without an idea of friendly and inimical behavior on which to base appropriate reactions. At the domestic level, notions such as "sovereignty as responsibility" turn established principles upside down in the search for better guidelines for behavior. During the transition, such notions also reinforce uncertainty (Deng et al. 1996; Obasanjo 1991). It is unclear where activities to manage and resolve conflict, and the principles that should guide them, fit into this context of uncertain order.

In the absence of a world order to defend, there is no sense of appropriate solutions. While most mediators work toward any solution that the parties to a conflict will accept, they usually have some guidelines of appropriateness and some notions of stability. Third parties in the Namibian and Rhodesian conflicts would accept any outcome acceptable to the parties as long as it was independence, and they were ultimately successful; mediators in the Eritrean, Cypriot, and Sri Lankan conflicts were not so sure where stability lay, and they failed. The same absence of clear solutions has dogged the many attempts at mediation throughout much of the former communist world, from Chechnya to Yugoslavia. Mediators and parties alike are still experimenting with the requirement for stability in solutions. Elections are deemed the appropriate mechanism for conflict resolution and the symbolic indication of conflict management from violent to political means, but the aftermath of such elections remains unclear. The Angolan experience of 1992 taught that a winner-take-all outcome was not wise, yet the Mozambican election of 1994 was followed by a winner-take-all government. When norms for management and resolution are under change or still being worked out, conflicts are hard to handle.

Since contemporary conflicts tend to be internal, the legitimacy of intervention is questionable. In a democratic age, people are sovereign and they get the government they deserve. In the absence of law-based world rule, violence is still the ultimate means of asserting basic internal rights and values, and so there is a strong argument for letting conflict run its course. Some things are worth fighting for—and against. The weak international law that does exist protects the sovereignty of states and their internal affairs from foreign interference, and for good reason: Relaxing the inhibitions on internal interference leaves power unrestrained and invites the strong to overrule the weak. The prohibition also protects would-be intervenors from involvement in cultures and arenas that are not their own. Ultimately, all these arguments are half-sound, reasoned justifications for inaction that are trumped by the need for action and responsibility.

In the absence of established systems of order and consensus on solutions, one defends one's own interests. Yet there is no clear sense of interest in dealing with the present era's many conflicts. It is clear to decision makers and the public alike that Rwanda does not fall into the geographic area of U.S. interests, and the one outside state that seems concerned—France— is widely decried for its involvement. It is not even clear to many that the former Yugoslavia fits into U.S. interests, as it resides just outside the area of the North Atlantic Treaty Organization's purview; even those European countries that see themselves concerned—Germany and France—are criticized for their narrow-minded engagement. The compelling interest to get involved in messy internal conflicts, where peacemaking, peacekeeping, and peace enforcement are likely to be viewed as unfriendly behavior by all sides, is nowhere apparent.

The lack of a clear sense of interest and legitimacy results in an absence of public commitment. All these doubts and arguments, repeated authoritatively by world leaders, feed the reaction behind which the leaders hide. Yet many polls have shown that the public is strongly committed to the management and resolution of international conflicts for reasons of both morality and interest, under these specific conditions: when leaders show that they know what they are doing, have a plan, explain it confidently, and pursue it deliberately (Yankelovich 1994; Nelson 1992). Conflict management and resolution are good politics, good business, and good morality, and need to be sold as such. A commitment to these goals allows leaders to turn conflict into an occasion for decisiveness and allows parties to get on with productive activity. It reduces debilitating conflict in three ways: by dealing with the specific conflict; by contributing to the construction of the principles of order; and, in turn, by reducing the ambiguity and uncertainty that give rise to conflict. It is a calling of courage and compassion, a hard defense of basic interests under dangerous conditions, a contribution to local reconciliation and global leadership.

The contribution of this book is to display the tools and skills available when that calling is exercised. It begins with Lewis Rasmussen's survey of the changes in the environment of global politics and how they have reshaped conflict resolution approaches. This is followed by an understanding of how the field of conflict resolution has evolved into such a broad discipline, as described by Louis Kriesberg. The current state of the art has built explicit bodies of knowledge, concepts, and prescriptions out of a number of components, combining politics, psychology, sociology, economics, and historical experience. Both hard-nosed interest and soft-handed charity join in providing insights and inspiration on human behavior. These insights come together at a time when there is a greater—if challengingly incomplete—knowledge about human interaction and an increased—if imperfectly coordinated—involvement of many levels of society in the interactions of foreign relations.

Officials undertake three major types of activity to manage and resolve conflicts, as presented by Daniel Druckman, Jacob Bercovitch, and Richard Bilder. Although these activities in international conflict resolution are generally carried out by states and their representatives, the mechanisms, effects, and relations are just as applicable in interpersonal relationships and are based on a well-grounded understanding of social and human behavior. Bargaining and negotiation compose the processes parties undertake to resolve their differences directly, overcoming conflict and establishing cooperation. Parties need specific tactics and strategies to move from conflicting to reconciling mindsets and behavior. When they are unable to do so, they need the involvement of third parties through mediation and conciliation. The introduction of a third party creates a triangle of relationships that complicates—but also helps to facilitate—reconciliation, requiring special tactics and relations. When parties are unable to reconcile or be reconciled, but only plead their antagonistic causes, the reconciling decision is transferred to another third party, an arbitrator or adjudicator. This action makes the third party's decision binding, leaving it to the external third party, rather than to the adversaries themselves, to find an appropriate solution to the problem.

In the interstices of these activities lie other approaches to conflict resolution, generally practiced by nonofficials, as presented by Herbert Kelman, Ronald Fisher, and Cynthia Sampson. Reconciliation efforts deal with the affective aspects of conflict, which are often more powerful driving forces than the cold items at issue. While the escalation and de-escalation of conflict alone cannot resolve the issues in contention, they provide the context and atmosphere that serve to admit resolution into the equation. Interactive conflict resolution uses the third party to help conflicting parties work out the nest of relationships in which the conflict is situated. It presents techniques whereby the third party can take a facilitating role in improving the relations among the parties. Faith-based approaches dig most deeply into the ambiance surrounding the conflict and into the motivations of third parties, whatever their specific role.

In the third part of this book, practitioners, represented by Cameron Hume, Andrew Natsios, and Eileen Babbitt, evaluate their roles in international conflict resolution. Official diplomacy at its best combines the techniques of two-party and third-party negotiation and mediation with the insights of reconciliation and the motives of dedication. Self-interest and others' interests need to be combined to move the parties (including one's own state) off the course of conflict and toward other means of achieving goals. Nongovernmental organizations occupy a gamut of positions from unofficial (private) diplomacy to quasi-state action, usually without the means of negative pressure that a state can sometimes wield and often without even the means of positive inducement, other than appeals to the parties' enlightened self-interest and heightened self-esteem. Training programs convey these skills and approaches in packages that range from short courses to longer training sessions to higher education programs. In so doing, they, too, practice conflict resolution, building skills and reflexes in preparation for the real thing.

KNOWLEDGE AND PRACTICE

Conflict

The very notion of training is based on a belief, still current since the writings of the encyclopedists in the late eighteenth century, that conflict resolution is a skill that can be transmitted, not (as earlier believed) an inborn personality trait (de Felice 1987; de Callières 1963). But myths die slowly, and even today some practitioners believe their skills cannot be analyzed or transmitted. While some personalities are certainly better suited to managing conflict than others, management and resolution comprise such a broad range of activities that there is a role for just about any personality, and all of them can benefit from analysis, training, and the study of seized and missed opportunities. While any situation—like any person—has its unique elements, no situation—like any person—is totally unique. Keys to understanding how to deal with a situation come from examining it in a comparative or generalized (conceptual) context.

The knowledge we have about what works and what does not work in conflict resolution is based primarily on studies of what practitioners do. (The only other source of data is experiments, whose relevant results are presented in Daniel Druckman's chapter.) That information is either examined for regularities, correlations, and causal sequences—that is, used inductively—or used to test ideas, hunches, and hypotheses—that is, used deductively. Only when information about practitioners' activities becomes ordered and focused does it become knowledge, and only as knowledge—not as isolated anecdotes—can it be useful in the maintenance and improvement of conflict resolution practices. So the cycle runs from practice to knowledge and back again, and that is the only way humanity improves itself in any field.

The knowledge reported in this work is new when seen as an accumulation. Probably none of the isolated acts that provide data for this knowledge is new, however; even the most modern twist on conflict resolution has doubtless been used somewhere in the past, perhaps accidentally, perhaps consciously. What is new is the discovery of regularities, correlations, and causal sequences on the basis of newly accumulated, ordered, and focused information, an aspect of the entire subject that is every bit as exciting as the resolution of a particular conflict by a practitioner. Indeed, the field of conflict resolution was only recently identified by name during the interwar period, and the component activity of negotiation was so named (in that meaning) only in the eighteenth century. (Several languages have not even named either term as yet.) Other components of the field—prenegotiations, conflict management, positive-sum outcomes, ripeness, formulas, to name a few—have been discovered and identified only in the past few decades, although of course they have existed—unnamed— as long as there has been human interaction.

Epistemologically, an object does not exist until it has a name, and it cannot be the subject of meaningful communication until its name, with its attendant definition, has been broadly accepted. In this new field, many aspects require definition at the outset. The subject of this work, conflict resolution, refers to removing the causes as well as the manifestations of a conflict between parties and eliminating the sources of incompatibility in their positions. This process is a long-term proposition, for, in the last analysis, only time resolves conflicts. Conflict management refers to eliminating the violent and violence-related means of pursuing the conflict, leaving it to be worked out on the purely political level. Conflict transformation means replacing conflict with positive relationships, such as satisfaction, cooperation, empathy, and interdependence, between parties. Peace-related terms are defined by their UN usage: "peacemaking" refers to diplomatic efforts to handle conflict according to Chapter VI of the UN Charter; "peacekeeping," to forces interpositioned with the parties' consent to monitor a peace agreement not specifically mentioned in the charter; "peace-enforcement," to military efforts to bring conflicting parties under control, as provided for under Chapter VII; and "peacebuilding," to structural measures to preclude a relapse into conflict (Boutros-Ghali 1995, 45–46).

By identifying important questions and seeking appropriate answers, we discover explanations for outcomes produced in the past and therefore prescriptions on how to produce outcomes desired in the future. Such explanations and prescriptions are likely to become more and more complex as we discover variables that intervene between cause and effect. That complexity brings explanations closer to reality but must be balanced against simplicity and directness in order to be useful and nonidiosyncratic. More and more knowledge is being created about the ways of conflict resolution; that very knowledge, in turn, opens up more opportunities to ask new questions, create new countermeasures, and find new answers. Such knowledge is not a procrustean bed, a fixed set of rules and regulations, or a body of incontrovertible doctrine and dogma. Rather, it invites better creativity and constructive innovation to employ an economy of knowledge to make better solutions to conflict.

One major objection can be validly raised, however, to the claim that knowledge is accumulating. The claim assumes that, despite changing world conditions, human interactions are similar enough for knowledge to accumulate and be relevant across time. Specifically, many of the lessons about conflict resolution were formulated during the Cold War, therefore findings from that era are claimed to be applicable to post–Cold War conflict resolution. That claim needs to be examined critically. Where findings about conflict management depend on a structural context defined by two superpowers, those findings should be reevaluated. Where the findings are independent of a specific structural context, however, they can be considered relevant and examined for the insights they bring.

Yet, even bipolar confrontations have been studied in comparison with other conflicts and found to yield useful knowledge (Armstrong 1993; Kriesberg 1992). Much of the conflict resolution literature derives from a tradition and an approach independent of the Cold War and offers even more contexts for comparative assessments of conflicts now that the bipolar era has passed. In short, the Cold War was the aberration in international conflict, not in the ongoing efforts at conflict resolution.

Resolution

Conflict demands resolution, but not because of the evil of its perpetrators—although incorrigibility and venality often make things worse. Were evil alone the problem, exemplars of the international community could band together, level a collective finger against them, and ban their nefarious machinations. Such was the prevailing wisdom in a previous era among such seasoned but idealistic statesmen as President Woodrow Wilson, Secretary of State Frank Kellogg, and French premier Aristide Briand. The experience of the intervening hot and cold wars has taught us not only something about how to resolve conflicts, but also that such earlier hopes were misguided. Conflict is a permanent feature of social and political interaction, and it often occurs for good reasons (Coser 1956; Bernard et al. 1957). The resolution of conflict depends on recognizing the concerns of the parties. "[T]he great secret of negotiation is to bring out prominently the common advantage to both parties of any proposal, and so to link these advantages that they may appear equally balanced to both parties, . . . to harmonize the interests of the parties concerned," wrote François de Callières to Louis XV in one of the first and still authoritative writings on negotiation (de Callières 1963, 110).

Thus, conflict resolution depends on a recognition that parties have at least some interest in the conflict, even though they may also be caught up in it in ways beyond their interests, and that these interests need to be met, outweighed, and reduced in order to be reconciled (Udalov 1995; Zartman 1995b). Parties' interests need to be addressed and their interest in reconciliation enhanced. Before this can take place, though, the parties must be brought to understand that reconciliation is not surrender (otherwise, conflict resolution would have a deservedly bad name) and interests are not the same as needs. Some approaches have suggested that a conflict can be transformed (and as a result disappear) only after the basic human needs of one or both of the sides are satisfied (Burton 1990; Azar and Burton 1986). Yet human needs are ever only temporarily satisfied: those sated today may be hungry tomorrow, the people who know who they are today may wonder tomorrow, those who have found dignity today may lose it tomorrow, and so on. Since only time resolves conflicts, time can also invent or revive conflict. If human agents can help time resolve by providing postconflict outcomes that at least address the question of durability—producing solutions that are processes and mechanisms, not judgments and awards—they will have made a respectable contribution to the well-being of the conflict's inheritor generation, which will be thereafter on its own.

Parties to the conflict may be able to do this by themselves, although someone—an internal party of "doves," the opponent in the conflict, or a friendly third-party adviser—needs to draw each conflicting party's attention away from the conflict itself as a means of attaining its interests and toward alternative means through reconciliation. If conflicting parties have interests, so do intervening third parties. Again, some external parties may well have an interest in continuing the conflict, and others may have an interest in one side in the conflict (Touval and Zartman 1985; Zartman and Touval 1996). Were the intervenors who favored resolution without any interests of their own in reconciliation, they would be disarmed indeed.

Even the "mediators without muscle," humanitarian agencies and goodwilled individuals, have an interest in defending their own efforts and profession by bringing conflict away from violence and toward resolution. The Vatican had powerful interests in mediating the Beagle Channel dispute between Argentina and Chile, the Carter Center had strong interests in mediating a cease-fire in southern Sudan, and the conflict management programs at George Mason University and Johns Hopkins University's School of Advanced International Studies had their own interests in their diverse efforts at reconciliation in the Liberian civil war (see Princen 1992; Touval and Zartman 1989). These interests may be simply in arriving at an agreement, not in any particular agreement, although most third parties also have an idea of what constitutes a stable and durable resolution and thus have an interest in seeing it achieved for the sake of their reputations.

Conflict resolution needs all the help it can get. Since parties to a conflict typically are already well entrenched in their conflicting behavior, for reasons they have often repeated to themselves to justify their resistance toward the other party, all the knowledge that can be brought to bear in favor of conflict resolution is badly needed and all the hands that can be brought to the task can be helpful. The only requirement is that multiple efforts be well coordinated so that they do not work against one another or allow conflicting parties to play the mediators against one another. At the official level, this requirement means cooperation among assisting parties. On a broader level, it means cooperation between official and unofficial efforts.

While some agencies are better organized for conflict resolution than others, and some states better positioned to handle a particular conflict than others, conflict resolution is everybody's business. It should be part of the role of global leadership and be shared among concerned states and international agencies. Above all, since conflict resolution is a crucial component of global leadership, it should be a leading plank in the foreign policy of the state with the widest global interests, the United States. It can be done quietly or assertively, directly or indirectly, unilaterally or cooperatively, as the particular circumstances require. However it is done, U.S. political leaders must always be cognizant of the fact that it is the country's role, part of America's traditions and calling, and expected by other members of the community of nations. The United States is best placed to help other parties out of their conflicts, and U.S. foreign policy has been at its finest when it has done so.

A cooperative security system, which enlists the collaboration of the major powers in conjunction with regional security organizations, is needed to meet the challenge of the decade (Zartman and Kremenyuk 1995). Conflict management and resolution should be the leitmotif in every major state's foreign policy, helping each other in the process. The U.S.-mediated negotiations at Dayton, which produced the Bosnian peace agreement in Paris, were the occasion for unseemly squabbles among the two host countries and others regarding which one had made the largest contribution to peace.

In fact, all of them were gravely deficient in peacemaking earlier and could claim significant contributions to the peace process only in the end.

But states, too, need help in their efforts to resolve conflicts. They need help both in practicing the calling and in focusing on broader, positive-sum benefits rather than narrow interpretations of their interests. Private parties can prepare and supplement state efforts and may have an advantage in overcoming problems of legitimacy in officials' efforts to deal with internal conflicts. Because private actors are not geared to producing final results in the same sense as official mediation, they can work on the problem longer. The Sant'Egidio community undertook mediation that no state could do in the Mozambican and Algerian conflicts (although it was backed and surrounded by official efforts in the first case), and Professor Herbert Kelman's long efforts preparing Israelis and Palestinians for the peace process have gradually come to fruition in the 1990s, as analyzed in this volume. Official and unofficial parties need to recognize the legitimate roles the other can play. Once they recognize these roles, they must cooperate.

Dilemmas

It would be good to end here, with a clarion call for more and better cooperation in resolving conflict according to the state of the art and practice summarized here (see also Raiffa 1982). But that step would come too soon, because a final caveat is needed if the righteousness and self-interest that has so often dogged the field is to be avoided. Not only is there a lot that analysts and practitioners still do not know and practice about conflict resolution, but even when the preaching is well practiced, there are inherent dilemmas that have no easy answers.

One is the dilemma of legitimacy. How can intervention be justified if it runs up against the conflicting parties' own interest to pursue the conflict? Even more so, is intervention by anyone in the type of conflict that dominates the 1990s—internal conflict and civil war—legitimate under international law and norms? In response, third parties and the international community can well ask whether the means conflicting parties use to pursue their interests are justifiable as well, whether the use of violence to oppress populations or resist government is not an abuse of a state's or a people's sovereignty. Third parties can arrogate the right to enter these debates, as thinking world citizens should, but they need to recognize the preeminent right of parties to set their own goals and interests.

A second dilemma concerns justice. Peace is sometimes the enemy of justice, and conflict can be ended only at the price of objectively fair outcomes. Such peace, so the objection goes, is illusory: there is no lasting peace without justice. But justice has many referents and is ultimately subjective (Zartman et al. 1996; Kolm 1997). A conflict resolution that perfectly combines peace and justice is as rare as other moments of perfection in human action. Mediators are often—perhaps usually—troubled by the choice between a peace, however temporary, that saves lives and continuing efforts in order to better reconcile interests. Conflict resolution among consenting parties is likely to be achieved only at the cost of letting some of the villains go free, often as the price for their signature. But how much injustice is peace worth?

A third dilemma involves management. Even if the other two dilemmas are avoided, efforts at reducing violence by managing conflict may actually impede its resolution. Eliminating violence in the pursuit of conflict may do nothing to resolve it and may even continue the conflict by rendering it economical to do so. Conflicts that cost little have little reason for settlement; they just simmer along, waiting for the moment when they can boil over. The best moment for resolution would appear to be when the parties to the conflict are stalemated at a high level of intensity from which they cannot unilaterally escalate their way out (Zartman 1989). But conflict management can work against such mutually hurting stalemates.

The fourth is the dilemma of force. Conflict resolution is peacemaking and peacebuilding. But it may also be peace enforcing; even in peacemaking there may be a need for force and threats of force. "*Si vis pacem para bellum* (If you want peace, prepare for war)," said the Romans, who knew something about both. Mediators in the most active phase of intervention (just as the best manipulators will tell you) may have to reinforce the stalemate that makes the parties come to terms: it took the 1973 October War to start the peace process in the Middle East, and nothing less than NATO bombing drove Bosnian combatants to peace in fall 1995. Yet parties cannot be forced to resolve conflicts in the absence of other interests and perceptions. How much force and when it should be applied remain eternal dilemmas of foreign policy, themselves unresolved by the good intentions of peacemakers.

The fifth is the dilemma of power. A myth is circulating that peacemaking is the opposite of power (see Burton 1995). Power is an action designed to move another party in an intended direction (Rubin and Zartman 1996; Dahl 1969; Simon 1969; Tawney 1964; Russell 1938). Persuasion is a form of power. Those who inveigh against "power politics" (a redundant term) merely want to put power in their own hands. Conflict resolution requires power to work, as does any other effort at changing a party's course. The dilemma arises when conflicting parties' actions are changed, or blocked, without their changing their minds. In this case, the mediator or the reconciling party has exercised enough power to accomplish only a postponement—rather than a deep resolution—of conflict. This dilemma confronted the Camp David peacemakers, who had to wait a decade and more before the next round of the peace process, starting at Madrid, could begin to work on the minds of the parties as well. Even then, conflict resolution arouses the nostalgia for conflict, as witnessed in the popularity of Hamas and Likud.

The last is the dilemma of prevention. The ultimate in conflict resolution, it would seem, is conflict prevention, which recognizes conflict's causes and deals with them before the conflicts have a chance to become violent. Governance is indeed conflict management, and most conflicts at the heart of politics never become violent because they are handled (within states) by normal politics or (among states) by normal diplomacy (Zartman 1996). But many conflicts that become crises in international relations could have been prevented had they been the subject of more intense diplomatic attention earlier. But how can the attentions of public and government be mobilized by potential crises when they are still cold? And how can one distinguish a conflict that will become a crisis and therefore needs prevention, from one that will burn out on its own and blow away without causing damage? The business of conflict resolution, for all its pride of accomplishment, needs the humility—and the excitement—to recognize that there are many more worlds to discover.

REFERENCES

Armstrong, Tony. 1993. *Breaking the Ice*. Washington, D.C.: United States Institute of Peace Press.

Azar, Edward E. and John W. Burton, eds. 1986. *International Conflict Resolution*. Brighton, U.K.: Wheatsheaf.

Bernard, Jessie et al. 1957. *The Nature of Conflict*. Paris: United Nations Educational, Scientific, and Cultural Organization.

Boutros-Ghali, Boutros. 1995. *An Agenda for Peace*. New York: United Nations.

Boutwell, Jeffrey, Michael Klare, and Laura Reed, eds. 1995. *Lethal Commerce: The Global Trade in Small Arms and Light Weapons*. Cambridge, Mass.: American Academy of Arts and Sciences.

Burton, John W., ed. 1990. *Conflict: Human Needs Theory*. New York: St. Martin's Press.

————. 1995. "Conflict Provention as a Political System." In *Beyond Confrontation*, ed. James Vasquez et al. Ann Arbor: University of Michigan Press.

Coser, Lewis. 1956. *The Functions of Social Conflict*. New York: Free Press.

Dahl, Robert. 1969. "The Concept of Power." In *Political Power*, ed. David Edwards et al. New York: Free Press.

Damrosch, Lori F., ed. 1993. *Enforcing Restraint: Collective Intervention in Internal Conflicts*. New York: Council on Foreign Relations.

de Callières, François. 1963 [1716]. *On the Manner of Negotiating Among Princes*. South Bend, Ind.: University of Notre Dame Press.

de Felice, Fortune Barthelemy. 1987 [1778]. "Negotiations, or the Art of Negotiating." In *The 50% Solution*, ed. I. William Zartman. New Haven: Yale University Press.

Deng, Francis et al. 1996. *Sovereignty as Responsibility*. Washington, D.C.: Brookings Institution.

Kolm, Serge C. 1997. *Modern Theories of Justice*. Cambridge, Mass.: MIT Press.

Kriesberg, Louis. 1992. *De-Escalation and Transformation of International Conflicts*. New Haven: Yale University Press.

Lake, David and Donald Rothchild, eds. 1997. *The International Spread and Management of Ethnic Conflict*. Princeton: Princeton University Press.

Nelson, Joan. 1992. "Poverty, Equity, and the Politics of Adjustment." In *The Politics of Economic Adjustment*, ed. Stephen Haggard and Robert R. Kaufman. Princeton: Princeton University Press.

Obasanjo, Olasegun. 1991. *The Kampala Document*. New York: African Leadership Forum.

Princen, Thomas. 1992. *Intermediaries in International Conflict*. Princeton: Princeton University Press.

Raiffa, Howard. 1982. *The Art and Science of Negotiation*. Cambridge, Mass.: Harvard University Press.

Rubin, Jeffrey Z. and I. William Zartman, eds. 1996. *Power and Asymmetry in Negotiation*. Laxenburg, Austria: International Institute of Applied Systems Analysis.

Russell, Bertrand. 1938. *Power*. London: Unwin.

Simon, Herbert. 1969. "Notes on the Observation and Measurement of Power." In *Political Power*, ed. David Edwards et al. New York: Free Press.

Tawney, R. H. 1964. *Equality*. London: Unwin.

Touval, Saadia and I. William Zartman, eds. 1985. *International Mediation in Theory and Practice*. Boulder, Colo.: Westview Press.

————. 1989. "Mediation in International Conflicts." In *Mediation Research: The Process and Effectiveness of Third-Party Intervention*, ed. Kenneth Kressel and Dean G. Pruitt. San Francisco: Jossey-Bass.

Udalov, Vadim. 1995. "National Interests and Conflict Reduction." In *Cooperative Security: Reducing Third World Wars*, ed. I. William Zartman and Victor A. Kremenyuk. Syracuse, N.Y.: Syracuse University Press.

Yankelovich, Daniel. 1994. "Shaping a New Communications Strategy." New York: Public Agenda. Mimeograph.

Zartman, I. William. 1989. *Ripe for Resolution*. 2d ed. New York: Oxford University Press.

————. 1995a. "Systems of World Order and Regional Conflict Reduction." In *Cooperative Security: Reducing Third World Wars*, ed. I. William Zartman and Victor A. Kremenyuk. Syracuse, N.Y.: Syracuse University Press.

————, ed. 1995b. *Elusive Peace: Negotiating an End to Civil Wars*. Washington, D.C.: Brookings Institution.

————, ed. 1996. *Governance as Conflict Management: Politics and Violence in West Africa*. Washington, D.C.: Brookings Institution.

Zartman, I. William, and Victor A. Kremenyuk, eds. 1995. *Cooperative Security: Reducing Third World Wars*. Syracuse, N.Y.: Syracuse University Press.

Zartman, I. William, and Saadia Touval. 1996. "International Mediation in the Post–Cold War Era." In *Managing Global Chaos: Sources of and Responses to International Conflict*, ed. Chester A. Crocker, Fen Osler Hampson with Pamela Aall. Washington, D.C.: United States Institute of Peace Press.

Zartman, I. William et al. 1996. "Negotiation as a Search for Justice." *International Negotiation* 1 (1):79–98.

PART ONE

MAPPING THE FIELD

1

PEACEMAKING IN THE TWENTY-FIRST CENTURY

New Rules, New Roles, New Actors

J. Lewis Rasmussen

INTRODUCTION

From World War II until the end of the Cold War, the game of global politics was relatively unambiguous. The rules and issues of a bipolar system were, for the most part, clearly defined, as were the relationships between allies and enemies and between official and unofficial actors. The number of players was manageable, and they knew their roles. Conflicts around the globe largely took the form of superpower proxy wars, in which Third World client states vied for power and influence in regions outside the immediate spheres of influence of the United States and the Soviet Union. In short, there was a constancy, a simplicity, and a predictability to international life that was rather reassuring.

Today, ours is a turbulent world in transformation. The waning of bipolarity in world politics has unleashed violent global disorder in the form of unchecked and often undisciplined passions for sociopolitical change that had long been suppressed. Foreign affairs professionals—governmental representatives; academicians; journalists; members of business, religious, and humanitarian assistance communities; and many others—all struggle to both formulate relevant questions and seek answers in what has become a period of greater global uncertainty than at almost any other time during this century.

One of the single greatest challenges confronting us today is how to understand the dynamics of contemporary political disputes and violent conflict in the international realm and how to better prevent, manage, and resolve such discord. The hard reality, though, is that difficult political, economic, and social choices must be made while the world community faces numerous and diverse challenges.

This chapter briefly explores how the study of international relations and the practice of foreign affairs are undergoing a profound epistemological change. Realism, the dominant way of explaining and predicting international behavior, is no longer singularly capable of interpreting the forces that determine political relations among nations and other relevant actors. Borrowing from the work of Thomas Kuhn (1970), we can speak of a paradigmatic shift in how we explain and influence interactions in the international realm because the existing dominant paradigm (realism) cannot account for changes in global political interaction.

The deficiencies of realism as a descriptive rubric are revealed in the following examination of how international conflict has changed since the paradigm established its primacy in international political theory. The chapter also examines realism's shortcomings as a prescriptive device for foreign policy practitioners who are confounded by the vicissitudes of numerous post–Cold War conflicts. Finally, the chapter explores notions of conflict transformation and sustainable peace. Overall, this chapter attempts to construct a holistic conceptual framework from the insights of noted academic scholars of international relations, leading scholar-practitioners in the conflict resolution field, and experienced diplomats who have devoted a major portion of their careers to scholarly reflection on how statecraft can be improved to cope with the increasing complexity in international affairs. As an approach for better understanding contemporary conflict and its resolution within the larger context of global politics, this framework should assist academics and practitioners in examining where, when, and how to intervene in a conflict.

THE LIMITS OF REALISM

Proponents of realism argue that international politics is based on several fundamental tenets:

- The state is the only significant actor in the international system
- The system resembles the "state of nature" and is governed by the principle of self-help, which holds that states compete with one another and act only on the basis of self-interest
- States are equal only in terms of their sovereignty
- The state will exercise its power (defined primarily in terms of military capability) to either maintain its place or advance in the hierarchy of states
- The system's distribution of power determines the likely behavior of states at any given time

Realism as a framework for understanding international politics was introduced by Edward Hallett Carr (1964) in his critique of idealism, *The Twenty Years Crisis, 1919-1939*. His interpretation of events surrounding the failure of the Kellogg-Briand Pact and the League of Nations—and the underlying current of Wilsonian idealism—carried sufficient explanatory power to propel realism toward its current status as the dominant paradigm in international relations.

The onset of the Cold War continued to validate realism's focus on balance-of-power politics, and U.S. foreign policy openly embraced the language of immediate national interest and power maximization around the world to defend against encroachments by its new Soviet rival. During this period, foreign policy practitioners joined academic theorists in the search for a conceptual framework that would not only explain and predict international behavior but also provide reliable principles on which to base foreign policy. Hans Morgenthau was the first to bridge the modern theory/practice divide. Interpreting world politics in the aftermath of a U.S.-led Allied victory, he described the structure of international politics and a course of foreign policy that justified continued U.S. dominance. This mutually supportive relationship prospered to the extent that the practice of *Realpolitik* in turn legitimized "a realist theory of international politics"— the title of his first chapter in *Politics Among Nations* (1956).

The approach purported to "detect and understand the forces that determine political relations among nations, and to comprehend the ways in which those forces act upon each other and upon international political relations and institutions" (Morgenthau 1956, 14). In other words, realism's proponents considered it a universal guide for interpreting all international political behavior.

However, just as the Wilsonian foundation of international relations faltered, realism also fell short in its ability to explain all facets of world politics.

Emerging in response to the tragedies of the two world wars, the new approach was decidedly "reformist and prescriptive and burdened with the primary task of resolving war. . . . It was not concerned with uncovering laws which would assist in the comprehension of an infinitely complex reality" (Little 1980, 6–7). Moreover, realism was, and remains, largely incapable of explaining aspects of international politics other than state-centric organized warfare. Specifically, realism was unequipped to explain sociopolitical change in the international system—a definite handicap, given that the modern discipline of international relations was initially established to help policymakers generate ideas about international law and organization to aid in their efforts to end warfare.

Unfortunately, from World War II through the end of the Cold War, much of the writing on realism focused on the causes of international war and great power wars. Three major arguments have justified this imbalance: (a) "any theory of international politics must necessarily be based on the great powers, for they define the context for others as well as themselves"; (b) "many of our theories of war and international behavior in general are disproportionately influenced by a small handful of cases of great power war"; and (c) "the great power bias in the theoretical literature on war pertains primarily to systemic-level theories of war, those that trace war to the structure of the international system and the relationships among states" (Levy 1989, 215).

While these arguments were perhaps appropriate when they were first advanced, international behavior in the post–Cold War era no longer supports such premises. Since 1989, the world has witnessed remarkable social and political changes, some nonviolent, others anything but peaceful. International wars have largely ceased to be the agents of change in the international system, giving way to the current plethora of internal conflicts over ethnic and religious identity, human rights, and basic human needs. At the core of contemporary conflict are fundamental disputes over the control of resources, the affirmation of identity, and the assurance of security. Beyond these basic differences is the fundamental change in the dominant system of world order—or, rather, the lack thereof: The bipolar system of the Cold War has disappeared without a clear succession.

One major outcome of this sea change has been to force policymakers; academics; members of business, religious, and nongovernmental communities; and everyday citizens alike to reexamine the world. It has caused us to rethink how we think, to reevaluate and adjust our mental frames for viewing and understanding social and political phenomena in the international realm. In other words, the world's changing political landscape has brought with it new concerns that demand new approaches toward the study and conduct of global political relations.

In sum, realism can no longer singularly serve as a guide for understanding the complex dynamics of internal sociopolitical conflict and its myriad interrelated problems. Cultural, demographic, developmental, economic, ecological, educational, religious, and psychological factors, in addition to those of a more traditional political-military nature, must be considered as significant sources of post–Cold War instability. As such, they also have a profound effect upon the external behavior of states (Haass 1995), whether manifested in conventional diplomatic relations; situations of nascent conflict; or full-scale conflagrations, where states are involved either as combatants or external third parties. Therefore, we should not be too quick to discard realism entirely; rather, we should integrate relevant insights into a more refined theoretical approach. In doing so, we will be better able to capture the complexity of contemporary international behavior, rendering it relatively more understandable and enabling us to formulate appropriate policy in a drastically changing global environment (Rosenau 1990).

IN SEARCH OF A NEW PARADIGM

Over the past several decades, realists have sought to portray themselves and their approach as "value free." Their insistence on separating out normative considerations was an attempt to imbue their approach with the certitude of positivism's scientific rationality. Yet even in its value-free explanations of international politics, realism betrayed a distinct set of values on how nations should behave in international society.

> There is a clear, if unstated, normative position underlying [realist] analysis. . . . [T]he avoidance of catastrophic war is the most important of values. In order to secure this, they are prepared to assume as irrational the value hierarchies of those for whom the risks of war might be preferable to the perpetuation of unbearable political, economic, and social conditions (Ferguson and Mansbach 1988, 46).

Consequently, there is not only an opportunity but a need to expand the scope of inquiry and to shift attention toward violent conflict—and its causes—short of great power war or interstate warfare in general. In other words, international relations, as an academic discipline, has to shift its focus from order among states to more readily include order within states.

A study conducted by the Association of Professional Schools of International Affairs highlights the "rich ferment within international relations as the passage is made from Cold War coherence via an intense examination of what will distinguish and unify international relations as a scholarly discipline into the next century." The resulting "intellectual space for a more pluralist approach" to international politics contains nine areas for new research, including rethinking the utility of realist tenets of international relations, expanding the security studies paradigm, searching for more effective regimes of international policy cooperation and coordination, accepting the relationship between domestic and international politics, and exploring the theory and practice of official and unofficial inter- and intra-national mediation (Goodman and Mandell 1994, 2–3).

From the late 1980s through the end of this century will constitute another redefinitional period like the post–World War II era, when the theory and practice of Morgenthau's realism became closely intertwined. When the status quo is so challenged and such efforts attain prominence, theory emerges to reflect and legitimize that type of political interaction (Mansbach and Ferguson 1992). During this transition, the theory and practice of conflict resolution may well become the warp and weft of the new international relations. The emerging paradigm will have to account for internal conflicts that, in a variety of ways, elude the confines of borders. Balance-of-power considerations cannot adequately explain the religious, ethnic, and other identity-based sources of contemporary international conflict. As a consequence, the new paradigm will be much more value-laden in its service as a prescriptive device—quite a different role from realism's emphasis on global superpower war.

Under the new paradigm, we must ask a fundamental question: What do we want to do about conflict in general? More specifically, should we resolve, settle, manage, regulate, mitigate, escalate, de-escalate, contain, terminate, prevent, avoid, or ignore it? The late Jim Laue would note that all are legitimate options under one set of circumstances or another, and one's choice regarding any given conflict is ultimately based on values. How does the situation and the proposed treatment fit into an intellectual or theoretical, moral or theological, or political framework? What interests are at stake, and how does this framework support those interests?

A period of global transition is a time to examine critically attitudes and perceptions toward conflict, options toward its resolution, and the meanings of "resolution." The transition permits horizons to the possible to be broadened to open the way to creative and critical thinking about confronting violent conflict. Stephen Brookfield eloquently elaborated on such a skill:

> Learning to think critically is one of the most significant activities of adult life. When we become critical thinkers we develop an awareness of the assumptions under which we, and others, think and act. We learn to pay attention to the context in which our actions and ideas are generated. We become skeptical of quick-fix solutions, of single answers to problems, and of claims to universal truth. We also become open to alternative ways of looking at, and behaving in, the world (Brookfield 1987, ix).

Such rethinking is not only possible, it is increasingly necessary. The short- and long-term cost of violent conflict (measured in human lives, productivity, natural resources, social infrastructure, capital, institutions, mechanisms of governance, and generations of the human psyche) between and within states strains the capacity of global community. How many crises could have been prevented from reaching such pandemic proportions? Many challenges facing preventive action, including linking response systems to early warnings, prioritizing values, and generating a sustained political will, "could be diminished or circumvented if [governments] were to reorient [their] thinking" (Lund 1996, 197).

Weighing competing interests and choosing among them is a constant process in the practice of foreign affairs. Involvement in conflict situations is not without costs, notwithstanding the moral weight that supports some interventions. Over $2 billion each was spent on the deployment of the UN Transitional Authority in Cambodia (UNTAC) and the second UN Operation in Somalia (UNOSOM II). Over $5 million dollars per day went to the peacekeeping operation in the former Yugoslavia before the United Nations handed the mission to the North Atlantic Treaty Organization (NATO). But is that the best way to spend that money? Might not earlier action do a better job at less cost? How can such complex problems be addressed more effectively? If the world community were less reactive and more proactive in its response to incipient conflicts, could not some conflicts be prevented? What impact might economic and social development projects have in any area with a budget of $5 million a day?

THE CHANGING NATURE OF CONTEMPORARY CONFLICT

Distinguishing between International War and Intergroup Conflict

Wallensteen and Sollenberg (1995) note that although the world has witnessed ninety-four armed conflicts between 1989 and 1994, the total number of armed conflicts since the end of the Cold War has decreased slightly—as of 1994, there were forty-two ongoing conflicts, down from forty-six in the previous year. And of the ninety-four conflicts occurring during 1989–94, only four were considered traditional, interstate conflicts; however, the number of minor and intermediate-level conflicts significantly increased. Thus, at a time when the "peace dividend" is supposed to be paying off, we still face a significant level of violent conflict and a rise in small-scale warfare.

To be sure, it is the *type* of conflict plaguing international society today—the nature of the belligerents and the location of the battlefield—that poses analytical and prescriptive problems for scholars and foreign policy practitioners. Mass violence now is waged not so much by states against each other as by more amorphous groups whose members are contesting the states and borders that contain them. Nearly two-thirds of the ongoing conflicts in 1993 could be defined as "identity-based" (Regehr 1993), constituting a direct challenge to existing state authority as their salient characteristic (Wallensteen and Sollenberg 1995).

Another distinction between international war and contemporary intergroup conflict is the manner in which they are waged. International wars are typically fought between states' professional armies roughly following standardized rules of engagement. Legal conventions governing the proper moral conduct of states and their armies leading up to and during war have existed for centuries. The principles of international law still provide the legal rationale for the state's pronouncements regarding the legality and moral justification for going to war and the legality (and, to a lesser extent, the morality) of conduct once engaged in war.

Internal conflicts, on the other hand, usually involve paramilitary formations that typically do not adhere to the agreed-upon, legally binding rules governing behavior in times of war. Even professional armies, when so engaged, are likely to reflect this unconventional behavior. National and other identity groups typically define their actions as consistent with their own interpretation of legal conventions. They argue that since the conflict is internal, their actions fall outside the realm of international law, and since they are challenging the constituted order, their actions fall outside the realm of domestic law.

When such conventions are ignored, fighting becomes, by definition, highly unconventional. Civilians are frequently targeted (women and children are typically the most victimized), "collateral damage" is often intentional, and human rights are frequently violated, as evidenced in Bosnia, Chechnya, Rwanda, and elsewhere. For example, the use of land mines is indiscriminate and the ramifications horrendous. Mines not only bar military passage along roads, paths, fields, and farmland, they also prevent civilians from undertaking normal, everyday activity and leave their countless victims without life or limb. Unfortunately, it is common for minefields to be poorly mapped—or not mapped at all. Mine clearing is tedious, costly (some mines cost as little as $5 to manufacture, but up to $1,000 each to remove), and extremely dangerous. After an area is cleared, new mines are easily and frequently relaid. The countless remaining mines become a lingering impediment to the reconstruction of and reconciliation in many war-torn societies.

In many contemporary conflicts, waves of refugees and displaced persons are left without means to support themselves, without homes, and without a general ability to function normally. Most are forced to live in makeshift camps without adequate shelter, medicine, food, water, and other necessities of daily life. Fear of retribution prevents many from even attempting to return home, despite repatriation efforts and the poor conditions in camps.

The intensity of the ethnic conflicts plaguing such diverse areas as Northern Ireland and Africa's Great Lakes region leaves the communities in place paralyzed with fear, effectively shutting down many normal societal functions, even though the infrastructure is left intact. Some conflicts render the infrastructure (and often its environment) useless, because the belligerents typically resort to scorched-earth tactics, as in Cambodia and Chechnya.

Since many current conflicts generate racial, religious, or cultural hatred and the ensuing "security dilemma"—the growing ethnic awareness makes groups take security measures that only make other groups feel more insecure—"ethnic cleansing" is occurring more frequently. In Rwanda, upwards of eight hundred thousand people were slaughtered in a series of massacres between Tutsis and Hutus "protecting" themselves against each other in the mid-1990s, and the situation remains volatile. Neighboring Burundi has gradually descended into the same vicious spiral of ethnic violence. The unearthing of mass graves and stockpiling of human skulls in Bosnia is gruesomely reminiscent of the senseless hatred that devastated Cambodia in the 1970s and continues to plague Khmer society.

Another difference is that conflict is no longer restricted to the advanced industrialized countries. In fact, there is a highly positive correlation between underdevelopment and armed conflict (Boutros-Ghali 1995b). According to the 1995 *Armed Conflicts Report*, most of the major armed conflicts occurred in 47 percent of those countries in the bottom half of the

1994 Human Development Index. Thirteen percent of states ranking in the top half of the index were host to one major armed conflict, although the vast majority of these states would be labeled "developing" by most industrialized countries (Project Ploughshares 1995).

Finally, recent international wars tend to be short, with specific and identifiable goals. Internal conflicts are much more prolonged (often lasting for decades) and may have historical roots that reach back over centuries, as in Northern Ireland, Sri Lanka, the former Yugoslavia, Sudan, Africa's Great Lakes region, parts of the Middle East, Guatemala, Cyprus, and Kashmir.

Such protracted social conflict (Azar 1990) or deep-rooted conflict (Burton 1987, 1990a) is characterized as bitter, hostile interaction among groups, where hatred, political and economic oppression, and other forms of victimization (perceived or actual) run along ethnic or other identity-based lines and periodically flare up in acts of extreme violence. Resolving protracted sociopolitical conflicts is extremely difficult, given such enduring problems as economic and technological underdevelopment and inequitable social and political systems. Resolving the deeper causes of such conflict requires changing the social order. The dilemma is that effective change in such systems requires recognition and tolerance of diversity, as well as access to participation in the processes that determine the conditions of security and identity.

Understanding the Sources and Dynamics of Conflict

Conflict can be defined as escalated competition at any system level between groups whose aim is to gain advantage in the area of power, resources, interests, values, or needs, and at least one of these groups believes that this dimension of the relationship is based on mutually incompatible goals (Laue 1991).

Since the characteristic conflict of our age is internal, it involves groups. Belonging to a group creates a sense of social identity; people form or join specific groups to enhance their effectiveness, self-esteem, and social worth (Tajfel 1982; Taylor and Moghaddam 1987). Since group identification is manifested in peoples' attitudes, beliefs, values, and behavior, a major function of groups is to enhance impact and stability through its members' conformity and operation within broader established social norms; groups tend to operate in society the way people operate in groups. Yet in some circumstances, group cohesion is established through the collective abandonment of the society's status quo norms. Value conflicts often arise over politics, religion, culture, or ideology, and are extremely difficult to deal with insofar as they resist efforts toward compromise (Burton 1990b). Moreover, the evaluation of identity tends to be based on comparisons with other social groups, leading to in-group favoritism and out-group denigration. In other words, "who we are" is very much a product of "who we are not."

Both social-comparison and relative-deprivation theories indicate that dissatisfaction and conflict occur when group identity is not sufficiently distinct and positive, and when the group suffers from shortfalls in the expected distribution of social resources in comparison to other groups. The group typically focuses on members of another group as responsible, individually or collectively, for its plight by either creating exclusionary barriers or enjoying a more favorable position in society. Because the "victimized" group also believes that it is feasible to acquire what it lacks, it attempts to change the intergroup situation—either peacefully, through dialogue, negotiation, and other democratic means, or by force, if it believes the other group(s) to be unyielding (Taylor and Moghaddam 1987; Fisher 1990a).

Many, if not most, current conflicts stem from the failure of political, economic, and social institutions to pay sufficient attention to the grievances and perceived needs of significant groups in the population. Yet there is no agreement over what specific needs are relevant, whether they are universal or relative in a specific context or cultural setting, whether they are different from simple wants or demands, whether they can be hierarchically ranked, whether they are mutable, and whether they are absolute or negotiable. However, needs theory can "serve as a checklist, and a warning of possible basic problems that may ensue if priorities are organized in such a way that important classes of basic needs are pushed into the background for large sections of the society and for considerable periods of time" (Galtung 1990, 311–12).

What are these needs? They include material and nonmaterial needs, such as physical and psychological security; basic survival needs, such as food and shelter; identity needs, such as dignity and respect for distinct cultural and linguistic identity; economic well-being in terms of educational and economic opportunity; the need for political participation; and the freedom to control one's own life (for example, the panoply of democratic rights, such as freedom of speech, movement, religious preference, and association) (see Burton 1990b).

The denial of such basic human needs is a significant source of conflict. While equating the origin of all conflict with unfulfilled human needs may seem reductionist, the agent of satisfaction for these needs must also be considered. For example, an ethnic group's need for status and increased social recognition could be satisfied by government policies that tolerate linguistic diversity and do not discriminate against minorities; satisfaction could also result from a competitive political system that permits the formation of new parties. If government policies or the broader political system cannot satisfy basic needs, it becomes necessary to find additional satisfiers internationally or in civil society. "As long as alternative satisfiers that are non-damaging to others are, in principle, available, then conflict resolution is possible" (Mitchell 1990, 167). If needs cannot be satisfied collectively, the aggrieved group may take the task into its own hands. One group's particular satisfier may be perceived as threatening to another group; the challenge is to strike an acceptable balance, since all needs of all groups can never be equally satisfied.

Needs have a greater chance of being met when relevant groups are (or perceive themselves to be) represented in the society's government; a society sharply divided into distinct identity groups may require political powersharing to meet this condition. Sisk points out that powersharing is predicated on an acceptance by the groups in conflict "of a *shared or common destiny*" and an expectation that they "will in fact go on living together." They must also adopt "a pragmatism that leads to collaborative problem solving through negotiation (that is, when negotiation is chosen not as a course through which to subdue the opponent, but for the purposes of jointly determining solutions)" (1996, 78 [emphasis in original]). The lack of a powersharing option was a major determinant in Jonas Savimbi's decision for the National Union for the Total Liberation of Angola (UNITA) to breach the 1991 settlement that temporarily ended Angola's civil war; the inclusion of a powersharing option was a major component of the 1994 Lusaka Agreement that terminated the renewed fighting.

However, identity needs may be so high within groups that powersharing is impossible, and even democratic mechanisms can exacerbate conflict. For example, national reconciliation in Cambodia was a primary objective of UNTAC, whose mission was to create a neutral, safe environment in which free and fair elections could be held. Indeed, reconciliation was viewed as both an input and an outcome of the national elections that were held in May 1993. However, the effort to promote a much-needed sense of national reconciliation created a paradox that still threatens to plunge Cambodia back into the chaos of its war-ravaged past: The very same elections were viewed quite differently by the four major factions competing for the right to claim a percentage of legitimate political, economic, and military power. For many of the players (particularly at the top level), the election process was—and politics remains—less about national reconciliation than about political and personal gain, not to mention survival.

The transition toward a peaceful democracy must be premised on a sense of national reconciliation from the bottom up and from the top down. In divided societies, a peace process must not only broaden "the moderate political center [by] persuading rejectionist parties to participate in negotiations," elections, and the renewed social institutions that follow, but must also deepen the practice of moderation within the society as a whole (Sisk 1996, 85). The philosophy, and the values and beliefs, necessary to support a democratic society must be given time to take root and sprout; above all, they must be nurtured before, during, and after elections. While the first new election in an emerging democracy is important, the second and third elections are even more so.

To this analysis must be added another approach, realistic conflict theory, which suggests that conflict is primarily the result of incompatible interests or competition for scarce resources (including territory) and of groups' or nations' attempts to maximize their positions, rewards, or outcomes. Based on a rational-economic model, this theory holds that the social-psychological aspects of intergroup behavior are determined by the compatibility or incompatibility of "real" interests (Taylor and Moghaddam 1987; Fisher 1990b). In protracted conflicts, groups (and individuals) initiate plans, policies, and even laws designed to satisfy in-group (and individual) needs. In situations of resource scarcity, including intense competition for the political and military power to rule, the denial of basic human needs is logical, since out-groups are viewed as competitors. However, strategies to ensure domination do not necessarily result in control. In fact, the ensuing out-group anger, hostility, and deep psychological need for structural change to control some resources frequently result in exacerbated and prolonged conflict.

Perceptions of self and other based on in-groups and out-groups can exacerbate conflict, as they are often distorted by inaccurate projections and attributions (Jervis 1976; Janis 1982; Mitchell 1981, 99–119). Under extreme conditions, members of an in-group vilify and dehumanize members of an out-group, rationalizing and justifying such behavior with deeply internalized images of a moral self and a diabolical enemy (White 1970, 1984). Again, under certain conditions, the need to identify deeply with a group or a nation can actually create the need for an enemy (Mitchell 1981, 71–98; Volkan 1985). In such protracted conflicts, the dominant group's attempt to consolidate its power base often leads it to create highly centralized and exclusionary socioeconomic and political structures that also

increase alienation. In addition, conflicts over clashing interests are usually accompanied by threats, either real or perceived. These real or perceived threats from an out-group increase in-group solidarity and the awareness of group identity, which, in turn, may lead to increased vilification
and, in the case of ethnic groups, ethnocentrism. The typical result is drastically reduced trust between the government (or dominant group) and the
nondominant group(s)—often to the extent that trust in a system of participatory politics and prospects for peaceful change are also drastically diminished.

When the rebel group UNITA appeared headed for defeat in Angola's
1992 supervised elections, it rejected the results and plunged the former
Portuguese colony back into its decades-long civil war. The society was so
ravaged that

> it has not been able to forge a solid consensus on basic issues of governance
> and has not established enough confidence in the political system to make
> all citizen groups feel that their interests can largely be taken care of if they
> do not control political power. In the absence of consensus and common
> vision, therefore, the question of who controls power becomes a life and death
> issue and the win/lose character of multiparty elections only exacerbates that
> battle (Assefa 1993, 27).

When "normal politics" fails to manage and resolve fundamental differences, "war is not simply an act of violence, but an allocation mechanism"
(Vasquez 1993, 47–48). In the extreme case of collapsed states, violent interaction is often perceived as a replacement for authoritative decision-
making procedures in the absence of normal mechanisms of governance.
"[V]iolence becomes an attractive instrument because it provides a way of
escaping interdependent decision making. . . ." (Vasquez 1993, 35).

This view highlights the difficulty of ending conflict based on rational
approaches alone. The links between needs and opposing interests, between
psychological factors and overt sociopolitical differences and the social and/
or military means through which they are addressed, often render a protracted conflict so complex that it is seemingly intractable (Kriesberg,
Northrup, and Thorson 1989). Hence, the first step requires the relevant
parties to alter their perceptions of the conflict and their role in it and
consequently shift their objectives. If the relationships can be redirected,
parties are more able to move from the belief that it is possible to win
everything on the battlefield to a realization that it is possible only to mini-
mize losses and salvage some gain at the bargaining table.

However, belligerents are seldom so rational, often believing instead that continued conflict is the most effective means to achieve their objectives. Thus the perception of a violent conflict's stalemate (which can be described as *plateaus* and *precipices*) is crucial in attempting to end the conflict. A belligerent reaches a plateau when it sees the conflict as unending, uncomfortable terrain stretching far into the horizon, with no possibility of respite. Correspondingly, the precipice represents the realization that matters will quickly get worse, if not catastrophic, if the options of negotiation and reconciliation are not explored (Zartman 1985). When the parties in a conflict perceive unilateral solutions (outright victory) to be blocked (a perception frequently produced by a leveling of the power asymmetry between the main adversaries), the conflict has "ripened" to the point of being a "mutually hurting stalemate" (Zartman 1985; Stedman 1991; Haass 1990). In such a situation paths toward joint solutions must become not only visible but believable. In other words, the conflicting parties must agree that the "risks of peace are less than the dangers of war" (Hume 1994, 147).

PUTTING THE "PEACES" TOGETHER

New actors, new rules, and new roles have given rise to uncertainty as we struggle to derive a new conceptual frame for analyzing and developing policies to address contemporary conflict. The post–Cold War era thus presents us with renewed opportunities not only to stop the progress of such conflict but to attempt to ameliorate its underlying causes.

Lewis Coser's sociological perspective suggests that the current spate of conflict should be understood as the international system's adjustment to major change, rather than a reversion to primitive anarchy and chaos. Ironically, such conflict may be a necessary prelude to the construction of a new peaceful order in international society.

> Conflict acts as a stimulus for establishing new rules, norms, and institutions, thus serving as an agent of socialization. . . . Furthermore, conflict reaffirms dormant norms and thus intensifies participation in social life. . . . As a stimulus for the creation and modification of norms, conflict makes the readjustment of relationships to changed conditions possible (Coser 1956, 128).

Thus it is not the protracted conflict of the post–Cold War era that is new, but rather, the absence of an effective and appropriate system of world order. To deal with basic internal conflicts, where the conflict management capabilities are weak, a strong global system must provide for new actors, new rules, and new roles. The colonial and Cold War eras are cases in point. In the 1990s, a strong global system is absent, and it is not clear what type of order will succeed the Cold War's bipolar system. While the United Nations provides a likely mechanism, the United States and other members of the world community have not allowed it to grow into that role. As a result, conflict is handled by disparate measures, rather than by a fully articulated system. Since there is no system to call them to order, such measures flourish. Thus, the growing array of conflict-resolution approaches is both a sign of transition from a past system and a prelude to a yet unknown new one.

The deployment of a peacekeeping mission is one such innovation in a half-century of learning how to respond to conflict and illustrates the changes not only in the type of conflicts waged but in the international community's response to the transition in world order. The number and size of UN peacekeeping missions have expanded dramatically since the end of the Cold War. Since 1988, twenty missions, more than all deployed over the previous forty years combined, have been launched, and all have had expanded personnel and mandates (Asada 1995). The early missions, or "first-generation peacekeeping" as they are sometimes called, ranged from several hundred to several thousand troops, and the majority of mission mandates were restricted to observing or monitoring cease-fires and separating the combatants. More recent peacekeeping missions have had significantly larger deployments: UN forces in Somalia during UNOSOM II ranged between 20,000 and 40,000; the deployment of the UN Confidence Restoration Operation in Croatia (UNCRO) alone had over 12,000 peacekeeping troops until December 1995; NATO's operation in Bosnia put nearly 60,000 troops in the former Yugoslav republic, with 20,000 coming from the United States alone.

Generally, the size of the force is determined by the nature of the mandate and the expected level of cooperation from the warring parties. Mission mandates now include a greater nonmilitary dimension: human rights education and monitoring; supervision of elections; assisting with judicial reform and civil administration; training public officials at various levels of government; providing humanitarian relief; repatriation and resettlement of refugees and displaced persons; demining; reconciliation; and postconflict reconstruction (Ratner 1995).

Primarily because of changes in the nature and functions of peacekeeping missions, more recent operations have acquired a new label—"peace operations." The main difference between traditional peacekeeping and what some call "second-generation" peacekeeping is that the latter seeks to implement peace, not just freeze conflicts in place. One major aspect of the international community's learning process in the transitional period is that peacekeeping operations should not preserve the status quo but should facilitate movement toward comprehensive resolution and, ultimately, a deeper transformation of the conflict (Rikhye and Skjelsbaek 1990).

Just as peacekeeping is designed to create an opportunity for negotiating a peace accord, a well-crafted settlement should serve as a guideline for a deeper resolution of the conflict. Consequently, the terms of the agreement should spell out provisions or provide mechanisms to help initiate and sustain the peace process. For example, the South African Peace Accords established institutional mechanisms for preventing and managing disputes and conflicts—including differences in interpreting the terms of the accord—at the local, regional, and national levels. A National Peace Committee (NPC) was set up to oversee the implementation of the peace accords. A National Peace Secretariat (nine members representing a wide range of political interests) was established as a liaison between the NPC and Regional and Local Dispute Resolution Committees (RDRCs and LDRCs). The peace accords called for the country to be rezoned into eight regions. RDRCs were established in each of the regions and were to oversee the establishment of LDRCs in as many villages, towns, and townships as feasible. Both the RDRCs and LDRCs were staffed with representatives from various tribal authorities, political organizations, churches, the business community, the police, and defense forces. Representing a cross-section of official and unofficial interests, the RDRCs and LDRCs were effective instruments in the South African peacemaking and peacebuilding processes (Gastrow 1995).

The conflicts in Cambodia, Mozambique, and El Salvador, the Israeli-Palestinian dispute, and current efforts in Bosnia serve as additional reminders that the problems leading up to and sustaining conflict must be addressed in the terms of a peace agreement and, in particular, during the implementation period. This process is critical and difficult. Laue (1991) counsels that for an implementation process to have any chance of success, the settlement itself must be

- a joint agreement that sufficiently satisfies the underlying needs and interests of all parties and does not sacrifice any key values of the parties

- enduring, so that the parties will not repudiate the agreement, even in periods of political change

- largely self-implemented and monitored, since agreements are not likely to hold up if elaborate enforcement mechanisms are required over an extended period
- built on standards of fairness and justice and not solely on compromise
- of sufficient advantage to all parties, so that adhering to the agreement will be more beneficial than not

Only with the successful implementation of the terms of settlement can there be a genuine resolution of the conflict, which means that the causes as well as the manifestations of a conflict are removed. This resolution phase broadly represents the period during which the terms of the settlement are implemented. Because successful implementation depends entirely upon the (re-)establishment and maintenance of enduring functional relationships and institutional capabilities, it is during this phase that postconflict reconciliation and reconstruction must occur. Moreover, the momentum supporting the peace process must be maintained during this period.

As we have learned from Angola, Cambodia, El Salvador, Rwanda, and numerous other examples, peace beyond the accord is difficult to achieve but is of paramount importance. This dimension of peacebuilding becomes preventive, defending against the calamity of a backslide into renewed fighting.

> Peace cannot be enforced where social and economic conditions fail to sustain it; it must instead be built. . . . Societies incapable of meeting their citizens' needs are most vulnerable to breakdown and conflict; conflict, in turn, does lasting damage to the political, social, and economic foundations of stable and prosperous societies (Project Ploughshares 1995, 3).

Following the Dayton Accords, postconflict activity in Bosnia represents movement from the settlement period toward the resolution phase. During NATO's yearlong peacekeeping operation, considerable planning has been devoted to the civilian handoff. For example, the U.S. government has held regular coordination meetings among representatives from various executive branch agencies and nongovernmental organizations (NGOs) under the auspices of the National Security Council. Also, the U.S. Information Agency has developed projects designed to supplement the country's educational system with teacher training and curriculum development in civic education. The U.S. Agency for International Development and the World Bank have undertaken or assisted public and private projects designed to help rebuild Bosnia's economic infrastructure, while supporting reconciliation efforts are aimed at assisting communities in reestablishing the economic, social, and cultural ties necessary for their citizens' integration into an emerging civil society.

Peacebuilding, whether in the postconflict resolution phase or as efforts to prevent the eruption of nascent conflict, depends on the ability to transform the conflict situation from one of potential or actual mass violence to one of cooperative, peaceful relationships capable of fostering reconciliation, reconstruction, and long-term economic and social development. Subsuming the "conflict family" of terms (conflict prevention, management, settlement, and resolution) and the partially overlapping "peace family" (Boutros-Ghali 1995a) used by the United Nations (peacekeeping, peace enforcing, peacemaking, and peacebuilding), "conflict transformation" is a more comprehensive process that goes beyond "conflict resolution." By themselves,

> quick fixes in protracted conflicts rarely lead to sustainable solutions. . . . Specifically, a crisis-driven response to a conflict, which measures success in the arresting of disease, starvation and the achievement of a cease-fire, must be embedded within the painstaking tasks of relationship and confidence building, of design and preparation for social change, all of which ultimately provide a basis for sustaining conflict transformation (Lederach forthcoming, 36).

Transformation implies a deliberate process of embedding or "nesting" changes in a conflict's manifestation at the personal, relational, structural, and cultural levels (Lederach forthcoming, 127–30). At the personal level, a transformational approach focuses on changes in perceptions of and attitudes toward the conflict, and in the conditions reflecting individuals' physical, psychological, and spiritual well-being. This suggests an intervention strategy designed to lessen immediate suffering and other psychologically destructive effects of the conflict. At the relational level, improvements in interaction and communication can increase mutual understanding and reduce fear and stereotyping, forcing parties to confront the terms of mutual interdependence and make difficult decisions regarding the extent to which they can redefine such social transactions. Transformation concerns not only psychological aspects of group relations but social, economic, political, and military relations as well.

The structural dimension focuses on the social environment necessary to fulfill basic human needs; access to religious, economic, political, and administrative resources; and opportunities to participate in decision-making procedures. It also refers to developing or enhancing mechanisms for change in structural inequities along the lines of the peacebuilding concept.

The cultural dimension refers to the deeply embedded values and beliefs that support the mechanisms and patterns of sociopolitical interaction within a society. Transformation at the cultural level is about identifying and reshaping the patterns that contribute to increased incidents of violent conflict and promoting the indigenous resources and mechanisms that are effective in responding constructively to disputes and conflict.

Analyzing conflict as a dynamic phenomenon, with its own life cycle and the ability to move back and forth along a time continuum of more or less intractability, broadens the peacemaker's repertoire of techniques for intervening effectively in a conflict. Regardless of the point of entry, the intervention strategy should be developed with the understanding of the events that have preceded and will follow it. The intended activity becomes but one part of a longer term, multidimensional process—one that has neither neat and distinct beginning or end points. It is therefore critical "to identify and cultivate the conditions of change from intractability to tractability. The message—prepare the ground—is as relevant to the foreign office as to the community activist" (Boulding 1989, ix–x).

New Actors in Conflict Resolution

Not only is the transition from one system of world order to another marked by diverse mechanisms to handle successive stages of conflict, it is also marked by diverse actors to carry out these functions. In addition to official interaction, the presence of unofficial actors is increasingly visible and valuable. James Rosenau depicts the shift from the Cold War to the post–Cold War eras as a "bifurcation of world politics" between a sovereignty-bound world and a sovereignty-free world whose dynamics and interactions can best be analyzed at three levels. The *micro level* refers to the cognitive and behavioral skills by which people, regardless of professional or socioeconomic status, "link themselves to the macro world of global politics." The *macro*, or *structural*, level refers to the "constraints embedded in the distribution of power among and within the collectivities of the global system." The *mixed level* "focuses on the nature of authority relations that prevail between individuals at the micro level and their macro collectivities" (Rosenau 1990, 10).

The bifurcation of world politics has not pushed the state out of the picture. Rather, the state is simply forced to share the stage with the sovereignty-free actors, whose pluralistic world has its own structures, processes, and decision rules. Competition and cooperation exist among actors within and across the sovereignty-bound and sovereignty-free worlds. The sovereignty-free world is virtually chaotic, as opposed to the mere anarchy of the sovereignty-bound world. "In the multi-centric world, relations among actors are on more equal footing, are more temporary and ad hoc, and more susceptible to change, but are less symmetrical and less constrained by power differentials, formal authority, and established institutions" (Rosenau 1990, 249). Actors from both worlds, including everyday citizens, are involved in both conflict and coping with the challenge of managing conflict within and between the two worlds. Their interplay becomes even more difficult to manage since each world is guided by a different set of rules governing agenda formation, policy objectives, and the choices available to achieve those objectives (Hirsch and Oakley 1995; Seiple 1996). Nowhere was this situation clearer than in the interactions among political, military, and humanitarian actors in Somalia, Haiti, Rwanda, and Bosnia in the 1990s.

When protracted or deep-rooted conflict becomes internalized in the everyday life of a society, people begin to accept the conflict as a normal part of life. Conflict can become habitual insofar as the roles of victim and victimizer become integral to social and political identity. Such deeply entrenched, complex situations require an intervention strategy that accounts for their complexity. A multitrack approach to peacemaking integrates activity on nine tactical levels: government, NGOs, business/commerce, private citizen, research/education and training institutes, advocacy organizations, religious communities, philanthropic organizations, and the media (Diamond and McDonald 1993).

In order to wage peace effectively, it is important to create a climate of support among policymakers, the elites who influence policymaking, and the populace. Support must exist for decision makers who take considerable personal and professional risks when pursuing official peace and reconciliation agreements with current or former enemies. Moreover, a climate of peacemaking at the local level is critical when it comes time to implement such agreements. Successful peacemaking is the product of various coordinated interventions carried out over time by official and unofficial actors working at all levels of society.

Unofficial actors, in what is known as Track Two diplomacy, perform a range of supplemental or parallel functions to help improve relationships at various levels and among different individuals. These Track Two diplomats can thus facilitate the successful conduct of official state relations (Track One diplomacy)—as witnessed in the Oslo component of the Middle East peace process. This is true across all points on a conflict continuum, regardless of whether the objective is to prevent, manage, or work toward the resolution of a conflict (Berman and Johnson 1977; Montville and Davidson 1981–82; Saunders 1988; Volkan, Montville, and Julius 1991).

In conflict interventions, government officials are often required to work with officials of the host government and public and private representatives of local communities on the dissemination of information, public opinion, and the economic, social, political, and military factors as they affect or are affected by a conflict. Most unofficial actors are largely unencumbered by the political baggage their official counterparts carry and thus can be more effective at times in providing networking capabilities among parts of societies that are "off limits" to most government personnel. In addition, unofficial actors serving as neutral parties can help provide a bridge within divided societies; unofficial activities are often the only means through which members of opposing parties or factions can safely meet.

An unofficial environment often permits members of opposing sides in a conflict to come together more easily to explore mutual fears, grievances, and demands. Such a purposeful, nonbinding environment

> allows for certain statements to be made, . . . offers floated, linkages explored and confidence-building measures exchanged that in [an official setting], because of political, personal, and psychological constraints, are most likely beyond the realm of possibility. . . . [I]f individuals participate with deep knowledge of the attitudes, policies and positions of their respective governments, the results of the [activities] can be useful for real policy planning and decisionmaking strategies (Rasmussen and Oakley 1992, 11–12).

Unofficial explorations of de-escalation and resolution efforts can obviate the consequences of failure if such interaction were to take place among official decision makers.

John Paul Lederach (forthcoming) adopts a pyramidal model to illustrate the interaction of public and private actors. At the top level of leadership, a few key political or military leaders represent (or claim to represent) legitimate governments or opposition movements. The midlevel leadership represents a much broader constituency—leaders from the country's business, religious, education, and other communities integral to the normal functioning of society. These people are frequently well connected informally with top-level leaders and are even better connected with the populace that the top leaders claim to represent. It is at the grassroots level where the conflict's origins and everyday impact can be best understood, since unfulfilled basic human needs give rise to and support the passions of hatred and despair that characterize contemporary conflict.

However, while local leaders are best connected to a conflict, they are also often quite removed from the official decision-making process. The difficulty in securing the cooperation of certain Bosnian mayors in implementing the Dayton-Paris agreement exemplifies the folly of ignoring such actors. It also points out the utility of Lederach's conceptual frame. The pyramidal model can be applied to systems of local governance as well. How can midlevel people and everyday citizens become more effective peacemakers? After all, they provide the supportive foundation, the absence of which not only hinders the implementation process but can cause an agreement to unravel, either in the immediate or longer term.

Conflicts typical of the transitional, post–Cold War era require a frame of reference that considers the legitimacy, uniqueness, and interdependency of grassroots, midlevel, and top-level needs and resources in constructing a comprehensive peace process (Lederach forthcoming). Guiding peaceful social and political change requires concerted and creative approaches toward developing and maintaining crucial relationships among bodies politic across the official/unofficial divide within and between countries, including representatives from governments, regional organizations, NGOs, business communities, religious orders, academia, and private citizens. Successful peacemaking can best be accomplished through coordinated efforts that work vertically in a top-down, bottom-up, and middle-out strategy, as well as horizontally within each level.

CONCLUSION

Like the world order system in transition, the conceptual lenses we use to interpret our world and to orient our actions are undergoing remarkable change. Not yet in a successor system or a new set of concepts, we are somewhere between paradigms.

Traditional concepts such as state, power, national interest, and diplomacy appear in a much wider frame. The capabilities and foreign policy decisions of individual states must *broaden* to cover more extensive relationships among bodies politic the world over. This step entails "seeing relations between nations as a political process of continuous interaction between significant elements of whole societies" (Saunders 1990, 2). Given the fact that nations face problems that they are unable to solve by themselves or even within the narrow confines of the interstate system, a broader, more comprehensive approach is needed to guide peaceful change in the international realm.

This approach challenges us to develop a conceptual framework that integrates rather than fragments understandings of the relationships among a variety of international actors, including states, regional organizations, public and private organizations, and individuals. Relations among nations "are increasingly a continuous political process of complex interaction among policymaking and policy-influencing communities on both sides of a relationship" (Saunders 1990, 9). Social and political change occurs through many levels of interaction rather than mainly through a linear series of government actions and responses. The issue is not whether states or nonstate actors are more important (states usually are), but whether more complex coalitions of actors affect more outcomes in contemporary international politics (Nye 1990, 177–179). The need to deal with internal, protracted conflicts as much as with interstate wars sets the stage for innovative as well as historic measures and approaches, and provides the basis for constructing a new system of world order. The post–Cold War era thus presents us with renewed opportunities not only to stop the progress of such conflict but to attempt to rectify the underlying causes.

The perspectives underlying analysis, and those underlying decisions regarding action or inaction, differ greatly across the political, military, and humanitarian communities—even more so when we distinguish among the analyst, the external parties to a conflict, those directly involved as combatants, and those directly affected by the conflict. The observer and the actor are both left holding kaleidoscopes through which each looks at a conflict and attempts to rationally diagnose the situation and think about policy recommendations that affect not only the implementation of a chosen policy but, ultimately, the order and functioning of the society in question. No matter how one turns the kaleidoscope, dealing with violent conflict and its transformation remains highly value-laden and involves political acts.

In the end, when we ask ourselves that simple yet provocative question, "What do we want to do about conflict?" we are left with two very different, although not inimical, precepts: *Si vis pacem para bellum* (if you want peace, prepare for war) and *Si vis pacem para pacem* (if you want peace, prepare for peace). However, as Saunders (1990, 2) reminds us, we cannot simply "drop one paradigm for another, but we can steadily transform concepts and instruments that no longer work well [and integrate those that do] into a new paradigm that meets the challenge of a future in the making."

REFERENCES

Asada, Masahiko. 1995. "Peacemaking, Peacekeeping, and Peace Enforcement: Conceptual and Legal Underpinnings of the UN Role—A Japanese Perspective." In *UN Peacekeeping: Japanese and American Perspectives*, ed. Selig S. Harrison and Masashi Nishihara. Washington, D.C.: Carnegie Endowment for International Peace.

Assefa, Hizkias. 1993. *Peace and Reconciliation as a Paradigm*. NPI Monograph Series, no. 1. Nairobi, Kenya: Nairobi Peace Initiative.

Azar, Edward E. 1990. "Protracted International Conflicts: Ten Propositions." In *Conflict: Readings in Management and Resolution*, ed. John Burton and Frank Dukes. New York: St. Martin's Press.

Berman, Maureen R., and Joseph E. Johnson, eds. 1977. *Unofficial Diplomats*. New York: Columbia University Press.

Boulding, Elise. 1989. Foreword to *Intractable Conflicts and their Transformation*, ed. Louis Kriesberg, Terrel R. Northrup, and Stuart J. Thorson. Syracuse, N.Y.: Syracuse University Press.

Boutros-Ghali, Boutros. 1995a. *An Agenda for Peace*. New York: United Nations.

———. 1995b. *An Agenda for Development*. New York: United Nations.

Brookfield, Stephen. 1987. *Developing Critical Thinkers: Challenging Adults to Explore Alternative Ways of Thinking and Acting*. San Francisco: Josey-Bass.

Burton, John. 1987. *Resolving Deep-Rooted Conflict: A Handbook*. Lanham, Md.: University Press of America.

———. 1990a. *Conflict: Resolution and Provention*. New York: St. Martin's Press.

———, ed. 1990b. *Conflict: Human Needs Theory*. New York: St. Martin's Press.

Carr, Edward Hallett. [1945] 1964. *The Twenty Years Crisis, 1919–1939*. 2d ed. reprint. New York: Harper and Row.

Coser, Lewis. 1956. *The Functions of Social Conflict*. New York: Free Press.

Diamond, Louise, and John McDonald. 1993. *Multi-Track Diplomacy: A Systems Approach to Peace*. 2d ed. Washington, D.C.: Institute for Multi-Track Diplomacy.

Ferguson, Yale H., and Richard W. Mansbach. 1988. *The Elusive Quest: Theory and International Politics*. Columbia: University of South Carolina Press.

Fisher, Ronald J. 1990a. *The Social Psychology of Intergroup and International Conflict Resolution*. New York: Springer-Verlag.

———. 1990b. "Needs Theory, Social Identity, and an Eclectic Model of Conflict." In *Conflict: Human Needs Theory*, ed. John Burton. New York: St. Martin's Press.

Galtung, Johan. 1990. "International Development in Human Perspective." In *Conflict: Human Needs Theory*, ed. John Burton. New York: St. Martin's Press.

Gastrow, Peter. 1995. *Bargaining for Peace: South Africa and the National Peace Accord*. Washington, D.C.: United States Institute of Peace Press.

Goodman, Louis W., and Brian S. Mandell. 1994. *International Conflict Resolution for the 21st Century: Preparing Tomorrow's Leaders*. Washington, D.C.: Association of Professional Schools of International Affairs.

Haass, Richard N. 1990. *Conflicts Unending*. New Haven: Yale University Press.

———. 1995. "Paradigm Lost." *Foreign Affairs* 74, no. 1 (January/February): 43–58.

Hirsch, John L., and Robert B. Oakley. 1995. *Somalia and Operation Restore Hope: Reflections on Peacekeeping and Peacemaking*. Washington, D.C.: United States Institute of Peace Press.

Hume, Cameron. 1994. *Ending Mozambique's War: The Role of Mediation and Good Offices*. Washington, D.C.: United States Institute of Peace Press.

Janis, Irving L. 1982. *Groupthink*. 2d ed. Boston: Houghton Mifflin.

Jervis, Robert. 1976. *Perception and Misperception in International Politics*. Princeton: Princeton University Press.

Kriesberg, Louis, Terrel R. Northrup, and Stuart J. Thorson, eds. 1989. *Intractable Conflicts and Their Transformation*. Syracuse, N.Y.: Syracuse University Press.

Kuhn, Thomas. 1970. *The Structure of Scientific Revolutions*. 2d ed. Chicago: University of Chicago Press.

Laue, James H. 1991. "Contributions of the Emerging Field of Conflict Resolution." In *Approaches to Peace: An Intellectual Map*, ed. W. Scott Thompson and Kenneth M. Jensen. Washington, D.C.: United States Institute of Peace Press.

Lederach, John Paul. Forthcoming. *Building Peace: Sustainable Reconciliation in Divided Societies*. Washington, D.C.: United States Institute of Peace Press.

Levy, Jack. 1989. "The Causes of War: A Review of Theories and Evidence." In *Behavior, Society, and Nuclear War*, vol. 1, ed. Philip E. Tetlock et al. New York: Oxford University Press.

Little, Richard. 1980. "The Evolution of International Relations as a Social Science." In *The Study and Teaching of International Relations*, ed. Randolph Kent and Gunnar Nielsson. London: Francis Pinter.

Lund, Michael S. 1996. *Preventing Violent Conflicts: A Strategy for Preventive Diplomacy*. Washington, D.C.: United States Institute of Peace Press.

Mansbach, Richard, and Yale Ferguson. 1992. "The Subject Is Politics." Paper presented at the annual meeting of the International Studies Association, March 31–April 4, Atlanta, Georgia.

Mitchell, Christopher R. 1981. *The Structure of International Conflict*. New York: St. Martin's Press.

———. 1990. "Necessitous Man and Conflict Resolution." In *Conflict: Human Needs Theory*, ed. John Burton. New York: St. Martin's Press.

Montville, Joseph, and William D. Davidson. 1981–82. "Foreign Policy According to Freud." *Foreign Policy* 45 (Winter): 145–57.

Morgenthau, Hans J. 1956. *Politics Among Nations*. 2d ed. New York: Alfred A. Knopf.

Nye, Joseph S., Jr. 1990. *Bound to Lead: The Changing Nature of American Power*. New York: Basic Books.

Project Ploughshares. 1995. *Armed Conflicts Report 1995*. Waterloo, Ontario: Institute of Peace and Conflict Studies, Conrad Grebel College.

Rasmussen, J. Lewis, and Robert B. Oakley. 1992. *Conflict Resolution in the Middle East: Simulating a Diplomatic Negotiation between Israel and Syria.* Washington, D.C.: United States Institute of Peace Press.

Ratner, Steven. 1995. "Peacemaking, Peacekeeping, and Peace Enforcement: Conceptual and Legal Underpinnings of the UN Role—An American Perspective." In *UN Peacekeeping: Japanese and American Perspectives,* ed. Selig S. Harrison and Masashi Nishihara. Washington, D.C.: Carnegie Endowment for International Peace.

Regehr, Ernie. 1993. *War After the Cold War: Shaping a Canadian Response.* Project Ploughshares Working Paper 93-3. Waterloo, Ontario: Institute of Peace and Conflict Studies, Conrad Grebel College.

Rikhye, Indar Jit, and Kjell Skjelsbaek, eds. 1990. *The United Nations and Peacekeeping: Results, Limitations, and Prospects.* New York: International Peace Academy.

Rosenau, James N. 1990. *Turbulence in World Politics: A Theory of Change and Continuity.* Princeton: Princeton University Press.

Saunders, Harold H. 1988. "Beyond Us and Them." Unpublished manuscript. Washington, D.C.: Brookings Institution.

———. 1990. "An Historic Challenge to Rethink How Nations Relate." In *The Psychodynamics of International Relationships,* vol. 1, ed. Vamik Volkan et al. Lexington, Mass.: Lexington Books.

Seiple, Chris. 1996. *The U.S. Military/NGO Relationship in Humanitarian Interventions.* Carlisle, Penn.: U.S. Army Peacekeeping Institute.

Sisk, Timothy D. 1996. *Powersharing and International Mediation in Ethnic Conflicts.* Washington, D.C.: United States Institute of Peace Press.

Stedman, Stephen J. 1991. *Peacemaking in Civil War: International Mediation in Zimbabwe, 1974-1980.* Boulder, Colo.: Lynne Rienner.

Tajfel, Henri, ed. 1982. *Social Identity and Intergroup Relations.* New York: Cambridge University Press.

Taylor, Donald M., and Fathali M. Moghaddam. 1987. *Theories of Intergroup Relations.* New York: Praeger.

Vasquez, John A. 1993. *The War Puzzle.* New York: Cambridge University Press.

Volkan, Vamik D. 1985. "The Need to Have Enemies and Allies: A Developmental Approach." *Political Psychology* 6: 219–47.

Volkan, Vamik D., Joseph V. Montville, and Demitrious A. Julius, eds. 1991. *Unofficial Diplomacy at Work.* Vol. 2 of *The Psychodynamics of International Relationships.* Lexington, Mass.: Lexington Books.

Wallensteen, Peter, and Margareta Sollenberg. 1995. "After the Cold War: Emerging Patterns of Armed Conflict, 1989–1994." *Journal of Peace Research* 32: 345–60.

White, Ralph K. 1970. *Nobody Wanted War: Misperception in Vietnam and Other Wars.* Garden City, N.J.: Doubleday.

————. 1984. *Fearful Warriors: A Psychological Profile of U.S.-Soviet Relations.* New York: Free Press.

Zartman, I. William. 1985. *Ripe for Resolution: Conflict and Intervention in Africa.* 2d ed. New York: Oxford University Press.

2

THE DEVELOPMENT OF
THE CONFLICT RESOLUTION FIELD

Louis Kriesberg

Conflict resolution (CR) is oriented toward conducting conflicts constructively, even creatively, in the sense that violence is minimized, antagonism
between adversaries is overcome, outcomes are mutually acceptable to the
opponents, and settlements are enduring. CR includes long-term strategies, short-term tactics, and actions by adversaries as well as by mediators.
It is based on the work of academic analysts and official and nonofficial
practitioners. As such, the rapidly expanding CR field is not a narrowly
defined discipline, but a general approach.

The first part of this chapter distinguishes and analyzes the major phases
in the growth of the CR approach. The second part of the chapter discusses the current status of the field and likely future developments, particularly the ways the CR approach and international relations theory and
practice influence and complement each other.

PHASES IN THE DEVELOPMENT OF CONFLICT RESOLUTION

Conflict resolution is a complex field of endeavor, with many interdependent kinds of activities. This is the natural consequence of the many tasks
its practitioners seek to accomplish and the diverse sources of its emergence

and expansion. This section discusses the contributions made by various scholars, practitioners, and organizations within four distinct periods, according to the years of their initial primary contribution: 1914–45, when ideas and actions prepared the way for the emergence of the CR field; 1946–69, a period of early efforts and basic research; 1970–85, a period of crystallization and expansion; and 1986–present, a time of extension, diffusion, and institutionalization.

However, the periods are not discrete; events and developments in later years have antecedents in earlier periods, and what begins in one period stretches into later years. The developments and events are discussed in terms of particular years not to indicate origin so much as salience. For a chronological listing of major events in the field, see the appendix. Events in the United States are given particular attention for various reasons, including the central role they have played in what is becoming an increasingly global endeavor.

1914–45: Precursors

The outbreak of World War I greatly undermined liberal optimism that spreading economic development, democracy, and trade would produce a relatively harmonious world in the not too distant future. Wilsonian idealism briefly revived such expectations in the postwar era, but they were short lived. The Great Depression, the rise of fascism, and the horrors and devastation of World War II further undermined faith in the attainment of enduring peace. These developments provided the context for some early work that contributed to the beginnings of modern CR.

One major body of work that helped prepare the ground for the CR field encompassed analyses of the eruption of large-scale conflicts. This work included studies of class-based struggles, particularly revolutions, as exemplified in the work of Crane Brinton (1938). This period also witnessed analyses of conflicts within organizations, particularly in labor-management relations. In this regard, the work of Mary Parker Follett (1942) notably helped lay the groundwork for contemporary CR. Finally, academic studies examined the outbreak of particular wars; foremost among the quantitative analyses of the incidence of wars was Quincy Wright's (1942) monumental study.

A major theme in this work was the importance of nonrational feelings in the outbreak of large-scale conflicts. Much of the research on the causes of war at this time focused on mass emotions aroused by nationalist politicians who mobilized their followers for armed struggle. This phenomenon was evident in various social movements and their attendant conflicts during this period, when personal attributes of national leaders served as powerful political symbols (Lasswell 1930). For some analysts, the rise of Nazism seemed to exemplify this aspect of national development.

In addition to analyzing the causes of intense conflicts, considerable work was done on ways conflicts could be managed and their destructive escalation avoided. First appearing in the 1930s, these analyses of social-psychological and group processes in ethnic, industrial, family, and other conflicts left a legacy of methods and issues on which CR scholars have built (Lewin 1948).

To some extent, the nonrational aspects of many conflicts made them amenable to management, since they were not based entirely on a clash of objective interests. The human relations approach to industrial conflict built on this assumption (Roethlisberger and Dickson 1943). Other work in industrial organization stressed the way struggles based on differences of interests could be controlled by norms and institutions if asymmetries in power were not too large. The experience with regulated collective bargaining provided a model for this possibility.

1946–69: Early Efforts and Basic Research

In the 1950s and 1960s, rapid growth in many CR-relevant scholarly and practitioner activities provided the foundations for further CR research. Some of the work was spurred by the specter of nuclear annihilation that the Cold War evoked, but many other components of the CR foundation had independent origins. Basic research in many academic disciplines helped establish a solid base for the later applications of CR. An early locus for such work was the University of Michigan, where the *Journal of Conflict Resolution* began publication in 1957 and the Center for Research on Conflict Resolution was established in 1959 (Harty and Modell 1991).

Obviously, social context profoundly affects the course of social conflicts and the way analysts and partisans think about them. For many years after the end of World War II, nations were preoccupied with economic reconstruction and growth, followed by an era largely distinguished by concerns about justice, autonomy, and equality in the 1960s. National liberation movements suddenly sprouted in the great powers' colonies; the United States was the scene of mass social unrest over civil rights and the country's involvement in Vietnam; and student demonstrations and national revolutions seemed to be engulfing the world's political landscape. Many analysts as well as activists viewed these struggles as based on valid grievances and worthy of support.

The Cold War was an important part of everyone's social context; it profoundly structured world politics and the ways analysts thought about conflict resolution for over four decades, but its character changed greatly over that time. For the purposes of this discussion, this era is divided into two periods. Some analysts use the 1962 Cuban Missile Crisis to mark the fundamental shift in the Cold War, but 1969 seems more appropriate, since it marks a relatively stable change in several areas. First, the antagonism between the Soviet Union and the People's Republic of China had become especially intense, as revealed in bloody skirmishes along their border. Second, the Social Democratic Party came to power in West Germany and instituted its policy of accommodation with Eastern Europe and the Soviet Union (*Ostpolitik*). Third, Richard Nixon became president of the United States and, partly as a way to end U.S. engagement in the war in Vietnam, undertook a policy of détente with the Soviet Union.

Spurred by concerns about the possible eruption of nuclear as well as non-nuclear wars, an important body of scholarly work based on quantitative methods flourished during this period. Systematic data began to be collected in an effort to examine the incidence and correlates of wars (Richardson 1960; Singer 1972). In addition, quantitative data on conflicting and cooperative interactions among countries began to be collected. These data continue to be analyzed, testing CR as well as traditional international relations concepts (McClelland 1968; Isard 1988; Leng 1993; Vasquez 1993).

Another important body of work focused on the ways cooperative activities and institutions could and did provide a basis for increasing international integration that lessened the possibility of destructive conflict. Much of this work consisted of examining variations in the levels of integration and cooperation among countries, finding that highly integrated countries formed communities with little likelihood of war, as documented in the work of Karl Deutsch et al. (1957). An important strand of thought argued that functional integration among countries would help create the reality of a common interest in peace (Mitrany 1943). Ernst B. Haas (1958) empirically analyzed how this occurred in the case of the European Coal and Steel Community, established in 1951, which gradually evolved into the present-day European Union.

Game theory has also been influential in the development of CR. It has helped analysts think about the conflict implications of various payoff matrices and the strategies chosen by interacting players (Rapoport and Chammah 1965). The prisoner's dilemma payoff matrix especially has been the basis of much work. Rather than assuming a zero-sum game, in which one side wins what the other loses, the variable-sum or mixed-motive game of the prisoner's dilemma type has been the subject of considerable analysis and experimentation. In the prisoner's dilemma game, each side can choose to cooperate or to defect (and seek unilateral advantage). In the payoff matrix, if one side cooperates and the other does not, the player who cooperates loses a great deal and the defecting player gains a great deal. If they both cooperate, they both gain a considerable amount; if they both defect, they both lose much. From the perspective of either party, with no additional information about what the other side will do, the best strategy is to defect; but if both sides do that, they both lose. Many experiments have been conducted to discern what factors affect the likelihood that people will follow one strategy or the other. Thomas Schelling's (1960) influential work, also drawing from game theory, examined the logic of bargaining.

During this period, traditional diplomacy was also subjected to careful analysis, inferring principles of practice that could be used to create policy in a nuclear age (Iklé 1964). The increasing attention to the new conditions of international politics created by nuclear weapons, especially for the purpose of deterrence, stimulated growing interest in the nonrational components in foreign-policy decision making and crisis behavior (Jervis 1976; Jervis, Lebow, and Stein 1985).

Considerable research was done in the 1950s and 1960s on factors that affect relations between potentially contending groups and how overt struggle can be prevented or, failing that, waged constructively and resolved amicably. Research methods included public opinion surveys, field observations, and small-group experimentation. For example, much work was done on race and ethnic relations, producing the well-documented finding that equal-status interaction among members of different ethnic groups reduces prejudice and antagonistic behavior among them. Another relevant finding centered on how the development of superordinate goals can bring contending groups into a cooperative relationship (Sherif 1966). A variety of experimental work on constructive and destructive conflict processes was conducted by Morton Deutsch (1973), helping to set the agenda for much subsequent work.

Also during this period, many sociologists analyzed the processes of industrial, community, ethnic, and other kinds of conflicts (Coleman 1957). Moreover, some analyses treated social conflicts as generic phenomena, noting similarities as well as differences among them (Coser 1956). Recognizing the ubiquity of conflicts, many of these sociologists directed their attention to the various functions of different conflicts and how they were waged and settled. Some anthropologists studied dispute settlement processes in societies with and without formal legal systems (Nader 1965; Gulliver 1979).

The analysis of nonviolent action provided another significant element to the development of CR (Sharp 1973). As articulated by some leaders of nonviolent campaigns, committing violence made future negotiation and reconciliation much more difficult. Instead, they argued, waging a nonviolent struggle enhanced the likelihood of later attaining an enduring and mutually acceptable outcome.

An additional influence in the development of CR has been the diverse field of peace research (Stephenson 1989), which makes several kinds of contributions. It draws attention to how people in different cultures and roles are socialized to believe that certain ways of waging conflicts are proper and others are not. Peace research also examines the social and institutional bases of war, including the military-industrial complex and other vested interests that influence the decision to pursue external conflicts; in so doing, this school of research contributes to the demystification of large-scale conflicts. Particularly germane to CR is the peace research community's analyses of how protracted conflicts may be de-escalated. For example, the idea underlying Graduated Reciprocation in Tension-Reduction (GRIT) is that de-escalation of tensions between adversaries can occur if one side announces it is undertaking conciliatory actions, invites reciprocation, and persists in conciliatory moves even when there is no immediate reciprocation (Osgood 1962). This idea has been influential among scholars and practitioners in the CR field, and there is much evidence that, under certain conditions, it has been an effective instrument in peacemaking when applied to protracted international conflicts (Etzioni 1967; Goldstein and Freeman 1990).

In addition to academic work, actual CR practice underwent significant change during 1946–69, when unofficial diplomacy became increasingly important in international affairs. For example, in 1957, nuclear physicists and others engaged in the development of nuclear weapons from the United States, Great Britain, and the Soviet Union began to meet to exchange ideas about reducing the chances that nuclear weapons would be used again (Pentz and Slovo 1981). The first meetings were held at the summer home of Cyrus Eaton in Pugwash, Nova Scotia, and developed into what have come to be called the Pugwash Conferences on Science and World Affairs. From the 1950s through the 1970s, the exchange of ideas and information at these meetings contributed to the signing of the Partial Test-Ban Treaty, the Nonproliferation Treaty, the Biological Weapons Convention, and the Antiballistic Missile Treaty. In 1995, the Pugwash Conferences and Joseph Rotblat, their executive director, won the Nobel Peace Prize.

Other regular, nonofficial meetings between well-connected persons from adversarial parties also played significant roles in opening up new channels of communication for discussing solutions to contentious issues. In the domestic context, this communication usually occurs in community relations through interethnic and interreligious councils or dialogue groups. One important international example is the Dartmouth Conference (Chufrin and Saunders 1993). At the urging of President Dwight D. Eisenhower, Norman Cousins, then editor of the *Saturday Review*, brought together a group of prominent U.S. and Soviet citizens as a means of keeping communications open when official relations were especially strained. The first of many such meetings was at Dartmouth College in 1960.

Practice was also changing in the domestic sphere. For example, in the United States, the civil rights struggle gave new salience to the power of nonviolent action. Efforts to mitigate the civil strife associated with the protests and demonstrations, for example, were carried out by the U.S. Justice Department and included not only observation and oversight, but also quiet mediation.

1970–85: Crystallization and Expansion

During this period, the practice of contemporary CR began to flourish. As new fields of CR activity were cultivated and expanded, publications disseminated CR ideas, and reports of experience with the more and more specialized types of mediation were published. Academic and relevant nonacademic institutions added training in negotiation and mediation to their programs.

A consensus on many of the core ideas of CR crystallized during this period. Part of this consensus included the idea that conflicts often could be restructured and reframed so that partisans would regard the conflict as a shared problem that had mutually acceptable solutions. The consensus did not preclude the option of coercive struggle to help bring about such change. Another core idea is that intermediaries can and do provide many services in assisting adversaries to construct mutually acceptable agreements to settle and ultimately resolve their conflicts. Furthermore, part of the consensus included the idea that negotiators and mediators could learn to improve their skills to manage and settle disputes in ways that would enhance the adversaries' relationships.

The rapid expansion of CR in the United States was in many ways a social movement, whose origins could be traced to the convergence of several other social movements, including the post-1960s appeal of local self-government and community activism (Adler 1987; Scimecca 1991). CR as a social movement was also fostered by the peacemaking and mediation activities of religious organizations, particularly those associated with the Society of Friends (Quakers) and the Mennonites. In addition, the expansion was furthered by the growth of the legal profession, litigation, and the ensuing congestion of the American court system. The emerging alternative dispute resolution (ADR) movement seemed attractive to some lawyers and many nonlawyers as an alternative to adversarial proceedings and to some of the judiciary as a way to reduce the burden on the courts (Ray 1982). Also, CR seemed to offer peace movement members, whose numbers soared in the early 1980s, a practical alternative to the nation's reliance on military options (Lofland 1993). Finally, CR ideas arising from research and theory provided a theoretical basis and intellectual justification for CR practices.

During this period, the Cold War underwent profound changes as well. Official détente began to crumble in the mid-1970s and collapsed by the end of the decade. The Cold War intensified greatly, spurred by the rhetoric and policies of the Reagan administration. But the growing integration of the world economy and sociocultural relations undermined the premises of the superpower rivalry. Suffering economic stagnation, the Soviet Union began a radical course of reform with the accession to power of Mikhail Gorbachev in 1985, eventually leading to the demise of the Soviet Union and the end of the Cold War during 1989–91.

One important development in CR during the 1970–85 period was the great expansion of CR work in many parts of the world. Notable contributions to theory and practice emerged from European peace research. In Germany, several peace and conflict research institutes were established after the Social Democratic Party came to power in 1969. Ideas about nonoffensive defense and how military defense could be structured so that the other side was not threatened spread across the continent; such ideas included a new generation of possible confidence-building measures. Finally, the earlier work of Gene Sharp on nonviolent action evolved into the idea of a civilian-based defense.

Feminist theory and research was another source of ideas in the development of CR. Feminist thought provided a critique and an alternative to the prevailing emphasis on hierarchy and coercive power as the essential mode of decision making in social life, including the international realm (Harris and King 1989). The feminist critique, viewing the traditional perspective largely as a product of men's socialization and dominance, sought to emphasize the importance of nonhierarchical social relations and the possibility of reaching integrative agreements through relatively consensual decision-making processes. In addition, feminist theory highlighted the many contributions of women in public as well as private life, even in a patriarchal world. In many ways, these feminist ideas were congenial with CR and provided additional rationales for its development.

Additional contributions to CR during this period stemmed from further scholarly investigations of game theory. For example, Snyder and Diesing (1977) analyzed international crises and found that the variation in representative payoff matrices of the crises helped explain their outcomes. Another body of work was based on the payoff matrix for the prisoner's dilemma game. Computer simulations and other evidence indicated that cooperation would result if one party followed a tit-for-tat strategy in an extended series of reiterated games (Axelrod 1984). In an analysis of interactions among the Soviet Union, the United States, and the People's Republic of China, however, the GRIT model seemed to provide a better fit with movement toward de-escalation and cooperation than did tit-for-tat (Goldstein and Freeman 1990).

An extensive body of social-psychological theory and research also has made important contributions to CR. Testing a variety of theories pertaining to cognition, interaction, and personality, among others, the research methodology has been predominantly small-group experimentation. Some work, for example, has focused on how entrapment contributes to escalating conflicts and how the process can be interrupted (Brockner and Rubin 1985). A great deal of work, in many CR disciplines, focused on the negotiation process itself during this period (Druckman 1977; Zartman 1978).

Another important source of contributions to the development of CR is the considerable work done on social movement theory and research (Tilly 1978; Toch 1965). The influential resource-mobilization approach stresses the importance not only of grievances as a source of conflict, but the belief that such grievances can be redressed. The emergence and transformation of large-scale conflicts, therefore, can be regarded as a function of the apparent strength of the opposition, the capabilities of the social movement's members, and the leaders' formulation of credible goals.

Peace movement actions during the period 1970–85 manifested themselves in traditional ways, such as mass public demonstrations, but they also took on new forms, such as various kinds of civil disobedience. The anti–Vietnam War demonstrations and resistance ended as U.S. military forces were withdrawn. After years of quiescence, peace movement actions were renewed in the early 1980s, with new goals and different forms, including demonstrations and political mobilization in the United States in favor of a bilateral freeze on the production, testing, and deployment of nuclear weapons (Marullo and Lofland 1990; Meyer 1990). In many west European countries, protest demonstrations and political pressure were directed at preventing the deployment of the North Atlantic Treaty Organization's cruise and Pershing II missiles against the Soviet Union. In addition, a groundswell of people-to-people diplomacy occurred during this period, as large numbers of U.S. citizens visited the Soviet Union and U.S. cities developed ties with Soviet counterparts (Lofland 1993).

Also during this period, interactive problem-solving workshops became increasingly popular. In this method of conflict resolution, a convenor (in most cases, an academic) brings together a few members of a conflict's opposing sides to guide and facilitate their discussions about the conflict (Kelman 1992). The participants typically have ties to the leadership of their respective sides or have the potential to become members of the leadership in the future. The workshops usually go on for several days, moving through several distinct stages.

John Burton, Leonard Doob, Herbert Kelman, Edward Azar, Ronald Fisher, and others are responsible for developing the workshop concept as a method of conflict resolution (Fisher 1996). Workshops typically have been held in relation to protracted internal and international conflicts, such as those in Northern Ireland, Cyprus, and the Middle East.

The workshops' participants themselves sometimes become quasi-mediators upon returning to their adversary group, but as workshop participants, they do not attempt to negotiate agreements (Kriesberg 1995). Sometimes they become participants in negotiations later on, as was the case in the negotiations between the Palestine Liberation Organization (PLO) and the Israeli government following the workshops organized by Herbert Kelman over the course of the struggle (Kelman 1995).

Problem-solving workshops are one element of what is often referred to in international relations as Track Two diplomacy (Montville 1991). Track One consists of the mediation, negotiations, and other official exchanges between governmental representatives. Track Two actually includes much more than problem-solving workshops and is best viewed as multitrack (McDonald 1991). Among the many unofficial multitrack channels are transnational organizations within which members of adversarial parties meet and discuss matters pertaining to the work of their common organizations. Another kind of track includes ongoing dialogue groups with members from the adversary parties discussing contentious issues between their respective countries (or communities or organizations).

Finally, the practice of ADR also greatly expanded during this period, as community dispute resolution centers were established in many parts of the United States. CR was also increasingly used in public disputes over environmental issues, such as disposal of radioactive waste, water use, and landfills (Susskind 1987).

1986–Present: Extension, Diffusion, and Institutionalization

In the past decade, CR has extended into more and more phases of conflicts, not simply the negotiation stage. Thus, increasing attention has been devoted to the prenegotiation phase, or the process of getting adversaries to the table (Stein 1989). Work at even earlier phases, before a conflict escalates, is also gaining attention, as is the postsettlement phase, involving the development of stable political structures and methods of reconciliation between the conflict's adversaries. All this is part of viewing conflicts in a long-term perspective, including the avoidance of a conflict's becoming intractable, the transformation of protracted conflicts into tractable ones, and reconciliation (or other kind of resolution) between adversaries after the conflict's transformation.

CR is also being applied in many new settings. For example, training and practice in mediation is increasingly finding its way into all levels of education, private corporations, and government agencies. CR techniques are also being introduced in more and more countries; for example, in eastern Europe and the former Soviet Union, as illustrated by the activities of the U.S.-based Partners for Democratic Change.

Furthermore, CR is growing more institutionalized. In the United States, CR's practice is legislatively mandated in certain circumstances; for example, in the development of certain federal regulations and in child custody cases in some jurisdictions. Institutionalization is also evident in the establishment of many research centers, several of the more prominent ones based at universities and originally funded by the William and Flora Hewlett Foundation. In addition, many universities provide graduate training in conflict analysis and resolution, including certificate programs within professional schools and graduate degree programs, as well as master's and doctoral programs in conflict resolution. Many independent and university-based centers also provide training as well as consulting services in conflict resolution and mediation.

The growth of CR has generated considerable research assessing the use and effects of various kinds of mediation in international and other types of conflicts (Mitchell and Webb 1988; Kressel and Pruitt 1989; Bercovitch and Rubin 1992; and Princen 1992). Research examining the conditions that lead to de-escalating efforts, whether mediated or not, has also expanded. Many elements must converge for conflicts to undergo a transition to de-escalation, including the adversaries' belief that they cannot gain what they want unilaterally or that efforts to do so would be too painful. Another important element is the possibility of an agreement among the adversaries, offering a mutually acceptable alternative (Touval and Zartman 1985). Policy-relevant research is often framed in terms of discerning the right time to undertake various kinds of de-escalating strategies (Zartman 1989; Kriesberg and Thorson 1991).

Finally, the nature and context of conflicts have changed as well. For example, conflicts among groups identifying themselves in terms of ethnicity, religion, language, and other communal attributes have become more salient in the current era. Also, technological advances and the increased integration of the global market have increased the competition among states and among classes, communities, and groups within states.

All these changes have affected CR ideas and practices. The rise of complex communal, environmental, and socioeconomic conflicts—often without clear right and wrong sides—has enhanced the pertinence of the CR approach and processes to find and maximize mutual benefits for all groups in a conflict. Some of these conflicts, particularly those involving ethnic differences, have been especially brutal and destructive. These developments have directed increased attention to the social construction of cultural attributes as the source of both communally based conflicts and their management (Rubinstein and Foster 1988; Cohen 1991; Faure and Rubin 1993; Ross 1993; Lederach 1995; Zartman 1996).

In addition, these developments have renewed attention to the emotional factors in conflicts and their resolution (Scheff 1994). Memories of past atrocities and humiliations often evoke feelings of revenge to regain lost honor and ease emotional traumas. Several academics and practitioners have developed CR methods that incorporate alternative ways of addressing such feelings (Volkan 1988).

Various CR practitioners have also begun to pay more attention to institutional arrangements for managing recurrent conflicts before they become protracted and destructive. Their work applies in a variety of conflict-prone venues, ranging from large industrial enterprises to multiethnic societies (Ury, Brett, and Goldberg 1988).

The practice of CR continues to evolve. In the domestic arena, applications have increased in areas relating to deep-rooted ethnic and other communal antagonisms, often exacerbated by immigration, and to deeply held value differences, such as those relating to abortion. These issues often require long-term strategies to build mutually respectful relations and legitimate institutionalized procedures to manage conflicts and to achieve a sense of justice for all parties involved.

In the international realm, the engagement of outside unofficial intermediaries in conflicts within and among other countries has increased. This CR method requires considerable sensitivity to elicit and adapt local approaches rather than impose methods developed in another setting (Lederach 1995). This type of international response to conflict has been parallelled by an increase in conventional interventions by international governmental organizations and individual governments into the internal affairs of other countries, particularly in cases of humanitarian crises and extreme violations of human rights; hence the UN and U.S. interventions in Somalia, Iraq, Haiti, and Rwanda during the early 1990s. Such governmental actions raise profound questions over the existence of shared standards and conceptions regarding sovereignty and human rights (Damrosch 1993; Deng et al. 1996).

The language of CR has permeated many arenas and subjects, as when partisans speak of finding a win/win solution. Furthermore, a variety of CR practices have become widely accepted in coping with conflicts. These practices include establishing informal dialogue groups, incorporating brainstorming periods in negotiations, and using various intermediaries.

CURRENT AND FUTURE ISSUES

Having considered the recent developments of the CR approach, we can now examine areas of broad consensus and sharp disagreement within the field. Following this examination, the remainder of the section will discuss how international relations theory and practice and CR are converging and complementing each other. The discussion will attempt to show how the diversity of CR activities stimulates innovation and critical thinking, and thus provides opportunities for complementary work.

Consensus and Dissensus within the CR Field

As CR activities have evolved, crystallized, and become institutionalized, some elements of consensus have emerged among those working in the field. Yet the great variety of conflicts to which CR is applied and the wide range of sources of CR ideas make universal agreement on CR precepts and techniques unlikely.

Matters of Consensus. There is general agreement, at least in principle, that there are specific CR strategies and tactics for particular kinds of conflicts and conflict stages. Thus, long-term strategies that combine a variety of methods typically are required to prevent a conflict from escalating destructively. More attention has been devoted to the various methods that are appropriate for intermediaries trying to hasten de-escalation at different stages of a conflict, referred to as the "contingency approach" (Keashly and Fisher 1995; also see Kriesberg 1997).

Also, the CR community generally recognizes the important influence adversaries have on each other in both escalating and de-escalating a conflict. Partisans, however, frequently attribute the cause and course of a conflict to the other side's internally driven characteristics or to characteristics within the larger social system that cannot be affected (Jervis 1976; Kelley and Michela 1980). The CR approach stresses that both sides affect the relationship and focuses on what each party can do to influence the course of a struggle.

Finally, there is growing recognition among CR practitioners that every social conflict involves many parties and issues (Putnam 1988; Kriesberg 1982). Viewed as such, social conflicts share certain elements and are thus interlocked. The changing salience of one conflict relative to another serves as a source of escalation and de-escalation; consequently, reframing a conflict so that its salience is reduced often promotes its settlement and resolution.

Matters of Dissensus. Many CR practitioners and those outside the field have subjected many aspects of the approach to sharp critiques. The internal debates are emphasized here. CR practitioners differ in the emphasis they place on "conflicts" versus "disputes" and on their settlement, resolution, or transformation. *Dispute* sometimes refers to contestations over matters that are negotiable and contain the elements of compromise, while *conflict* is about issues that involve deep-rooted human needs (Burton 1990). According to this view, *conflict resolution* means solving the problems that led to the conflict, and *transformation* means changing the relationships between the parties to a conflict; *conflict settlement* refers to suppressing the conflict itself, without dealing with deeper causes and relations. Not all CR practitioners make such a sharp distinction; they generally regard some types of contestations as more limited than others but recognize that disputes may also be episodes in a larger conflict. The settlement of disputes, then, may contribute to changes in the relationship between adversaries and the gradual transformation of their conflict.

CR practitioners also differ in the importance they accord to coercion and violence in the way conflicts are conducted and settled or resolved. Some analysts reason that any reliance on coercion is antithetical to a problem-solving resolution of a conflict. Traditional "realists," on the other hand, tend to assume that all conflicts are ultimately resolved by coercion. Many CR practitioners, believing that power differentials are an inescapable fact of all relationships, take a middle ground. They stress the varieties of power, such as the ability to employ positive and negative sanctions, normative or persuasive inducements, and altruism and shared identity (Boulding 1989). They also emphasize how conflicts are reframed, and the parties' self-identity redefined, in the course of a struggle and the effort to resolve it.

Some observers argue that CR may be used as an instrument of control by the dominant party in a conflict. Without taking sides in this debate, we must concede that insofar as parties are unequal in status, power, or other resources, the weaker party tends to give up more in a mediated or negotiated agreement (Nader 1991). But this is perhaps more likely to be true if the dispute is settled by other procedures.

Finally, practitioners disagree about when various methods of conflict escalation and resolution may be appropriate (Laue and Cormick 1978). Some would not try to mediate or otherwise facilitate a settlement between parties in a highly asymmetrical relationship. Indeed, many feminists and others criticize CR practitioners for their tendency to ignore power differences in their haste to employ CR techniques (Taylor and Miller 1994). However, others in the field believe there is no alternative when seeking to mediate conflicts with power inequalities, since conflict parties rarely are equal in their resources and capabilities. These CR practitioners may even regard facilitating the adversaries' recognition and acceptance of the realities of their relationship as contributing to a settlement. One way to work around the dilemmas these views pose is to incorporate constructive ways of waging a struggle into the repertoire of CR techniques. Thus, some practitioners emphasize ways of redressing power imbalances without denying the grievances or interests of the opposition, which is the appeal of nonviolent action for many people (Wehr, Burgess, and Burgess 1994). However, CR also refers to strategies and tactics of mediators to help balance negotiations (Deutsch 1973; Zartman and Rubin 1996; Zartman 1987).

Convergence and Complementarity between
Conflict Resolution and International Relations

The fields of CR and international relations are converging, in part simply because of the radically changing nature of global politics and conflicts' role in it. Also, practitioners and academics in both disciplines, regardless of their approaches, have sought to build links to the other community. Professional associations, foundation-supported meetings, and the efforts of many academic and nonacademic institutions, such as the United States Institute of Peace, have facilitated this convergence.

However, CR and conventional international relations theory and practice will and should remain somewhat divergent, which should not be (and generally is not) interpreted to mean that they are antagonistic or even that they are alternative ways of managing conflicts. The approaches should be viewed as complementary.

Convergence. Many CR ideas have gone beyond the confines of academia to the general public and official and unofficial practitioners. One notable example is the idea that adversaries can achieve win/win outcomes. Thus, the transmission of German and other European peace researchers' ideas about nonoffensive defense to Soviet leaders in the early and mid-1980s played an important role in Gorbachev's "new thinking" and its acceptance within the Soviet military and foreign-policy bureaucracies (Kriesberg 1992).

Innovative ideas and practices in international relations have contributed to some noteworthy CR developments, resulting in some rather useful and enduring syntheses. For example, analyses of actual cases of mediation in international conflicts have broadened the concept of the mediator's role and mediation activities. When officials of major states serve as mediators, their access to economic, military, and status resources, and their interest in the outcome of the mediation, all contribute to the process (Princen 1992). Despite the myth that mediators must strive for neutrality and be careful to facilitate, experience with mediation in many arenas reveals that mediators are often quite active in shaping both the process and the agreement (Kolb et al. 1994). The great variety of mediation activities that can be combined differently in manifold roles, and the diversity of persons who provide some of those services—inside as well as outside those roles—are beginning to be explored (Kriesberg 1995).

Another example of synthesis derives from the attention traditional international relations has devoted to the study of institutions. Recent analyses of normative regimes and an array of other formal and informal institutional arrangements that have been negotiated to resolve problems related to weapons, human rights, environmental protection, and many other issues enrich the repertoire of options when adversaries can consider for ways out of a destructive conflict. Increasingly, CR practitioners are focusing not only on the process of de-escalation and negotiation, but on the fairness and durability of the outcomes as well. Such a focus leads them to consider possible formulas that not only can settle a dispute, but settle it in a way that makes it unlikely to recur.

Finally, the profound changes in the nature of the world system, noted at the outset of this chapter, have impelled convergence. This result may be seen in the increasingly crucial role played by nongovernmental agents as both partisans and intermediaries in many transnational conflicts (Chatfield, Pagnucco, and Smith forthcoming).

Complementarity. Peacemaking practices of CR and international relations often complement each other, sequentially or simultaneously. Many examples of sequential complementarity can be cited, usually when the CR practice involves nonofficial or Track Two methods that precede the more traditional diplomatic approaches, since Track Two diplomacy may prepare the groundwork for official negotiations. At other times, negotiations are initiated in a Track Two channel and then handed off to an official negotiating forum. Sometimes, the traditional diplomatic channel reaches an impasse, and a new track is opened informally. When progress is made, the negotiations are then transferred back to the official channel. This was the case in the 1993 negotiations between Israelis and PLO representatives conducted in Oslo, Norway.

Another example can be seen in the work deriving from one of the task forces established under the auspices of the Dartmouth Conference in 1982. Following the collapse of U.S.-Soviet détente, members of the conference established task forces on arms control and regional conflicts to examine what had gone wrong. Reflection on the process and the phases of the conference's development provided the basis for two members of the regional conflicts task force, Gennady Chufrin and Harold Saunders, to co-chair the Tajikistan Dialogue (Saunders 1995). The dialogue brought together a wide range of Tajiks in 1993, following the first round of a vicious civil war that erupted after the Soviet Union dissolved and Soviet Tajikistan became independent. Meeting several times a year, the dialogue group's members moved back and forth across five distinct stages: (a) deciding to engage in dialogue to resolve mutually intolerable problems;

(b) coming together to map the elements of the problems and the relationships that perpetuate the problems; (c) uncovering the underlying dynamics of the relationships and beginning to see ways to change them; (d) planning steps together to change the relationships; and (e) devising ways to implement their plan. In practice, participants may remain at one stage for several meetings and even return to an earlier stage when circumstances change. Some of the Tajiks from different factions participated in the official negotiations undertaken only after the Tajikistan Dialogue had met several times.

In some instances, organizers of short-term problem-solving workshops have turned the workshops into a series, constituting a continuing workshop with the same participants. This was the case with the continuing Israeli-Palestinian workshop organized by Rouhana and Kelman (1994). Meeting four times between November 1990 and July 1992, each workshop lasted three or four days and followed ground rules designed to facilitate analytical discussion of the issues that encouraged joint thinking about the conflict. The third-party facilitators, following an intervention model, steered the participants through two major phases: first, the presentation of concerns and needs; then, joint thinking about satisfying them and overcoming the barriers to doing so.

These and earlier workshops involving Israeli Jews and Palestinian Arabs contributed in several ways to the later official negotiations between the Israeli government and the PLO (Kelman 1995). For example, understandings about each other's points of view and concerns, and possible ways to reconcile them, provided the basis for officials on each side to believe a mutually acceptable formula could be found.

CR efforts sometimes complement relatively traditional international relations activities when carried out simultaneously as well as sequentially. One way this occurs is when unofficial tracks parallel official negotiating tracks, as was the case in the Pugwash and Dartmouth meetings during the years of U.S.-Soviet negotiations regarding arms control.

The multiplicity of intermediary efforts, however, can also hamper effective de-escalation and the achievement of enduring, mutually acceptable agreements. Too many uncoordinated efforts can undermine one another as they convey different messages to the adversaries about what different intermediaries have in mind regarding the future course of the conflict. Or one or more of the adversaries may try to play off one intermediary against another. In addition, intermediaries may compete for attention and strain the capability of the adversaries' representatives to provide an adequate response.

Nevertheless, in large-scale conflicts various intermediaries and approaches generally need to be combined to be effective. If they are well coordinated, their effectiveness enhances the efforts of any one approach. Such coordination includes actions pursued simultaneously and sequentially, as exemplified in the 1989–92 peace process that ended Mozambique's civil war (Hume 1994). In the course of its missionary and humanitarian work in Mozambique, the Community of Sant'Egidio, a Catholic lay order based in Rome, had developed ties with both the government of Mozambique and the insurgent Resistencia Nacional Mocambicano (RENAMO) forces. Both sides found various possible international governmental organizations to be unacceptable mediators, even as they both began to consider ways of ending the war. Yet Sant'Egidio was accepted to act as a facilitative mediator. Since it was not a state actor, it could provide a setting for negotiations that did not raise issues about the status of the adversaries.

A four-person team acted as mediators: two members of Sant'Egidio, the archbishop of Beira, and a member of the Italian parliament who had previous foreign ministry service. During the negotiations, however, representatives of many governments assisted in the peace process. The Italian government helped with the arrangements and consulted with the negotiating parties. Representatives of the governments of France, Portugal, the United Kingdom, and the United States, and representatives of the United Nations, consulted with the mediators and with representatives of RENAMO and the Mozambican government. In 1992, the representatives joined the formal negotiations as observers. In addition, the governments of neighboring countries contributed to the process. For example, President Mugabe of Zimbabwe helped arrange the first meeting and handshake between Mozambique president Joaquim Chissano and RENAMO leader Alfonso Dhlakama. In addition, nongovernmental organizations, including those providing humanitarian assistance, actively consulted during the negotiations. As the process evolved, the various intermediaries consulted with each other and coordinated their efforts. Ultimately, a peace agreement was signed in Rome on October 4, 1992.

CONCLUSION

Some disagreements about what can and should be done regarding specific conflicts usually arise from strongly held values. People assign different priorities to values, such as achieving and maintaining freedom and economic well-being and upholding the value of human life under any circumstances. The priority given to such values affects preferences about the timing of de-escalation and peacemaking efforts; for example, whether to equalize the power differential between belligerents before trying to settle the conflict. Values also affect preferences about which parties should participate in negotiating a settlement; for example, whether to exclude especially hardline factions on one or more sides.

At a time when so many peoples the world over have the opportunity to realize their own values, there comes the realization that choices must be made among conflicting values. Such trade-offs inevitably pose moral dilemmas. For example, how much pain and suffering should be borne (and by whom) to continue fighting to perhaps gain a better settlement later? The CR approach cannot solve such moral dilemmas. However, CR tends to favor long-term processes and outcomes that take into account all sides of a conflict and that maximize the participation of the people directly affected.

CR is a vigorous, evolving field of endeavor, encompassing a great variety of perspectives and methods; its many advocates are familiar with interdisciplinary strife as well as cooperation. The diversity is natural and even beneficial, since no single perspective or method suits every conflict during every phase of its course. A familiarity with the many possible methods of CR is valuable, since proper policymaking in response to conflict requires a large repertoire of possible strategies and techniques. Some are suitable for one person or organization and not another, and rarely can any single person or group transform a conflict or resolve it. Many people contribute a bit, and in this new era of relative political instability among and within nation-states, many more people must contribute if destructive conflicts and oppressive outcomes are to be avoided or reduced.

APPENDIX

Significant Events and Dates in the Development of Conflict Resolution

1942   Mary Parker Follett, *Dynamic Administration*
        Quincy Wright, *A Study of War*
        National War Labor Board established

1947   Federal Mediation and Conciliation Service established as independent
        agency

1948   UN Educational, Scientific, and Cultural Organization initiates Project
        on Tensions Affecting International Understanding

1952   Elmore Jackson, *Meeting of Minds: A Way to Peace Through Mediation*

1956   Lewis Coser, *The Functions of Social Conflict*

1957   *Journal of Conflict Resolution*, based at the University of Michigan, begins publication

Karl Deutsch, et al., *Political Community and the North Atlantic Area*

Pugwash Conferences on Science and World Affairs holds first meeting

1959   Center for Research on Conflict Resolution established at the University of Michigan

International Peace Research Institute (PRIO) founded in Oslo, Norway

1960   Lewis Richardson, *Statistics of Deadly Quarrels*

Thomas Schelling, *The Strategy of Conflict*

1961   Theodore F. Lentz, *Towards a Science of Peace*

1962   Kenneth E. Boulding, *Conflict and Defense*

Charles E. Osgood, *An Alternative to War and Surrender*

1964   *Journal of Peace Research* begins publication, based at PRIO

International Peace Research Association founded

1965   Anatol Rapoport and A. Chammah, *The Prisoner's Dilemma*

John Burton and others organize a problem-solving workshop with representatives from Malaysia, Indonesia, and Singapore

1966   Muzafer Sherif, *In Common Predicament*

1969   John W. Burton, *Conflict and Communication: The Use of Controlled Communication in International Relations*

1970   Leonard W. Doob, *Resolving Conflict in Africa: The Fermeda Workshop*

Consortium on Peace Research, Education, and Development founded

Program on Nonviolent Conflict and Change established at Syracuse University

1971   Adam Curle, *Making Peace*

1972   J. David Singer and Melvin Small, *The Wages of War, 1816–1965*

1973   Department of Peace Studies, awarding graduate degrees, established at the University of Bradford, England

Morton Deutsch, *The Resolution of Conflict: Constructive and Destructive Processes*

Louis Kriesberg, *The Sociology of Social Conflicts* (*Social Conflicts*, 1982 rev. ed.)

Gene Sharp, *The Politics of Nonviolent Action*

Society of Professionals in Dispute Resolution holds inaugural conference

1979   P. H. Gulliver, *Disputes and Negotiations: A Cross-Cultural Perspective*

1981   Roger Fisher and William Ury, *Getting to YES*

1983   National Conference on Peacemaking and Conflict Resolution holds first meeting

1984   United States Institute of Peace established

Robert Axelrod, *The Evolution of Cooperation*

The William and Flora Hewlett Foundation establishes a program to support work in conflict resolution theory and practice

1985   Saadia Touval and I. William Zartman, eds., *International Mediation in Theory and Practice*

I. William Zartman, *Ripe for Resolution: Conflict and Intervention in Africa*

The Network for Community Justice and Conflict Resolution established in Canada

1986   Christopher W. Moore, *The Mediation Process*

1988   Lawrence Susskind and Jeffrey Cruikshank, *Breaking the Impasse*

George Mason University begins offering Ph.D. in conflict resolution

1989   Kenneth Kressel and Dean G. Pruitt, eds., *Mediation Research*

Partners for Democratic Change founded, linking university-based national centers in Sofia, Prague, Bratislava, Budapest, Warsaw, and Moscow

1991   First European Conference on Peacemaking and Conflict Resolution, held in Istanbul

1992   Instituto Peruano de Resolucion de Conflictos, Negociacion, y Mediacion established in Peru

1993   Marc Howard Ross, *The Management of Conflict: Interpretations and Interests in Comparative Perspective*

1994   Anita Taylor and Judi Beinstein Miller, eds., *Conflict and Gender*

1995   John Paul Lederach, *Preparing for Peace: Conflict Transformation Across Cultures*

REFERENCES

Adler, Peter S. 1987. "Is ADR a Social Movement?" *Negotiation Journal* 3 (1): 59–66.

Axelrod, Robert. 1984. *The Evolution of Cooperation*. New York: Basic Books.

Bercovitch, Jacob, and Jeffrey Z. Rubin, eds. 1992. *Mediation in International Relations*. New York: St. Martin's Press.

Boulding, Kenneth E. 1962. *Conflict and Defense*. New York: Harper and Row.

———. 1989. *Three Faces of Power*. Beverly Hills, Calif.: Sage.

Brinton, Crane. 1938. *The Anatomy of Revolution*. New York: W. W. Norton.

Brockner, Joel, and Jeffrey Z. Rubin. 1985. *Entrapment in Escalating Conflicts*. New York: Springer-Verlag.

Burton, John W. 1969. *Conflict and Communication: The Use of Controlled Communication in International Relations.* London: Macmillan.

———. 1990. *Conflict: Resolution and Provention.* New York: St. Martin's Press.

Chatfield, Charles, Ronald Pagnucco, and Jackie Smith, eds. *Solidarity Beyond the State: The Dynamics of Transnational Social Movements.* Forthcoming. Syracuse, N.Y.: Syracuse University Press.

Chufrin, Gennady I., and Harold H. Saunders. 1993. "A Public Peace Process." *Negotiation Journal* 9 (2): 155–77.

Cohen, Raymond. 1991. *Negotiating Across Cultures.* Washington, D.C.: United States Institute of Peace Press.

Coleman, James. 1957. *Community Conflict.* New York: Free Press.

Coser, Lewis. 1956. *The Functions of Social Conflict.* New York: Free Press.

Curle, Adam. 1971. *Making Peace.* London: Tavistock.

Dahrendorf, Ralf. 1959. *Class and Class Conflict in Industrial Society.* Stanford, Calif.: Stanford University Press.

Damrosch, Lori F. 1993. *Enforcing Restraint: Collective Intervention in Internal Conflicts.* New York: Council on Foreign Relations.

Deng, Francis, et al. 1996. *Sovereignty as Responsibility.* Washington, D.C.: Brookings Institution.

Deutsch, Karl, et al. 1957. *Political Community and the North Atlantic Area.* Princeton, N.J.: Princeton University Press.

Deutsch, Morton, 1973. *The Resolution of Conflict: Constructive and Destructive Processes.* New Haven: Yale University Press.

Doob, Leonard W., ed. 1970. *Resolving Conflict in Africa: The Fermeda Workshop.* New Haven: Yale University Press.

Druckman, Daniel, ed. 1977. *Negotiations: Social-Psychological Perspectives.* Beverly Hills, Calif.: Sage.

Etzioni, Amitai. 1967. "The Kennedy Experiment." *Western Political Quarterly* 20 (June): 361–80.

Faure, Guy Olivier, and Jeffrey Z. Rubin, eds. 1993. *Culture and Negotiation.* Beverly Hills, Calif.: Sage.

Fisher, Roger, and William Ury. 1981. *Getting to YES.* Boston: Houghton Mifflin.

Fisher, Ronald J. 1996. *Interactive Conflict Resolution: Pioneers, Potential, and Prospects.* Syracuse, N.Y.: Syracuse University Press.

Goldstein, Joshua S., and John R. Freeman. 1990. *Three-Way Street: Strategic Reciprocity in World Politics.* Chicago: University of Chicago Press.

Gulliver, P. H. 1979. *Disputes and Negotiations: A Cross-Cultural Perspective.* New York: Academic Press.

Haas, Ernst B. 1958. *The Uniting of Europe*. Stanford, Calif.: Stanford University Press.

Harris, Adrienne, and Ynestra King, eds. 1989. *Rocking the Ship of State: Toward a Feminist Peace Politics*. Boulder, Colo.: Westview Press.

Harty, Martha, and John Modell. 1991. "The First Conflict Resolution Movement, 1956–1971: An Attempt to Institutionalize Applied Interdisciplinary Social Science." *Journal of Conflict Resolution* 35 (4):720–58.

Hume, Cameron. 1994. *Ending Mozambique's War*. Washington, D.C.: United States Institute of Peace Press.

Iklé, Fred Charles. 1964. *How Nations Negotiate*. New York: Harper and Row.

Isard, Walter. 1988. *Arms Races, Arms Control, and Conflict Analysis: Contributions from Peace Science and Peace Economics*. New York: Cambridge University Press.

Jackson, Elmore. 1952. *Meeting of Minds: A Way to Peace Through Mediation*. New York: McGraw-Hill.

Jervis, Robert. 1976. *Perception and Misperception in International Politics*. Princeton: Princeton University Press.

Jervis, Robert, Richard Ned Lebow, and Janice Stein. 1985. *Psychology and Deterrence*. Baltimore: Johns Hopkins University Press.

Keashly, Loraleigh, and Ronald J. Fisher. 1995. "Complementarity and Coordination of Conflict Interventions: Taking a Contingency Perspective." In *Resolving International Conflicts*, ed. Jacob Bercovitch. Boulder, Colo.: Lynne Rienner.

Kelley, Harold, and John Michela. 1980. "Attribution Theory and Research." *Annual Review of Psychology* 31: 457–501.

Kelman, Herbert C. 1992. "Informal Mediation by the Scholar Practitioner." In *Mediation in International Relations*, ed. Jacob Bercovitch and Jeffrey Z. Rubin. New York: St. Martin's Press.

———. 1995. "Contributions of an Unofficial Conflict Resolution Effort to the Israeli-Palestinian Breakthrough." *Negotiation Journal* 11 (1): 19–27.

Kolb, Deborah M., et al. 1994. *When Talk Works: Profiles of Mediators*. San Francisco: Jossey-Bass.

Kressel, Kenneth, and Dean G. Pruitt, eds. 1989. *Mediation Research*. San Francisco: Jossey-Bass.

Kriesberg, Louis. 1973. *The Sociology of Social Conflicts*. Englewood Cliffs, N.J.: Prentice-Hall (1982 rev. ed. *Social Conflicts*).

———. 1992. *International Conflict Resolution*. New Haven: Yale University Press.

———. 1995. "Varieties of Mediating Activities and of Mediators." In *Resolving International Conflicts*, ed. Jacob Bercovitch. Boulder, Colo.: Lynne Rienner.

———. 1997. "Preventing and Resolving Destructive Communal Conflicts." In *The International Politics of Ethnic Conflict: Theory and Evidence*, ed. Patrick James and David Carment. Pittsburgh, Penn.: University of Pittsburgh Press.

Kriesberg, Louis, and Stuart J. Thorson. 1991. *Timing the De-Escalation of International Conflicts.* Syracuse, N.Y.: Syracuse University Press.

Lasswell, Harold D. 1930. *Psychopathology and Politics.* Chicago: University of Chicago Press.

Laue, James, and Gerald Cormick. 1978. "The Ethics of Intervention in Community Disputes." In *The Ethics of Social Intervention,* ed. Gordon Bermant, Herbert C. Kelman, and Donald P. Warwick. Washington, D.C.: Halsted.

Lederach, John Paul. 1995. *Preparing for Peace: Conflict Transformation Across Cultures.* Syracuse, N.Y.: Syracuse University Press.

Leng, Russell J. 1993. *Interstate Crisis Behavior, 1816–1980.* New York: Cambridge University Press.

Lentz, Theodore F. 1961. *Towards a Science of Peace.* New York: Bookman Associates.

Lewin, Kurt. 1948. *Resolving Social Conflicts.* New York: Harper and Brothers.

Lofland, John. 1993. *Polite Protesters: The American Peace Movement of the 1980s.* Syracuse, N.Y.: Syracuse University Press.

Marullo, Sam, and John Lofland, eds. 1990. *Peace Action in the Eighties.* New Brunswick, N.J.: Rutgers University Press.

McClelland, Charles A. 1983. "Let the User Beware." *International Studies Quarterly* 27:169–78.

McDonald, John W. 1991. "Further Explorations in Track Two Diplomacy." In *Timing the De-Escalation of International Conflicts,* ed. Louis Kriesberg and Stuart J. Thorson. Syracuse, N.Y.: Syracuse University Press.

Meyer, David S. 1990. *A Winter of Discontent.* New York: Praeger.

Mitchell, Christopher R., and K. Webb. 1988. *New Approaches to International Mediation.* Westport, Conn.: Greenwood.

Mitrany, David. 1943. *A Working Peace System: An Argument for the Functional Development of International Organization.* New York: Oxford University Press (reprinted in 1966 as *A Working Peace System.* Chicago: Quadrangle Books).

Montville, Joseph V. 1991. "Transnationalism and the Role of Track-Two Diplomacy." In *Approaches to Peace: An Intellectual Map,* ed. W. Scott Thompson and Kenneth M. Jensen. Washington, D.C.: United States Institute of Peace Press.

Nader, Laura, ed. 1965. "The Ethnography of Law." Special issue of *American Anthropologist* 67, no. 6 (part 2).

———. 1991. "Harmony Models and the Construction of Law." In *Conflict Resolution: Cross-Cultural Perspectives,* ed. Kevin Avruch, Peter W. Black, and Joseph A. Scimecca. New York: Greenwood Press.

Osgood, Charles. 1962. *An Alternative to War or Surrender.* Urbana: University of Illinois Press.

Pentz, Michael J., and Gillian Slovo. 1981. "The Political Significance of Pugwash." In *Knowledge and Power in a Global Society*, ed. Eilliam M. Evan. Beverly Hills, Calif.: Sage.

Princen, Thomas. 1992. *Intermediaries in International Conflict*. Princeton: Princeton University Press.

Putnam, Robert. 1988. "Diplomacy and Domestic Politics: The Logic of Two-Level Games." *International Organization* 42 (Summer): 427–53.

Rapoport, Anatol, and Albert M. Chammah. 1965. *The Prisoner's Dilemma: A Study in Conflict and Cooperation*. Ann Arbor: University of Michigan Press.

Ray, Larry. 1982. "The Alternative Dispute Resolution Movement." *Peace and Change* 8 (Summer): 117–28.

Richardson, Lewis. 1960. *Statistics of Deadly Quarrels*. Pittsburgh, Penn.: Boxwood Press.

Roethlisberger, Fritz Jules, and William J. Dickson. 1943. *Management and the Worker*. Cambridge, Mass.: Harvard University Press.

Ross, Marc Howard. 1993. *The Management of Conflict: Interpretations and Interests in Comparative Perspective*. New Haven: Yale University Press.

Rouhana, Nadim N. 1995. "The Dynamics of Joint Thinking Between Adversaries in International Conflict: Phases of the Continuing Problem-Solving Workshop." *Political Psychology* 16 (2): 321–45.

Rouhana, Nadim N., and Herbert C. Kelman. 1994. "Promoting Joint Thinking in International Conflicts—An Israeli-Palestinian Continuing Workshop." *Journal of Social Issues* 50 (1): 157–78.

Rubenstein, Robert A., and Mary LeCron Foster, eds. 1988. *The Social Dynamics of Peace and Conflict*. Boulder, Colo.: Westview Press.

Saunders, Harold H. 1995. "Sustained Dialogue on Tajikistan." *Mind and Human Interaction* 6:123–35.

Scheff, Thomas J. 1994. *Bloody Revenge: Emotions, Nationalism, and War*. Boulder, Colo.: Westview Press.

Schelling, Thomas C. 1960. *The Strategy of Conflict*. Cambridge, Mass.: Harvard University Press.

Scimecca, Joseph A. 1991. "Conflict Resolution in the United States: The Emergence of a Profession?" In *Conflict Resolution: Cross-Cultural Perspectives*, ed. Kevin Avruch, Peter W. Black, and Joseph A. Scimecca. New York: Greenwood Press.

Sharp, Gene. 1973. *The Politics of Nonviolent Action*. Boston: Porter Sargent.

Sherif, Muzafer. 1966. *In Common Predicament*. Boston: Houghton Mifflin.

Singer, J. David. 1972. "The Correlates of War Project: Interim Report." *World Politics* 24 (2): 243–70.

Stein, Janice Gross, ed. 1989. *Getting to the Table*. Baltimore: The Johns Hopkins University Press.

Stephenson, Carolyn M. 1989. "The Evolution of Peace Studies." In *Peace and World Order Studies: A Curriculum Guide.* 5th ed. Edited by Michael Klare and Daniel C. Thomas. Boulder, Colo.: Westview Press.

Susskind, Lawrence. 1987. *Breaking the Impasse: Consensual Approaches to Resolving Public Disputes.* New York: Basic Books.

Taylor, Anita, and Judi Beinstein Miller, eds. 1994. *Conflict and Gender.* Cresskill, N.J.: Hampton Press.

Tilly, Charles. 1978. *From Mobilization to Revolution.* Reading, Mass.: Addison-Wesley.

Toch, Hans. 1965. *The Social Psychology of Social Movements.* 2d ed. New York: Bobbs Merrill.

Touval, Saadia, and I. William Zartman, eds. 1985. *International Mediation in Theory and Practice.* Boulder, Colo.: Westview Press.

Ury, William L., Jeanne M. Brett, and Stephen B. Goldberg. 1988. *Getting Disputes Resolved.* San Francisco: Jossey-Bass.

Vasquez, John A. 1993. *The War Puzzle.* New York: Cambridge University Press.

Volkan, Vamik D. 1988. *The Need to Have Enemies and Allies.* Northvale, N.J.: Jason Aronson.

Wehr, Paul, Heidi Burgess, and Guy Burgess. 1994. *Justice Without Violence.* Boulder, Colo.: Lynne Rienner.

Wright, Quincy. 1942. *A Study of War.* Chicago: University of Chicago Press.

Zartman, I. William. 1987. *Positive Sum: Improving North-South Negotiations.* New York: Transaction Publishers.

———. 1989. *Ripe for Resolution: Conflict and Intervention in Africa.* 2d ed. New York: Oxford University Press.

———, ed. 1978. *The Negotiation Process: Theories and Applications.* Beverly Hills, Calif.: Sage.

———, ed.. 1996. *Elusive Peace: Negotiating an End to Civil Wars.* Washington, D.C.: Brookings Institution.

Zartman, I. William, and Jeffrey Z. Rubin. 1996. *Power and Asymmetry in International Negotiations.* Laxenburg, Austria: International Institute of Applied Systems Analysis.

PART TWO

APPROACHES TO PEACEMAKING

3

Negotiating in the International Context

Daniel Druckman

According to *Webster's New Collegiate Dictionary*, to negotiate is "to hold intercourse with a view to coming to terms; to confer regarding a basis of agreement." Despite its apparent straightforwardness, this definition has taken on a variety of meanings, especially during the past thirty years. Some view the process of negotiating as a puzzle to be solved, others see it as a bargaining game involving an exchange of concessions, some consider it a way of reconciling differences within and between organizations, and still others think of it as a means for implementing governmental policies. (For other metaphors, see the inaugural issue of *International Negotiation* [1996].) These views have developed into distinct frameworks for research with their own community of researchers who develop specialties in the fields of game theory, social psychology, organizational behavior, and international relations, respectively. Each field has contributed important insights into the process of negotiating.

These insights apply to a wide range of circumstances in which negotiation takes place. National leaders often make demands or exchange proposals from a distance. Well-known historical examples include the bilateral exchanges between the United States and the Soviet Union over the 1948–49 blockade of Berlin, between Kennedy and Khrushchev in 1962 over Soviet missile bases in Cuba, and between Carter and Khomeini concerning the American hostages in Iran in 1979–80. Leaders and their representatives also often confront each other face-to-face to discuss their conflicting interests over security, monetary and trade, or environmental issues. These meetings usually consist of formal summits, such as the meeting between Reagan and Gorbachev in 1986 at Reykjavík, or more protracted sessions, such as the long series of talks between their countries' representatives over arms control, beginning with the Strategic Arms Limitation Talks (SALT) and winding up with the Strategic Arms Reduction Talks (START). They also occur between allies concerning their shared and conflicting interests on bilateral trade or military issues.

Other examples include talks among more than two nations. Sometimes they occur between blocs, such as the NATO–Warsaw Pact discussions during the 1970s over mutual and balanced force reductions. They may take the form of trilateral discussions at which simultaneous bilateral negotiations take place. A current example is the discussion among Iceland, Norway, Russia, and the Faroe Islands over fishing rights in the North Atlantic: While Icelandic negotiators rejected the Russo-Norwegian offer, they reached an agreement with the Faroes; the Norwegians protested this agreement. They may also occur in multilateral conference settings, where representatives from many nations gather for discussions of regional, continental, or global issues. Notable examples are the Uruguay Round of the General Agreement on Tariffs and Trade (GATT), the negotiations establishing the European Community (referred to as the Single European Act), the ongoing discussions among members of the Organization for Security and Cooperation in Europe, the talks that led to the Montreal Protocol on ozone depletion, and the discussions that resulted in the Rio Declaration on the protection of the global environment.

These examples demonstrate that international negotiation takes many forms. It consists of communications exchanged from a distance or face-to-face. It occurs between two or more nations' representatives in bilateral, trilateral, and multilateral forums. It concerns matters in a great variety of issue-areas that may have local, regional, or global consequences. While there are some basic insights that apply widely to the many forms, there are also obvious differences of context and scope. These differences complicate the search for *a general theory* of negotiation. They account for the emergence of alternative perspectives but also serve as interesting variables whose impact on negotiating behavior can be ascertained. This chapter examines these perspectives, as well as the general patterns that characterize many types of negotiations through a survey of the broad literature on negotiating in the international context. Four dominant approaches to the study of negotiation are summarized, followed by a discussion of some important ideas about the distinct rhythms and patterns of negotiations found in these different approaches. Cases of arms control and environmental negotiations will illustrate how these ideas have been used in the analysis of complex negotiations. Many of these analyses have been done in the context of large projects on international negotiation developed at such institutions as the U.S. Foreign Service Institute (FSI), the International Institute of Applied Systems Analysis (IIASA), and the Harvard Program on Negotiation (PON). Yet, despite the advances in knowledge about this topic, there remains a gap between research and practice. Some progress in bridging this gap will be discussed before concluding the chapter with a look back at what has been accomplished and a look forward to promising directions for research and application.

THINKING ABOUT NEGOTIATION: FOUR PERSPECTIVES

Four ways of thinking about negotiation have become dominant frameworks for research and theory development. These approaches differ in terms of their emphasis and complexity, but they also differ according to the particular processes they focus on—moves and preferences, communication processes, intra- and interorganizational processes, and an international system of diplomatic politics. Each approach is summarized briefly in the following sections.

Negotiation as Puzzle Solving

Game and decision theorists think about negotiation as a puzzle to be solved and prescribe "solutions" based on the parties' preferences. The key question for game theorists is, How do people make optimal choices when these choices are contingent on what other people do? According to the classical theory advanced by Von Neumann and Morgenstern (1944), players choose strategies, or courses of action, that determine an outcome. In its original form, the theory is static because it says little about the processes by which players' choices unfold to yield an outcome.

Recently, Brams (1993) added a dynamic element to the classical theory. His "theory of moves" takes into account the tendency of players to look ahead before making a move or decision. By doing so, the theory seems to capture several aspects of actual strategic encounters between antagonists and allows for the possibility that players have only incomplete information.

As such, Brams's theory assumes that players can rank outcomes in terms of preferences but cannot necessarily attach utilities to them, and allows for the use of threats and cycling of moves to wear down an opponent.

The most prominent puzzle for game theorists is the well-known prisoner's dilemma game, which involves two suspected criminals who face the following consequences: If one confesses and the other remains silent, the confessor goes free and the silent suspect gets a ten-year sentence; if both confess, they each get five-year sentences; if both remain silent, they get one-year sentences. Four possible outcomes are represented in a two-by-two matrix: compromise, conflict, and a "win" for either of the two suspects (see Figure 3.1). In classical game theory, both suspects have dominant strategies of confessing, resulting in the conflict outcome. Brams's theory of moves shows how the same dilemma can lead to the compromise outcome. By taking foresight into account, Brams shows that most initial states (compromise, one or the other suspect wins) produce the compromise outcome. However, he also allows for the possibility that players possess incomplete information, which can lead to misperception. For example, in the Iran hostage crisis, President Carter believed that selecting the option of military intervention would force Ayatollah Khomeini to select negotiation in order to improve his payoff, at which point Carter could also choose negotiation to obtain his best payoff in the compromise outcome, which was also better for Khomeini. This was not the case. Brams (1993) showed that in the real (correctly perceived) payoff matrix, Khomeini could not be swayed from his dominant strategy of selecting obstruction. In fact, the outcome of the crisis remained at Carter's choice of negotiation and Khomeini's choice of obstruction—which was more favorable to Khomeini than to Carter—until the hostages were released (see Figure 3.2).

Brams uses his formulation to demonstrate some consequences of actions taken by players who move simultaneously. He does not document the consequences of strategies used by opponents when they play the game. Evidence is provided from Axelrod's (1984) studies of the iterated prisoner's dilemma game. He concludes that while no one strategy is optimal, the "tit-for-tat" approach fares best over the long term, when the value of future payoffs is important and when the other players' strategies are not known. Such an approach is successful, according to Axelrod, because it avoids provocation, makes exploitation impossible, is forgiving, and is simple. Brown (1986) notes, however, that the strategy may be viewed as an attempt to coerce rather than as an effort to stimulate cooperation, and may, in fact, lead to downward spirals in relations between nations. A more effective strategy, according to Brown, is to "follow two tracks: a tough

©1993 by Tom Dunne. Reproduced from Brams (1993) with permission of the artist.

Figure 3.1. The Prisoner's Dilemma. The Prisoner's Dilemma has been used to model behavior in a variety of strategic situations. The model involves two suspected criminals who face the following consequences: If one confesses and the other remains silent, the confessor goes free (the best payoff of 4) and the silent suspect gets a ten-year sentence (the worst payoff of 1). If both confess, they each get five-year sentences (the next-worse payoff of 2). If both remain silent, they get one-year sentences (the next-best payoff of 3). Four possible outcomes are represented in the two-by-two matrix: compromise, conflict, and a "win" for either of the two suspects.

responsive strategy on substantive issues, and an unconditionally cooperative policy on process issues" (1986, 381). This approach sends two messages to an adversary, namely, that we encourage a stable working relationship but will not be exploited.

Another class of problems connected with negotiation concerns decision making under conditions of uncertainty in noninteractive, noncompetitive situations. Raiffa and his colleagues at Harvard have developed an approach, known as "decision analysis," that takes these conditions into account in its applications to negotiation. Like game theory, decision analysis concentrates on players' preferences for alternative outcomes. Unlike

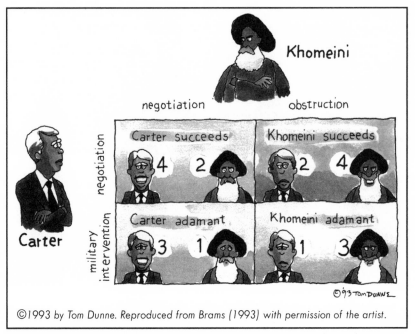

©1993 by Tom Dunne. Reproduced from Brams (1993) with permission of the artist.

Figure 3.2. A Real-World Dilemma. Incomplete information about players' motives leads to misperception and faulty assessments of their strategies. In the Iran Hostage crisis, President Carter incorrectly assessed Iran's internal politics, believing that selecting the option of military intervention would force Ayatollah Khomeini to select negotiation to improve his payoff. Yet in the real payoff matrix shown above, Khomeini could not be swayed from his dominant strategy of selecting obstruction. The outcome, shown in the lower right box, gave Khomeini his next-best payoff of 3 and Carter his worst payoff of 1.

game theory, it analyzes decisions one player at a time (i.e., it does not derive from a premise of interdependence among the decision makers). The solution to the puzzle is to use each player's stated preferences to arrive at outcomes acceptable to both (all) parties. This type of analysis has been used during the preparation stage to assist negotiators in deciding where to offer a compromise or concession, and where to remain adamant.

Ulvila (1990) illustrates decision analysis in a five-step procedure as it applies to the Philippines base-rights talks. First, the positions of Philippine and U.S. delegations were identified on each of six issues (including command and control, compensation, and criminal jurisdiction). Second, the impact of each issue on both delegations' key interests (e.g., sovereignty, economic development, and security) was estimated. Third, possible compromise options, located between the parties' initial positions, were identified (e.g., $1.1 billion in compensation, a figure between the U.S. position of $700,000 and the Philippine position of $1.5 billion). Fourth, the options were expressed in numerical terms, where various compromises were "scaled" (at 50 for a "true" compromise) in relation to either delegation getting its own way (assigned a score of 100); this step enables an analyst to evaluate alternative package deals. For example, it was shown that the United States came out best if it compromised on three of the issues (command and control, jurisdiction, and number of facilities), obtained its own position on the security issue, and yielded to the Philippines on the compensation and human rights issues. Finally, the alternative packages were evaluated in terms of payoffs to each delegation and were represented graphically in order to highlight the one package that would produce the largest *joint* gain. In this case, the package that proved best for the United States was also shown to be the one that resulted in the greatest joint gains; a somewhat better package for the Philippines, but not for the United States, entailed settling four issues on the Philippine delegation's terms, two on the U.S. delegation's terms, and no compromises. For other case applications of this approach, see Raiffa (1982), Ulvila and Snyder (1980), and Spector (1994).

Negotiation as a Bargaining Game

Another way of thinking about negotiation is in terms of a process influenced by forces that promote or detract from agreements. Negotiation is thus viewed as a bargaining game in which opponents exchange concessions, and where the exchange is influenced by the situation in which it takes place. This approach is descriptive: Laboratory situations are created to explore hypothesized determinants of bargaining behavior. Starting roughly with the seminal work of Siegel and Fouraker (1960), experimentalists in social psychology have sought an understanding of the conditions that drive the bargaining process. According to this view, negotiation is a process by which parties move gradually from their own initial positions toward the positions of others. In its simplest form, this process occurs between a single buyer and a unique seller who have total control over their interaction; the field of microeconomics refers to this situation as "bilateral monopoly." In their research on bilateral-monopoly bargaining, Siegel and Fouraker found that the best outcomes obtain when (1) there is a prominent optimal outcome; (2) there is complete information so that the prominent outcome can be identified; (3) each party has veto power, ensuring that the outcome is mutually acceptable; and (4) there are only two parties involved. Further analyses of this approach by Kelley and Schenitzki (1972) showed that maximum joint profits can be attained only when bargainers make concessions in a systematic manner.

What happens, however, when there is no prominent optimal outcome or when it is difficult to find? Who concedes first? Which party makes the larger concession? The bargaining becomes a contest of wills between tactical adversaries, each trying to pressure the other into conceding first or more frequently. A good deal of the research on two-party bargaining has focused on this situation, and the findings have identified tactics that could tilt the contest in favor of one or the other bargainer. Examples are commitment tactics, alternating from initially tough to subsequently soft postures, the tactical use of deadline pressures, and distinguishing between "white-hat" (good guy) negotiators and "black-hat" (bad guy) constituents. Tactics such as these could lead to an agreement that favors the more effective tactician. Used effectively by both parties, however, the tactics could produce a deadlock. Other work in this area includes Rubin and Brown (1975) and Pruitt and Carnevale (1993).

Negotiation as Organizational Management

Organizational theorists view negotiation as a process of building consensus among diverse constituencies with stakes in the outcome. Key constituencies are the principals or power-holders within the organizations represented in the negotiation. The process is dynamic, consisting of "two- (or multi-) way" communication among negotiators, constituents, and principals before and during the interparty negotiations. This conception renders negotiation a two- (or multi-) tiered process, also referred to as a two-level game (Putnam 1988): An intraparty (or domestic) negotiation occurs simultaneously with the interparty (or international) negotiation.

This view of negotiation recognizes its complexity. In particular, it recognizes the negotiator's dilemma of being caught between the often conflicting expectations of his or her constituents at home and those of the negotiation's other parties. This dilemma, known as "boundary-role conflict," was identified initially by Walton and McKersie (1965, chapter 8) in the context of labor-management negotiations. These authors highlight both the conditions for internal conflict and the tactics that may be used to resolve the dilemma. Two applications of this concept to international negotiations are Druckman's (1977a) formal model of dual responsiveness and Hopmann's (1977) analysis of the Mutual and Balanced Force Reduction (MBFR) talks. The former depicts the way a representative constructs a negotiating package that is acceptable to the other party, while at the same time taking into account the various bureaucratic agencies that seek to influence the contents of that package. The latter demonstrates how the multiple layers of bargaining within and between alliances were partially responsible for the long-term stalemate that entrapped the talks. We will examine boundary roles further in the section on rhythms and patterns.

The importance of bureaucratic politics in negotiation is made evident in both journalistic (Talbott 1979, 1984; Smith 1980) and analytical (Jonsson 1979; Jensen 1988) treatments of arms-control negotiations. By taking into account the organizational "embeddedness" of international negotiators' positions and performances, Kahn (1991) suggests a number of ways organizational theory can contribute to an understanding of negotiations among representatives of nation-states. There seems to be little doubt that negotiators "are motivated in large part by organizationally mediated rewards and penalties, the hope of organizational preferment, organizationally generated feelings of solidarity with others, identification with organizationally defined missions, and organizationally determined standards and values" (Kahn 1991, 149). Similarly, Winham's (1977) conceptualization of negotiation as a management process and Lax and Sebenius's (1986) depiction of management as a negotiation process illustrate clearly how well organizational phenomena reflect the complexity of negotiations between nations. These analyses urge us to pay more attention to the influence of role demands on the process and outcomes of negotiation.

Negotiation as Diplomatic Politics

A fourth perspective views negotiation as another setting for playing the game of international politics. Viewed as such, negotiations are microcosms of international relations, where parallel interactions or cross-linkages among many types of diplomatic activities occur, each influencing the other. This is the perspective of policy analysts and international relations scholars who are interested in how a particular negotiation fits into a broadly conceived foreign policy. The actors are governments whose actions are driven by policy prerogatives and structural elements of the international system.

By placing negotiation in the context of international relations, the analyst develops an appreciation for a variety of objectives served by negotiation, precedents or predilections that constrain negotiators, the linkages established among different negotiating venues, and the influence of external events on the negotiating process. Iklé (1964) illustrated how the type of agreement sought—for example, whether to extend an earlier agreement or to normalize a relationship—influences the main characteristics of the negotiating process. Of particular interest is his discussion of negotiating for side effects, where the parties seek to bolster a relationship, obtain intelligence, or affect the actions of third parties, rather than seeking an agreement. Kelleher (1976) showed that the legacy of past agreements often determines the way nations negotiate, especially when domestic constituencies emphasize the logic of precedent. Attempts to link an ongoing negotiation to others in progress or completed illustrate the connectedness of talks within an issue-area. Linkages are also often used tactically to break or create impasses, as shown in Tollison and Willett's (1979) analysis of economic negotiations and in Jensen's (1988) treatment of arms-control talks. More generally, international negotiators are influenced by specific external events, as demonstrated by the research reported by Hopmann and his colleagues (Hopmann and King 1976; Hopmann and Smith 1978) and discussed further below. These influences support the view that negotiations are embedded within an international system. (For an extreme statement of this view, see Kremenyuk 1991.)

Whereas the other approaches concentrate on the process of negotiating, this perspective focuses primarily on the international politics surrounding the negotiation. For the scholar of international relations, negotiation is one type of interaction among national representatives that impinges on the relationship between their nations. For the policymaker, negotiation is only one of several tools for implementing and developing foreign policies; others include official and unofficial diplomatic communications, ministerial meetings, meetings of international organizations, and summitry. For both scholar and practitioner, negotiation is a dynamic process that complements other activities initiated (or participated in) by governments. The *results* of these activities are evaluated in relation to broad policy objectives (e.g., Rubin 1981; Zartman 1989).

RHYTHMS AND PATTERNS OF NEGOTIATION

Research on negotiation processes has sought to determine whether a particular pattern characterizes most negotiations and has produced an interesting debate about stages: Does negotiation proceed in a linear fashion? If so, through how many distinct stages? If not, what other model best describes the process? Researchers have construed transitions from one stage to another in terms of turning points, and their chief interests revolve around identifying the occurrence of turning points and the circumstances that bring them about. The "circumstances" can be regarded as influences that drive the process toward or away from agreement. This section will present alternative conceptions of stages and turning points and will also summarize the research on key variables that influence the process.

Stages and Turning Points

Credit for introducing the concept of stages is usually given to Douglas (1957), who suggested that industrial negotiations pass through three stages: establishing the bargaining range, reconnoitering the range, and precipitating the decision crisis. More elaborate renditions of the concept appear in the literature. Gulliver's (1979) eight stages are the most elaborate model proposed to date. Druckman's (1983, 1986b) model consists of five stages: an agenda debate, a search for guiding principles, defining the issues, bargaining to arrive at an acceptable concession change, and a search for implementing details. Even more refined models have been suggested; Pruitt's (1981) distributive/coordinative distinction may be the most basic (see also Morley and Stephenson 1977; Walton and McKersie 1965).

Certain elements are found in each of the schemes: (1) sequential progression, in chronological and conceptual time; (2) alternating antagonistic and coordinative behavior within and across stages; (3) interconnected and overlapping stages rather than rigid and precise steps to an outcome; and (4) synchronization problems between the bargainers. Although disagreement exists on whether the stages are prescriptions for getting agreements or descriptions of processes observed in many cases, they tend to be both, reflecting how it is done, and how it is done well.

The stage concept can be a useful device for negotiators and analysts: It can be used to chart progress, to identify disjunctures in the process, and to provide a recognized pattern of expectations and behavior. Gulliver (1979) and Pruitt (1981) note the necessity of experiencing stages to know what is possible and to evaluate alternative agreements. According to Gulliver (1979, 177), "The parties need to experience the process and gain the experience of each other and of themselves so that they come to accept a particular outcome as satisfactory." It is also a tool for managing cognitive complexity, a function of particular relevance to international negotiations.

Applied to international negotiations, the stage concept has been used to describe a process that moves from the general to the specific. Pruitt

(1981) explains the progression as having two functions: to organize the intellectual efforts of the bargainers and to deal efficiently with basic differences in outlook. International negotiators are often required to consider several issues simultaneously. To do this effectively, they must consider ways to simplify the intellectual task. One procedure is to identify a set of general issues and principles on which they agree. This procedure is the first stage of Zartman's (1975) two-stage model of negotiation: development of an abstract formula followed by the details needed to implement this formula. (Zartman and Berman [1982] extend this model to three stages, adding a diagnostic process before a formula is developed.) One study that tests this model against concession/convergence behavior is Hopmann and Smith (1978).

As the negotiation passes through stages, momentum builds toward a conclusion, referred to as the endgame. It is useful to think about the progression in terms of turning points, defined as events or processes that mark the passage from one stage to the next, signaling progress from earlier to later phases. This concept has been used to depict progress in such diverse negotiations as the base-rights talks between the United States and Spain (Druckman 1986b), the North American Free Trade Agreement negotiations (Tomlin 1989), the Intermediate Nuclear Forces (INF) talks (Druckman et al. 1991), and eleven cases of multilateral environmental negotiations that took place from 1972 to 1992 (Chasek 1994). Examples are resolving impasses, signing framework agreements, developing formulas and then bargaining over details, and absorbing events outside the talks by either changing evaluations of the terms on the table or resolving the decision dilemma in the endgame. Defined more precisely, turning points have been shown to be useful analytical devices for assessing relationships between aspects of the verbal exchanges and key events (e.g., Druckman 1986b). Similar concepts have been used productively to capture transitions in team development, especially when major "jumps in progress" occur (Gersick 1988) or when shared perspectives have been achieved (Dechant and Marsick 1992).

Issues of timing occur also with regard to the decision to negotiate. The question of interest arises when the parties are ready to negotiate or to seek mediation. Fisher's (1990) conflict stages are instructive. He depicts the way international conflicts escalate in terms of four stages: discussion, polarization, segregation, and destruction. At each stage, the relationship between disputants changes. The preferred method of conflict management becomes increasingly competitive, going from joint decision making in stage one to attempts at destruction in stage four. Intervention activities also change: assisting communication through negotiation in the first stage, improving relationships through consultation in the second stage, controlling hostility through "muscled" mediation in stage three, and controlling violence through peacekeeping in stage four. Less is known about the right time to intervene or to undertake an effort to make a desired change— whether early, when the costs are low, or late, when the moment is "ripe."

One well-known approach emphasizes the importance of a "mutually hurting stalemate" (Touval and Zartman 1985). Parties are more likely to come to the table when they are offered the prospect of a way out of a situation of increasing costs, coupled with decreasing prospects of winning. However, other factors may also lead parties to make de-escalatory moves. Kriesberg (1991) has identified three conditions for de-escalation. One concerns relations between the adversaries, including relative power, level of cooperative exchanges, and extent of shared interests and values. Another condition involves domestic circumstances, including support for reducing antagonism, changes in government leadership, economic difficulties, and changes in support for a military-based security regime. A third condition is the international context, which consists of the impacts of other conflicts and the readiness of various governmental and nongovernmental actors to serve as intermediaries in the conflict. These factors are likely to combine in various ways to make the situation conducive (or nonconducive) to de-escalation. Kriesberg also mentions the prospect of positive benefits from de-escalation.

Less is known about the relationship between the dynamics of conflict and the stages through which negotiations proceed. Although conditions may be conducive to entering into negotiation, the negotiation process itself may facilitate or hinder the relationship between the adversaries, leading either to further de-escalation or to the next stage in Fisher's (1990) ladder of escalation. It facilitates the relationship to the extent that it proceeds through the negotiation stages outlined above. It hinders the relationship to the extent that the process is characterized by frequent impasses rather than turning points. Whether the process gathers momentum toward agreement or ends in stalemate depends on many of the factors discussed in this chapter as well as the kinds of strategies of de-escalation— based on parties, inducements, and issues—proposed by Kriesberg (1991). Further research is needed to increase our understanding of the role played by negotiation in resolving international conflicts as well as the impact of those conflicts on the negotiation process.

Constraints: Boundary Roles

The international negotiator occupies several roles simultaneously. As a representative of his or her government's interests, the negotiator must be responsive to its demands or requests. The negotiator must also take into account the interests of the other governments involved in the talks. Referred to as a "boundary-role conflict" (Walton and McKersie 1965; Frey and Adams 1972; Druckman 1977a; Walton et al. 1994), this dilemma often confounds the main objective of the negotiator, who must try to resolve the different interests in order to attain an agreement. The dilemma is further complicated by a lack of consensus within the negotiator's own government and by the presence of multiple parties, including alliance partners, opponents, and third parties and their own interests in particular agreements. Another aspect of this dilemma is the frequent absence of key stakeholders, particularly in negotiations that involve governments and intranational actors that may lack legitimacy. Multilateral negotiations magnify the dilemma further, placing the negotiator in a managerial role that requires consensus building, leadership, and horse trading much in the manner of a lobbyist. Putnam (1988) and Evans and colleagues (1993) analyze negotiation as a linked, two-level process, in which the key to international agreement lies in the concordance of proposals with domestic interest coalitions.

Boundary roles place complex information-processing and tactical demands on the negotiator. With regard to information processing, negotiators monitor other sides' moves for evidence of position change. They also monitor their own side for evidence of changes in positions on issues or preferences for various parts of the negotiation package. These monitoring activities have been conceived in different ways: the former as concession-making functions, the latter as utility functions. Neither type of function is simple, and both depend on the results of monitoring. Negotiators have been shown to adjust their strategies (making more or fewer concessions) following an evaluation of the others' moves, as depicted, for example, by Coddington's (1968) model. They alter (or maintain) their positions also in response to changes in agency or constituent evaluations: The more accountable they are to those agencies, the more likely they are to respond to these changing preferences (Druckman 1978).

At the same time, negotiators are not passive observers of the process. They are also tacticians who attempt to bring about change in both directions—influencing both their opponents and their constituents or principals. This is the "art" of impression management, described by Walton and McKersie (1965) in terms of three types of tactics. One type is intended to increase the negotiator's flexibility, for example, by limiting constituent participation in the formulation of proposals. Another type is intended to reduce constituents' aspirations by invoking rational arguments or using tacit communication to elicit the opponent's cooperation. A third set of tactics serves to reduce the discrepancy between constituents' expectations and performance. These tactics include limiting opportunities for surveillance, obscuring concessions, and exaggerating the level of achievement. The successful execution of these tactics depends on the extent to which negotiators have both control over the process and complete information about their side's preferences and strategies. By reducing the negotiators' latitude through scripting and monitoring and by withholding information, the principals can limit the negotiators' control over the process. To the extent that negotiation is a two- (or multi-) sided struggle for control, the negotiators are also limited by their opponents' control over the process.

The end of the Cold War has widened the domains and structures for negotiation. More issues, more actors, and new formats have served to increase the complexity of international negotiations. These changes have implications for monitoring and control over the process. With regard to monitoring, the negotiator must keep track of many more positions and changed preferences. With regard to control, negotiators have less influence over decisions made in multilateral forums, but they also have more flexibility in developing positions and strategies due to the enlarged negotiating agendas facing governments. In light of these developments, the challenge is less a matter of dealing with conflicting demands of constituents or principals and opponents, and more a matter of keeping track of ongoing developments. Negotiation is becoming more like the management-process metaphor proposed by Winham (1977).

Preparing: Strategizing or Studying

Preparing for the negotiation is a central activity during the prenegotiation phase. Experimental evidence suggests that prenegotiation activities affect both the prospects for entering negotiations and the ease with which parties negotiate. Thibaut (1968) demonstrated the delicate balance of power among the parties needed to preserve a common interest in negotiation. Parties are more likely to enter into a negotiation when the talks can help them avoid a breakdown in their relationship; for example, when one party is in a better position to be exploitative, as in the case of a powerful nation demanding a high price for armaments from a weaker ally, and when another party is in a better position to be disloyal, as in the case of the weaker nation threatening to leave an alliance. Results indicate that most protective contracts were entered into when these threats were highest.

Bass (1966) and Druckman (1968) demonstrated the impact of the way bargaining teams prepare prior to negotiation. Bargaining was facilitated to the extent that parties avoided intensive strategy preparation and focused on the issues per se during prenegotiation caucuses. Moreover, it made little difference whether the caucuses were unilateral (teammates only) or bilateral (members of opposing teams). Informal, issue-oriented discussion was more effective than both tactical preparation and no prenegotiation communication among teammates or with opponents (see also Klimoski 1972). The effects on indicators of flexibility or the willingness to compromise are particularly strong: Among ten variables analyzed in a recent meta-analysis of bargaining experiments, type of preparation produced the second-strongest effect size (Druckman 1994). Issue-oriented discussions may further increase the level of cooperation during the process and produce even better outcomes if they include efforts to understand the underlying values that divide the parties (Druckman et al. 1988). However, whether these results are due primarily to increased understanding or camaraderie among the negotiators remains to be explored; further research is needed to distinguish effects between the cognitive and the emotional aspects of planning. (See Druckman and Broome 1991 for a start along these lines.)

These results have implications for Dean's (1986) analysis of the preparation of U.S. negotiators for arms-control talks with the Soviet Union. He stresses the importance of bringing the negotiator "into the U.S. concept at the outset." However, such training should be done as part of informal and issue-oriented discussions. While negotiators' participation in the development of national positions may give them a better understanding of the country's position, it may also enhance their commitment to those positions, as the laboratory research suggests. Development of a negotiating concept would also benefit from exploratory discussions with the other side prior to the formal talks. Dean recognizes the importance of such nonbinding exchanges for the formulation of opening positions, taking into account differences and similarities in the parties' objectives.

Prenegotiation activities may also contribute to the "atmospherics" of the negotiation. For example, attention must be paid to the physical setting of the talks, including both their symbolic significance and the facilities used, and to the provision of adequate logistical support. Changes in the way parties interact may lay the foundation for constructive negotiation; alternative channels of communication may be opened for sending up trial balloons and for widening the range of options under consideration.

Effective use of prenegotiation preparations may spell the difference between successful and unsuccessful outcomes.

More broadly, the prenegotiation phase has taken on increasing importance as nations discuss complex issues in global forums where difficult conceptual problems must be resolved before bargaining can occur. Chasek's (1994) comparative analysis of multilateral environmental negotiations makes clear that the prenegotiation phase is not simply preparatory in the narrow sense of planning for an eventual negotiation but contributes, in a larger sense, to developing a framework that can make agreement possible. As such, prenegotiation activities are indeed a part of the negotiation process, as Saunders (1984) has proposed. They fill important functions, clarifying the agenda, parties, supports, budgets, costs and risks, and other requirements that are necessary before negotiations can begin (Stein 1989).

Framing: Developing Sets and Orientations

Pruitt (1965) has highlighted the importance of the ways international actors define or perceive their situation. Of particular relevance for negotiation are perceptions of the task as being either competitive (win-lose) or cooperative (problem solving). A number of experimental studies have demonstrated that these perceptions were heavily influenced by the situation and, in turn, influenced the negotiating process and outcome (Druckman 1968; Zechmeister and Druckman 1973; Druckman et al. 1988). For example, in the Druckman study (1968), strategic planning prior to the negotiation produced competitive perceptions that resulted in frequent deadlocks. Similar correlates of negotiating behavior have been found for such perceptions as whether the negotiating climate is viewed as futile or productive, tolerant or hostile, and whether the opponent is seen as fair or unfair, trusting or suspicious (Druckman et al. 1988).

In a number of bargaining experiments, the investigator induced the negotiator's orientation through instructions from the experimenter or from constituents (e.g., Summers 1968; Organ 1971). In some studies, orientation was "selected" by recruiting subjects who indicated cooperative or competitive attitudes prior to the experiment (e.g., Wall 1975; Lindskold et al. 1983). Taken together, these experiments show strong effects for this variable: Of ten variables compared in a recent meta-analysis, orientation had the strongest impact on compromise behavior. The impacts were considerably stronger for studies that induced orientations than for those that selected for them (Druckman 1994).

Orientations toward negotiation may be induced in subtle ways. A series of experiments (Neale et al. 1987; Neale and Bazerman 1985) showed that negotiating behavior can be affected by simply framing the bargaining task in terms of "gains to be realized" (potential profits) or "losses to be avoided" (potential costs). Negotiators with a gains orientation typically complete more transactions or conclude more agreements than those with a losses orientation. They do so, however, largely because they are willing to make larger compromises, not because they arrive at integrative agreements that result in high joint profits. Additionally, the larger compromises are thought to be due to an aversion to taking risks (e.g., escalating the conflict or causing impasses) induced by the gains orientation. Indeed, risk aversion may account for the plethora of compromise agreements arms-control negotiators have achieved over the years (Jensen 1988).

At a somewhat deeper level, negotiators may be influenced by the metaphors that are evoked by negotiating situations. A recent analysis indicated that subjects who viewed a simulated conflict in ideological terms also perceived the bargaining process as resembling an arms race, and this perception correlated with their being less willing to compromise and less satisfied with the outcome. The arms-race metaphor illustrates the importance of mental models in negotiation. Some models, or analogies, may lead subjects to cooperate in seeking an agreement, while others may lead them to compete for advantage. We need to learn more about the way such imagery influences conflict behavior, leading toward or away from satisfactory agreements. Moreover, negotiation may be more effective to the extent that negotiators develop a shared model of the task and their roles in it. The recent work on the way teams develop shared mental models would seem to be particularly relevant, especially in the context of the new problem-solving formats of global environmental conferences. Orasanu and Salas found that effective (compared to ineffective) teams were characterized by "[shared] knowledge enabling each person to carry out his or her role in a timely and coordinated fashion, helping the team to function as a single unit with little negotiation of what to do and when to do it" (1993, 7). When asked to account for a team's success, coaches will often say that the team members play well together or that they anticipate each other's moves. These sorts of shared understandings developed among team members may also develop among negotiators from different countries, especially as they continue to interact in long-term conferences.

Bargaining and Concessions

Bargaining and concession making are common features of most, if not all, negotiations. Although the term *bargaining* is often used interchangeably with *negotiation*, it can also refer to one phase in a process that consists of many other activities (Druckman 1983). Bargaining occurs during the discussions over details, where parties exchange concessions or trade items of value (Zartman 1975). This section examines several aspects of bargaining that have received attention in the research literature: the concession-making "dance," negative spirals and starting mechanisms, driving factors, and the role of values.

The Concession-Making Dance. Since the publication of the study by Siegel and Fouraker (1960), students of bargaining behavior have devoted considerable attention to the effects of alternative concession-making strategies for eliciting concessions from an opponent. A tough strategy, recommended by Siegel and Fouraker, is likely to work if it produces concessions from the opponents, for example, when they are under time pressure and have weak alternatives to a settlement; it will not work if it leads opponents to reciprocate toughness, as when they worry about being exploited or perceive an unfair advantage. Similarly, a softer approach, recommended by Osgood (1962), will work if it produces reciprocation from the opponent who is anxious to conclude a fair agreement; it will not work if the opponent responds with fewer concessions in an attempt to exploit the other's softness. Central to these strategies is the issue of responsiveness: Do bargainers reciprocate, exploit, or ignore the other's concessions (Bartos 1978; Pruitt 1981)? This question has been addressed in analyses of international negotiations.

These analyses sought to ascertain the extent to which international bargainers reciprocated each other's concessions. In his analysis of base-rights talks between the United States and Spain, Druckman (1986b) discovered a pattern in which, following a comparison of mutual concessions in the initial round, negotiators attempted to "close the gap" in the next round by reducing their concessions when the other side failed to concede (i.e., they reciprocated each other's tough postures). A similar pattern, referred to as comparative responsiveness, was found by Stoll and McAndrew (1986) in the ten years of talks between the Soviet Union and the United States over limiting strategic weapons (SALT I and II). In addition, analyses of seven international negotiations for which concession data were available (including the Nuclear Test Ban talks, SALT I and II, and postwar disarmament talks), conducted by Druckman and Harris (1990) demonstrated that among the ten models of responsiveness examined (namely, simple tit-for-tat, five variants on monitoring trends in the other's concessions, and four variants on comparing previous mutual concessions), the comparative pattern best depicted the way negotiators responded to each other's moves; negotiators evaluate the size of the difference between their own positions and those of other sides and then respond. This pattern resembles Coddington's (1968) bargaining cycle of expectations-evaluations-adjustments, also known as "threshold adjustment." (Snyder and Diesing 1977 provide further elaboration of these cycles.) Although the adjustments can be made in the direction of either increased toughness or softness, the cases examined were characterized by moves that increased mutual toughness, often leading to impasses. Of interest is the challenge of reversing this pattern, moving the negotiation down a path toward agreement rather than stalemate.

Negative Spirals and Starting Mechanisms. Only one case analyzed in the Druckman and Harris (1990) study showed a pattern in which bargainers adjusted their moves in the direction of the "softer" opponent. This case occurred during the final two years of discussion between the Soviet Union and the United States over a partial nuclear test ban and resulted in an agreement (Hopmann and Smith 1978). The agreement was marked by President Kennedy's 1963 announcement of a suspension of U.S. nuclear tests and an appeal for a relaxation of East-West tension. Regarded as a unilateral initiative, the announcement broke a long impasse in negotiations that lasted from 1958 to 1963. Laboratory and historical case studies have identified some conditions under which unilateral initiatives are likely to produce the desired cooperative responses.

The laboratory evidence suggests that such initiatives are likely to be more effective when the initiator clarifies the intention behind the move, when reciprocity is not required too soon, when it is rewarded, and when it is difficult for the other party to explain away the initiatives (Lindskold et al. 1986). Favorable circumstances include perceived dependence of the intended recipient on the initiator, a perception that the initiating party cannot be exploited, and the recipient's judgment that the benefits of cooperation outweigh those of competition. Historical evidence presented by Rose (1988) adds other favorable conditions: a clear signaling of demands by the initiating party, no internal bureaucratic conflicts within the recipient, and no threats to political status, security, economic, or military capabilities. Of these conditions, the most important concern was risk to security; a nation that perceived itself at risk did not reciprocate its adversary's cooperative move.

Unilateral initiatives are actions usually taken outside of negotiation. They can be used as starting mechanisms to get talks back on track or to break impasses (note Osgood's [1973] proposal of Graduated Reduction in Tensions for MBFR). They can also be used as alternatives to formal negotiations, such as Adelman's (1984–85) proposed strategy for achieving arms control without treaties. The former is directed primarily toward getting agreements; the latter is intended to improve relationships. In some cases, both purposes are served by one party's initiatives; one example is Gorbachev's stream of unilateral moves leading to the Intermediate-Range Nuclear Forces (INF) agreement and to a markedly changed relationship between the superpowers. The extraordinary events that preceded the fall of the Soviet Union have provoked analysts to reexamine their assumptions about the benefits of formal negotiation, at least in the area of arms control (see Ramberg 1993).

Driving Factors in Bargaining. The research discussed above concentrates primarily on the effects of the other party's concession making, demonstrating that bargainers respond to each other's moves. However, such responsiveness is only one of several factors that drive the bargaining process. Many other variables have been found in experimental studies to affect bargaining. These effects are summarized in a recent meta-analysis of the literature (Druckman 1994), in which ten aspects of the bargaining situation were compared for their relative impacts on compromise in bargaining. Beyond a competitive or cooperative orientation, the strongest effects were obtained for whether bargainers strategized or studied prior to bargaining, whether or not the bargaining occurred under a deadline, and whether the distance between initial positions was large or small. The weakest effects were obtained for whether the issue was considered "large" or "small," and whether or not audiences were present during the bargaining session. It appears that the way bargainers define their task, as a competitive contest or problem to be solved, has a particularly strong influence on their attempts to secure an agreement.

Further analyses of the experimental findings suggest insights into the way different aspects of the situation combine to produce various effects. The question most frequently asked in this regard is: When do bargainers stick to their positions? The answers are varied: (a) when they prepare strategies in cohesive groups for a negotiation in which few issues are being contested and no deadline exists; (b) when competitive orientations are induced during the bargaining by bureaucratic "superiors" and are linked explicitly to bargaining strategies; (c) when they negotiate in the presence of an audience that creates strong face-saving pressures; and (d) when there are no time limits to reach agreement and no "strike costs" while the bargaining takes place. These are some of the conditions for intransigence; as such, they are aspects of the situation that can be manipulated as part of a tactical approach to negotiating beneficial agreements.

The Role of Values in Bargaining. Bargaining interactions are also influenced by the types of issues under discussion. In international negotiations, parties typically discuss their interests in matters of security, territory, or trade. These issues are usually well defined, allowing for the sorts of exchanges characteristic of bargaining over tangible items. Were it this simple, however, the record would show many agreements emerging from a fairly predictable process in many ways akin to collective bargaining in labor-management disputes. Unfortunately, this is seldom the case in international negotiation. Impasse is a major concern in international negotiations, and the process does not exhibit a predictable pattern from one case to another. In part, this situation is due to the role values play in defining the issues at stake.

Differences in values enter the discussions in several ways. One is when government representatives address issues concerning their countries' relationship, as occurs often in regions undergoing political transformation (Druckman 1980). Another is when agendas are expanded to deal with "larger" issues, as, for example, when Spain demanded that the United States broker its entry into NATO during the course of the 1975–76 talks about renewing base rights (Druckman 1986b). A third example is when issues of national sovereignty are raised in talks about establishing trade or security regimes, economic unions, or regional organizations; the new entities provoke anxieties about the extent to which independence must be sacrificed for the advantages of interdependence (Zartman 1991). Finally, a fourth example is when parties are divided along ideological lines, as in negotiations to resolve internal conflicts between insurgent groups asserting their claims for power and regimes bent on preserving the political order (Zartman 1995).

These issues are rarely the direct subjects of negotiation. They are often regarded as non-negotiable, as issues to be discussed but not compromised. As such, they exacerbate the conflict by making it difficult for parties to resolve their differences over interests. This is especially the case when the link between value differences and interests or positions is made explicit by one or another party, as illustrated in a series of experiments by Druckman and colleagues. The experimental results showed that conflicts were easier to resolve when value differences were either not introduced or essentially "de-linked" from interests (Druckman et al. 1977). However, they also showed that when values were separated from interests, the negotiating process was more competitive than when value differences were confronted and discussed in prenegotiation sessions (Druckman et al. 1988). Further experiments showed that the facilitating effects of the prenegotiation discussions were due to the increased camaraderie and familiarity gained during those meetings (Druckman and Broome 1991). These results underscore an important contribution of prenegotiation sessions, namely, to acknowledge differences of values without letting those differences hinder subsequent talks over specific interests (Stein 1989).

Over the longer term, there may be a broader interplay between values and interests that produces cycles of polarized and depolarized conflicts between parties. The cycles reflect diverging and converging positions owing to repeated attempts to resolve conflicting interests; agreements serve to reduce value differences, which, in turn, makes it easier to negotiate future conflicts. Similarly, stalemates can exaggerate value differences, serving to hinder future negotiations. Earlier theoretical work has described the process in the form of propositions (Druckman and Zechmeister 1973), which were later usefully applied to depict the bargaining and related interactions between conflicting groups in the Philippines (Druckman and Green 1995).

EXPANDING THE DOMAIN

As noted throughout this chapter, much of our knowledge about negotiation is based on the results of laboratory experiments, supplemented by a rich literature of case studies. An advantage of the experimental approach is that it focuses attention on relationships between precisely defined variables, such as the influence of time pressure on agreements. Such a setting also has the feature of cumulative knowledge, allowing an investigator to compare across experiments the relative impacts of several variables on negotiating behavior (Druckman 1994). A disadvantage of the laboratory approach is a kind of myopic focus that renders the findings only partially relevant to complex cases of international negotiation. The knowledge comes in parts, with each part—a line of experiments—revealing only those aspects of negotiation that are isolated for "microscopic" investigation. A challenge for future research will be to link or synthesize the parts into a broader picture. One way to do this is through the development of frameworks.

Frameworks

A good deal of the conceptual work on negotiation has consisted of identifying the various parts of the process. These are general dimensions that can be used to describe a variety of cases. The primary contributions of this approach are those found in most taxonomic work, namely, to define a field, to distinguish among similar and dissimilar cases, and to identify connections or hypothesized relationships among the categories. These functions have been served by the frameworks proposed by Sawyer and Guetzkow (1965), which relates preconditions to processes, conditions, and outcomes, and by Randolph (1966), which organize the aspects of negotiation into the categories of prenegotiation, negotiation, agreement, and implementation.

Sawyer and Guetzkow (1965) used their framework to organize the empirical work on negotiation done in the 1950s and 1960s. Since then, it has served to guide research and application, including Ramberg's (1977) study of tactics used in the talks over demilitarization of the deep seabed; Bonham's (1971) analysis of factors influencing the 1955 East-West talks in the UN Disarmament Subcommittee; Druckman and Hopmann's (1991) models of the MBFR process; Druckman's (1973, 1977a) efforts to organize the social-psychological literature on bargaining processes and influences; and, most recently, Weiss's (1994a, 1994b) framework for organizing cross-cultural research on international business negotiations (see also Graham et al. 1994). The Sawyer-Guetzkow framework has also served as a basis for Fisher's (1983) conceptualization and organization of the literature on third-party consultation.

These frameworks do have their shortcomings. By itself, an organizing framework lacks sufficient penetration of details to capture subtle processes in particular cases; it is also, at least initially, a taxonomic, not an analytical, exercise. Recognizing these shortcomings, projects have recently been undertaken to move beyond the defining and organizing functions of frameworks. A number of projects, conducted as part of the Processes of International Negotiation program at IIASA, are examples of attempts to bridge analysis and synthesis. These projects fall within the initial framework established by the program, analyzing negotiation according to actors, structures, processes, strategies, and outcomes (Kremenyuk 1991).

Framework categories were used in the design of a simulated conference on environmental regulation (Druckman 1993a). The exercise captured processes of international negotiation—as described by frameworks—without forfeiting the essential properties of experimental design. By developing scenarios that resembled the real-world talks (at each of several negotiating stages), role players (scientists and diplomats) were confronted with contingencies similar to those facing the actual delegates. By "unpacking" the key variables in each scenario, using a pair-comparison procedure, the relative impacts of those variables (in each stage) on decisions about position movement, tactics, and perceptions were compared. Results were expressed in the form of trajectories of factors that influenced decisions in each stage. For example, a path toward agreement was as follows: friendly relations with other delegations (stage one) —> talks held at a peripheral location (stage two) —> talks given limited media attention (stage three) —> talks given limited media attention (stage four). These factors increased flexibility leading to an agreement at the end of the process. Other factors served to decrease flexibility, leading to stalemate at the end: a lack of familiarity with the other delegations (stage one) —> talks held at a central location (stage two) —> talks given wide media attention (stage three) —> talks given wide media attention (stage four). These factors can also be altered or manipulated for impact—that is, as levers of negotiating flexibility.

Another project used framework categories as interview questions for comparative case analysis (Druckman 1997). Members of Austrian national delegations to a variety of bilateral and multilateral talks were asked about several aspects of the negotiation: its structure, the composition of the delegations, bureaucratic support, the issues, the negotiating situation, the process, the outcomes, and the influence of events outside the negotiation. Building on the computer model developed by Bloomfield and Beattie (1971) for conflict analysis, the research used statistical procedures to discover similarities and dissimilarities among the cases as well as the critical factors that distinguished them. The key distinguishing factor among the cases was conference size. Smaller conferences were more likely to result in binding agreements or treaties than larger, multilateral conferences. Smaller conferences were characterized by low turnover of delegates, private forums, a stage-like process, packaging of issues, and relatively weak deadline pressures. These factors facilitate choosing among the "available terms" (Ikle 1964, 60). As such, they may be a more cost-effective forum for negotiation than large multilateral talks since they have fewer transaction costs and produce better outcomes. Multilateral talks, however, offer other advantages. One is alliance coordination. Another is the creation of communities of opinion that serve as regimes regulating transactions among regional or global actors. These advantages are a result of conference diplomacy, not negotiation intended to create binding agreements.

The differences between bilateral and multilateral structures also have implications for analysis. Zartman (1994) identifies six characteristics of multilateral negotiations, including multiple parties (but not fixed at a given number), many issues that allow for complex trade-offs, a considerable variety of roles among the parties in the negotiation, outcomes that concern rules more than redistributive issues, and the organization of parties into coalitions that often change during the course of the talks. These features complicate analyses of relationships between processes (or strategies) and outcomes and require an expanded framework, drawing on insights provided by game and decision theory, organization theory, small-group analysis, coalition approaches, and leadership analysis. Each of these approaches addresses how parties manage the complexity of the encounter in order to produce an outcome. By emphasizing a particular aspect of the multilateral process, each approach is limited. By combining these aspects into a broader perspective, a synthesis of the approaches provides the range and scope needed to understand the way multilateral processes lead to outcomes. The increasing popularity of multilateral forums in the post–Cold War world encourages further progress in developing a useful analytical paradigm.

A fourth project created a computer program for diagnosing parties' flexibility and projecting probable outcomes of ongoing negotiations (Druckman 1993b). Users were asked questions in each of five categories: the issues, the parties, the delegations, the situation, and the process. The questions varied in terms of the extent to which they correlated with flexibility; each question was assigned a weight based on research evidence about its impact on flexibility. The answers and weights were combined by the program to yield a judgment of each party's flexibility. These judgments were then used as estimates of likely outcomes, including optimal agreements for both parties, fair but less-than-optimal agreements, capitulation by one party to another, impasses, and continuation without agreement. Among the program's features is the ability to make comparisons among different cases and among different "theories" of negotiation. With regard to cases, users can answer the questions for each of several negotiations and compare their location on a "flexibility grid"; regarding theories, users can compare the flexibility judgments resulting from answers to questions in each of the categories. In a recent application, a very high correspondence was discovered between the hypothesized outcomes of nine completed cases (Panama Canal, nuclear test ban, INF, and acid rain talks, among others) and the actual outcomes obtained in those negotiations, attesting to the validity of the diagnostic (framework) categories (see Druckman 1993b).

Activities that occur after an agreement has been negotiated are receiving increasing attention. Regarded as a stage in an extended process of negotiation and renegotiation, these activities include ratification, monitoring the parties for compliance with the provisions or verification of the agreement, and continuing negotiation of the terms or issues still to be resolved. In their study of environmental agreements, Spector and Korula (1992) divide postagreement processes into domestic and international aspects. The domestic aspects include ratification, rule making to protect the agreement, implementation and resistance, and monitoring. The international components consist of the formation, operation, and adjustment of the regimes that come into being as a result of the agreements. Environmental negotiations are embedded within a larger institutional context; complex issue packages and linkages among issue-areas and sectors make them difficult to negotiate and sustain.

Less complex, perhaps, is the implementation of bilateral arms-control and base-rights agreements. A key issue for arms control is verification of the agreed reductions, although issues concerning the emergence of security regimes are also relevant (Jervis 1983). Base-rights provisions are often of shorter duration and are renegotiated periodically. (See Iklé's [1964] discussion of extension negotiations.) Domestic ratification and relational issues are also important in this arena (Druckman 1990). These are examples of activities to be included in an expanded framework of negotiation.

In addition to postnegotiation processes, an enlarged framework should take into account the various activities that precede negotiation, as discussed earlier, as well as the multilateral (and global) structures characteristic of many current venues, discussed above. Such an enlarged framework should also recognize that negotiations occur between various types of identity groups within and independent of nation-states. Although little attention has been paid to these negotiation processes, a good start in developing a framework, based on diverse cases, has been made in Zartman's (1995) work on internal negotiations.

Complex Cases

Frameworks also guide qualitative analyses of cases. This is illustrated by the series of case studies done by the Foreign Policy Institute (FPI) at Johns Hopkins University's School for Advanced International Studies and by the Pew Project, based at Georgetown University's Center for the Study of Diplomacy; and those reported in *Negotiation Journal*, edited by Harvard's PON, and in the new journal *International Negotiation*, edited by the Washington Interest in Negotiation (WIN) group. The FPI cases are structured in terms of a common framework for analyzing the negotiation process, and their narratives seem to capture the dynamics of complex bilateral and multilateral negotiations. Following a background summary, each case narrative focuses on the parties and their sources of power and interests, leading to a discussion of the underlying and immediate precipitants that brought about negotiation. The next sections deal with process, beginning with prenegotiations and culminating in a decision on whether to negotiate. The process continues with a search for a formula that provides a basis for working out the details of an agreement, including the tactics and decisions involved in ending the talks with a mutually satisfactory outcome. The authors' attempts to identify turning points and to provide insights into the impacts of pressures exerted by the parties contribute to compelling lessons for negotiating behavior. Examples of bilateral cases are the 1972 Simla talks between India and Pakistan, the 1904–05 peace talks between Russia and Japan, the Panama Canal negotiations, and the Beagle Channel dispute between Chile and Argentina. Analyses of the multilateral cases provide additional insights into the process of managing complexity: for example, the Stockholm Conference on Security and Cooperation in Europe, the Mediterranean Action Plan, the Contadora peace process, and the Convention on Transboundary Air Pollution.

Although not structured in terms of a common framework, the Pew case studies and those reported in *Negotiation Journal* and *International Negotiation* also use guiding concepts to provide insights into the process. In discussing lessons learned from four international cases (the U.S.-Canada Free Trade Agreement, a hostage release following a 1970 skyjacking in Jordan, the 1971 quadripartite agreement on Berlin, and the Washington Naval Conference), Salacuse and Rubin note that they all "identify phases . . . and point to the importance of timing and ripeness in beginning a negotiation and then moving from one phase to another" (1990, 316). The cases illustrate the shaping influence of external events, or the international environment, and the need for negotiators to manage them. They also highlight the technique of linkage, or managing the complexity of different issues by combining them into packages. Other *Negotiation Journal* case studies document the importance of turning points in the life cycle of a negotiation (Druckman et al. 1991), making credible conciliatory gestures to signal a willingness to terminate conflict (Mitchell 1991), acting when the moment is ripe (Dupont 1990), and being sensitive to the timing of multilateral conferences (Koh 1990). Cases in a special issue of *International Negotiation* dealing with the former Soviet Union and Eastern Europe show the effects of past styles and images and of current contextual features (*International Negotiation* 1996). Together, the cases analyzed in the journals identify processes and influences that could be the basis for a general framework for analyzing international negotiation.

Comparative Analyses

Two projects undertaken by FSI's Center for the Study of Foreign Affairs emphasized comparative analysis in the study of negotiation. The project's examination of diverse cases for similarities and differences generated some important lessons for the research community. In one project, an attempt was made to derive lessons from the experiences of negotiators in four cases: the Panama Canal treaties, the Falkland/Malvinas Islands dispute, the Cyprus dispute, and negotiating Zimbabwe's independence (Bendahmane and McDonald 1986). The diversity of the cases provided a rich set of lessons about many aspects of negotiation as well as the interplay of local, regional, and international politics. Among the more interesting insights are those concerning formal and informal diplomacy, conditions for negotiation, procedures, endgame tactics, and strategies for sustaining an agreement. Different procedures and tactics were shown to be effective at different stages. As Druckman notes, "It was the combination of choice of technique and its skillful use together with a changing political context, recognized as favorable when it became so, that provided the key to success in Panama and in Zimbabwe" (1986a, 287).

Another FSI project, undertaken in collaboration with members of the WIN group, developed lessons from three cases of separate base-rights negotiations involving the United States and Spain, Greece, and the Philippines (McDonald and Bendahmane 1990), which were noted more for their comparability than for their diversity. The analyses offered insights into the impact of delegation composition, procedural flexibility, the use of certain tactics, and the role played by language in the endgame and in sustaining the agreement. The two sets of cases also illustrate the interplay of context and process. Context is highlighted in the earlier cases, rooted as they were in international politics. Process is emphasized in the base-rights cases, where the bilateral relationship is adjusted through periodic negotiations. These projects illustrate the value of *inducing* lessons from experience. This is an alternative analytical approach to *using* a framework for case analysis, as was done in the projects described above. The lessons do, however, contribute to the development of frameworks as we go back and forth between inductive and deductive approaches to understanding negotiation processes.

THE "GREAT DIVIDE": THE NEGOTIATOR MEETS THE RESEARCHER

In his recent book, *Bridging the Gap*, Alexander George writes that "members of these two communities (academic and policymaking) define their interest in international relations somewhat differently; they pursue different professional goals and have difficulty communicating with each other" (1993, 135). He then proposes strategies for generating policy-relevant knowledge, among them: Include in the research variables over which policymakers have some control, do not define concepts at too high a level of abstraction, and seek conditional generalizations. With regard to negotiation, Druckman and Hopmann (1989) describe similar difficulties in the relationship between scholars and practitioners and also suggest approaches for generating relevant knowledge. Although many communication problems still exist, progress has been made in tailoring conceptual knowledge and research to the needs of negotiators or diplomats and their support staffs. Several projects serve to illustrate how this is done.

The FSI projects described above are examples of attempts by scholars to derive lessons of value to practitioners. The lessons are insights derived from past experience and recast as prescriptions or guidelines for action. Although limited to only a few cases, and made in hindsight, the lessons do alert practitioners to pitfalls in the negotiation process and may serve as an aid to planning. The FPI case studies, also described above, are examples of scholar-practitioners analyzing their cases in terms of a conceptual framework of negotiation stages described in some detail by Zartman and Berman (1982). The lessons are insights derived from using the framework to analyze the details of the various cases. Although used primarily for teaching, the case studies are valuable for the participating practitioners, who were challenged to think about their cases in terms of the Zartman-Berman framework. More generally, framework categories help organize the complex set of activities that occur in negotiation and also facilitate comparing cases in terms of similar and dissimilar processes.

Advances in information technology have provided a number of useful tools for negotiators. The work of Druckman and Hopmann (1991) on content analysis illustrates how the method can be used to keep track of statements made throughout the course of a long negotiation (monitoring), anticipate key events such as the tabling of a proposal (signaling), anticipate reactions to one's own statements or moves (predicting and posturing), and construct plausible packages based on areas where compromise is likely. Applications of decision analysis to several cases illustrate its usefulness as a tool for generating options and evaluating those options as plausible alternative agreement packages. Examples are the U.S.-Philippines base-rights talks described above (Ulvila 1990), the Panama Canal talks (Raiffa 1982), the International Conference on Tanker Safety and Pollution Protection (Ulvila and Snyder 1980), the Uruguay Round of the GATT talks (Spector 1994), the Single European Act of the European Community (Spector 1994), and the UN Conference on Environment and Development (Spector 1991). The two approaches are complementary, one (content analysis) focusing on process and the other (decision analysis) on preferences. They can be used in tandem, first to assess progress and then to update the configuration of preferences as these change during the course of negotiation.

Computer programs can also be used as diagnostic aids. Druckman (1993b) describes "Negotiator Assistant," a program developed with support from the United States Institute of Peace. The program provides negotiators and analysts with estimates of each party's flexibility and the extent to which alternative outcomes are likely to occur. It is used to compare cases and "theories" about the key influences on negotiation, evaluate alternative scenarios by allowing a user to perform "what if" exercises, and provide advice on tactics for impasse resolution. Earlier work by Hammond and associates (1975) contributed computer aids designed to help negotiators think analytically about the problem, diagnosing their own bases for making judgments and clarifying the sources of differences between the parties. This research was found to be especially useful in clarifying the technical aspects of negotiation and, as such, particularly relevant to negotiations over complex issues. These are only a sampling of decision-support tools available for negotiation. Andriole (1993) calls attention to a wide array of existing or emerging technologies that can support the negotiation process, ranging from electronic mail to group-decision support systems. His effort to match aspects of the process with tasks and tools provides a way to think about tools in relation to negotiation: Different tools should be designed for different negotiating functions. It also brings the engineering technologies into closer contact with the conceptual work on negotiation and, as such, holds promise for bridging the gap between practitioners and researchers in the social sciences.

While computer aids provide analytical support to negotiators, there are many aspects of negotiation that are not analytical, which negotiators learn about from experience; these include the effects of emotions, value differences, and cultural factors. In these areas, too, research contributes to understanding. With regard to the role of emotions, Johnson's (1971) research calls attention to the way alternating expressions of warmth and coldness influence expectations and concessions. More recently, Pearson (1990) found that sincere acknowledgments of the others' perspectives may facilitate the process of obtaining agreements by increasing feelings of affinity (positive affect) and trust among the parties. Also, the research on responsiveness, discussed above, makes clear the importance of synchrony in bargaining exchanges; bargainers seek equivalence in moves made by themselves and others (Druckman and Harris 1990). They may also imitate the others' expressions, as shown in the current work on socially induced affect (McIntosh 1994).

With regard to values, the studies reviewed above illustrate what happens when value differences are linked to the interests in dispute. They also show that those differences can be addressed in prenegotiation sessions, leading to more satisfactory settlements and improved relationships between the parties. Many studies document the importance of culture in negotiation. For example, in one study, Indian subjects bargained more competitively than cohorts in comparable age groups from other cultures, at least in part because of their early experiences with resource scarcity (Druckman et al. 1976). In another study (Mushakoji 1972), Japanese negotiators used relative-gain and gain-maximizing strategies more often than Americans, perhaps because of more general approaches to conflict management preferred by these cultures (Ohbuchi and Takahashi 1994). Nonexperimental analyses of national styles, such as Solomon's (1985) study of Chinese negotiating tactics and Whelen's (1979) study of changing Soviet diplomacy, illustrate the importance of culture as an influence on negotiating strategies and processes. (See Druckman and Hopmann 1989 for a review of this literature.)

The research underscores the tendency to confuse opponents' intentions (often attributed to negative motives) with their customary ways of behaving in negotiation. Taking into account these influences, Janosik (1987) and Weiss (1994a; 1994b) offer frameworks for thinking about several ways in which culture influences process. Druckman and Hopmann (1989) argue that culture is context, not process, and that it shapes behavior but is not synonymous with it. Practitioners could find the frameworks and the findings quite useful and could incorporate them into training packages and role-playing exercises designed to sensitize negotiators to the human dimensions of negotiation. The training techniques used by Danielian (1967) and Brislin (1986) are good examples. By explaining events and behaviors from the other's point of view, these techniques allow a trainee to internalize the values and norms of different cultures. Such exercises could contribute further to bridging the gap between the research and practitioner communities.

It may also be the case, however, that the practitioners themselves define a subculture that influences their negotiating behavior. These subcultures may reduce the impacts of national styles on the negotiating process. As Alger's (1963) study of diplomats interacting within a UN committee and Modelski's (1970) survey of foreign ministers suggest, a common socialization may produce a cadre of diplomats who are more similar to one another than to their compatriots. To date, we know little about this phenomenon or about its significance for national styles of negotiating behavior. It is a topic that needs to be examined, perhaps in the manner of Schein's (1985) probes of an organization's values and operating assumptions.

LOOKING BACK AND LOOKING FORWARD

This chapter surveys the basic and applied research literatures on negotiating in the international context. At its core is a discussion of the processes and influences on negotiation as it occurs in diverse settings and issue-areas. Negotiation is viewed in terms of four perspectives, each of which contributes to our understanding of the various parts of the broader domain. Together, the perspectives present a more complete picture than any one taken alone.

Advances in game and decision theory contribute to strategic thinking about negotiation. From game theory, we learn about the immediate and long-term consequences of alternative moves. From decision theory, we learn about the implications of combining preferences to produce desirable, if not optimal, outcomes. Using simple bargaining games as tools for understanding, experimentalists have identified concession tactics that influence others' responses leading toward or away from acceptable outcomes. Expanding "inward," organizational theorists have made evident the importance of boundary dilemmas confronted by negotiators. Negotiation is best construed as a two- (or multi-) level game, in which negotiators must address simultaneously often conflicting demands made by those sitting across the table (other national delegations) and those sitting behind them (representatives from agencies of their own government). Expanding outward, international relations scholars have emphasized the negotiating context, particularly the diplomatic politics among nations with stakes in the outcomes and the linkages that are made among issues discussed in different negotiating venues.

To a large extent, our knowledge about these processes has been gained through research stimulated by these perspectives and conducted in laboratory and field settings. Laboratory studies have provided insights into the impact of preparing, framing, and bargaining exchanges as well as constraints imposed by role demands. Case analyses have illuminated sequences of events in terms of stages and turning points, showing how certain contexts and processes create impasses, while other processes provide the momentum needed to forge agreements. The laboratory studies have been useful in documenting various forces impinging on the negotiation process; the case analyses have provided a more detailed understanding of the unfolding processes. Further contributions to knowledge have come from applications of advanced statistical techniques. More precise estimates of impacts have come from meta-analyses; similarities and dissimilarities among processes that occur in different cases have been discovered through the use of multidimensional scaling.

The analyses' contributions to knowledge are impressive, but to what extent have they contributed to practice? This is a field where scholars have developed practical tools; progress has been made in bridging the gap between researchers and practitioners. Working relationships between scholars and professional diplomats have, for example, produced lessons from past experience that will be invaluable to future generations of negotiators. New information technologies have been tailored to assist negotiators in evaluating alternative options and diagnosing various situations. In addition, the research on the effects of emotions, values, and cultural factors provides insights into the nonanalytical aspects of negotiation. These and other findings gain further relevance as they are incorporated into the development of training packages.

Looking back, we can applaud the accomplishments made by the community of negotiation scholars. Looking forward, we can offer a rich agenda for further research, both basic and applied. The agenda is shaped in part by changes that have occurred in international relations. A larger number of actors and relationships among those actors in the international system have increased the complexity of analysis and practice. Our conceptual frameworks must now encompass the trend toward multilateralism in international affairs as well as the burgeoning number of internal conflicts. We are only beginning to develop frameworks to guide research on multilateral negotiations and the wider web of constituencies that complicate the negotiator's boundary role dilemmas (see Zartman 1994). As we focus more on the highly charged negotiations among groups seeking new sources of identity in failed states and countries undergoing profound social and economic change, the role of values and emotions in negotiation will undoubtedly receive more attention (see Zartman 1995). As we encourage comparative case analyses, we must also view negotiation both as a larger process that includes prenegotiation and implementation stages and as part of a larger strategy that includes unilateral initiatives, mediation, multi-track activities, and even elements of coercive diplomacy.

REFERENCES

Adelman, Kenneth L. 1984–85. "Arms Control with and without Agreements." *Foreign Affairs* 62 (Winter): 240–63.

Alger, Chadwick F. 1963. "United Nations Participation as a Learning Experience." *Public Opinion Quarterly* 27 (Fall): 411–26.

Andriole, Stephen J. 1993. "Information Management Support for International Negotiations." *Theory and Decision* 34 (3): 313–28.

Axelrod, Robert. 1984. *The Evolution of Cooperation.* New York: Basic Books.

Bartos, Otomar J. 1978. "Simple Model of Negotiation: A Sociological Point of View." In *The Negotiation Process: Theories and Applications,* ed. I. William Zartman. Beverly Hills, Calif.: Sage.

Bass, Bernard M. 1966. "Effects on Subsequent Performance of Negotiators of Studying Issues or Planning Strategies Alone or in Groups." *Psychological Monographs,* whole no. 614.

Bendahmane, Diane B., and John W. McDonald, eds. 1986. *Perspectives on Negotiation: Four Case Studies and Interpretations.* Washington, D.C.: Foreign Service Institute.

Bloomfield, Lincoln P., and Robert Beattie. 1971. "Computers and Policymaking: The CASCON Experiment." *Journal of Conflict Resolution* 15:33–46.

Bonham, G. Matthew. 1971. "Simulating International Disarmament Negotiations." *Journal of Conflict Resolution* 15 (September): 299–315.

Brams, Steven J. 1993. "Theory of Moves." *American Scientist* 81 (November/December): 562–70.

Brislin, Richard W. 1986. "A Culture General Assimilator: Preparation for Various Types of Sojourns." *International Journal of Intercultural Relations* 10 (2): 215–234.

Brown, Scott. 1986. "The Superpowers' Dilemma." *Negotiation Journal* 2 (4): 371–84.

Chasek, Pamela. 1994. "From Stockholm to Rio: An Analysis of 20 Years of Multilateral Negotiation in the United Nations System." Ph.D. diss., School for Advanced International Studies, Johns Hopkins University, Washington, D.C.

Coddington, Alan. 1968. *Theories of the Bargaining Process.* Chicago: Aldine.

Danielian, Jack. 1967. "Live Simulations of Affect-Laden Cultural Cognitions." *Journal of Conflict Resolution* 11 (September): 312–24.

Dean, Jonathan. 1986. "MBFR: From Apathy to Accord." *International Security* 7 (4): 116–39.

Dechant, Kathleen, and Victoria J. Marsick. 1992. "How Groups Learn from Experience." Unpublished paper, Teacher's College, Columbia University.

Douglas, Ann. 1957. "The Peaceful Settlement of Industrial and Intergroup Disputes." *Journal of Conflict Resolution* 1 (March): 69–81.

Druckman, Daniel. 1968. "Prenegotiation Experience and Dyadic Conflict Resolution in a Bargaining Situation." *Journal of Experimental Social Psychology* 4 (October): 367–83.

———. 1973. *Human Factors in International Negotiations: Social-Psychological Aspects of International Conflict*. Sage Professional Papers in International Studies, Number 02-020. Beverly Hills, Calif.: Sage.

———. 1977a. "Boundary Role Conflict: Negotiation as Dual Responsiveness." *Journal of Conflict Resolution* 21 (4): 639–62.

———. 1978. "The Monitoring Function in Negotiation: Two Models of Responsiveness." In *Contributions to Experimental Economics: Bargaining Behavior*, ed. Heinz Sauermann. Tubingen, West Germany: J.C.B. Mohr.

———. 1980. "Social-Psychological Factors in Regional Politics." In *Comparative Regional Systems: West and East Europe, North America, the Middle East, and Developing Countries*, ed. Werner J. Feld and Gavin Boyd. New York: Pergamon.

———. 1983. "Social Psychology and International Negotiations: Processes and Influences." In *Advances in Applied Social Psychology*, ed. Robert F. Kidd and Michael J. Saks. Vol. 2. Hillsdale, N.J.: Erlbaum.

———. 1986a. "Four Cases of Conflict Management: Lessons Learned." In *Perspectives on Negotiation: Four Case Studies and Lessons Learned*, ed. Diane B. Bendahmane and John W. McDonald. Washington D.C.: Foreign Service Institute.

———. 1986b. "Stages, Turning Points, and Crises: Negotiating Military Base Rights, Spain and the United States." *Journal of Conflict Resolution* 30 (2): 327–60.

———. 1990. "Three Cases of Base-Rights Negotiations: Lessons Learned." In *U.S. Bases Overseas*, ed. John W. McDonald and Diane B. Bendahmane. Boulder, Colo.: Westview.

———. 1993a. "The Situational Levers of Negotiating Flexibility." *Journal of Conflict Resolution* 37 (2): 236–76.

———. 1993b. "Statistical Analysis for Negotiation Support." *Theory and Decision* 34 (3): 215–33.

———. 1994. "Determinants of Compromising Behavior in Negotiation: A Meta-Analysis." *Journal of Conflict Resolution* 38 (3): 507–56.

————. 1997. "Dimensions of International Negotiations: Structures, Processes, and Outcomes." *Group Decision and Negotiation* 6 (5).

————, ed. 1977b. *Negotiations: Social-Psychological Perspectives*. Beverly Hills, Calif.: Sage.

Druckman, Daniel, Alan A. Benton, Faizunisa Ali, and J. Susana Bagur. 1976. "Cultural Differences in Bargaining Behavior: Argentina, India, and the United States." *Journal of Conflict Resolution* 20 (3): 413–52.

Druckman, Daniel, and Benjamin J. Broome. 1991. "Value Differences and Conflict Resolution: Familiarity or Liking?" *Journal of Conflict Resolution* 35 (4): 571–93.

Druckman, Daniel, Benjamin J. Broome, and Susan H. Korper. 1988. "Value Differences and Conflict Resolution: Facilitation or Delinking?" *Journal of Conflict Resolution* 32 (3): 489–510.

Druckman, Daniel, and Justin Green. 1995. "Playing Two Games: Internal Negotiations in the Philippines." In *Elusive Peace: Negotiating an End to Civil Wars*, ed. I. William Zartman. Washington, D.C.: Brookings Institution.

Druckman, Daniel, and Richard Harris. 1990. "Alternative Models of Responsiveness in International Negotiation." *Journal of Conflict Resolution* 34 (2): 234–51.

Druckman, Daniel, and P. Terrence Hopmann. 1989. "Behavioral Aspects of Negotiations on Mutual Security." In *Behavior, Society, and Nuclear War*. Edited by Philip E. Tetlock, Jo L. Husbands, Paul C. Stern, and Charles Tilly. Vol. 1. New York: Oxford University Press.

————. 1991. "Content Analysis." In *International Negotiation: Analysis, Approaches, Issues*, ed. Victor A. Kremenyuk. San Francisco: Jossey-Bass.

Druckman, Daniel, Jo L. Husbands, and Karin Johnston. 1991. "Turning Points in the INF Negotiations." *Negotiation Journal* 7 (1): 55–67.

Druckman, Daniel, Richard Rozelle, and Kathleen Zechmeister. 1977. "Conflict of Interest and Value Dissensus: Two Perspectives," In *Negotiations: Social-Psychological Perspectives*, ed. Daniel Druckman. Beverly Hills, Calif.: Sage.

Druckman, Daniel, and Kathleen Zechmeister. 1973. "Conflict of Interest and Value Dissensus: Propositions in the Sociology of Conflict." *Human Relations* 26 (August): 449–66.

Dupont, Christophe. 1990. "The Channel Tunnel Negotiations, 1984–1986: Some Aspects of the Process and Its Outcome." *Negotiation Journal* 6 (1): 71–80.

Evans, Peter B., Harold K. Jacobson, and Robert D. Putnam, eds. 1993. *Double-Edged Diplomacy: International Bargaining and Domestic Politics*. Berkeley: University of California Press.

Fisher, Ronald J. 1983. "Third-Party Consultation as a Method of Intergroup Conflict Resolution: A Review of Studies." *Journal of Conflict Resolution* 27 (2): 301–34.

————. 1990. *The Social Psychology of Intergroup and International Conflict*. New York: Springer-Verlag.

Frey, Robert L., and J. Stacy Adams. 1972. "The Negotiator's Dilemma: Simultaneous Ingroup and Outgroup Conflict." *Journal of Experimental Social Psychology* 8 (July): 331–46.

George, Alexander. 1993. *Bridging the Gap: Theory and Practice in Foreign Policy*. Washington, D.C.: United States Institute of Peace Press.

Gersick, Connie J. G. 1988. "Time and Transition in Work Groups: Toward a New Model of Group Development." *Academy of Management Journal* 31 (1): 9–41.

Graham, John L, Alma T. Mintu, and Waymond Rodgers. 1994. "Explorations of Negotiation Behaviors in Ten Foreign Cultures Using a Model Developed in the United States." *Management Science* 40 (1): 72–95.

Gulliver, P. H. 1979. *Disputes and Negotiations: A Cross-Cultural Perspective*. New York: Academic Press.

Hammond, K. R., T. R. Stewart, L. Adelman, and N. Wascoe. 1975. "Report To The Denver City Council and Mayor Regarding the Choice of Handgun Ammunition for the Denver Police Department." Report No. 179, Program of Research on Judgment and Social Interaction, University of Colorado, Boulder.

Hopmann, P. Terrence. 1977. "Bargaining within and between Alliances on MBFR: Perceptions and Interactions." Paper presented at the International Studies Association, March 16–20, St.Louis, Mo.

Hopmann, P. Terrence, and Timothy King. 1976. "Interactions and Perceptions in the Test Ban Negotiations." *International Studies Quarterly* 20 (1): 105–42.

Hopmann, P. Terrence, and T. C. Smith. 1978. "An Application of a Richardson Process Model: Soviet-American Interactions in the Test Ban Negotiations, 1962-63." In *The Negotiation Process: Theories and Applications*, ed. I. William Zartman. Beverly Hills, Calif.: Sage.

Iklé, Fred C. 1964. *How Nations Negotiate*. New York: Harper and Row.

International Negotiation. 1996. Inaugural issue on "Negotiation Metaphors: Framing International Negotiations Anew." Vol. 1 (1).

Janosik, Robert J. 1987. "Rethinking the Culture-Negotiation Link." *Negotiation Journal* 3 (4): 385–96.

Jensen, Lloyd. 1988. *Bargaining for National Security: The Postwar Disarmament Negotiations*. Columbia: University of South Carolina Press.

Jervis, Robert. 1983. "Security Regimes." In *International Regimes*, ed. Stephen D. Krasner. Ithaca: Cornell University Press.

Johnson, David W. 1971. "Role Reversal: A Summary and Review of the Research." *International Journal of Group Tensions* 1 (October): 318–34.

Jonsson, Christer. 1979. *Soviet Bargaining Behavior: The Nuclear Test Ban Case*. New York: Columbia University Press.

Kahn, Robert L. 1991. "Organizational Theory." In *International Negotiation: Analysis, Approaches, Issues*, ed. Victor A. Kremenyuk. San Francisco: Jossey-Bass.

Kelleher, Catherine. 1976. "Predilections in Negotiations." Unpublished manuscript. University of Maryland, College Park.

Kelley, Harold H., and D. P. Schenitzki. 1972. "Bargaining." In *Experimental Social Psychology*, ed. Charles Graham McClintock. New York: Holt.

Klimoski, Richard J. 1972. "The Effects of Intragroup Forces on Intergroup Conflict Resolution." *Organizational Behavior and Human Performance* 8 (December): 363–83.

Koh, Tommy. 1990. "The Paris Conference on Cambodia: A Multilateral Negotiation that 'Failed.'" *Negotiation Journal* 6 (1): 81–87.

Kremenyuk, Victor A., ed. 1991. *International Negotiation: Analysis, Approaches, Issues*. San Francisco: Jossey-Bass.

Kriesberg, Louis. 1991. "Introduction: Timing Conditions, Strategies, and Errors." In *Timing the Deescalation of International Conflicts*, ed. Louis Kriesberg and Stuart J. Thorson. Syracuse, N.Y.: Syracuse University Press.

Lax, David A., and James K. Sebenius. 1986. *The Manager as Negotiator: Bargaining for Cooperation and Competitive Gain*. New York: Free Press.

Lindskold, Svenn, Brian Betz, and Pamela S. Waters. 1986. "Transforming Competitive or Cooperative Climates." *Journal of Conflict Resolution* 30 (March): 99–114.

Lindskold, Svenn, Pamela S. Waters, and Helen Koutsourais. 1983. "Cooperators, Competitors, and Response to GRIT." *Journal of Conflict Resolution* 27 (September): 521–32.

McDonald, John W., and Diane B. Bendahmane, eds. 1990. *U.S. Bases Overseas: Negotiations with Spain, Greece, and the Philippines*. Boulder, Colo.: Westview.

McIntosh, Daniel. 1994. "Socially-Induced Affect." In *Learning, Remembering, Believing: Enhancing Human Performance*, ed. Daniel Druckman and Robert A. Bjork. Washington, D.C.: National Academy Press.

Mitchell, Christopher R. 1991. "A Willingness to Talk: Conciliatory Gestures and De-Escalation." *Negotiation Journal* 7 (4): 405–30.

Modelski, George. 1970. "The World's Foreign Ministers: A Political Elite." *Journal of Conflict Resolution* 14 (June): 135–75.

Morley, Ian E., and Geoffrey M. Stephenson. 1977. *The Social Psychology of Bargaining*. London: Allen and Unwin.

Mushakoji, Kinhide. 1972. "The Strategies of Negotiation: An American-Japanese Comparison." In *Experimentation and Simulation in Political Science*, ed. J. A. Laponce and Paul Smoker. Toronto: University of Toronto Press.

Neale, Margaret A., and Max H. Bazerman. 1985. "The Effects of Framing and Negotiator Overconfidence on Bargaining Behaviors and Outcomes." *Academy of Management Journal* 28 (1): 34–49.

Neale, Margaret A., Vandra L. Huber, and Gregory B. Northcraft. 1987. "The Framing of Negotiations: Contextual versus Task Frames." *Organizational Behavior and Human Decision Processes* 39 (2): 228–41.

Ohbuchi, Ken-Ichi, and Yumi Takahashi. 1994. "Cultural Styles of Conflict Management in Japanese and Americans: Passivity, Covertness, and Effectiveness of Strategies." *Journal of Applied Social Psychology* 15:1345-66.

Orasanu, Judith, and Eduardo Salas. 1993. "Team Decision Making in Complex Environments." In *Decision Making in Action: Models and Methods*, ed. Gary A. Klein, Judith Orasanu, and R. Calderwood. Norwood, N.J.: Ablex Publishing Co.

Organ, Dennis. 1971. "Some Variables Affecting Boundary Role Behavior." *Sociometry* 34 (December): 524–37.

Osgood, Charles. 1962. *An Alternative to War or Surrender*. Urbana: University of Illinois Press.

———. 1973. "GRIT for MBFR: A Proposal for Unfreezing Force-Level Postures in Europe." Testimony to the Subcommittee on Europe of the House Committee on Foreign Affairs, June 26.

Pearson, Tamara. 1990. "The Role of 'Symbolic Gestures' in Intergroup Conflict Resolution: Addressing Group Identity." Ph.D. diss., Harvard University.

Pruitt, Dean G. 1965. "Definition of the Situation as a Determinant of International Action." In *International Behavior: A Social-Psychological Analysis*, ed. Herbert C. Kelman. New York: Holt, Rinehart, and Winston.

———. 1981. *Negotiation Behavior*. New York: Academic Press.

Pruitt, Dean G., and Peter J. Carnevale. 1993. *Negotiation in Social Conflict*. Pacific Grove, Calif.: Brooks/Cole.

Putnam, Robert. 1988. "Diplomacy and Domestic Politics: The Logic of Two-Level Games." *International Organization* 43 (3): 427–60.

Raiffa, Howard. 1982. *The Art and Science of Negotiation*. Cambridge, Mass.: Harvard University Press.

Ramberg, Bennett. 1977. "Tactical Advantages of Opening Positioning Strategies: Lessons from the Seabed Arms Control Talks, 1967–1970." *Journal of Conflict Resolution* 21 (4): 685–700.

———, ed. 1993. *Arms Control without Negotiation: From the Cold War to the New World Order*. Boulder, Colo.: Lynne Rienner.

Randolph, Lillian. 1966. "A Suggested Model of International Negotiation." *Journal of Conflict Resolution* 10 (September): 344–53.

Rose, William M. 1988. *U.S. Unilateral Arms Control Initiatives: When Do They Work?* Westport, Conn.: Greenwood Press.

Rubin, Jeffrey Z., ed. 1981. *Dynamics of Third-Party Intervention: Kissinger in the Middle East*. New York: Praeger.

Rubin, Jeffrey Z., and Bert R. Brown. 1975. *The Social Psychology of Bargaining and Negotiation*. New York: Academic Press.

Salacuse, Jeswald W., and Jeffrey Z. Rubin. 1990. "Negotiation Processes at Work: Lessons from Four International Cases." *Negotiation Journal* 6 (4): 315–17.

Saunders, Harold H. 1984. "The Prenegotiation Phase." In *International Negotiation: Art and Science*, ed. Diane B. Bendahmane and John W. McDonald. Washington, D.C.: Foreign Service Institute.

Sawyer, Jack, and Harold Guetzkow. 1965. "Bargaining and Negotiation in International Relations." In *International Behavior: A Social-Psychological Analysis*, ed. Herbert C. Kelman. New York: Holt.

Schein, Edgar H. 1985. *Organizational Culture and Leadership*. San Francisco: Jossey-Bass.

Siegel, Sidney, and Lawrence E. Fouraker. 1960. *Bargaining and Group Decision Making: Experiments in Bilateral Monopoly*. New York: McGraw-Hill.

Smith, Gerard C. 1980. *Doubletalk: The Story of SALT I*. New York: Doubleday.

Snyder, Glenn H., and Paul Diesing. 1977. *Conflict among Nations: Bargaining, Decision-Making, and System Structure in International Crises*. Princeton N.J.: Princeton University Press.

Solomon, Richard H. 1985. *Chinese Political Negotiating Behavior*. Report No. R-3295. Santa Monica, Calif.: Rand Corporation.

Spector, Bertram I. 1991. "Preference Adjustment and Opportunities for Agreement: A Contingency Analysis of the UNCED Prenegotiation Process." Working Paper. Laxenburg, Austria: International Institute for Applied Systems Analysis.

———. 1994. "Decision Theory: Diagnosing Strategic Alternatives and Outcome Trade-Offs." In *International Multilateral Negotiation*, ed. I. William Zartman. San Francisco: Jossey-Bass.

Spector, Bertram I., and Anna R. Korula. 1992. "The Post-Agreement Negotiation Process: The Problems of Ratifying International Environmental Agreements." Report WP-92-90. Laxenburg, Austria: International Institute for Applied Systems Analysis.

Stein, Janice Gross, ed. 1989. *Getting to the Table: The Processes of International Prenegotiation*. Baltimore: Johns Hopkins University Press.

Stoll, Richard J., and William McAndrew. 1986. "Negotiating Strategic Arms Control, 1969–1979." *Journal of Conflict Resolution* 30 (2): 315–26.

Summers, David A. 1968. "Conflict, Compromise, and Belief Change in a Decision-Making Task." *Journal of Conflict Resolution* 12 (June): 215–21.

Talbott, Strobe. 1979. *Endgame: The Inside Story of SALT II*. New York: Harper and Row.

———. 1984. *Deadly Gambits*. New York: Alfred A. Knopf.

Thibaut, John. 1968. "The Development of Contractual Norms in Bargaining: Replication and Variation." *Journal of Conflict Resolution* 12 (March): 102–12.

Tollison, Robert D., and Thomas D. Willett. 1979. "An Economic Theory of Mutually Advantageous Issue Linkages in International Negotiations." *International Organization* 33 (4): 425–49.

Tomlin, Brian W. 1989. "The Stages of Prenegotiation: The Decision to Negotiate North American Free Trade." In *Getting to the Table: The Processes of International Prenegotiation*, ed. Janice Gross Stein. Baltimore: Johns Hopkins University Press.

Touval, Saadia, and I. William Zartman, eds. 1985. *The Man in the Middle: International Mediation in Theory and Practice*. Boulder, Colo.: Westview.

Ulvila Jacob W. 1990. "Turning Points: An Analysis." In *U.S. Bases Overseas*, ed. John W. McDonald and Diane B. Bendahmane. Boulder, Colo.: Westview.

Ulvila, Jacob W., and Warren D. Snyder. 1980. "Negotiation of International Oil Tanker Standards: An Application of Multiattribute Value Theory." *Operations Research* 28 (1): 81–96.

Von Neumann, John, and Oskar Morgenstern. 1944. *Theory of Games and Economic Behavior*. Princeton: Princeton University Press.

Wall James A., Jr. 1975. "Effects of Constituent Trust and Representative Bargaining Orientation in Intergroup Bargaining." *Journal of Personality and Social Psychology* 31 (6): 1004–12.

Walton, Richard E., and Robert B. McKersie. 1965. *A Behavioral Theory of Labor Negotiations: An Analysis of a Social Interaction System*. New York: McGraw-Hill.

Walton, Richard E., Joel Cutcher-Gershenfeld, and Robert B. McKersie. 1994. *Strategic Negotiations: A Theory of Change in Labor-Management Relations*. Boston: Harvard Business School Press.

Weiss, Stephen E. 1994a. "Negotiating with 'Romans' - Part I." *Sloan Management Review* 35 (2): 51–61.

———. 1994b. "Negotiating with 'Romans' - Part II." *Sloan Management Review* 35 (3): 85–99.

Whelen, Joseph. G. 1979. "Soviet Diplomacy and Negotiating Behavior: Emerging New Context For U.S. Diplomacy." Report prepared by the Congressional Research Service for the House Committee on Foreign Affairs. Washington D.C.: Government Printing Office.

Winham, Gilbert R. 1977. "Complexity in International Negotiation." In *Negotiations: Social-Psychological Perspectives*, ed. Daniel Druckman. Beverly Hills, Calif.: Sage.

Zartman, I. William. 1975. "Negotiations: Theory and Reality." *Journal of International Affairs* 9 (1): 69–77.

———. 1989. *Ripe for Resolution: Conflict and Intervention in Africa*. 2d ed. New York: Oxford University Press.

————. 1991. "Regional Conflict Resolution." In *International Negotiation: Analysis, Approaches, Issues*, ed. Victor A. Kremenyuk. San Francisco: Jossey-Bass.

————, ed. 1994. *International Multilateral Negotiation*. San Francisco: Jossey-Bass.

————, ed. 1995. *Elusive Peace: Negotiating an End to Civil Wars*. Washington, D.C.: Brookings Institution.

Zartman, I. William, and Maureen R. Berman. 1982. *The Practical Negotiator*. New Haven: Yale University Press.

Zechmeister, Kathleen, and Daniel Druckman. 1973. "Determinants of Resolving a Conflict of Interest: A Simulation of Political Decision Making." *Journal of Conflict Resolution* 17 (March): 63–88.

4

Mediation in International Conflict

An Overview of Theory, A Review of Practice

Jacob Bercovitch

How can states manage their conflicts, internal as well as international? Broadly speaking, we can identify four very different strategies: violence and compellence, deterrence, adjudication, and accommodative strategies (e.g., bargaining and mediation).

Although states reserve, and often exercise, the right to resort to violence and compellence, there is clearly a very strong expectation and normative commitment, as well as something of an international consensus, regarding the necessity and desirability of managing conflicts in other ways. Article 2(3) of the UN Charter states that "All member states shall settle their international disputes in such a manner that international peace and security, and justice, are not endangered." In 1982, the UN General Assembly adopted a Declaration on the Peaceful Settlement of Disputes, which emphasized "the need to exert utmost efforts in order to settle any conflict and dispute between States exclusively by peaceful means." The importance of the principle of peaceful settlement of conflicts can hardly be overemphasized.

The available methods of *peaceful* settlement of international conflicts are listed in Article 33 of the UN Charter, requesting that the "parties to

any dispute, the continuance of which is likely to endanger the maintenance of international peace and security, shall, first of all, seek a solution
by negotiation, inquiry, mediation, conciliation, arbitration, judicial settlement, resort to regional agencies or arrangements, or other peaceful means
of their choice."

Essentially, the UN Charter recognizes the existence of three basic techniques for the peaceful management of international conflicts, whatever
their form, and asks all states to use any one of them. The three techniques
are direct negotiation among the conflicting parties; various forms of mediation, good offices, and conciliation; and arbitration and adjudication, in
which a third party makes the decision. Each technique has its own characteristics, strengths, and disadvantages, and each is suited to different conflicts. This chapter explores the particular techniques of mediation, how
mediation works, its unique features, who can undertake mediation activities, the problems mediators typically encounter, and how mediation can
contribute to resolving conflicts and preventing their escalation in a new
international environment.

MEDIATION: THE SEARCH FOR A DEFINITION

For many years, the study of mediation has suffered from conceptual impre-
cision and a startling lack of information. Practitioners of mediation, formal or informal, in the domestic or international arena were keen to sustain its image as a mysterious practice taking place behind closed doors;
scholars of mediation themselves did not think their specialty was susceptible to a systematic analysis. In short, neither group believed that it could
discern any pattern of behavior in mediation's various forms, or that any
generalizations could be made about the practice in general.

The prevalent agnosticism toward analysis and the desire to maintain
the intuitive mystique of mediation are best exemplified in the comments
of two noted American practitioners. Arthur Meyer, commenting on the
role of mediators, notes that "the task of the mediator is not an easy one.
The sea that he sails is only roughly charted, and its changing contours are
not clearly discernible. He has no science of navigation, no fund inherited
from the experience of others. He is a solitary artist recognizing at most a
few guiding stars, and depending on his personal powers of divination"
(Meyer 1960, 160). William Simkin, an equally respected practitioner of
mediation, comments in a slightly less prosaic but no less emphatic fashion
that "the variables are so many that it would be an exercise in futility to
describe typical mediator behavior with respect to sequence, timing or the

use or non-use of the various functions theoretically available" (Simkin 1971, 118).

The mystery and uniqueness of mediation acted like something of a ghost that haunted many of us for too long. There may be little consensus on how best to practice or study mediation, but, mercifully, there is very broad agreement that this particular ghost should be exorcised. Mediation can, and should, be studied properly, and the lessons derived from such a study should serve as signposts in the quest for more effective conflict management.

The most helpful approach to mediation links it to a related strategy—negotiation—but at the same time emphasizes its unique features and conditions. The parameters of such an approach were established by Carl Stevens and Thomas Schelling. Stevens (1963, 123) states that "mediation, like other social phenomena, is susceptible to systematic analysis. The key to analysis is in recognizing that where mediation is employed it is an integral part of the bargaining process. . . . [A]n analysis of mediation is not possible except in the context of general analysis of bargaining negotiations." In a similar vein, Schelling (1960, 22) notes that a mediator "is probably best viewed as an element in the communication arrangements, or as a third party with a payoff structure of his own."

Mediation is, at least structurally, the continuation of negotiations by other means. What mediators do, can do, or are permitted to do in their efforts to resolve a conflict may depend, to some extent, on who they are and what resources and competencies they can bring to bear. Ultimately, though, their efforts depend on who the parties are, the context of the conflict, what is at stake, and the nature of their interaction. "Mediation," as Stulberg so rightly notes, "is a procedure predicated upon the process of negotiation" (Stulberg 1981, 87). Mediation is, above all, adaptive and responsive. It extends the process of negotiation to reflect different conflicts, different parties, and different situations. To assume otherwise is to mistake wishful thinking for reality.

What, then, are the unique features or characteristics of mediation? A number of these are listed below:

1. Mediation is an extension and continuation of peaceful conflict management.
2. Mediation involves the intervention of an outsider—an individual, a group, or an organization—into a conflict between two or more states or other actors.
3. Mediation is a noncoercive, nonviolent and, ultimately, nonbinding form of intervention.

4. Mediators enter a conflict, whether internal or international, in order to affect it, change it, resolve it, modify it, or influence it in some way.

5. Mediators bring with them, consciously or otherwise, ideas, knowledge, resources, and interests of their own or of the group or organization they represent. Mediators often have their own assumptions and agendas about the conflict in question.

6. Mediation is a voluntary form of conflict management. The actors involved retain control over the outcome (if not always over the process) of their conflict, as well as the freedom to accept or reject mediation or mediators' proposals.

7. Mediation operates on an ad hoc basis only.

Mediation differs from other accommodative strategies such as negotiation (in its dyadic rather than triadic structure) and arbitration (in its nonbinding character). Different definitions of mediation address these differences by purporting to (a) capture the gist of what mediators do or hope to achieve, (b) distinguish between mediation and related processes of third-party intervention (i.e., arbitration), and (c) describe mediators' attributes. It is worth looking at a few definitions of mediation and assessing their implications.

Focusing on what mediators hope to achieve and how they may go about achieving it, Oran Young offers a definition of mediation as "any action taken by an actor that is not a direct party to the crisis, that is designed to reduce or remove one or more of the problems of the bargaining relationship, and therefore to facilitate the termination of the crisis itself" (Young 1967, 34). In much the same vein, Chris Mitchell defines mediation as any "intermediary activity . . . undertaken by a third party with the primary intention of achieving some compromise settlement of the issues at stake between the parties, or at least ending disruptive conflict behavior" (Mitchell 1981, 287). And in a somewhat more detailed fashion, Blake and Mouton define mediation as a process involving "the intervention of a third party who first investigates and defines the problem and then usually approaches each group separately with recommendations designed to provide a mutually acceptable solution" (Blake and Mouton 1985, 15).

Other definitions are less outcome-oriented and focus on the act of the intervention itself. Ann Douglas defines mediation as "a form of peacemaking in which an outsider to a dispute intervenes on his own or accepts the invitation of disputing parties to assist them in reaching agreement" (Douglas 1957, 70). Moore defines it as "an extension and elaboration of the negotiation process. Mediation involves the intervention of an acceptable, impartial, and neutral third party who has no authoritative decision making power to assist contending parties in voluntarily reaching their own mutually acceptable settlement" (Moore 1986, 6). And Linda Singer defines it as a "form of third-party assistance [that] involves an outsider to the dispute who lacks the power to make decisions for the parties" (Singer 1990, 20).

Still other definitions focus on neutrality and impartiality as the distinguishing features of mediation. Bingham defines mediation as the "assistance of a 'neutral' third party to a negotiation" (Bingham 1985, 5). Folberg and Taylor see mediation "as the process by which the participants, together with the assistance of a neutral person or persons, systematically isolate disputed issues in order to develop options, consider alternatives, and reach a consensual settlement that will accommodate their needs" (Folberg and Taylor 1984, 7). Moore draws attention to the process of mediation and the neutrality of a mediator in the following definition: "the intervention into a dispute or negotiation by an acceptable, impartial and neutral third party who has no authoritative decision-making power to assist disputing parties in voluntarily reaching their own mutually acceptable settlement of issues in dispute" (Moore 1986, 14). Finally, Spencer and Yang see mediation as "the assistance of a third party not involved in the dispute, who may be of a unique status that gives him or her certain authority with the disputants; or perhaps an outsider who may be regarded by them as a suitably neutral go-between" (Spencer and Yang 1993, 1495).

These definitions (and they are but a sample) exemplify the enormous scope of mediation. Mediation may take place in conflicts between states, within states, and between groups of states, organizations, and individuals—and may be further complicated by conflicts among ethnic groups. Mediators enter a conflict to help those involved to achieve an outcome—or a better outcome—that they would not be able to achieve otherwise. Once involved in a conflict, mediators may use a wide variety of behaviors to achieve their objectives. Some mediators make suggestions for a settlement, others refrain from doing so. Some mediators are interested in achieving a compromise, others are not. Above all, some mediators are neutral, others are not. Henry Kissinger and President Jimmy Carter were far from neutral in mediating various conflicts while in office, but they were decidedly successful and effective mediators.

Some may consider this quibbling over definitions or aspects of neutrality to be a futile exercise in semantic ambiguity. It is most emphatically not so. The myriad of possible mediators and the range of mediation roles and strategies are so wide as to defeat many attempts to understand, as we seek to do here, the "essence" of mediation. A corollary is the tendency to assume that mediators can adopt only one role (e.g., a go-between) or one strategy (e.g., offering proposals). This does not help us to understand the reality of international mediation. Assigning an exclusive role or strategy to one kind of mediation neglects the dynamics of the process. It is also detrimental to the search for common and divergent dimensions of mediation in international and other social contexts and the effort to draw general lessons from mediation experience.

The reality of international mediation is that of a complex and dynamic interaction between mediators who have resources and an interest in the conflict or its outcome, and the protagonists or their representatives. In any given conflict, mediators may change, their role may be redefined, issues may alter, indeed even the parties involved in the conflict may and often do change. A comprehensive definition seems to be a primary requisite for understanding this reality. The following broad definition provides suitable criteria for inclusion (and exclusion) and serves as a basis for identifying differences and similarities. Mediation is here defined as a process of conflict management, related to but distinct from the parties' own negotiations, where those in conflict seek the assistance of, or accept an offer of help from, an outsider (whether an individual, an organization, a group, or a state) to change their perceptions or behavior, and to do so without resorting to physical force or invoking the authority of law.

This may be a broad definition, but it is one that can be generally and widely applied. It forces us to recognize, as surely we must, that any mediation situation comprises (a) parties in conflict, (b) a mediator, (c) a process of mediation, and (d) the context of mediation. All these elements are important in a mediation. Together they determine its nature, quality, and effectiveness, as well as why some mediations succeed while others fail.

THE INCIDENCE OF MEDIATION

It is interesting to note just how widespread the resort to mediation really is in international relations. Although it may not always be apparent, most international conflicts experience some form of mediation. Several scholarly studies address this issue. Northedge and Donelan (1971) identify 50 international conflicts from 1945 to 1970, finding that some form of mediation was involved in 31 (or 62 percent) of these disputes and achieved a successful settlement in 7 of these conflicts (or 23 percent of mediated conflicts). A more comprehensive study conducted by Holsti (1983) lists 94 international conflicts in the post–1945 period, noting that mediators were involved in 42 (or 45 percent) of these disputes and that their involvement achieved some measure of success in 30 disputes (71 percent of mediated conflicts). Mark Zacher (1979), who focuses more specifically on the conflict management activities of regional organizations, finds that such organizations were involved in 40 international disputes (35 percent of all disputes between 1945 and 1977), and that in 21 of these disputes (53 percent), such interventions produced a successful outcome.

Butterworth's study of international conflict resolution (1976) offers an even more complete picture of the extent of third-party mediation in international conflict. He identifies 310 international conflicts between 1945 and 1974, and notes that in 255 of these disputes (or 82 percent) there was some form of mediation. Bercovitch (1989) identifies 72 major international disputes in the postwar period and finds that 44 of these (or 61 percent) experienced one or more mediation attempts. A more recent paper (Bercovitch 1996) identifies 241 international disputes in the 1945–1990 period and finds that 145 of these disputes (60 percent) were mediated. The total number of mediations in the same period—international and domestic—was tallied at 593 cases; but the actual number of cases is much higher, since so many informal mediation activities undertaken by individuals or nongovernmental organizations (NGOs) are simply not reported in the news.

What all these studies point out quite unmistakably is that, whichever way we look at it, mediation can hardly be described as being in a state of disuse; it is frequently resorted to by actors of the most diverse kind. Mediation is, on the face of it, an effective strategy that can deal with all types of conflicts.

The challenges of the post–Cold War era, with its increased uncertainty, its sudden change in many of the accepted rules of the game, and the proliferation of intense ethnic and other identity-based conflicts, will no doubt require us to resort to mediation even more often than we have in the past. Mediation may well be the closest thing we have to an effective technique for dealing with conflicts in the twenty-first century. For this reason alone, it behooves us to study mediation seriously and systematically. In an interdependent and increasingly fractious world, conflicts affect us all; their proper management is everyone's business.

THE STUDY OF INTERNATIONAL MEDIATION

The literature on international mediation has attracted many scholars and reflects a great diversity in terms of approaches and perspectives (see Kolb and Rubin 1991). These approaches—and there is a seemingly endless variety of them—range from purely scholarly studies to policy implications to the reflections of mediators themselves, and to studies suggesting that academics should act as third parties in mediation efforts. Sometimes these approaches offer implications for practical involvement, at other times they focus on descriptions and theory development. The following can be identified as the four main traditions in the study of international mediation:

1. The first group of studies is essentially prescriptive and is devoted to offering advice on what constitutes good conflict management in real-world situations (e.g., Fisher and Ury 1981). These studies, mostly developed by scholars associated with the Program on Negotiation at Harvard University, generate books and manuals on how mediators and negotiators should behave, what constitutes good negotiation or mediation, and how conflicts—serious or otherwise—can be resolved.

2. Some studies of mediation in a variety of contexts are based on theoretical notions and the participation of academic practitioners in a variety of actual conflicts, with the aim of testing ideas and developing a generic theory for the resolution of social conflicts. These studies use a variety of interaction and problem-solving techniques to combine political action with scientific experimentation and thus contribute to the development of a set of rules that can address all (not just international) conflicts. Some of this research (Burton 1969, 1972, 1984; Doob 1971; Fisher 1983; Kelman 1992; Walton 1969) has generated valuable insights, but much of it is still in a pioneering phase.

3. There are many studies of mediation by economists and game theorists who develop mathematical models to examine how people, under conditions of maximum rationality and knowledge, would behave in conflict situations. These studies (e.g., Raiffa 1982) are mostly illustrative of the best strategies for making concessions and agreements.

4. The fourth set of studies is based on actual descriptions and empirical examinations of mediation cases. These studies seek to develop theories and to offer general guidelines through (a) the detailed description of a particular case of international mediation (e.g., Ott 1972; Rubin 1981), (b) laboratory and experimental approaches to mediation (e.g., Bartunek et al. 1975; Rubin 1980) to discover how parties and mediators behave

in controlled circumstances, and (c) large-scale systematic studies that draw on numerous cases of international mediation to formulate and test propositions about effective mediation and to assess the conditions under which mediation can be made to work better (e.g., Bercovitch and Rubin 1992; Touval and Zartman 1985). This tradition, in many ways the most fruitful approach and the one that can produce the most relevant policy implications for decision makers, forms the basis of this chapter.

THE MOTIVES FOR MEDIATION

These different approaches often complement, and sometimes contrast with, one another. They can all, however, provide useful insights on the three most relevant questions in mediation: Why mediate? How does one mediate? When is mediation most likely to be successful? The following examines these questions in detail.

As an instrument of diplomacy and foreign policy, mediation has become almost as common as conflict itself. It is carried out daily by such disparate actors as private individuals; government officials; religious figures; regional, nongovernmental, and international organizations; ad hoc groupings, or states of all sizes. Each of these mediators brings to the mediation situation its own interests, perceptions, and resources. Each of them may adopt behavior that ranges from the very passive, through the facilitative, to the highly active. The form and character of mediation in a particular international conflict are determined by the context of both the international system and the conflict itself, the issues, the parties involved, and the identity of the mediator. The importance of this reciprocal influence can hardly be overemphasized.

As a legitimate form of international peacemaking and an expression of international concern, mediation is particularly appropriate when (a) a conflict is long, drawn out, or complex; (b) the parties' own conflict-management efforts have reached an impasse; (c) neither party is prepared to countenance further costs or loss of life; and (d) both parties are prepared to cooperate, tacitly or openly, to break their stalemate.

When these conditions prevail, the presence of a mediator can secure a peaceful outcome. But why would a mediator wish to intervene in other people's conflicts, and why, for that matter, would states in conflict (or parties in dispute) accept a mediator?

Traditional approaches to mediation assume that a conflict's parties and a mediator share one compelling reason for initiating mediation: a desire to reduce, abate, or resolve a conflict. To this end, both sides may invest considerable personnel, time, and resources in the mediation. This shared humanitarian interest may be the only genuine reason in a few instances of mediation, but normally even this interest intertwines with other, less altruistic, motivations.

When the mediator is an unofficial individual (e.g., President Carter in North Korea in 1994), the motives for initiating mediation may include a desire to (a) be instrumental in changing the course of a long-standing or escalating conflict, (b) gain access to major political leaders and open channels of communication, (c) put into practice a set of ideas on conflict management, and (d) spread one's own ideas and thus enhance personal stature and professional status. The presence of one or more of these motives (which may be conscious or subconscious) in an opportune situation provides a very strong rationale for an individual to initiate unofficial mediation.

Where a mediator is an official representative of a government or an organization, as is often the case, another set of motives may prevail. Such persons may wish to initiate mediation because (a) they have a clear mandate to intervene in disputes (e.g., the charters of the Arab League, the Organization of African Unity, and the Organization of American States each contain an explicit clause mandating that their members seek mediation in regional disputes), (b) they may want to do something about a conflict whose continuance could adversely affect their own political interests, (c) they may be directly requested by one or both parties to mediate, (d) they may wish to preserve intact a structure of which they are a part (e.g., the frequent mediation attempts by the United States in disputes between Greece and Turkey, two valued NATO member-states), or (e) they may see mediation as a way of extending and enhancing their own influence by becoming indispensable to the parties in conflict or by gaining the gratitude (and presumably the political goodwill) of one or both protagonists (e.g., the frequent efforts by the United States to mediate the Arab-Israeli conflict).

Mediators are political actors; they engage in mediation and expend resources because they expect to resolve a conflict and gain something from it. For many actors, mediation is a policy instrument through which they can pursue some of their interests without arousing too much opposition (Touval 1992a). The relationship between a mediator and disputants is thus never entirely devoid of political interest. To overlook this aspect is to miss an important element in the dynamics of mediation.

Adversaries in conflict have a number of motives for desiring mediation: (a) mediation may actually help them reduce the risks of an escalating conflict and get them closer to a settlement, (b) each party may embrace mediation in the expectation that the mediator will actually nudge or influence the other party, (c) both parties may see mediation as a public expression of their commitment to an international norm of peaceful conflict management, (d) they may want an outsider to take much of the blame should their efforts fail, or (e) they may desire mediation because a mediator can be used to monitor, verify, and guarantee any eventual agreement. One way or another, parties in conflict—and a mediator—have pretty compelling reasons for accepting, initiating, or desiring mediation.

Whether we are studying ethnic, internal, or international conflict, we should resist the tendency to think of mediation as a totally exogenous input, as a unique role and a distinct humanitarian response to conflict in which a well-meaning actor, motivated only by altruism, is keen to resolve a conflict. A mediator, through the very act of mediating, becomes a legitimate actor in a conflictual relationship. This relationship involves interests, costs, and potential rewards and exemplifies certain roles and strategies. A mediator's role is part of this broad interaction. To be effective, the mediator's role must reflect and be congruent with that interaction. This is how mediation should be seen, studied, and considered in international relations.

THE MEDIATOR'S ROLES AND BEHAVIOR

Mediation has been a prevalent form of international conflict management for many years. It is linked to the development of international negotiations and diplomacy, and it is embedded in the creation of institutions, regimes, and formal organizations to help states deal with many aspects of their relationships. But what do mediators actually do? Do they change behavior merely by chairing meetings and carrying messages, or do they possess more active roles and functions?

Considerable attention has been devoted to the question of mediator roles, functions, and behavior. Some scholars see these aspects as the most useful criteria by which to evaluate the success of mediation. In an exhaustive review of the literature, Wall (1981) identified more than a hundred specific mediation functions and behaviors. All these forms of behavior arise from the fact that the negotiators concerned cannot reach an agreement, and their stated purpose is to change, modify, settle, or resolve a conflict. Enacting these behaviors constitutes the "heart" of mediation.

To make sense of the many forms of behavior mediators may undertake, a number of role categories that encompass related forms of behavior are suggested. Mediators' roles may be characterized in a number of ways (e.g., Jabri 1990; Princen 1992). The late Jeffrey Rubin of Tufts University and the Fletcher School of International Law and Diplomacy, for instance, offered a set of mediation roles and distinguished between formal mediation (e.g., by the UN secretary-general) and informal mediation (e.g., by academic practitioners such as John Burton and Herb Kelman), individual mediation (e.g., by Lord Owen) and mediation by a representative of a state (e.g., by the U.S. secretary of state), invited mediation and noninvited mediation, advisory mediation and directive mediation, permanent mediation and temporary mediation, and resolution-oriented mediation and relationship-oriented mediation. Each of these types of mediators has different interests, resources, and capabilities, and the behavior of each may lead to different outcomes (Rubin 1981). Stulberg, writing in a more traditional vein, lists the following as mediators' roles: (a) catalyst, (b) educator, (c) translator, (d) resource-expander, (e) bearer of bad news, (f) agent of reality, and (g) scapegoat (Stulberg 1987). Susskind and Cruickshank, whose conception of mediation is that of "assisted negotiation," introduce a dynamic element into the discussion by identifying a number of roles (e.g. representation, inventing options, monitoring) and relating these to the various stages of the conflict (Susskind and Cruickshank 1987).

Another, and some would argue a more useful, approach for categorizing what mediators actually do is that of a mediation strategy, which Kolb defines as "an overall plan, approach or method a mediator has for resolving a dispute. . . . [I]t is the way the mediator intends to manage the case, the parties, and the issue" (Kolb 1983, 24). Which are the most important mediation strategies, and do different mediators choose different strategies?

There are a number of ways of thinking about mediation strategies. Kolb distinguishes two kinds of strategies: deal-making strategies (affecting the substance of a conflict) and orchestration strategies (managing the interaction) (Kolb 1983), similar to Rubin's resolution- and relationship-oriented roles. Stein, in her study of successive American mediations in the Middle East, talks about incremental strategies, or segmenting a conflict into smaller issues, and comprehensive strategies, which deal with all aspects of a conflict (Stein 1985). Carnevale, a social psychologist, suggests that mediators may choose from among four fundamental strategies: integration (searching for common ground), pressing (reducing the range of available alternatives), compensation (enhancing the attractiveness of some alternatives), and inaction (which, in effect, means allowing the parties to go their own way) (Carnevale 1986). Kressel, in one of the most widely used typologies, presents three general strategies: reflexive (discovering issues, facilitating better interactions), nondirective (producing a favorable climate for mediation), and directive (promoting specific outcomes) (Kressel 1972).

Touval and Zartman's typology of mediation strategies is the most apposite for the scholar or practitioner of international mediation. They identify three discrete categories of behavior, on an ascending level of involvement, that can describe the full range of mediation techniques. This typology is particularly useful because it is derived deductively from a general framework of mediation relationships that includes information, decision making, and influence. It can also be examined empirically through either observations or postmediation questionnaires. Above all, though, it includes all dimensions of mediator behavior within three categories: communication, formulation, and manipulation (Touval and Zartman 1985). This typology overcomes many of the limitations of past research.

Some of the specific interventions associated with each category are listed below.

1. *Communication strategies*
    - make contact with parties
    - gain the trust and confidence of the parties
    - arrange for interactions between the parties
    - identify underlying issues and interests
    - clarify the situation
    - avoid taking sides
    - develop a rapport with the parties
    - supply missing information
    - transmit messages between parties
    - encourage meaningful communication
    - offer positive evaluations
    - allow the interests of all parties to be discussed

2. *Formulation strategies*
    - choose the meeting site
    - control the pace and formality of the meetings
    - control the physical environment
    - establish protocol

- ensure the privacy of mediation
- suggest procedures
- highlight common interests
- reduce tensions
- control timing
- deal with simple issues first
- structure the agenda
- help devise a framework for an acceptable outcome
- help parties save face
- keep the process focused on the issues
- make substantive suggestions and proposals
- suggest concessions parties can make

3. *Manipulative strategies*
   - keep parties at the table
   - change parties' expectations
   - take responsibility for concessions
   - make parties aware of the costs of nonagreement
   - supply and filter information
   - help negotiators to undo a commitment
   - reward concessions made by the parties
   - press the parties to show flexibility
   - promise resources or threaten withdrawal
   - offer to verify compliance with the agreement
   - add incentives and threaten punishments
   - threaten to withdraw mediation

Touval and Zartman's typology permits us to analyze and understand what mediators actually do when they get involved in a conflict. The choice of any form of mediation behavior or strategy is rarely random. Rather, it is influenced by factors peculiar to the conflict and internal to the mediator. Mediators try to vary their behavior to reflect the conflict at hand. In low-intensity conflicts, for instance, communication strategies may be more effective; high-intensity conflicts may call for more active, manipulative strategies. Time pressure, mediator rank, and previous relations between the parties all may determine the choice of a strategy. To be effective, mediation strategies and behavior must be truly congruent with the nature of a conflict and the objectives and interests of a mediator.

Whichever intervention strategy mediators use, their underlying objectives in any conflict are to change: (a) the physical environment of conflict management (e.g., by maintaining secrecy, or imposing time limits, as President Carter did at Camp David); (b) the perception of what is at stake (e.g., by structuring an agenda and/or identifying and packaging new issues); and (c) the parties' motivation to reach a peaceful outcome by, for example, using subtle pressure. Any international conflict presents opportunities for some form of mediation. To be effective, however, mediation strategies must reflect the reality of the conflict and the resources of the mediator. To that extent international mediation is truly a contingent and reciprocal political activity.

WHO MAY MEDIATE?

Given the inevitability and omnipresence of conflict, a limited range of widely accepted procedures for dealing with it, and the unwelcome reality of the scope of its potential destructiveness, it is hardly surprising that so many actors, each adopting different strategies and tactics, are keen to mediate and undertake peacemaking activities. In an international environment lacking a centralized authority, the range of mediators and the diversity of mediation are truly immense. To make some sense of the bewildering range of possible mediators, I suggest that we think of them as falling within one of the following three categories: individuals, states, and institutions and organizations. Let us examine the characteristics of each.

Individuals

The traditional image of international mediation, one nurtured by the media and popular accounts, is that of a high-ranking official, shuttling from one place to another in an attempt to search for understanding and to restore communication between hostile parties or to help settle their conflict directly. This image is only partly accurate. The individual mediator who engages in such behavior is normally an official representing his or her government in a series of formal interactions with high-level officials from the disputing countries. This image cannot be accurately described as individual mediation.

By individual mediation, I mean mediation that is carried out by individuals who are not government officials or political incumbents. Although individual mediation exhibits greater variety and experimentation than other forms of mediation, it essentially consists of only two kinds: formal and informal. Informal mediation refers to the efforts of mediators who have a long-standing experience of, and a deep commitment to, international conflict resolution (e.g., the Quakers; see Yarrow 1978) or to the efforts of knowledgeable scholars whose background, attitudes, and professional experience give them the opportunity to engage in mediation with real conflict parties (the efforts of scholars such as Burton, Doob, and Kelman are some notable examples). Such individuals approach a conflict as private citizens, not as official representatives. They utilize their academic competence, credibility, and experience to facilitate communications, gain a better understanding of the conflict, and work toward its resolution.

The process of informal mediation usually begins when mediators enter a conflict on their own initiative. The format and arrangements of such mediation are, to say the least, novel. Present in a personal capacity only, mediators rely mostly on communication-facilitation strategies; the whole tone of mediation is free and flexible and can serve as a useful input to a more formal mediation. The efforts of two Israeli academics, Ron Pundak and Yair Hirschfeld, as well as Terje Roed-Larsen of Norway, exemplify the potential benefits of informal mediation through their paving the way for formal discussions between the Israeli government and the Palestine Liberation Organization.

Another example of informal mediation is the assistance given to parties in conflict by the International Negotiation Network (INN) at the Carter Center. This initiative was created by President Carter in 1976, with assistance from other international leaders, to fill a major mediation gap. Most states and international organizations are prevented from intervening in the internal affairs of another sovereign state. Yet, since the vast majority of recent serious conflicts have been largely internal rather than interstate, a clear need existed for an informal network of prestigious individuals (including former heads of state and UN secretaries-general) to offer additional mediation resources to the disputants. The INN's informal mediation can range from offering facilities to clarifying issues to providing a "face-saving" option by bringing parties either into mediation or out of a conflict. The INN has been actively involved in various mediation and consultation efforts in Ethiopia, Liberia, Cyprus, Zaire, Burma (Myanmar), Cambodia, and Sudan (Spencer and Yang 1993). In short, the INN has shown just how much can be achieved through informal mediation by individuals.

Formal mediation, on the other hand, takes place when a political incumbent, a government representative, or a high-level decision maker acts in an *individual* capacity to mediate a conflict between the *official* representatives of other states (e.g. Dennis Ross in his role as the State Department's Special Middle East Coordinator, and Richard Holbrooke in Bosnia). It invariably occurs within a formal structure, such as a conference, a political forum, or other official arenas, and is much less flexible than informal mediation. Formal mediation is also less susceptible to the impact of personality. Its loss of flexibility, however, is more than matched by its immediacy of access to influential decision makers. As such, formal mediation is often indistinguishable from diplomatic intercourse; its range of roles is more limited than that of informal mediation, but its impact on outcomes is more direct.

States

Individual mediation, although significant, is not common at the international level. Most mediation is carried on by states (or, to be more accurate, their representatives) and regional and international organizations.

When a state is invited to mediate a conflict, or when it initiates mediation, the services of one of its top decision makers are normally engaged. In these cases, figures such as Henry Kissinger; Presidents Carter or Clinton; former secretary of state Christopher, former assistant secretary of state Chester Crocker, or Lord Carrington; or special representatives like Gunnar Jarring or Philip Habeeb all fulfill mediation roles, usually in the full glare of the international media, as representatives of their countries.

Mediation, at any level and in all its guises, is essentially a voluntary process. This dimension is particularly important in the relations between states where any unwelcome intervention may be strenuously resisted. For mediation between states to be effective, even the most highly placed decision makers must be seen as impartial, acceptable to the disputants, and deserving of their trust. The absence of any one of these attributes may well lead to a failed mediation. States will submit their conflict to mediation only when they believe that the mediator can act fairly and recognize the importance of their interests. When we talk about mediation by states, we normally distinguish between small states and large states. Each claims legitimacy and authority on the basis of different attributes. Small states such as Algeria, Switzerland, and Austria (see Slim 1992) have been involved in a disproportionate number of international mediations. Their very size and presumed lack of clout make them appear nonthreatening and ideally positioned to carry out mediations between adversaries. Small states usually wait for an invitation to mediate. When they do intervene, their efforts tend to be confined to regional conflicts, and their strategies tend to be mostly low-profile strategies of dialogue and communication. This is where small states can be most useful in mediation efforts.

Large states, by contrast, often create the opportunity to mediate and use the mediation as a vehicle to protect or promote their own interests (Touval 1992a). Large states have a greater complement of resources and can select from a wider range of strategies. Because of their global interests, large states get involved in many conflicts in various parts of the world. When large states mediate a conflict, they can use their greater resources to wield a variety of carrots and sticks. They can generate and maintain a momentum toward a settlement by offering a neutral environment (e.g., Camp David or Dayton), pressing for concessions, offering proposals, and generally altering the disputants' payoffs and motivations.

Mediation, whether it is conducted by small or large states, is not pre-scribed by international law. It is unpredictable and ever changing, and its precise form and characteristics are negotiated and renegotiated with each passing phase. There is little that is predetermined about the course of out-comes when states mediate a conflict.

Institutions and Organizations

The complexity of the international environment is such that states can no longer facilitate the pursuit of all human interests or satisfy the demands for a shrinking range of public sector goods and services the world over. Consequently, we have witnessed a phenomenal growth in the number of international and transnational organizations, all of which may affect is-sues of war and peace. These organizations have become, in some cases, more important providers of services than states. They have also become, in the modern international system, very active participants in the search for mechanisms and procedures conducive to peacemaking and conflict reso-lution. We would expect these organizations to have a greater impact on the mediation of international conflicts.

Three kinds of organizations play an important role in the area of peace-making and conflict resolution: regional, international, and transnational. Regional and international organizations, such as the Organization of American States (OAS), the Organization of African Unity (OAU), and the United Nations, represent ensembles of *states* that have signified their intention to fulfill the obligations—including those of formal mediation—

of membership as set forth in a formal treaty. Transnational organizations (e.g., Amnesty International) represent *individuals* from different countries who have similar knowledge, skills, or interests, and who meet on a regular basis to promote their common interests through various means, including informal mediation.

Of the international organizations now in existence, none has been more active in resolving conflicts through negotiations and mediation than the United Nations, whose charter specifically commits it to provide the answers to global problems of conflict and security. In the post–Cold War era's outbreaks of low-level violence, civil wars, and ethnic conflicts, the United Nations is often seen as the only actor capable of resolving conflict independently. The *Agenda for Peace*, released by Secretary-General Boutros-Ghali (1995), recognizes the future challenges the United Nations is likely to encounter and places great emphasis on preventive diplomacy, peacemaking, and postconflict peacebuilding as priorities for the world organization.

The United Nations is quickly becoming a center for initiating concerted efforts to deal with the deep-rooted causes of conflict—to resolve conflicts, not merely stop them in their tracks—and will undoubtedly use its new political latitude to expand its mediation and conflict resolution activities. Recent UN peacemaking efforts in Somalia, Bosnia, Cambodia, Liberia, Afghanistan, Angola, and Rwanda show the extent to which this once largely ineffectual and much-criticized organization is now prepared to involve itself in all kinds of difficult and intractable conflicts. Once involved, the United Nations can offer a wealth of related resources unavailable to most other mediators, including a forum, skilled support personnel, and the ability to mobilize an international consensus on a particular outcome.

Regional organizations, like the European Union (EU), the OAS, the OAU, and the Arab League, all adhere to the principles of negotiation and mediation as their preferred means of resolving conflicts. Because most conflict occurs between regional neighbors, it is not surprising that these organizations have always had a great latitude in the field of conflict resolution. Some, like the EU and the Organization for Security and Cooperation in Europe (OSCE), have made conflict resolution a major component of their structure. Regional organizations usually engage in collective mediation; their strength undoubtedly owes to their members' common background, culture, and experience. They may not have the capacity or resources of the United Nations, but they are all involved in some current peacemaking activities: the EU in Bosnia, the OAU in Somalia, and the OAS in El Salvador.

Transnational organizations, such as Amnesty International, the Quakers' Friends Peace Committee and Friends World Committee for Consultation, and the International Committee of the Red Cross, operating independently of states, embody many of the elements commonly associated with impartiality. With limited resources and fewer strategies available to them, these organizations often find themselves involved in what are termed humanitarian interventions (where the victims are hostages, refugees, or prisoners). When strict secrecy or a high degree of impartiality is required and when neither governments nor international organizations can gain access to a conflict, transnational organizations come into their own. New organizations, like the London-based International Alert and the Atlanta-based International Negotiation Network, exemplify the growing number of institutions and organizations committed to peacemaking, mediation, and conflict resolution.

TOWARD MORE EFFECTIVE MEDIATION

Given the diversity of conflicts, circumstances, and actors, there cannot possibly be a "right way" to manage or mediate international conflicts. However, it is possible to generalize from various studies on mediation and to reflect on lessons learned in order to identify some factors and conditions that impede mediation or help it to become more effective.

Mediation is not a panacea to all the social problems and conflicts in the world. It cannot be successful (whatever that means) in each and every conflict. Clearly, it can be effective in some situations and less effective in others, and scholars and practitioners alike have devoted considerable attention to the conditions under which mediation can be more effective.

In an overview of mediation, Jeffrey Rubin notes that "For international mediation—indeed, for any form of intervention in any conflict setting—to be effective, three things are required: disputant *motivation* to settle or resolve the conflict in question, mediator *opportunity* to get involved, and mediator *skill*" (Rubin 1992, 251). The parties' motivation and commitment to accept and engage in mediation undoubtedly affect the outcome of mediation. When disputants are unenthusiastic about mediation or believe they can get what they want through unilateral action, the likelihood of a successful mediation is extremely low. Effective mediation requires consent, high motivation, and active participation.

From the perspective of a would-be mediator, a number of features can be indicative of the parties' genuine motivation and serious commitment to mediation. Foremost among these is the receipt of a joint request. When only one party requests mediation, the chances of a successful outcome are pretty slim. Mediation offers more rewarding opportunities when it is requested by both parties in conflict rather than by one party only or by the mediator. A joint request may well be a condition for effective international mediation (Bercovitch 1984; Hiltrop 1989).

International mediation is also more likely to be effective when certain conditions and circumstances are present. These include relative power parity between the states or other actors in conflict (Young 1967), the absence of ideological issues or those of general "principle" from the mediator's scope (Bercovitch and Langley 1993), a clear identification of the parties in conflict (which is not always as straightforward as it may appear), the absence of severe internal disorganization or civil war in the country or countries where the conflict is taking place, the exclusion of the nature and history of the parties' previous relationship from the mediation (Bercovitch 1989), and the presence of a ripe moment constituted by a "hurting stalemate."

Empirical research (Bercovitch 1986) suggests that neither premature nor belated mediations are especially likely to be effective. The most propitious time to initiate mediation is roughly halfway through the life cycle of a conflict, and certainly after the parties' own efforts have failed. At this stage the parties' motivation to settle is at its highest, and so an opportunity is present—a ripe moment. The timing of mediation is a crucial factor affecting the chances of its success. Conflicts, like all other social processes, have their own life cycles (which may stretch across days, months, or years). There are times when a conflict is "ripe for mediation" (Zartman 1985), and times when mediation can only make a conflict worse and harm the credibility of the mediators (Haass 1990). Assessing when a conflict is ready for mediation may not be easy, varying from case to case and depending on many dynamic factors. Yet the existence of a "hurting stalemate" (e.g., a military setback, a change in power relations, or a failure to impose a unilateral outcome) remains the best benchmark in a conflict for deciding when to initiate mediation. The parties reach a hurting stalemate when their own efforts to manage the conflict are going nowhere and when the costs, both human and economic, of pursuing the conflict begin to mount. These and other conditions affect the chances of the mediation's success. Being able to identify these conditions may affect mediators' decisions to initiate or forego mediation as well as its likely course and outcome. Knowing when to use mediation may be more important than how often it is used.

Another factor affecting mediation is the mediator's identity and skills. Mediation is a voluntary process, so only an appropriate mediator is likely to be effective. There is wide agreement among scholars and practitioners that appropriate mediators should possess intelligence, tact, skills in drafting formal proposals, and a sense of humor, in addition to specific knowledge of the conflict at hand. Mediators who possess these attributes are likely to be acceptable to all sides in a conflict and consequently enhance the parties' motivation to reach a peaceful settlement.

A related aspect of mediator identity that can aid in distinguishing potentially effective from ineffective mediators is that of rank. It is important to recall that some mediators, such as a president, a prime minister, or a secretary of state, are better able to marshal resources in the course of mediation than those of lesser stature. High-ranking mediators can be more persuasive than middle-level officials; they possess leverage and can use social influence that could be crucial in persuading the parties to make concessions or move toward an agreement. This notion is borne out in a series of empirical studies (Bercovitch and Houston 1993) that clearly show the positive association between high rank and successful mediation outcomes.

A related idea is that mediation roles and strategies may affect outcomes. Some (e.g. Burton 1969; Kelman 1992) advocate communication-facilitation strategies as most likely to achieve a successful outcome. Others (e.g., Touval and Zartman 1985) argue for more forceful mediation involving formulation and manipulation. Although much may depend on the nature and circumstances of a conflict, there is strong evidence (e.g., Bercovitch and Houston 1993) to suggest that more directive strategies are more likely to be effective. Active strategies can rely on the full gamut of influence, using reward, persuasion, legitimacy, and information to effect an outcome.

Mediators may appear to do little more than shuttle from here to there, chair meetings, and clarify issues. In most cases, though, they quickly begin to urge the parties to reach some agreement. Mediators have to do more than generate and share information if they are to have a desired impact on a conflict; they have to use more active strategies and change the ways the parties think and interact.

A number of conditions relating to a conflict, and some relating to a mediator, form the core of a comprehensive theory of mediation. This theory, in turn, can offer policy implications and guidelines that can be applied in specific cases; such a theory can ultimately explain and predict the success and failure of mediation across a wide range of conflicts. This fruitful area of research should prove invaluable in bringing scholars and practitioners together to construct an inventory of conditions that either impede or promote the successful mediation of a conflict.

EVALUATING INTERNATIONAL MEDIATION

We have seen that numerous actors and organizations may undertake and initiate international mediation, but is there any way of assessing just how much these different types of mediators can achieve? How can mediation outcomes be assessed, and how can the impact of a particular mediation be evaluated? If mediation is ultimately about changing or influencing a conflict, or the way parties in conflict behave, can such changes be discerned? Furthermore, if change has been effected and a satisfactory outcome of sorts has been achieved, can this outcome be attributed to the wisdom and experience of the mediator or to the motivation of the parties? Conversely, if the parties show no change whatsoever, should this be described as mediation failure? How much time should elapse before we can realistically expect results from the mediation? What is the norm? Six months, one year, three years, or longer? Will the criteria change depending on the nature of the conflict, the parties, and the mediator? In short, evaluating success and failure in mediation poses serious conceptual and methodological problems.

Because international mediation is not a uniform practice, it seems futile to draw up one set of criteria to cover the many objectives of all mediators. Individual mediators, for instance, may emphasize communication-facilitating strategies, be more concerned with the quality of interaction, and seek to create a better environment for conflict management. States, on the other hand, may seek to change the behavior of those in conflict and achieve a settlement of sorts. Such different objectives cannot be easily accommodated within a single perspective. To answer the question of whether or not mediation works, we need to know something about the various goals of mediation. Hence the need for two broad criteria, subjective and objective, to assess the contribution and consequences of any form of international mediation.

Subjective criteria refer to the parties' or the mediator's perception (and, to some extent, that of other relevant external actors) that the goals of mediation have been achieved or that a desired change has taken place. Using this perspective, we can suggest that mediation has been successful when the parties express satisfaction with the process or outcome of mediation, or when the outcome is seen as fair, efficient, or effective (Susskind and Cruickshank 1987).

Fairness of mediation, satisfaction with its performance, or improvement in the overall climate of the parties' relationship cannot be easily demonstrated, but they are undoubtedly consequences of successful mediation. They are subjective because they depend on the assessments of the parties in conflict. Even if a conflict remains unresolved, mediation—of any form—can do much to change the way the disputants feel about each other and lead, however indirectly, to both a long-term improvement in the parties' relationship and a resolution of the conflict.

Objective criteria for assessing the impact and consequences of mediation offer a totally different perspective. Objective criteria rely on substantive indicators that can be demonstrated empirically. Usually such criteria involve observations of change and judgments about the extent of change as evidence of the success or failure of mediation. Thus, one can consider a particular mediation effort successful if it contributed to a cessation or reduction of violent behavior and the opening of a dialogue between the parties. Or, one can call a mediation successful when a formal and binding agreement that settles the conflict's issues has been signed.

Evaluating the success or failure of international mediation in objective terms is a relatively straightforward task. Here one can measure success or failure in terms of the permanence of the agreement achieved, the speed with which it was achieved, the reduction in the level of hostilities between the disputants, the number of issues on which agreement was achieved, and so forth. On the face of it, objective criteria seem to offer a perfectly valid way to assess the impact, consequences, and effectiveness of international mediation.

However, it would be unwise to rely solely on objective criteria. Different mediators, and indeed different parties in conflict, have different goals in mind when they enter the realm of conflict management. Changing the behavior of the parties could well be only one among a set of goals. Some international mediators may focus on the substance of interactions, others may focus on its climate, setting, and decision-making norms. These goals cannot always be evaluated easily. Each mediation should, perhaps, be evaluated in terms of the criteria that are significant to its own efforts. The questions of whether or not mediation works and how best to evaluate it can be answered only by collecting information and making judgments in specific cases. There are just too many conceptual problems with these questions, and it seems that, on this issue at least, our theoretical ambitions must be tempered by the constraints of a complex reality.

CONCLUSION

Until ten or fifteen years ago, scholarly attempts to comprehend the nature and sources of human conflict in general, and the manner of its resolution in particular, were all too few in number and rather marginal in character. This situation has changed considerably. International conflict and conflict management have become subjects for systematic analysis. Scholarly tracts and practitioners' reflections have helped to institutionalize the field and enhance the individual and collective capacity to manage conflicts. The risks, costs, and tragedies of conflicts in the later part of our century have finally forced us to search for better ways to resolve them. The traditional reliance on power or avoidance are as far from being optimal ways of dealing with conflict as they are outdated. Negotiation and mediation are at last beginning to emerge as the most appropriate responses to conflict in its myriad forms and to the challenge of building a more peaceful world. Negotiation and mediation do not just happen. They are social roles subject to many influences; and, like other roles, they can be learned.

The shared quest for learning the principles and practices of mediation can make sense only if it is conducted within some kind of an intellectual framework, one that can explain the logic and reasoning behind this method of conflict management, in which the mediator is neither directly part of a conflict nor totally removed from it. This chapter has sought to provide such a framework and assess its basic dimensions.

The framework embodies my conviction that mediation is an aspect of the broader process of conflict management and that, irrespective of what the conflict is about or who the mediators are, mediation involves the intertwining of interests, resources, and positions in an attempt to influence outcomes. This relationship is critical for analyzing the dynamics of conflict and assessing the prospects of successful mediation. I have tried to unravel many aspects of this relationship and point out their influence on mediation. I do not assume that my analysis is exhaustive, but I believe that the foregoing presentation adequately integrates many findings that have a bearing on conflict resolution and provides answers to such questions as who may mediate conflicts, when mediation should be initiated, how it actually works, and how its impact can be evaluated.

The end of the Cold War and the emergence of an ever-increasing number of ethnic and internal conflicts provide many opportunities for a significant expansion in the use of mediation as an instrument of conflict resolution. The old techniques of power and deterrence seem increasingly less relevant to deal with the problems and conflicts confronting us until the end of the century and perhaps beyond. Mediation may well offer the most coherent and effective response to these issues. To ensure that it can also be successful, we need to develop a better understanding of the process and offer consistent guidelines to the many actors involved in mediation. This effort is still in its infancy, and many different fields and disciplines can contribute to its development. In this chapter, I have tried to take a few tentative steps in that direction. The challenge confronting us all is to recognize the diversity, strengths, and limitations of mediation, and then use its most effective range of tools where appropriate. Given the amount of destruction accruing from today's conflicts and tomorrow's potential crises, this is one challenge we cannot afford to ignore.

REFERENCES

Bartunek, Jean M., Alan A. Benton, and Christopher B. Keys. 1975. "Third Party Intervention and the Behavior of Group Representatives." *Journal of Conflict Resolution* 19 (3): 532–57.

Bercovitch, Jacob. 1984. *Social Conflicts and Third Parties: Strategies of Conflict Resolution*. Boulder, Colo.: Westview.

———. 1986. "International Mediation: A Study of Incidence, Strategies and Conditions of Successful Outcomes." *Cooperation and Conflict* 21 (3): 155–68.

———. 1989. "International Dispute Mediation." In *Mediation Research, The Process and Effectiveness of Third-Party Intervention*, ed. Kenneth Kressel and Dean G. Pruitt. San Francisco: Jossey-Bass.

———. 1996. "Understanding Mediation's Role in Preventive Diplomacy." *Negotiation Journal* 12 (3): 241–59.

Bercovitch, Jacob, and Allison Houston. 1993. "Influence of Mediator Characteristics and Behavior on the Success of Mediation in International Relations." *International Journal of Conflict Management* 4 (October): 297–321.

Bercovitch, Jacob, and Jeffrey Langley. 1993. "The Nature of the Dispute and the Effectiveness of International Mediation." *Journal of Conflict Resolution* 37 (4): 670–91.

Bercovitch, Jacob, and Jeffrey Z. Rubin. 1992. *Mediation in International Relations*. New York: St. Martin's Press.

Bingham, Gail. 1985. *Resolving Environmental Disputes*. Washington, D.C.: The Conservation Foundation.

Blake, Robert A., and Jane Srygley Mouton. 1985. *Solving Costly Organizational Conflicts*. San Francisco: Jossey-Bass.

Boutros-Ghali, Boutros. 1995. *An Agenda for Peace*. New York: United Nations.

Burton, John W. 1969. *Conflict and Communication*. London: Macmillan.

———. 1972. "The Resolution of Conflict." *International Studies Quarterly* 16 (March): 5-29.

———. 1984. *Global Conflict*. Brighton, Sussex: Wheatsheaf Books.

Butterworth, Robert L. 1976. *Managing Interstate Disputes, 1945-1974*. Pittsburgh: University of Pittsburgh Press.

Carnevale, Peter. 1986. "Strategic Choice in Mediation." *Negotiation Journal* 2 (1): 41-56.

Carnevale, Peter, and Richard Pegnetter. 1985. "The Selection of Mediation Tactics in Public Sector Disputes: A Contingency Analysis." *Journal of Social Issues* 41 (2): 65-81.

Doob, Leonard W. 1971. *Resolving Conflict in Africa*. New Haven: Yale University Press.

Douglas, Ann. 1957. "The Peaceful Settlement of Industrial and Intergroup Disputes." *Journal of Conflict Resolution* 1 (March): 69–81.

Fisher, Ronald J. 1983. "Third-Party Consultation as a Method of Intergroup Conflict Resolution." *Journal of Conflict Resolution* 27 (2): 301-44.

Fisher, Roger, and William Ury. 1981. *Getting to Yes*. Boston: Houghton Mifflin

Folberg, Jay, and Alison Taylor. 1984. *Mediation*. San Francisco: Jossey-Bass.

Haass, Richard N. 1990. *Conflicts Unending*. New Haven: Yale University Press.

Hiltrop, Jean M. 1989. "Factors Affected with Successful Labor Mediation." In *Mediation Research, The Process and Effectiveness of Third-Party Intervention*, ed. Kenneth Kressel and Dean G. Pruitt. San Francisco: Jossey-Bass.

Holsti, Kalevi J. 1983. *International Politics: A Framework for Analysis*. 4th ed. Englewood Cliffs, N.J.: Prentice-Hall.

Jabri, Vivienne. 1990. *Mediating Conflict: Decision Making and Western Intervention in Namibia*. Manchester: Manchester University Press.

Kelman, Herbert C. 1992. "Informal Mediation by the Scholar/Practitioner." In *Mediation in International Relations*, ed. Jacob Bercovitch and Jeffrey Z. Rubin. New York: St. Martin's Press.

Kolb, Deborah M. 1983. "Strategy and Tactics of Mediation." *Human Relations* 36 (3): 247–68.

Kolb, Deborah M., and Jeffrey Z. Rubin. 1991. "Mediation through a Disciplinary Prism." *Research on Negotiation in Organizations* 3:231–57.

Kressel, Kenneth. 1972. *Labor Mediation: An Exploratory Survey*. New York: Association of Labor Mediation Agencies.

Kressel, Kenneth, and Dean G. Pruitt, eds. 1989. *Mediation Research. The Process and Effectiveness of Third-Party Intervention*. San Francisco: Jossey-Bass.

Meyer, Arthur. 1960. "Functions of the Mediator in Collective Bargaining." *Industrial and Labour Relations Review* 13 (June): 159–65.

Mitchell, Christopher R. 1981. *The Structure of International Conflict*. London: Macmillan.

Moore, Christopher W. 1986. *The Mediation Process: Practical Strategies for Resolving Conflict*. San Francisco: Jossey-Bass.

Northedge, Fred S., and Michael D. Donelan. 1971. *International Disputes: The Political Aspects*. London: Europa Publications.

Ott, Mervin C. 1972. "Mediation as a Method of Conflict Resolution." *International Organization* 26 (4): 595-618.

Princen, Thomas. 1992. *Intermediaries in International Conflict*. Princeton: Princeton University Press.

Raiffa, Howard. 1982. *The Art and Science of Negotiation*. Cambridge, Mass.: Harvard University Press.

Rubin, Jeffrey Z. 1980. "Experimental Research on Third-Party Intervention in Conflict." *Psychological Bulletin* 87 (2): 379–91.

———. 1992. "International Mediation in Context." In *Mediation in International Relations*, ed. Jacob Bercovitch and Jeffrey Z. Rubin. New York: St. Martin's Press.

———., ed. 1981. *Dynamics of Third-Party Intervention: Kissinger in the Middle East*. New York: Praeger.

Schelling, Thomas. C. 1960. *The Strategy of Conflict*. Cambridge, Mass.: Harvard University Press.

Simkin, William E. 1971. *Mediation and the Dynamics of Collective Bargaining*. Washington, D.C.: Bureau of National Affairs.

Singer, Linda R. 1990. *Settling Disputes: Conflict Resolution in Business, Families, and the Legal System*. Boulder, Colo.: Westview.

Slim, Randa. 1992. "Small-State Mediation in International Relations: The Algerian Mediation of the Iranian Hostage Crisis." In *Mediation in International Relations*, ed. Jacob Bercovitch and Jeffrey Z. Rubin. New York: St. Martin's Press.

Spencer, Doyle E., and Huang Yang. 1993. "Lessons from the Field of Intra-National Conflict Resolution." *Notre Dame Law Review* 67:1495–1512.

Stein, Janice Gross. 1985. "Structure, Strategies and Tactics of Mediation." *Negotiation Journal* 1 (4): 331-47.

Stevens, Carl M. 1963. *Strategy and Collective Bargaining Negotiations*. New York: McGraw Hill.

Stulberg, Joseph B. 1981. "The Theory and Practice of Mediation: A Reply to Professor Susskind." *Vermont Law Review* 6:85–17.

———. 1987. *Taking Charge/Managing Conflict*. Lexington, Mass.: D.C. Heath.

Susskind, Lawrence, and Jeffrey Cruickshank. 1987. *Breaking the Impasses: Consensual Approaches to Resolving Public Disputes*. New York: Basic Books.

Touval, Saadia. 1992a. "The Superpowers as Mediators." In *Mediation in International Relations*, ed. Jacob Bercovitch and Jeffrey Z. Rubin. New York: St. Martin's Press.

————. 1992b. "Gaining Entry to Mediation in Communal Strife." In *The Internationalization of Communal Strife*, ed. Manus I. Midlarsky. London: Routledge.

Touval, Saadia, and I. William Zartman. 1985. "Mediation in Theory." In *International Mediation in Theory and Practice*, ed. Saadia Touval and I. William Zartman. Boulder, Colo.: Westview.

Wall, James A, Jr. 1981. "Mediation: An Analysis, Review and Proposed Research." *Journal of Conflict Resolution* 25 (1): 157–80.

Wallensteen, Peter, and Karin Axell. 1993. "Armed Conflict at the End of the Cold War, 1989-1992." *Journal of Peace Research* 30 (3): 331–46.

Wallensteen, Peter, and Margareta Sollenberg. 1995. "After the Cold War: Emerging Patterns of Armed Conflict, 1989–1994." *Journal of Peace Research* 32 (3): 345–60.

Walton, Richard E. 1969. *Interpersonal Peacemaking: Confrontations and Third-Party Consultation*. Reading, Mass.: Addison-Wesley.

Yarrow, C. H. 1978. *Quaker Experiences in International Conciliation*. New Haven: Yale University Press.

Young, Oran R. 1967. *The Intermediaries: Third Parties in International Crises*. Princeton: Princeton University Press.

Zacher, Mark W. 1979. *International Conflicts and Collective Security, 1946–1977: The United Nations, Organization of American States, Organization of African Unity, and the Arab League*. New York: Praeger.

Zartman, I. William. 1985. *Ripe for Resolution: Conflict and Intervention in Africa*. 2d ed. New York: Oxford University Press.

5

ADJUDICATION

International Arbitral Tribunals and Courts

Richard B. Bilder

INTRODUCTION

International adjudication is a method of international dispute settlement that involves the referral of the dispute to an impartial third-party tribunal—normally either an arbitral tribunal or an international court—for binding decision, usually on the basis of international law. In contrast with so-called political means of settlement, international adjudication usually involves a legal obligation on the part of the parties to the dispute to accept the third party's decision as settling the dispute. This chapter describes the general nature and role of international adjudication, some of its advantages and disadvantages as compared with other dispute-settlement techniques, and its prospects.

The vision of an international legal order in which all international disputes are subject to binding and impartial adjudication has strongly influenced thinking about international law and governance. Not surprisingly, national legal systems have furnished the model for people's expectations about a legally regulated international society. National experience and jurisprudence have traditionally accorded adjudication a preeminent status among dispute-settlement techniques. Indeed, it has generally been assumed that the hallmark and sine qua non of an effective domestic legal system is the compulsory settlement of disputes by permanent courts. Consequently, this is the goal many have set for the international legal system as well. Subjecting nations to the rule of law has often been equated with subjecting their behavior to the judgment of impartial international tribunals. For Americans in particular, a historical experience in which courts have played an important role in forging and maintaining an effective federal system shapes the view that international courts might play a similar role in helping to establish an effective international system.

By this standard, the achievement of an effective international legal order remains elusive. It is a fundamental principle of international law that no state need submit its disputes to impartial adjudication unless it wishes; unless all states involved in a particular dispute have given their consent, an international arbitrator or court has no jurisdiction to decide the dispute. Yet states have generally been reluctant to give such consent. While nations often pay lip service to the ideal of judicial settlement, in practice they have established only a few international courts—most notably, the International Court of Justice (ICJ) or "World Court"—and have entrusted relatively few significant disputes to international arbitral tribunals or courts. Much thought has been devoted to ways to encourage nations to make more use of international tribunals, but none have proved very successful.

While this discussion will urge encouraging and strengthening the role of adjudication in international dispute settlement, it may be useful to keep several caveats in mind.

First, as the other chapters of this book demonstrate, adjudication is only one of many possible ways of dealing with disputes. The usual and accepted methods of peaceful settlement are those listed in Article 33 of the UN Charter—negotiation, conciliation, arbitration, judicial settlement, resort to regional agencies or arrangements, and resort to UN or other international organization dispute-settlement procedures. In essence, a full list of methods reflects a spectrum of techniques that range from so-called diplomatic means, such as negotiation, consultations, good offices, mediation, and conciliation, which give control of the outcome primarily to the parties themselves, to so-called legal means, such as arbitration or judicial settlement, which give control of the outcome primarily to a third party (or parties). Of course, the various dispute-settlement techniques are not mutually exclusive, and a particular process of dispute resolution will often combine different methods. Indeed, negotiation—which is the predominant and preferred method of resolving disputes—typically plays at least some part in any dispute-settlement effort, including one ultimately resolved through adjudication. Thus, in deciding whether to use adjudication to resolve a particular international dispute, the states involved will have to weigh its advantages and disadvantages carefully against those of alternative available methods.

Second, it is open to question whether national legal systems, overseeing a wide variety of relations among millions or hundreds of millions of individuals coexisting in a close-knit society, are appropriate models for an international legal system, designed to meet very different problems of order and cooperation among less than two hundred nation-states. The special characteristics of the international political order—and in particular the inevitability of continuous interactions and relations among its members—may suggest the appropriateness of legal institutions, techniques, and responses very different from those found in national legal orders. In short, we are beginning to realize that there is no one way in which a legal system must work; instead, there are a number of ways of organizing a legal order, more than one of which may be effective.

Moreover, while adjudication plays a significant role in national legal orders, there is growing evidence that this role is probably different than commonly assumed. Recent studies, at least in the United States, suggest that the great majority of disputes are settled by means other than formal court decisions. Indeed, much of the evidence suggests that lawsuits function primarily as a spur to private settlement and that judges function significantly as mediators in encouraging such settlements, in addition to their more formal role as deciders of disputes. Consequently, legal scholars and practitioners have been devoting more attention to the role of nonadjudicatory techniques in the functioning of the legal order and to devising innovative alternative dispute-resolution techniques to meet the needs of an overburdened and often expensive judicial system.

Third, it is arguable that a focus on adjudication reflects a particularly Western bias toward methods of dispute settlement. For example, it has been said that Chinese, Japanese, and certain other non-Western societies traditionally emphasize nonadversarial techniques of mediation and mutual accommodation to deal with disputes and are generally reluctant to use adjudication or other adversarial or "legally oriented" methods. This situation suggests a need for sensitivity in any international dispute to the particular cultural attitudes and responses toward conflict and dispute settlement of the parties involved. Certainly, any conflict-management strategy must take into account such differing cultural perspectives in deciding on the appropriateness of adjudicatory versus other dispute-settlement approaches in particular contexts.

Finally, the U.S. position toward international adjudication has been and remains ambivalent, reflecting fluctuations in U.S. foreign policy between messianism, a belief that the United States should lead nations toward acceptance of the rule of law in international affairs, and chauvinism, or the distrust of international law and institutions and the belief that only realpolitik can safeguard the national interest. As we will see, while the United States pioneered the idea of international arbitration and was long one of the strongest advocates of international adjudication, its recent policy has been less clear—particularly in the wake of the ICJ's 1984 and 1986 judgments against the United States in the *Nicaragua* case.

THE NATURE OF INTERNATIONAL ADJUDICATION

What are international arbitral tribunals and courts, what do they do, and how do they work?

In contrast to the compulsory jurisdiction normally exercised by courts in national legal systems, the jurisdiction of international arbitral tribunals and courts is solely consensual. Absent special agreement, a state is under no international obligation to submit a dispute with another state—or, *a fortiori*, with an individual or nongovernmental organization—to legally binding settlement by an international court, arbitral tribunal, or other third party. Consequently, under international law, an international court or arbitral tribunal can render a binding decision regarding a dispute only in situations where the state or states concerned have expressly or implicitly consented to that court or tribunal exercising jurisdiction over the particular dispute or category of dispute. A state may give its consent either by special agreement at the time of the dispute or by agreement in advance in some other treaty or instrument. If a state does consent to arbitration or judicial settlement of a dispute with another state, it is bound by that consent, and the appropriate tribunal may exercise jurisdiction according to the terms of such consent.

In view of states' reluctance to relinquish control over the outcomes of their disputes to third parties, it is not surprising that, in general, international arbitral tribunals and courts have played a rather limited role in the settlement of international disputes. States have been particularly reluctant to obligate themselves in advance to the compulsory binding adjudication of potential disputes with other countries—especially over issues that may involve what they consider vital national interests. In general, they have been willing to do so only when their commitment to such compulsory jurisdiction is restricted in terms of subject matter or otherwise carefully circumscribed.

There are essentially two methods of international adjudication: arbitration and judicial settlement by an international court. The differences between the two methods lie principally in the permanence of the tribunal to which the dispute is referred, the scope of its jurisdiction or authority, and the extent to which the parties to the dispute can control the selection of the third parties—arbitrators or judges—who will rule on their dispute and the tribunal's jurisdiction and procedures.

Arbitration

Arbitration is a form of adjudication that involves the referral of a dispute or disputes to an ad hoc tribunal, rather than to a permanently established court, for binding decision. In this case, the parties, by their agreement (usually called a *compromis*), must establish the tribunal, which will decide their dispute "from scratch." The agreement defines the issue to be arbitrated and determines the method for selecting the arbitrator or arbitrators, the machinery and procedure of the arbitral tribunal, and the way of paying for the tribunal's costs. The arbitral tribunal is constituted to address only the particular issue or issues entrusted to it by the parties' agreement and is bound strictly by the terms of that agreement. Once the tribunal's work is completed, it ceases to exist. While arbitration tribunals typically are constituted to deal only with a single dispute, some important arbitral tribunals (sometimes called claims commissions) have been established to address a number of related disputes over a period of time, particularly involving claims by individuals or corporations that are nationals of one state against another state. A recent example is the Iran-U.S. Claims Tribunal, which was established at The Hague under the 1981 Algiers Accords between the two countries to deal with several thousand claims arising mostly out of the U.S.-Iran hostage crisis; the tribunal has still not completed its work.

Typically, an arbitral tribunal is composed of three arbitrators, one chosen by each party and the third, or "neutral," arbitrator selected by agreement of the two "national" arbitrators, or failing the parties' agreement, by an impartial third party such as the president of the International Court of Justice. (It is important to provide some "fallback" impartial appointment mechanism, since otherwise a recalcitrant party might try to block the arbitration process by refusing to agree to the selection of any particular neutral arbitrator.) However, the parties may wish to select a single arbitrator, such as the UN secretary-general; a tribunal of five, with three neutral arbitrators; or, as in the case of the nine-member Iran-U.S. Claims Tribunal, a larger number of arbitrators. The parties typically choose highly reputable judges, diplomats, former prominent government officials, international lawyers, or academics to serve as arbitrators. The parties and arbitrators also have to decide upon the tribunal's procedure, including its meeting times and places. In 1958, the UN General Assembly recommended to states a set of Model Rules of Arbitral Procedure, developed by the UN International Law Commission, which has provided a very useful and widely accepted basis for agreement on arbitral procedures. States may also draw upon other model procedural codes, such as the Arbitration Rules of the UN Commission on International Trade Law, which govern the procedure of the Iran-U.S. Claims Tribunal.

Since the parties must specifically agree to any arbitration—and are not likely to do so unless they believe that they can "live with" an adverse decision—it is not surprising that most states comply with arbitral decisions (usually called awards). However, disputes may occasionally arise with respect to arbitral judgments, particularly where a losing party claims that the tribunal exceeded its authority or failed to do what was asked under the *compromis* and that, consequently, its award is a nullity. A study of the execution of some three hundred arbitral awards between 1794 and 1936 uncovered only twenty cases of noncompliance, although there have probably been several more since 1936.

Arbitration is one of the oldest forms of international adjudication, dating back to the time of the early Greeks—indeed, some scholars say, to early Mesopotamia. More modern forms of international adjudication date back to the Jay Treaty of 1794 and the 1814 Treaty of Ghent between the United States and Great Britain, both of which established several arbitral commissions. The concept of international arbitration was broadly endorsed by the international community at the Hague Peace Conference of 1899, which, among other things, approved a Convention for the Pacific Settlement of International Disputes and the establishment of the so-called Permanent Court of Arbitration at The Hague. Despite its name, this institution is not really a court, but rather a bureau that maintains a roster of potential international arbitrators and, on request, provides services to an arbitral tribunal.

According to a recent scholarly survey, in the past two centuries there have been about 450 international arbitrations conducted between or among states (Stuyt 1990). Over this same period, the United States alone was involved in some 115 such international arbitrations, including the famous 1871–72 *Alabama Claims* arbitration with Great Britain, in which the tribunal decided that Great Britain had to pay compensation for damage caused by a Confederate warship that was built in Great Britain and permitted to sail from that country in violation of its obligation as a neutral during the American Civil War.

There have been at least several dozen significant arbitrations since 1945. They include the 1965 *Gut Dam* arbitration (United States and Canada); the 1968 *Rann of Kutch* arbitration (India and Pakistan); the 1977 *Beagle Channel* arbitration (Argentina and Chile); the 1986 *Rainbow Warrior* arbitration (France and New Zealand); the 1988 *Taba* arbitration (Egypt and Israel); three arbitrations involving air transport agreements between the United States and, respectively, France, Italy, and the United Kingdom; and the continuing series of decisions handed down by the still-functioning Iran-U.S. Claims Tribunal, which, as of October 1995, has issued some 566 awards involving over $2.6 billion. International arbitration has also recently assumed an important role in the adjustment of trade and investment disputes through specialized arbitrations occurring under the auspices and dispute-settlement procedures of the General Agreement on Tariffs and Trade (GATT, now the World Trade Organization, or WTO), the World Bank–sponsored International Centre for the Settlement of Investment Disputes (ICSID), the Canada-U.S. Free Trade Agreement, and, more recently, the North American Free Trade Agreement (NAFTA). Mention should also be made of the UN Compensation Commission, established by the United Nations to address claims against Iraq arising from Iraq's 1990–91 invasion and occupation of Kuwait.

Judicial Settlement

Judicial settlement is a form of adjudication that involves the referral of a dispute or disputes to a permanent judicial body for binding settlement. In the case of judicial settlement, the machinery and procedure of the tribunal, including the method of selecting the judges of the court, are already established by existing international instruments, such as the Statute and the Rules of the International Court of Justice. A permanent judicial tribunal is typically established to deal with a broad number and range of disputes submitted by a variety of states and continues in existence beyond its judgment in any particular case.

The first permanent international court was the little-known Central American Court of Justice, which was established by the Washington Peace

Conference of 1907 as part of its settlement of the conflict among Guatemala, El Salvador, and Honduras; between 1908 and 1918 the court heard ten cases. The first truly global international court was the Permanent Court of International Justice (PCIJ), which was formally inaugurated in 1922 at The Hague, Netherlands, under the aegis of the League of Nations as part of the post–World War I peace settlements. The PCIJ, housed in an elaborate building donated by Andrew Carnegie called the "Peace Palace," functioned from 1922 to 1940; it ceased to exist when the league was formally dissolved in 1946. The present world court, the International Court of Justice (ICJ), was established by the UN Charter as the principal judicial organ of the United Nations, and also has its seat in the Peace Palace. The ICJ is the legal successor to, and is in most respects similar to, the PCIJ, with a comparable statute and a shared and continuing jurisprudence. In view of the ICJ's importance, it will be discussed in greater detail in the next section.

While the ICJ is the most prominent international court and at present the only one with a general and global jurisdiction, there are also several other important international courts with more specialized functions and jurisdictions. They include the European Union's Court of Justice and the Court of First Instance (the latter established in 1989), operating in Luxembourg, Belgium, under the provisions of the Treaty of Rome and the Single European Act, respectively; the European Court of Human Rights, with its seat in Strasbourg, France, which operates under the European Convention for the Protection of Human Rights and Fundamental Freedoms and its various protocols; and the Inter-American Court of Human Rights, with its seat in San Jose, Costa Rica, which was established by the Organization of American States and functions under the American Convention on Human Rights. Each of these specialized courts plays a major role in its respective regional system, and each has addressed important cases and developed a significant jurisprudence. Moreover, each of these courts has unique and interesting jurisdictional and procedural features. For example, each of these courts can in certain circumstances hear cases brought by individuals—unlike the ICJ, which has jurisdiction solely over cases brought by states. Under Part XV of the UN Law of the Sea Convention, which has recently entered into force, a new International Tribunal for the Law of the Sea will be established, with its seat in Hamburg, Germany. Other continuing international tribunals include the administrative tribunals of the UN's specialized agencies, such as the International Labor Organization, the World Bank, and the International Monetary Fund, which deal with disputes between these organizations and their staff members.

Neither the ICJ nor any of the other international courts is authorized to exercise criminal jurisdiction over individuals. While international criminal courts are not, strictly speaking, primarily directed at resolving disputes between or among states, a brief survey of them may be relevant. Of course, the most important experiment in this respect was the post–World War II Nuremberg and Tokyo International Military Tribunals, established by the victorious Allied powers to try major Axis war criminals. Since that time, proposals for the establishment of a permanent international criminal court have been made repeatedly, both in the United Nations and by a number of unofficial bodies. Up until very recently, such proposals have had little result. However, the atrocities of the conflict in Bosnia have led to several significant developments in this regard. In May 1993, the UN Security Council established a sixteen-judge ad hoc International Tribunal for the former Yugoslavia, with jurisdiction to prosecute persons responsible for serious violations of international humanitarian laws committed in the region since 1991. As of May 1996, this tribunal, which has its seat in The Hague, has indicted over fifty individuals and has proceeded to hearings in its first case. In November 1994, the UN Security Council established an ad hoc International Tribunal for Rwanda to prosecute violations of humanitarian law occurring in that country. While largely separate, the Rwanda tribunal will share some elements with its counterpart for the former Yugoslavia, in particular its chief prosecutor, some of the prosecutor's staff, and some appellate judges.

Moreover, in 1994, the UN International Law Commission sent to the General Assembly, at its behest, a draft statute for a permanent International Criminal Court, with broad jurisdiction over at least certain categories of international crimes, such as acts of aggression, genocide, apartheid, exceptionally serious war crimes, systematic or massive violation of human rights, torture, hostage taking, hijacking, and trafficking in illicit narcotics. As of late 1995, international discussions and negotiations were continuing under General Assembly auspices over matters of common concern regarding the draft, including the method of establishing the court; whether the court will have concurrent jurisdiction with national courts; the role of the UN Security Council in deciding which cases should be brought before the court; and the court's composition, administration, and financing. Some states pressed for a diplomatic conference in 1997 for the purpose of agreeing on an international treaty to establish such a court. Whether an International Criminal Court should be established and whether it can play a significant role in avoiding, managing, or resolving international conflict remain important, controversial, and as yet unresolved questions.

Choosing between Arbitration and Judicial Settlement

Assuming that states are willing in principle to submit their dispute to binding third-party settlement, or that they are both parties to a treaty that contains a compromissory clause allowing a choice between arbitration and judicial settlement, how do they decide whether to submit their dispute to arbitration or judicial settlement? Of course, a relevant compromissory clause in a prior agreement expressly specifying only one or the other method of settlement, or submission of the dispute to a tribunal, will usually determine the matter. If not, the parties' choice will depend on considerations such as their particular attitudes and preferences, the relative physical convenience or cost of a particular method, the parties' past experience and familiarity with one or the other method, the relative expertise of potential arbitrators or judges to handle the particular issue, and other circumstances.

The principal advantage of arbitration is that it offers the parties maximum control and flexibility over the selection of the arbitrators who will hear the case, the scope of the issue before the tribunal, and the tribunal's procedures. In other words, by negotiating their own *compromis*, the parties can tailor the adjudicative process to meet their particular needs and concerns. This may be particularly useful when the issues to be placed before the tribunal are highly technical, as in disputes involving international trade, aviation, the law of the sea, and so forth; the parties may sometimes prefer that such issues be decided by an arbitrator or arbitrators with special background and expertise. States may sometimes prefer arbitration because one or both parties, or their relevant national constituencies, lack confidence in the competence or impartiality of an international court, such as the ICJ. Although there appear to be few, if any, recent cases in which states have agreed to allow an arbitral tribunal or court to decide a dispute *ex aequo et bono* (i.e., on the basis of what they consider a fair and reasonable solution rather than strictly on the basis of legal rights), some commentators have suggested that it might be easier to ask an arbitral tribunal than a court to do so; indeed, some believe that arbitral tribunals inherently tend to decide disputes this way, seeking compromise solutions. Arbitration can sometimes, if the parties wish, be conducted less expensively, less formally, and with less publicity than international court proceedings. Finally, since the jurisdiction of the ICJ is currently limited solely to disputes between states, any dispute in which one of the parties is not a state (either an international organization, a corporation, or an individual) must be referred to arbitration for binding settlement. (Individuals or corporations may, of course, under traditional international legal principles of state responsibility and diplomatic protection, persuade the state of their nationality to espouse or "take up" their claim against a foreign state and thus bring it within the ICJ's jurisdiction.)

Arbitration also has its drawbacks. The fact that parties must agree on both the constitution and jurisdiction of the arbitral tribunal and on the selection of the arbitrators may involve considerable additional effort and delay and perhaps even create more controversy between the parties. Part-time arbitrators may have less judicial experience and be less insulated from outside influence than permanent judges. Arbitration may also sometimes involve greater expense, since the parties themselves must share an arbitral tribunal's costs, which can be substantial. Finally, some commentators have suggested that, since arbitral tribunals are generally less prestigious than international courts, states may feel less pressure to comply with an arbitral award than a court judgment, and the award may be less enforceable as a consequence.

Conversely, the principal advantage of an international court is that it is already in existence and therefore readily available to states wishing to submit their dispute to impartial settlement. Moreover, the international community pays the court's costs. Finally, the judges on a court are usually full-time professionals who presumably have considerable judicial experience, a special commitment to impartiality, and an interest in the court's development of a consistent jurisprudence. On the other hand, a court has its disadvantages as well. One or both parties may lack confidence in the expertise, general competence, or impartiality of a particular international court or its judges. They may consider the court's location, traditions, or procedures inappropriate for the case. Finally, one or both parties might conceivably be concerned that a court would constitute too prestigious and conspicuous a forum; it may be more politically awkward for a losing party to fail to comply with a court's judgment than with an arbitral tribunal's award.

In practice, the differences between arbitration and judicial settlement may be narrower than portrayed here, and particular adjudicative procedures may incorporate elements of both methods. Thus, the Iran-U.S. Claims Tribunal, while technically an arbitral tribunal, has now functioned for over a decade and has assumed many of the characteristics of a permanent international court, including the development of its own unique and significant jurisprudence. Conversely, pursuant to the ICJ's rules, several recent cases have been submitted by the parties to a special chamber of the court, consisting of a limited number of judges (usually five), who are, in effect, selected with the approval of the parties.

"Legal" versus "Political" Disputes

In discussions of international disputes, a distinction is sometimes drawn between so-called legal or justiciable disputes and so-called political, non-legal, or nonjusticiable disputes. The implication is that certain disputes, such as those involving national honor, "vital" national interests, or the use of force, have inherent characteristics that make them particularly inappropriate for the use of adjudication as a dispute-settlement technique. Iran made such an argument in the *Tehran Hostages* case, as did the United States in the later *Nicaragua* case—both unsuccessfully.

A number of early treaties generally providing for the arbitration of disputes, in fact, made such distinctions. Certainly, nations are less willing to agree to binding third-party settlement of very politically sensitive disputes; in these cases, adjudication may indeed not be the most effective technique. However, since international law is, at least in theory, a complete system, it is difficult to argue that any particular type of dispute is inherently beyond the jurisdiction or capacity of a court or arbitral tribunal to decide, even if the parties so desire and have given the tribunal their consent to do so. Thus, at least in theory, all international disputes seem to be "justiciable" in this sense. Indeed, the World Court has never yet rejected a case on the grounds that it involved nonlegal issues or that it could more appropriately be resolved by a political organization such as the UN Security Council.

Nevertheless, this supposed distinction may be helpful in reminding the world community that some disputes are better settled through negotiations and decisions by the states directly concerned or by political bodies, and that effective adjudication of disputes requires both parties' genuine political acceptance and consent to such settlement. The hard fact remains that absent more effective international governance and enforcement mechanisms, it is very difficult for any international tribunal—or the international community at large—to impose an adverse judgment on an unwilling state.

THE INTERNATIONAL COURT OF JUSTICE

The most prominent and important international judicial institution—and the only one that presently exercises a general global jurisdiction—is the

International Court of Justice or "World Court." Indeed, when most people talk about international adjudication, they usually have the ICJ in mind. Consequently, it may be useful to look more closely at this court and its work.

The ICJ was established in 1945 by the UN Charter as the principal judicial organ of the United Nations and is governed by a special treaty called "the Statute of the Court," which is annexed to the UN Charter and to which all members of the United Nations are also parties. Under the charter, nonmember states may under certain conditions become parties to the court's statute; Switzerland has become a party pursuant to this provision. The court is composed of fifteen judges from different countries, elected for staggered terms of nine years each by the UN General Assembly and the Security Council, with a view to obtaining judges from diverse regions and with different ethnic and cultural backgrounds. (As of February 1997, the court was composed of judges from Algeria, the United States, Japan, France, Sri Lanka, Madagascar, Hungary, China, Germany, Sierra Leone, the Russian Federation, the United Kingdom, Venezuela, the Netherlands, and Brazil. As of July 1995, the court for the first time included a woman judge, Rosalyn Higgins of the United Kingdom.) Since each party to a case is entitled to choose an ad hoc judge if no judge of its nationality is otherwise on the court, there may be more than fifteen judges sitting on a particular case.

The judges serve in their capacity as jurists rather than representatives of their countries and are, of course, supposed to act impartially in deciding cases according to the rules of international law. As already mentioned, under the court's rules the parties to a case may also, by agreement, submit their dispute to a special chamber or panel of judges (usually five) rather than the full court—with the court "consulting" the parties as to the membership of the chamber; several recent cases have been heard by such chambers. In response to the growing importance of international environmental issues, the court has recently established a special Chamber on Environmental Matters; however, as of this writing, no cases have been referred to it.

The Court's Jurisdiction

The court's most important job is to deliver legally binding judgments in so-called contentious cases involving disputes between states. Only states can bring contentious cases before the court; neither the United Nations nor other intergovernmental organizations, nongovernmental organizations, or individuals can do so. Under the court's statute, the ICJ is required to decide such disputes in accordance with international law, applying treaties and other international agreements accepted by the parties, customary international law, and general principles of law recognized by the international community, unless the parties expressly agree that the court should decide the case *ex aequo et bono*. The ICJ does not exercise any criminal jurisdiction and has no authority to try or punish individuals for violations of international criminal law.

The court is also authorized by the UN Charter and its statute to give advisory opinions in response to requests from the UN General Assembly, the Security Council, or other organs of the United Nations or its specialized agencies so authorized by the General Assembly; currently, neither states, other intergovernmental organizations, nongovernmental organizations, nor individuals can request such opinions from the court. The court's delivery of such an advisory opinion is discretionary; it may refuse to give an opinion, for example, if it believes that the request is, in effect, an attempt by one party to obtain the court's legal ruling on a dispute over which it does not have the other party's consent to the court's jurisdiction. However, in almost all cases the court has complied with such requests. The court has, in fact, delivered a number of very important advisory opinions, including the 1949 opinion on *Reparation for Injuries*, the 1962 opinion on *Certain Expenses of the UN*, the 1971 *Namibia* opinion, and the 1975 opinion on the *Western Sahara*. Responding to a request by the UN General Assembly, the court issued an advisory opinion in July 1996 on the *Legality of the Threat or Use of Nuclear Weapons* stating that the threat or use of nuclear weapons would generally be unlawful (i.e., contrary to the rules of international law applicable to armed conflict), except possibly in extreme circumstances of self-defense in which the very survival of a state was at stake.

Like all international arbitral and judicial bodies, the court can hear and decide disputes only with the consent of the states involved. As set out in Article 36 of the court's statute, states can consent to the court's jurisdiction over a contentious case in several ways. First, they may conclude a special agreement providing for the court to decide an existing dispute. This is the most common way for states to submit cases and was the method, for example, by which the United States and Canada submitted the 1984 *Gulf of Maine* maritime boundary case to the court. Second, states may agree in advance, in a treaty's "compromissory clause," that the court shall have jurisdiction to decide any future dispute involving the interpretation or application of that treaty. As of 1985, there were some 250 treaties in force that included such compromissory clauses; the United States is party to at least 70 of these treaties (see International Court of Justice Yearbook

1985, 102–18). This was the basis on which the United States, for example, persuaded the court to assert jurisdiction over Iran in the 1980 U.S.-Iran *Hostages* case, since Iran was a party to several relevant treaties with the United States containing such compromissory clauses. Finally, under the provisions of the "optional clause" of Article 36(2) of the court's statute, any state may, by filing a declaration to this effect in advance, give the court "compulsory jurisdiction" to decide any dispute it may have in the future with any other nation that has also made such a declaration. As of early 1996, 58 of the 186 states that are currently members of the United Nations had accepted the compulsory jurisdiction of the court under the optional clause, although some of them had done so with significant reservations. Usually these reservations concern disputes involving "national security" or those arising before the declaration was filed; more recently, states have reserved the right under the optional clause to exclude "any given category or categories of dispute" upon making an appropriate notification to the UN secretary-general. In such cases, the court will have jurisdiction only to the extent that the parties' declarations are, in fact, reciprocal and coincide. Such parallel declarations were involved in the *Nicaragua* case, brought in 1984 by Nicaragua against the United States.

Where the parties to the dispute have specifically agreed to submit the dispute to the World Court, there is, of course, rarely any question as to the court's jurisdiction to hear the case. However, where one state seeks to bring another before the court on the basis that they both are either parties to a compromissory clause in a particular treaty or that they have both filed declarations under the optional clause, the respondent state may challenge the court's jurisdiction to hear the case by arguing, for example, either that it did not consent in advance to the court's jurisdiction over the particular type of dispute or that the applicant state has not so consented. In this event, the court will typically deal with the case in two stages: first, a "jurisdictional" phase, in which the court determines whether both states have, in fact, consented to its hearing the case, and then, if it determines that it does have jurisdiction, a "merits" phase, in which the court proceeds to decide the substance of the dispute. Sometimes an unwilling respondent state believes so strongly that the court is not entitled to hear a case brought against it that it refuses even to appear before the court. For example, Iceland refused to appear in the 1974 *Fisheries Jurisdiction* case brought against it by the United Kingdom and Federal Republic of Germany; France refused to appear in the 1974 *Nuclear Tests* case brought against it by Australia and New Zealand; Iran refused to appear in the 1980 *Tehran Hostages* case brought against it by the United States; and, as we will see, the United States refused to appear in the "merits" phase of the *Nicaragua* case, after the court held that it had jurisdiction to hear Nicaragua's claims. However, the court may hear a case even if the respondent state fails to appear, provided the court finds that it has jurisdiction. Under the court's statute, the court's own decision on whether it has jurisdiction is final and binding.

The ICJ has various other powers necessary to the performance of its functions. For example, even at the initial stages of a case, if the court believes the circumstances so require, it may "indicate" any provisional measures the parties should undertake in order to preserve their respective rights. Thus, as occurred in both the *Tehran Hostages* and *Nicaragua* cases, the court may request one or both parties to avoid actions that might add to the tensions between them or make it more difficult for the court to resolve the dispute. Again, the court may, under certain circumstances, permit third parties to intervene in contentious cases to which they are not initially a party.

Under the UN Charter and the court's statute, the ICJ's judgment is legally binding upon the parties. However, the court's statute makes clear that its decision has no binding force except between the parties and in regard to that particular case; that is, the ICJ has no doctrine of precedent binding on other parties, as is the case in the U.S. legal system. Article 94 of the UN Charter expressly provides that "Each Member of the United Nations undertakes to comply with the decision of the International Court of Justice in any case to which it is a party," and states have usually complied with this international obligation. Notable exceptions are Albania, which failed to comply with the judgment against it in the 1949 *Corfu Channel* case; Iran in the 1980 *Tehran Hostages* case; and the United States in the 1986 *Nicaragua* case. Each indicated that it would not comply with the court's adverse judgment. However, the United States, pursuant to the 1981 Algiers Accords, subsequently withdrew the *Tehran Hostages* case. And the new Chamorro government in Nicaragua, which replaced the Sandinista regime in 1990, withdrew the *Nicaragua* case in 1991. Consequently, neither Iran nor the United States is now in noncompliance.

Article 94 also stipulates, "If any party to a case fails to perform the obligations incumbent upon it under a judgment rendered by the Court, the other party may have recourse to the Security Council, which may, if it deems necessary, make recommendations or decide upon reasons to be taken to give effect to the judgment." There has thus far been little recourse to this provision, since states usually do comply with the court's judgments. Presumably, Article 94 permits the Security Council to decide on measures that are legally binding on all UN members, possibly including the use of sanctions or even military force, to bring about compliance with a judgment. However, any such decision by the Security Council would, of course, be subject to a permanent member's veto. As yet, the Security Council has never made a decision under Article 94.

The Court's Work

Over their history, the ICJ and its predecessor, the PCIJ, have decided relatively few cases. During the quarter-century of its existence, the PCIJ issued thirty-two judgments and twenty-seven advisory opinions; during the period 1946–1994, the ICJ has handed down fifty-five judgments and twenty advisory opinions (Carter and Trimble 1995, 297 and 300). Together, the ICJ and PCIJ have averaged only about two judgments or opinions per year. While some of these cases were of fairly minor importance, a number of cases have been of major significance both in terms of their usefulness in settling very troublesome disputes between the parties and for their impact on the development of international law. Somewhat remarkably, during the past few years there has been an apparent resurgence of interest among states in the ICJ, and the court has never been busier. As of December 1995, the court had nine contentious cases and two advisory opinions on its docket, had recently decided three other important cases, and had recently played an important role in the parties' own settlement of three more cases.* However, it is still to early to tell whether this signals a fundamental shift in states' attitudes towards judicial settlement and use of the court.

---

*As of December 1995, the following cases were on the court's docket: a case brought by Bosnia against Yugoslavia (Serbia and Montenegro) challenging Serbian actions in Bosnia as violating the Genocide Convention and certain other treaties and international law; two cases brought by Iran against the United States arising from U.S. actions in the Persian Gulf during the Iran-Iraq war—the U.S. shooting down of Iran Airlines Flight 655 by the U.S.S. *Vincennes* and U.S. attacks on Iranian oil platforms in the Gulf; a case brought by Hungary against Slovakia concerning the construction of a dam on the Danube River; cases brought by Libya against the United States and the United Kingdom concerning the two countries' efforts to force Libya to extradite two Libyan nationals alleged to have been responsible for the blowing up of Pan American Flight 103 over Lockerbie, Scotland in 1988; two cases concerning territorial claims and territorial or maritime delimitations between, respectively, Qatar and Bahrain, and Cameroon and Nigeria; and a case brought by Spain against Canada, challenging Canada's arrest of a Spanish fishing vessel just outside of Canada's exclusive economic zone.

Also, as of December 1995, there were, as indicated, two related requests for advisory opinions pending before the court: a request by the World Health Organization for an advisory opinion, asking the court whether "in view of the health and environmental effects, would the use of nuclear weapons by a state in war or other armed conflict be a breach of its obligations under international law including the WHO Constitution?" and a broader subsequent request

The United States and the Court

What is the attitude of the United States toward the court? As indicated, while it has long supported the broad concept of the peaceful settlement of disputes, the United States has often been ambivalent in its policy toward international adjudication and the court. In 1946, President Truman accepted the court's compulsory jurisdiction under the optional clause, albeit with broad reservations. Prior to 1984, the United States had been involved as both applicant and respondent in several cases before the court. The most significant of these was its suit against Iran in the 1980 *Tehran Hostages* case, in which the court ruled in favor of the United States. But the most important U.S. involvement with the court has been Nicaragua's 1984 suit against the United States, charging that U.S. support of the contras and other activities directed against the Sandinista regime violated international law.

Since the *Nicaragua* case has had considerable effect on recent U.S. policy regarding the court, it is worth briefly describing. Despite strong U.S. arguments to the contrary, the court decided in 1984 that it had jurisdiction over Nicaragua's claim against the United States and that the matter was admissible and appropriate for judicial consideration. The United States vigorously protested the court's jurisdictional decision and announced that it would not participate further in the case. Moreover, in view of its strong disagreement with the court's holding, the United States announced in October 1985 that it was terminating its acceptance of the court's

---

by the UN General Assembly asking the court "urgently to render its advisory opinion on the following question: 'Is the threat or use of nuclear weapons in any circumstance permitted under international law?'" The court at this time had also recently issued judgments involving important territorial and maritime disputes between Libya and Chad; El Salvador, Honduras, and Nicaragua; and Denmark and Norway; and had ruled that it could not adjudicate upon a dispute brought by Portugal against Australia concerning an Australia-Indonesia treaty concerning exploitation of the oil resources of the so-called Timor Gap's continental shelf. Moreover, at this time, the parties themselves, following preliminary rulings by the court, had recently settled a case brought by Finland against Denmark involving Denmark's construction of a bridge over the Great Belt in the Baltic Sea; a case brought by Nauru against Australia involving the alleged responsibility of Australia, the United Kingdom, and New Zealand for the exploitation of phosphates in Nauru during Australia's administration of that territory; and a case concerning the maritime delimitation between Guinea-Bissau and Senegal.

As this book goes to publication, significant subsequent developments have included the February 1996 settlement by the United States and Iran and discontinuance of the case involving the shooting down of Iran Airlines Flight 655; the May 1996 commencement by Botswana of a case against Namibia involving the delimitation of their boundary around Kasikiki/Sedudu Island; the July 1996 issuance by the court of its advisory opinion to the UN General Assembly on the threat or use of nuclear weapons; and the election in February 1997 of an American, Judge Stephen M. Schwebel, as president of the court.

compulsory jurisdiction under the optional clause, to take effect one year from that date. Despite U.S. nonappearance in the final phase of the *Nicaragua* case, the court proceeded to a hearing on the case's merits, as its statute permitted. In June 1986, the court issued its judgment, finding that U.S. support of the contras, as well as certain other actions, were in violation of international law; however, it withheld for further consideration a determination of damages. The Reagan administration again protested the court's *Nicaragua* decision, announced that the United States would not recognize the judgment, and vetoed a Security Council resolution calling upon the United States to do so. Thereafter, the case remained inactive until 1991, when Nicaragua's Chamorro government withdrew the case.

Since that time, the United States has been involved with the court on several other occasions. During 1987–89, the United States brought the so-called *ELSI* case against Italy—with the parties agreeing that the case should be heard by a special chamber of the court—and lost. It has also recently appeared before the court as respondent in two cases brought by Iran arising from U.S. actions in the Persian Gulf during the Iran-Iraq war, and in a case brought by Libya involving U.S. efforts to obtain extradition of two Libyan intelligence agents alleged to have participated in the bombing of Pan American Flight 103 over Lockerbie, Scotland. The United States has also participated in proceedings relating to several recent requests for advisory opinions by the court.

The Clinton administration has not yet clearly stated its policy regarding U.S. use of the court, or, more particularly, regarding reacceptance of the court's compulsory jurisdiction, as some groups and commentators have urged.

SOME PROS AND CONS OF ADJUDICATION

When is adjudication likely to be the most appropriate or sensible way of trying to resolve an international dispute, and when is it unlikely to be helpful? From the standpoint of the international community and the interests of both the states involved in a dispute, adjudication obviously offers both potential advantages and disadvantages compared with other methods of dispute settlement. Since national leaders and other state officials usually weigh these pros and cons carefully in deciding whether to use adjudication or other techniques to deal with a particular dispute, they are worth spelling out in some detail.

Some Advantages of Adjudication

Some possible advantages of adjudication include the following:

- *Adjudication is dispositive.* At least ideally, an arbitral or judicial decision puts an end to the dispute. Sometimes, it is important to the parties that a dispute simply be settled, regardless of how it is done. When negotiations are for some reason unsuccessful, adjudication provides a way for the parties to put the matter behind them and move on to other issues.
- *Adjudication is impartial and principled.* The basic idea of third-party adjudication is that an impartial arbitrator or judge will decide the dispute in a fair and just way, on the basis of neutral legal or equitable rules or principles—"the rule of law"—rather than the parties' respective power or the judges' bias or arbitrary whim. Decisions reached by impartial processes assert a strong claim to acceptability and legitimacy, both by the parties themselves and by the international community at large.
- *Adjudication is authoritative.* To the extent the parties have genuinely consented to third-party adjudication of a dispute, the tribunal is respected and its procedures are perceived as fair, the decision is likely to be viewed by the international community as authoritative and entitled to respect, buttressing expectations of and pressures for compliance with the judgment.
- *Adjudication is impersonal.* Since the decision is rendered by a neutral third party, the governments of the parties themselves cannot be held directly responsible for the outcome. Consequently, third-party settlement is a politically useful way foreign offices can dispose of certain politically sensitive issues without taking responsibility for losses or concessions. They can "pass the buck" for not "winning" a dispute submitted to a third-party tribunal, saying, in effect, "Don't blame us, blame the judge!"
- *Adjudication is serious.* Because adjudication is generally understood to be a complex, expensive, and somewhat intimidating process involving significant costs and risks for those involved, a state's proposal to submit a dispute to adjudication shows the other party and the international community that it takes the matter seriously and that it is prepared to go to considerable lengths to pursue its claim. Consequently, simply threatening or bringing an action in an international court may in itself buttress a party's credibility and bargaining strength in further negotiations. Such an act may make the other party pay more serious attention to the claim and increase pressure by other nations or by the international community at large on the other party to settle the dispute.
- *Adjudication is orderly.* The well-established structure of the adjudicative process provides a framework for the orderly presentation and development of the opposing parties' respective claims concerning the dispute.

Consequently, adjudication may lead to both a better understanding by the parties themselves of the respective merits of each other's positions and possibly their own negotiation of a settlement.

- *Adjudication may reduce tensions and buy time.* Agreeing to submit a dispute to adjudication demonstrates the parties' commitment to a peaceful and fair settlement and may "depoliticize" the dispute or serve as a politically acceptable way of buying time for the parties to make further attempts to seek a negotiated solution.

- *Adjudication can be precedential and help develop international law.* An authoritative arbitral or judicial decision not only settles the particular dispute before the tribunal, but may also provide guidance to both the parties and other states as to how they should conduct themselves in the future—that is, it serves as a guide to the relevant rules and expectations of the international community concerning particular kinds of international behavior.

- *Adjudication is system-reinforcing.* Impartial adjudication is widely viewed as symbolizing the international rule of law, and a nation's willingness to submit a dispute to judicial settlement is generally taken as a test of its respect for and commitment to international law. To the extent that many or most states demonstrate a commitment to international adjudication, international law and the international legal system are strengthened.

Some Risks of Adjudication

Adjudication also poses a number of risks and potential disadvantages, which parties considering arbitration or judicial settlement will also need to consider carefully. They include the following:

- *Adjudication involves the risk of losing.* Adjudication necessarily involves the possibility of an adverse decision. In contrast with other "nonlegal" or "political" methods of dispute settlement, submission to binding third-party settlement means that parties give up their ultimate control over outcomes, which foreign-policy officials and their political masters are loath to relinquish. Many nations are simply unwilling to take the chance that they may lose, particularly when the dispute involves what they consider important or "vital" national interests.

- *Adjudication may not be impartial.* The premise of adjudication is that the arbitrator or judge will be impartial. However, the process of selecting international judges may be influenced by political factors, and international tribunals typically include judges of one or both of the parties' nationalities; thus, some judges may be predisposed toward one party's position. International arbitration is less likely to raise this problem, since the parties have more control over selection of the tribunal's members and, in particular, the party-appointed arbitrators must usually agree on selection of the neutral arbitrator.

- *Adjudication is unpredictable.* The outcome of adjudication may be difficult to predict, either because there are no relevant rules of international law or because, as is often the case, existing rules are ambiguous or uncertain. Moreover, apart from the problem of deliberate bias by the tribunal, letting a third party decide a matter always involves an element of chance. No matter how careful the parties are in selecting an arbitrator or judge, and regardless of the judge's reputation, any judge may simply fail to understand the issue, have unconscious biases, try to avoid responsibility or criticism by compromising or "giving something to each side," or simply reach a wrong decision through incompetence or faulty reasoning.

- *Adjudicative settlement is imposed.* In contrast to a settlement reached by the parties themselves through negotiated agreements, a judicial tribunal imposes its own settlement on the parties. Even when a state has initially consented to adjudication, traditional notions of sovereignty and national pride may make it resist the idea that an international arbitrator or court can appropriately rule on its behavior or tell it how to behave or what to do.

- *Adjudicative settlement may be illusory or superficial.* A tribunal must focus narrowly on the immediate "legal" issue before it, which may have little to do with the underlying causes of the dispute or the true source of contention between the parties. In cases where the legal issue is only the symptom or symbol of a far more complex problem, the tribunal's judgment may not really settle, and may even exacerbate, the dispute.

- *Adjudication is adversarial and potentially escalatory.* Despite efforts by the international community to encourage judicial settlement, being "taken to court" may be regarded as a hostile and unfriendly act—something that nations wanting to continue doing business together are generally loath to do. When one party to a dispute does not want impartial adjudication, efforts by the other party to force judicial settlement upon it may increase ill will, discourage further negotiation, and sidetrack alternative attempts to reach solutions.

- *Adjudication may freeze the dispute and the parties' options.* Once a dispute is brought to court, the dispute will move, at least to some extent, outside the control of the parties. The case may acquire its own dynamic, and "winning" the case may become the only goal. In some cases, the tribunal may permit the matter to drag on, locking the parties into long-term contention and further exacerbating tensions. In other cases, the tribunal may have little choice but to move swiftly and remorselessly toward a decision, even if it is in the parties' mutual interest to let the dispute sit a while in the hopes that, with time and changing circumstances and perceptions, it will fade away. Moreover, the fact that adjudication is usually public and often newsworthy may serve to freeze the parties' positions, give the dispute a public prominence and significance neither desires, and obstruct possibilities for a compromise settlement.

- *Adjudication is inflexible.* In theory, adjudication is a zero-sum game—one party wins, the other party loses. But many problems are intrinsically resistant to such all-or-nothing solutions, or may be better resolved by compromise than by a "win-lose" decision. Where two states are necessarily engaged in continuous interaction, a decision that legally disposes of a particular dispute but leaves one party feeling it has been treated unfairly may ultimately do more harm than good. In this case, feelings of resentment and attempts to compensate in other areas for what is perceived as an unjust decision may hamper future relationships between the parties or even alienate the losing party from the legal or political system. If such a result is likely, techniques that permit reaching mutually acceptable and politically viable compromise settlements may be more useful and appropriate.

- *Adjudication is conservative.* Since adjudication is, at least in theory, only applied law, it looks for principles of what the law *is* rather than what the law *ought to be*. Thus, when one party is really demanding—perhaps with good reason—a change in the law, judicial tribunals may have difficulty providing an adequate or acceptable resolution of the dispute. While states may, in theory, instruct a tribunal to decide cases according to its sense of what is most reasonable and fair—*ex aequo et bono*—states have rarely chosen to do so. However, consistent with relevent customary international law, which indicates that states should settle their maritime delimitation disputes on equitable principles, the ICJ has generally tried to reach "an equitable result" in maritime boundary cases, and its decisions have been accepted by the parties.

- *Adjudication may be inconvenient and costly.* Arbitral or judicial proceedings may be complex, time-consuming, and expensive and may divert the energies of high-level officials from other important duties. For poorer nations, the legal costs of hiring sophisticated counsel (usually from Western countries) may be significant; although, as discussed below, the UN secretary-general has recently established a special fund to help poorer nations in this respect. Moreover, delays may be substantial; it is not uncommon for the decision of a case to take a number of years.

- *Adjudication may be too precedential.* The precedential nature of adjudication can pose risks as well as advantages. A party may be relatively indifferent to the outcome of a particular minor dispute, but not indifferent to the potentially precedential effect of a decision on similar or analogous disputes, either with the same or other parties, that may be of much greater and more lasting significance.

- *Adjudication may be used for propaganda or harassment purposes.* A nation may be concerned that adjudication may encourage other, unfriendly nations to abuse any available judicial processes by bringing frivolous suits in order to embarrass or harass it. However, it is not always easy to make a clear distinction between a "proper" and an "improper" use of international adjudication. Certainly, nations often seem to have a largely political or propaganda purpose in mind when resorting to the ICJ, in the sense that they usually hope, by legitimating their claim, to bring the force of the international community's opinion to bear on the other party's actions.

- *Adjudication may be ineffective.* Absent more effective international procedures for the enforcement of international arbitral or judicial decisions, a nation may be uncertain whether a favorable judgment will be carried out, particularly if one party is an unwilling litigant before the tribunal and has indicated in advance that it will not recognize either the tribunal's jurisdiction or its judgment.

THE CASE FOR INTERNATIONAL ADJUDICATION

This discussion suggests that international adjudication is not likely to play a major part in the settlement of international disputes for some time to come. Given the alternatives, the parties to a dispute often prefer to use negotiation and other nonadjudicative methods of settlement that entail fewer risks and allow them a greater degree of control. However, even if relatively few international disputes are actually resolved through international adjudication, this does not mean that it does not have a significant role or that we can afford to ignore it. There are a number of reasons why international adjudication deserves the international community's encouragement and support.

First, while adjudication may not be the best way of resolving every dispute, there are a number of situations in which arbitration or judicial settlement may be the best way of handling the problem and can perform a very useful dispute-settlement function. In practice, most disputes do not involve issues of significant or "vital" national concerns. In these cases, while each party may prefer to win the dispute, the stakes involved are limited and each can afford to lose; adjudication is a good way for the parties to achieve their most important objective—disposing of the dispute. Among the types of disputes particularly conducive to adjudication are the following:

- disputes that do not involve significant national interests and in which the governments concerned, for political or other reasons, are unable to make concessions or compromises in negotiations (e.g., substantively unimportant but emotionally volatile minor border disputes or issues of sovereignty over small or insignificant areas of territory or maritime boundaries);
- disputes involving difficult and complex factual or technical questions in which the parties may be prepared for a compromise solution but cannot themselves develop a basis for arriving at a viable compromise (e.g., again, certain complex border or related issues, such as delimitation of maritime areas, continental shelves, fisheries, or the deep seabed); and
- certain particularly awkward or dangerous disputes, in which the resort to judicial settlement may be a politically acceptable way of buying time and containing a volatile situation while solutions continue to be worked out.

As these categories suggest, a significant number of arbitrations and World Court judgments have, in fact, concerned territorial or maritime delimitation disputes.

Second, the very availability of international tribunals may help avoid disputes or induce their settlement. Even if states choose only infrequently to invoke the compromissory clauses in relevant agreements, or the ICJ's jurisdiction under the optional clause, this does not mean such commitments are useless. On the contrary, since each party to a dispute covered by such provisions knows that the other can resort to the World Court, a state that wishes to avoid adjudication will have more incentive to act reasonably and to reach a negotiated settlement. That is, where the parties have conferred potential jurisdiction on an international tribunal, their decisions and bargaining, like those of parties to domestic disputes, are more likely to occur "in the shadow of the law." As one prominent international legal scholar notes, "the value of arrangements for dispute settlement is not to be judged solely by the cases. For a provision for compulsory arbitration by its very existence can discourage unreasonable behavior and so may be useful even if it is never invoked" (Merrills 1991, 106).

Finally, it is important to note that, for many people throughout the world, international adjudication symbolizes civilized and ordered behavior and the rule of law in international affairs. Whatever the truth may be as to how the international legal system actually works, the public's perceptions of the relevance and effectiveness of international law are at least partly based on whether it sees impartial international tribunals, and particularly the International Court of Justice, as playing a significant role in international dispute settlement. If many states (particularly powerful ones) are willing to submit their disputes to impartial settlement by international arbitral tribunals and courts, the public will deem international law relevant and worthy of respect. If, on the other hand, powerful states show indifference or contempt for international adjudication and the World Court, the public is likely to conclude that international law has little significance or relevance and to withhold its support from efforts to promote international law and its institutions. Indeed, these public attitudes may over time reflect back on official and bureaucratic attitudes toward respect for international law; if the public believes international law "counts," public officials will be under political pressure to act accordingly. Consequently, if a state believes that its national interest will be furthered by wider global respect for international law, it will also have an interest in doing what it can to strengthen and support the role of international adjudication.

In sum, since adjudication can be a particularly useful device in the international community's toolbox of dispute-settlement techniques, it is important that it be readily available and employed to the fullest whenever its use is warranted. Even if adjudication is not a panacea for problems of world order, it makes sense to do all that we can to strengthen and encourage the greater use of judicial institutions and to improve their ability to respond in flexible ways to nations' dispute-settlement needs.

PROPOSALS TO ENCOURAGE ADJUDICATION

What kinds of steps might we take to facilitate and encourage the use of adjudicative techniques to resolve international disputes? A wide variety of measures have been proposed and are worth considering. They include the following:

- Establish new courts or other judicial mechanisms with jurisdiction over disputes arising in specialized contexts or particular regions, for example: (1) a new global International Human Rights Court or a new International Environmental Tribunal, operating within the UN framework and composed of judges with special expertise in those areas; and (2) a new regional African International Court or International Court for Latin America, dealing with disputes arising between states on these continents, perhaps with the ICJ serving an appellate function.

- Expand the number and scope of compromissory clauses—that is, provisions for the compulsory judicial settlement of disputes—in treaties. This could be accomplished by amending existing international agreements to add compromissory clauses where they presently lack such provisions and by ensuring that most new treaties include such provisions. Alternatively, states could consider developing a new "umbrella" Treaty on the Peaceful Settlement of Disputes, designed expressly to commit states to the compulsory judicial settlement of their disputes, either generally or perhaps where they are also parties to treaties lacking such compromissory clauses.

- Expand the advisory jurisdiction of the ICJ by, for example: (1) granting authority to seek advisory opinions from the court to additional UN-related bodies, such as the Human Rights Committee functioning under the International Covenant on Civil and Political Rights or the Committee on Racial Discrimination functioning under the UN Convention on the Elimination of Racial Discrimination; (2) amending the court's statute to permit additional applicants, such as the UN secretary-general, regional organizations, or even member states or national courts, to seek advisory opinions directly on questions of international law; and (3) establishing some procedure whereby states or national courts can indirectly obtain advisory opinions through an intermediary special committee of the UN General Assembly.

- Amend the court's statute to grant it jurisdiction over contentious cases brought by the UN secretary-general; other important international officials, such as the new UN high commissioner for human rights; other public international organizations, such as the European Union or the Organization of American States; and perhaps major nongovernmental organizations, or possibly even individuals. A general suggestion along these lines would be to broaden access and participation by concerned international and nongovernmental organizations and even individuals, through provisions for filing amicus curiae ("friend of the court") briefs in cases brought before the court.

- Make existing courts and arbitral arrangements more "user-friendly," particularly to newer, smaller, or poorer states, by simplifying and expediting procedures, broadening the parties' range of choice over arbitrators and judges, expanding available remedies, and reducing costs. Initiatives along these lines include the ICJ's 1978 revision of its rules expanding the availability and use of its chamber procedure, and the UN secretary-general's 1989 action establishing a trust fund to assist states seeking settlement of their disputes through the ICJ, designed to provide financial assistance to poorer states for expenses incurred in bringing cases before the court by special agreement. Other proposals of this type include: providing for more prompt and effective interim measures of relief; further developing standardized rules of arbitral procedure and authoritative and usable lists of experienced and competent arbitrators; and providing "legal aid" to newer and poorer states under the auspices of the International Law Association, national societies of international law, or the UN Institute for Training and Research.

- Encourage more states, including the United States, to accept the compulsory jurisdiction of the World Court under the optional clause of Article 36(2) of the court's statute—and to do so without crippling reservations. The American Society of International Law, the American Bar Association, and other concerned groups have made or are currently studying proposals for such U.S. reacceptance. Some proposals along this line suggest arrangements that would permit states to accept the court's compulsory jurisdiction on a step-by-step basis, starting with less risky obligations and gradually extending their commitment only as their confidence in the court develops.

CONCLUSION

In concluding this chapter, let me suggest why support of international adjudication seems very much in the U.S. national interest. From the foundation of the Republic, the principle of respect for law has been a firm tenet of U.S. foreign policy. The American public has generally believed that its country's and its children's future will be brighter and more secure in a world governed by law than in one where disputes are resolved solely through power and coercion. Moreover, considering the importance of the

United States in international affairs, there seems little likelihood of achieving an effective international legal order without firm U.S. commitment and participation.

One of the most vital ways the United States can demonstrate a commitment to international law is by supporting impartial dispute settlement and the role and work of the World Court. Such a policy would recognize not only the potential practical usefulness of international adjudication in advancing immediate U.S. foreign policy interests—as in its use of the ICJ in the Iran hostage crisis—but also the broader contribution that arbitration and judicial settlement can make in resolving international disputes, developing international law, and symbolizing the ideal of international order.

In his September 11, 1990 address to a joint session of Congress during the Persian Gulf crisis, President Bush noted that,

> A hundred generations have searched for this elusive path to peace, while a thousand wars raged across the span of human endeavor. Today that new world is struggling to be born. A world quite different from the one we have known. A world where the rule of law supplants the rule of the jungle. A world in which nations recognize the shared responsibility for freedom and justice. A world where the strong respect the rights of the weak.
>
> . . . .
>
> America and the world must support the rule of law. And we will.

A policy of strong U.S. support for international adjudication and the World Court could very well be an important step toward implementing this vision.

LIST OF CASES CITED

Case concerning Elettronica Sicula (ELSI)
United States v. Italy, 1989 ICJ 15.

Certain Expenses of the UN
(Advisory opinion) 1962 ICJ 151.

Fisheries Jurisdiction
United Kingdom v. Iceland; Federal Republic of Germany v. Iceland, 1974 ICJ 3, 175.

Gulf of Maine
Canada v. United States, 1984 ICJ 246.

Legality of the Threat or Use of Nuclear Weapons
(Advisory opinion) 35 ILM 809 (July 1996)

Namibia
(Advisory opinion) 1971 ICJ 16.

Nicaragua
Case concerning Military and Paramilitary Activities in and against Nicaragua
(Nicaragua v. United States), 1984 ICJ 392 (judgment of November 26,
1984, on jurisdiction and admissibility), 23 ILM 468 (1984); 1986 ICJ 14
(judgment of June 27, 1986, on merits), 25 ILM 1623 (1986).

Nuclear Tests
Australia v. France; New Zealand v. France. 1974 ICJ 253, 457.

Reparation for Injuries
(Advisory opinion) 1949 ICJ 174.

United States Diplomatic and Consular Staff in Tehran (Tehran Hostages)
United States v. Iran. 1980 ICJ 3.

Western Sahara
(Advisory opinion) 1975 ICJ 12.

REFERENCES

Carter, Barry. E., and Phillip R. Trimble. 1995. *International Law*. 2d ed. Boston:
Little, Brown.

International Court of Justice Yearbook, no. 39. 1985. The Hague: International
Court of Justice.

Merrills, John G. 1991. *International Dispute Settlement*. 2d ed. Cambridge, Mass.:
Grotius Publications.

Stuyt, Alexander M., ed. 1990. *Survey of International Arbitrations, 1794-1989*.
3d updated ed. Dordrecht, Netherlands: Martin Nijhoff.

ADDITIONAL READINGS

This chapter draws on certain of the author's other writings on this subject, in
particular: *Managing the Risks of International Agreement* (Madison: University of
Wisconsin Press, 1981); "An Overview of International Dispute Settlement," *Emory
Journal of International Dispute Resolution* 1 (1986): 1–32; "International Dispute
Settlement and the Role of International Adjudication," *Emory Journal of International Dispute Resolution* 2 (1987): 131–73, and in *The International Court of Justice
at a Crossroads*, ed. Lori F. Damrosch (Dobbs Ferry, N.Y.: Transnational Publishers,
1987), 155–80; "International Third Party Dispute Settlement," *Denver Journal of
International Law and Policy* 17 (1989): 471–503, and in *Approaches to Peace: An
Intellectual Map*, ed. W. Scott Thompson and Kenneth M. Jensen (Washington,

D.C.: United States Institute of Peace Press, 1991), 191–226; "The United States and the World Court in the Post–'Cold War' Era," *Catholic University Law Review* 40 (1991): 261–62; and "International Law in the 'New World Order': Some Preliminary Reflections," *Florida State University Journal of Transnational Law and Policy* 1 (1992): 1–21.

I

Some useful writings on the general topic of international adjudication are:

American Law Institute, Restatement of the Law Third, *The Foreign Relations Law of the United States* § 903 (International Court of Justice) and § 904 (Interstate Arbitration).

Bernhardt, Rudolf, ed. 1981. *Encyclopedia of Public International Law*. Vol. 1, *Settlement of Disputes*. Amsterdam: North Holland Publishing. Co. See especially the entries on "Arbitration," "The International Court of Justice," "International Courts and Tribunals," and "Judicial Settlement of International Disputes."

Janis, Mark W., ed. 1992. *International Courts for the Twenty-First Century*. Dordrecht, Netherlands: Martin Nijhoff.

Lauterpacht, Elihu. 1991. *Aspects of the Administration of International Justice*. Cambridge, Mass.: Grotius Publications.

Merrills, John G. 1991. *International Dispute Settlement*. 2d ed. Cambridge, Mass.: Grotius Publications. See especially chapters 5, 6, 7, and 11.

Prott, Lyndell V. 1979. *The Latent Power of Culture and the International Judge*. Abingdon, England: Professional Books.

Schachter, Oscar. 1960. "The Enforcement of International Judicial and Arbitral Decisions." *American Journal of International Law* 54.

United Nations. 1992. *Handbook on the Peaceful Settlement of Disputes Between States*. New York: United Nations. See especially pages 55–80 and 146–54.

II

Some useful writings on arbitration are:

Carlston, Kenneth S. 1946. *The Process of International Arbitration*. New York: Columbia University Press.

Lillich, Richard B., and Charles N. Brower, eds. 1993. *International Arbitration in the 21st Century: Towards "Judicialization" and Uniformity*. Irvington, N.Y.: Transnational Publishers.

Ralston, Jackson H. 1929. *International Arbitration from Athens to Locarno*. Stanford: Stanford University Press.

Schwebel, Stephen. 1987. *International Arbitration: Three Salient Problems*. Cambridge, Mass.: Grotius Publishers.

Simpson, John L., and Hazel Fox. 1959. *International Arbitration: Law and Practice*. London: Stevens.

Sohn, Louis B. 1963. "The Role of International Arbitration Today." *Hague Recueil des Cours* 108:1–113.

————. 1982–83. "The Role of Arbitration in Recent International Multilateral Treaties." *Virginia Journal of International Law* 23:171–86.

Stuyt, Alexander. M., ed. 1990. *Survey of International Arbitrations, 1794–1989.* 3d updated ed.

Waldock, C. M. H., ed. 1972. *International Disputes: The Legal Aspects.* London: Stevens. See chapter 2.

Wetter, J. Gillis. 1979. *The International Arbitral Process: Public and Private.* 5 vols. Dobbs Ferry, N.Y.: Oceana Publications

III

Some useful writings on the International Court of Justice are:

Damrosch, Lori F., ed. 1987. *The International Court of Justice at a Crossroads.* New York: Transnational Publishers.

Falk, Richard. 1986. *Reviving the World Court.* Charlottesville, Va.: University Press of Virginia.

Franck, Thomas M. 1986. *Judging the World Court.* New York: Priority Press Publications.

Gross, Leo., ed. 1976. *The Future of the International Court of Justice.* Dobbs Ferry, N.Y.: Oceana Publications.

Highet, K. 1991. "The Peace Palace Heats Up: The World Court in Business Again?" *American Journal of International Law* 85:646–54.

Jennings, Robert. 1995. "The International Court of Justice After Fifty Years." *American Journal of International Law* 89:493–505.

Merrills, John. 1993. "The Optional Clause Revisited." *British Yearbook of International Law* 64:197–244.

Rosenne, Shabta. 1985. *The Law and Practice of the International Court.* 2d rev. ed. Dordrecht, Netherlands: Martin Nijhoff.

————. 1995. *The World Court: What It Is and How It Works.* 5th rev. ed. Dordrecht: Netherlands: Martin Nijhoff .

IV

Some useful writings on certain of the more specialized international courts and arbitral procedures discussed in this Chapter are:

(1) On the Court of Justice of the European Union:

Schermers, Henry, and Dennis F. Waelbroeck. 1992. *Judicial Protection in the European Communities.* 5th ed. Boston: Klumer Law and Taxation Publishers.

Schermers, Henry. 1988. "The European Court of First Instance." *Common Market Law Review* 25:541–58.

Waelbroeck, Dennis F. 1990. "Role of the Court of Justice in the Implementation of the Single European Act." *Michigan Journal of International Law* 11:671–90.

(2) On the European Court of Human Rights:

Mahoney, Paul, and S. Prebensen. 1993. "The European Court of Human Rights." In *The European System for the Protection of Human Rights*, ed. Ronald St. J. Macdonald, Franz Matscher, and Harold Petzold. Dordrecht, Netherlands: Martin Nijhoff.

Merrills, John G. 1993. *The Development of International Law by the European Court of Human Rights*. 2d ed. Manchester, U.K.: Manchester University Press.

Walsh, Brian. 1987. "The European Court of Human Rights." *Connecticut Journal of International Law* 2:271–84.

(3) On the Inter-American Court of Human Rights:

Buergenthal, Thomas. 1982. "The Inter-American Court of Human Rights." *American Journal of International Law* 76:231–45.

Davidson, Scott. 1992. *The Inter-American Court of Human Rights*. Brookfield, Vt.: Gower Publishing Co.

(4) On Arbitration under the International Convention for the Settlement of Investment Disputes:

Broches, Aron. 1966. "The Convention of the Settlement of Investment Disputes: Some Observations on Jurisdiction." *Columbia Journal of Transnational Law* 5:263–80.

Delaume, Georges. 1987. "ICSID Arbitration." In *Contemporary Problems in International Arbitration*, ed. Julian Lew. Dordrecht: Netherlands: Martin Nijhoff.

(5) On arbitration under the U.S.-Canada Free Trade Agreement and North American Free Trade Agreement (NAFTA):

Horlick, Gary N., and F. A. DeBusk. 1993. "Dispute Resolution Under NAFTA." *Journal of World Trade* 27:21–41.

Huntington, D. S. 1993. "Settling Disputes Under the North American Free Trade Agreement." *Harvard International Law Journal* 34:407–43.

Lowenfeld, Andreas F. 1991. "Binational Dispute Settlement Under Chapter 19 of the Canada–United States Free Trade Agreement: An Interim Appraisal." *New York University Journal of International Law and Policy* 24:269–339.

Rosa, A. K. 1993. "Old Wine, New Skins: NAFTA and the Evolution of International Trade Dispute Resolution." *Michigan Journal of International Law* 15:255–305.

(6) On arbitration under the General Agreement on Tariffs and Trade (GATT) and the World Trade Organization (WTO):

Davey, William J. 1987. "Dispute Settlement in GATT." *Fordham International Law Journal* 11:51–109.

Hudec, Robert E. 1993. *Enforcing International Trade Law: The Evolution of the Modern GATT Legal System*. Salem, N.H.: Butterworth Legal Publishers.

————. Forthcoming. "Strengthening of Procedures for Settling Disputes." In *Remaking the World Trading System: The Uruguay Round Agreements From an Asian-Pacific Perspective*, ed. Hugh Corbet. Ann Arbor: University of Michigan Press.

Jackson, John H. 1989. *The World Trading System: Law and Policy of International Economic Relations*. Cambridge, Mass.: MIT Press.

(7) On the Iran-U.S. Claims Tribunal:

Avanessian, Aida B. 1993. *Iran-United States Claims Tribunal in Action*. Dordrecht, Netherlands: Martin Nijhoff.

Caron, David D. 1990. "The Nature of the Iran-United States Claims Tribunal and the Evolving Structure of International Dispute Resolution." *American Journal of International Law* 84:104–56.

Mapp, Wayne. 1993. *The Iran-United States Claims Tribunal: The First Ten Years, 1981–1991*. Manchester, U.K.: Manchester University Press.

(8) On the United Nations Compensation Commission:

Lillich, Richard B., ed. 1995. *The United Nations Compensation Commission*. Thirteenth Sokol Colloquium. Irvington, N.Y.: Transnational Publishers.

(9) On international commercial arbitration:

Craig, W. Lawrence, William W. Park, and Jan Paulsson. 1990. *International Chamber of Commerce Arbitration*. 2d ed. Dobbs Ferry, N.Y.: Oceana Publications.

Redfern, Alan, and Martin Hunter. 1986. *Law and Practice of International Commercial Arbitration*. London: Sweet and Maxwell.

V

Some organizations, as well as governmental and intergovernmental agencies, with particular expertise and interests concerning international adjudication, which might be able to supply relevant information, include:

The American Society of International Law
2223 Massachusetts Avenue, N.W.
Washington, D.C. 20008-2864

A.S.I.L. publishes two respected periodicals, the quarterly *American Journal of International Law* and *International Legal Materials* (six issues per year), both of which frequently include information on current developments concerning international adjudication.

The United Nations Association of the U.S.A.
485 Fifth Avenue
New York, NY 10017

Office of Legal Affairs
United Nations Secretariat
United Nations, New York 10017

Section of International Law and Practice
American Bar Association
1800 M Street, N.W. (Suite 450-South)
Washington, D.C. 20036-5886

Office of the Legal Adviser
U.S. Department of State
Washington, D.C. 20520

6

Social-Psychological Dimensions of International Conflict

Herbert C. Kelman

Social-psychological concepts and findings have by now entered the mainstream of theory and research in international relations. Explorations of the social-psychological dimensions of international politics go back at least to the early 1930s (see Kelman 1965 for a review of the earlier history and a series of contributed chapters on various topics in the field; see also Kelman and Bloom 1973, Kelman 1991, and Tetlock forthcoming, for reviews of later developments). Current work on foreign policy decision making and the cognitive, group, and organizational factors that help to shape it (see Holsti 1989; Fischhoff 1991; and Farnham 1992), on negotiation and bargaining (see Druckman and Hopmann 1989; and Rubin, Pruitt, and Kim 1994), on enemy images (see Holt and Silverstein 1989), on public opinion in the foreign-policy process (see Russett 1989), and on deterrence and other forms of influence in international politics (see Stein 1991) draws extensively on social-psychological research and theory.

Paralleling these theoretical and empirical developments, a new form of practice of international conflict resolution, anchored in social-psychological principles, has evolved over the past thirty years. The approach derives from the pioneering work of John Burton (1969, 1979, 1984). My colleagues and I have used the term *interactive problem solving* to describe the approach (Kelman 1986, 1992a, 1996; Rouhana and Kelman 1994). Ronald Fisher and other scholars in the field have referred to it as *third-party consultation* (for example, Fisher 1983, 1989) and more recently as *interactive conflict resolution*. Under the latter title, Fisher reviews the history, central features, and procedures of this approach in the next chapter in this volume.

The present chapter offers a social-psychological perspective on the analysis and resolution of international conflict—a perspective based in social-psychological theory and research, which, in turn, informs the practice of interactive problem solving described in the next chapter. A social-psychological analysis provides a special lens for viewing international relations in general and international conflict in particular. It is a different lens than that provided by the realist or the neorealist schools of international relations or other, more traditional approaches that focus on structural or strategic factors. It may, therefore, help to explain certain phenomena for which other approaches cannot adequately account, or introduce dimensions that these approaches have not considered. But a social-psychological approach is primarily designed to complement other approaches rather than substitute for them. It focuses on only some of the dimensions of what is clearly a larger, multidimensional landscape.

Thus, I do not advocate a social-psychological theory of international relations or international conflict as a comprehensive alternative theory for the field. What is needed is a *general* theory of international relations, but one in which analysis of the social-psychological dimensions is not merely an appendage, but an integral part. Several assumptions underlie this view.

First, psychological factors are pervasive in international conflict and international relations generally. Psychological processes at the individual and collective levels constitute and mediate much of the behavior of nations. Any general theory of international relations that fails to take cognizance of them is therefore incomplete. Indeed, political analysts and actors invariably make assumptions about such psychological processes—for example, when they talk about risk taking, decision making, intentions, reactions to threats or incentives, or the role of public opinion. What psychological analysis does is address such assumptions explicitly, critically, and systematically.

Second, the most relevant contributions of psychological analysis are at the social-psychological level. To be sure, general psychological processes—such as those concerned with cognitive functioning, reactions to stress, or the behavioral effects of reward and punishment—explain the behavior of decision makers and other individual actors in international affairs; but these individuals act within organized social structures. Social psychology provides the appropriate framework for analyzing such behavior since it focuses on phenomena at the intersection of psychological and institutional processes: social interaction and the relationship of individuals to social systems.

Third, "psychological" is not the opposite of "real." Psychological analysis of a conflict in no way implies that the conflict is unreal, a mere product of misperception or misunderstanding. In examining the emotional or cognitive processes in a conflict relationship, there is no presumption that these processes are unrealistic or irrational. The degree of realism or rationality varies from situation to situation. Indeed, psychological analysis is often concerned with enhancing the realism of perception (for example, White 1984) or the rationality of decision making (for example, Janis 1982). On the other hand, psychological analysis is based on the assumption that subjective factors play a role in the perception and interpretation of events. In a conflict relationship, such subjective elements may exacerbate the conflict by generating differences in the way the parties perceive reality and by imposing constraints on the rational pursuit of their interests.

Fourth, though pervasive and important, psychological factors must always be understood in context. International conflict and its resolution must be conceived as societal and intersocietal processes that come about through the actions and interactions of large numbers of individuals who, in turn, function through a variety of groups and organizations, and who are propelled by collective moods and states of consciousness with deep historical and ideological roots. Historical, geopolitical, and structural factors provide the context and set the constraints for the operation of psychological factors.

Finally, therefore, the contribution of a social-psychological perspective to understanding international conflict depends on identifying the appropriate points of entry for psychological analysis—those points in a theory of international relations where social-psychological propositions may provide particularly relevant levers for theoretical explanation. But it always must be kept in mind that these are points of entry into a larger theoretical framework that is, of necessity, multidimensional. A parallel assumption, at the level of practice, underlies interactive problem solving or similar social-psychologically based forms of unofficial diplomacy. Such approaches can make significant contributions to conflict resolution and ought to become integral parts of a comprehensive model of diplomacy. They do not, however, provide an alternative to official diplomacy or a substitute for binding negotiations. Their value, again, depends on identifying the appropriate points of entry into the larger diplomatic process where they can make a relevant contribution—for example, by providing opportunities for nonbinding exploration of options or creative reframing of issues.

Proceeding on the above assumptions, this chapter undertakes two tasks. It begins with a discussion of several propositions about the nature of international conflict that flow from a social-psychological perspective and that have clear implications for conflict resolution. It then describes social-psychological processes characteristic of conflict interaction that contribute to the escalation and perpetuation of conflict and that must be reversed if the conflict is to be resolved.

THE NATURE OF INTERNATIONAL CONFLICT

A social-psychological perspective suggests certain propositions about the nature of international conflict that expand on the view of the phenomenon emerging from more traditional approaches, such as the realist school of international relations. The first proposition holds that international conflict is *a process driven by collective needs and fears*, rather than entirely a product of rational calculation of objective national interests on the part of political decision makers. Second, international conflict is *an intersocietal process*, not only an interstate or intergovernmental phenomenon. Third, international conflict is *a multifaceted process of mutual influence*, not only a contest in the exercise of coercive power. And fourth, international conflict is *an interactive process with an escalatory, self-perpetuating dynamic*, not merely a sequence of action and reaction by stable actors.

Thus, without denying the importance of objectively anchored national interests, the primacy of the state in the international system, the role of power in international relations, and the effect of structural factors in determining the course of an international conflict, a social-psychological perspective enriches the analysis of international relations in a variety of ways: by exploring the subjective factors that set constraints on rationality; by opening the "black box" of the state as a unitary actor and analyzing the processes within and between societies that underlie state action; by broadening the range of influence processes (and, indeed, of definitions of power) that play a role in international politics; and by conceiving international conflict as a dynamic process, shaped by changing realities, changing interests, and changing relationships between the conflicting parties.

Conflict as a Process Driven by Collective Needs and Fears

International or ethnic conflict must be conceived as a process in which collective human needs and fears are acted out in powerful ways. Such conflict is typically driven by nonfulfillment or threats to the fulfillment of basic needs. These needs include not only obvious material ones, such as food, shelter, physical safety, and physical well-being, but also, and very centrally, psychological needs, such as identity, security, recognition, autonomy, self-esteem, and a sense of justice. "Need," as used here, is an individual-level concept; needs are attributes of individual human beings. But insofar as these needs become driving forces in international and intergroup conflict, they are needs of individuals articulated through important identity groups. The link of needs to groups—their collective aspect—is indeed an important and almost ubiquitous feature of human needs. The fulfillment of needs takes place to a considerable extent within the context of groups of different sizes. The ethnic group, the national group, and the state are among the collectivities that serve as important vehicles for fulfilling and protecting fundamental needs.

Closely related to these basic needs in intergroup conflict situations are fears about the denial of the needs—fears focusing, for example, on perceived threats to security or identity. In protracted conflicts between identity groups, such fears often take on an existential character, turning the conflict into a struggle over group survival. The Israeli-Palestinian conflict, for example, can be described as an existential conflict between two parties, each of which sees its very existence as a national group at stake in the conflict (Kelman 1987).

Identity, security, and similarly powerful collective needs, and the fears and concerns about survival associated with them, are often important causal factors in intergroup and intercommunal conflict. The causes of conflict generally combine objective and subjective factors, which are related to each other in a circular fashion. Conflicts focusing, for example, on issues like territory and resources almost invariably reflect and further magnify underlying concerns about security and identity. But, whatever their role in the causation of a conflict, subjective forces linked to basic needs and existential fears contribute heavily to its escalation and perpetuation. Such needs and fears create a resistance to change even in situations in which both parties, or significant elements of both parties, have concluded that it is in their best interests to end the conflict. Despite this perceived

interest, the parties are often unable to extricate themselves from the escalatory dynamic in which they are caught up.

Exploration of collective needs and fears is particularly helpful in understanding why it is so difficult for parties to change course in conflicts that
have become increasingly destructive and detrimental to their interests.
Although the parties may recognize that it is to their advantage to find a
negotiated solution, they are afraid to go to the negotiating table. Or, having reluctantly gone to the table, they are afraid to make the necessary
concessions or accommodations for the negotiations to move forward. They
worry that once they enter negotiations, or—having entered negotiations—
once they make certain concessions, they will find themselves on a slip-
pery slope: that they will inexorably be moving, concession after concession, toward an outcome that will leave their very existence compromised.
In short, the sense that their identity, security, and existence as a national
group are at stake contributes heavily to their resistance to negotiation or
to accommodation in the course of negotiations.

The role of such existential fears and needs is more pronounced in ethnic conflicts than in the kinds of interstate conflicts with which traditional
theories of international politics have been concerned. But collective needs
and fears play a part in all international conflicts and lie behind what are
usually described as national interests—essentially the interests perceived
by elites who control the operative definition of the national interest. These
perceptions are heavily influenced by objective factors. The fact that a state,
for example, lacks certain essential resources, or has an ethnically divided
population, or has no access to the sea, obviously plays a role in how the
elites define the state's interests. But such objective factors always combine
with subjective factors to determine how different segments of a society
perceive state interests, and what ultimately becomes the national interest
as defined by the dominant elites. The subjective determinants of perceived
national interests are the collective needs and fears of the society, as interpreted by the political leadership and other elites.

Similarly, it can be assumed that all conflicts represent a combination of
rational and irrational factors. Ethnic conflicts, though often portrayed as
uniquely irrational, resemble conflicts between states and even between
superpowers in that regard. Moreover, in each type of conflict the mix between rational and irrational elements may vary from case to case. Some
ethnic conflicts may be preponderantly rational, just as some interstate conflicts may be preponderantly irrational.

In all international conflicts, the needs and fears of populations are mobilized and often manipulated by the leadership. Collective needs and fears are often linked to individual needs and fears. For example, in ethnic conflicts characterized by a high level of violence, the fear of annihilation of one's group is often (and for good reason) tied to a fear of personal annihilation. Insofar as these personally tinged collective needs and fears are mobilized, they become the focus of collective action within a society. The mobilization and manipulation of collective needs and fears vary in the degree of demagoguery and cynicism they involve, but they are always seen as necessary tasks of leaders in a conflict situation. Furthermore, though mobilized and often manipulated, collective needs and fears must be viewed as real and authentic reactions within the population.

What does this conception of conflict as a process driven by collective needs and fears imply for conflict resolution? First, it follows from this view that genuine conflict resolution must address these needs and fears. If a conflict is to be resolved, in the sense of leading to a stable peace that both sides consider just and to a new relationship that is mutually enhancing and contributes to the welfare and development of the two societies, the solution must satisfy the fundamental needs and allay the deepest fears of the affected populations. The objective of conflict resolution is not to eliminate the conflict entirely, which is neither possible nor desirable as a general goal (since conflicts are potentially constructive forces within a society or region and serve as the basis for essential social change); rather, it is to eliminate the violent and otherwise destructive manifestations of conflict. But even these destructive elements cannot be made to disappear overnight in conflicts that have been pursued for many years—in some cases, for generations—and are marked by accumulated memories that are constantly being revived by new events and experiences. Conflict resolution does not imply that past grievances and historical traumas have been forgotten and a consistently harmonious relationship has been put in place. It simply implies that a process has been set into motion that addresses the central needs and fears of the societies and establishes continuing mechanisms to confront them.

From a normative point of view, the ultimate criterion for a successful, mutually satisfactory solution of a conflict is that it addresses the fundamental needs of both parties. Thus, what negotiation theorists mean by a win-win solution in a protracted conflict between identity groups is a solution that has, in fact, spoken—however imperfectly—to such needs and the fears associated with them: a solution in which neither side is required to sacrifice what it considers to be a vital need and both are reassured with respect to their deepest fears. It is in the search for such solutions that justice enters the picture in nonadversarial approaches to conflict resolution, such as interactive problem solving. Problem-solving workshops, for example, are governed by a no-fault principle, which eschews efforts to establish who is right and who is wrong from a legal or a moral standpoint. Although the parties' differing views of rights and wrongs must be discussed since they contribute significantly to the dynamics of the conflict, the assumption is that the parties cannot find a solution by adjudicating these differing views. Rather, they must move toward a solution by jointly discovering mutually satisfactory ways of dealing with the issues that divide them. Insofar as they arrive at a solution that addresses the fundamental needs of both parties, justice is being done—not perfect justice, but enough to ensure the prospects for a durable peace. Thus, commitment to a solution that is responsive to the basic concerns of the two parties is the operationalization of justice in a problem-solving approach.

An interesting implication of a human-needs orientation, first noted by John Burton (1988), is that the psychological or ontological needs on which it focuses—needs like identity, security, or recognition—are not inherently zero-sum. One party need not gain its identity or security at the expense of the other. In fact, much of the new thinking about security, exemplified by the concept of common security, is based on the proposition that each party's security is enhanced by the security of the other. Similarly, in a context of mutual recognition, the identity of one is enhanced by the identity of the other (Kelman 1987, 358). In intense conflicts, of course, there is a strong tendency to see these needs as zero-sum and to assume that one's own security and identity can be protected or enhanced only by depriving the other of security and identity. But since these needs are not by nature mutually exclusive, addressing them may offer possibilities for a mutually satisfactory solution. If the parties can probe behind their incompatible positions and explore the underlying needs that engender these positions, they may be able to shape an integrative solution that satisfies both sets of needs. Once such underlying needs have been addressed, issues like territory or resources—which are more inherently zero-sum in nature (although also susceptible to creative reframing)—can then be settled through distributive bargaining.

A final implication of the view that conflict is driven by collective needs and fears relates to the question of when the individual becomes the appropriate unit of analysis in international relations. Though the needs and fears that drive conflict are collectively expressed and must be satisfied at the collective level, they are experienced at the level of individual human beings. To address such needs and fears, therefore, conflict resolution must, at some stage, provide for certain processes that take place at the level of individuals and the interaction between individuals. One such process is empathy, or taking the perspective of the other, which is essential to any effort to move toward an accommodation that takes account of the needs and fears of both parties. Empathy develops in the interaction between individuals, and it is in the minds of individuals that the perspective of the other has to be somehow represented. Creative problem solving is another example of a process essential to conflict resolution that takes place in the minds of individuals and in the interaction between them as they move from analyzing the causes of a conflict to generating new ideas for resolving it. Insight and learning are further examples of individual-level processes that need to be part of a larger effort at conflict resolution. Problem-solving workshops and similar conflict-resolution activities provide a setting in which such processes can occur. They contribute to the larger process of conflict resolution by creating, through the interaction between the participating individuals, new insights and ideas that can be exported into the political debate and the decision-making processes within the conflicting societies. Thus, a problem-solving workshop can be thought of as a laboratory—indeed, as a workshop in the literal sense of the word—where a product is being created for export. Essentially, workshops represent a special micro-process that provides inputs into the macro-process of conflict resolution.

Conflict as an Intersocietal Process

A focus on the needs and fears of the population involved in conflict readily brings to mind a second social-psychological proposition: that international conflict is not merely an intergovernmental or interstate phenomenon, but an intersocietal phenomenon. The conflict, particularly in the case of protracted ethnic struggles, becomes an inescapable part of daily life for the members of the opposing communities. The conflict pervades the whole society and its component elements—not only when it takes the form of explicit violence, but even when the violence is muted. Thus, analysis of conflict requires attention not only to its strategic, military, and diplomatic dimensions, but also to its economic, psychological, cultural, and social-structural dimensions. Interactions along these dimensions, both within and between the conflicting societies, shape the political environment in which governments function. Intrasocietal and intersocietal processes define the political constraints under which governments operate and the resistance to change that these produce. For example, the leaders' attempts to respond to public moods, to shape public opinion, and to mobilize group loyalties often feed the conflict and reduce the options for conflict resolution.

A view of conflict as a process that occurs between two societies immediately prompts us to examine what happens *within* each society. In particular, this view alerts us to the role of internal divisions within each society. Although theories of international relations often treat states as unitary actors, the societies that states or other political organizations represent are never monolithic entities. Every political community is divided in various ways, and these internal divisions often play a major role in exacerbating or even creating conflicts *between* such political communities. The course of an intergroup conflict typically reflects the intragroup conflicts within both conflicting groups, which impose constraints on the political leaders. Leaders pursuing a policy of accommodation have to consider the reactions of opposition elements, who may accuse them of betraying the national cause or jeopardizing the nation's existence. They also have to be responsive to the anxieties and doubts within the general population, which opposition elements foster and from which they draw support. In all these ways, internal divisions introduce severe constraints on efforts at conflict resolution.

Although the intersocietal nature of conflict contributes to its perpetuation, it also creates certain necessities and opportunities for conflict resolution. The internal divisions within each society do indeed impose serious constraints on decision makers in the pursuit of peaceful solutions, but they also provide them with potential levers for change. Such divisions challenge the monolithic image of the enemy that parties in conflict tend to hold and enable them to deal with each other in a more differentiated way. They can come to recognize that even in a community mobilized for violent conflict, there may be elements amenable to an alternative approach who are potential partners for negotiation. This reality provides the opportunity, for example, of forming coalitions across the conflict lines—coalitions between elements on each side that are interested in negotiation. Indeed, problem-solving workshops and related activities can be conceptualized as part of a process of forming precisely such a coalition (Kelman 1993). A coalition across conflict lines, however, must of necessity remain an uneasy coalition. If it became overly cohesive, its members would lose their ability to influence the political decision making within their respective communities. By becoming too closely identified with their counterparts on the other side, coalition members might become alienated from their own co-nationals, lose credibility at home, and hence forfeit their political effectiveness and ability to contribute to another important precondition for conflict resolution: the development of a new consensus for a negotiated solution within their own community. If coalitions across conflict lines remain sensitive to the need to maintain the members' separate group identities and credibility at home, they represent a potentially effective way to capitalize on the divisions within the conflicting societies in the interest of conflict resolution, peacemaking, and, ultimately, building a new relationship between the former enemies.

Another implication of an intersocietal view of conflict is that negotiations and third-party efforts ideally should be directed not merely to a political *settlement* of the conflict in the form of a brokered political agreement, but to its *resolution*. A political agreement may be adequate for terminating relatively specific, containable interstate disputes, but it is inadequate for conflicts that engage the collective identities and existential concerns of the societies involved. Conflict resolution in this deeper, more lasting sense implies arrangements and accommodations that emerge out of the interactions between the parties themselves, that address the needs of both parties, and to which the parties feel committed. An agreement that is not widely accepted within the two societies is unlikely to lead to a durable peace. What is required, in short, is a gradual process conducive to change in structures and attitudes, to reconciliation, and to the transformation of the relationship between the two societies—the development of a new relationship that recognizes the interdependence of the conflicting societies and is open to cooperative, functional arrangements between them. The real test of conflict resolution in deep-rooted conflicts is how much the process by which agreements are constructed and the nature of those agreements contribute to transforming the relationship between the parties.

Finally, a corollary of an intersocietal analysis of conflict is a view of diplomacy as a complex mix of official and unofficial, formal and informal efforts with complementary contributions. The peaceful termination or management of conflict requires binding agreements that can be achieved only at the official level. But insofar as we think of conflict as not only an interstate, but also an intersocietal affair, many different sectors of the two societies have to be fruitfully involved in a more elaborate, integrated process of diplomacy. In this context, unofficial, noncommittal interactions can play a complementary role by exploring ways of overcoming obstacles to conflict resolution and helping to create a political environment conducive to negotiation and other diplomatic initiatives (Saunders 1988).

Conflict as a Multifaceted Process of Mutual Influence

Much of international politics entails mutual influence, whereby each party seeks to protect and promote its own interests by shaping the behavior of the other. Conflict occurs when these interests clash: when attainment of one party's interests (and fulfillment of the needs that underlie them) threatens, or is perceived to threaten, the interests (and needs) of the other. In pursuing the conflict, therefore, the parties engage in mutual influence, designed to advance their own positions and block the adversary's. Similarly, in conflict resolution—by negotiation or other means—the parties exercise influence to induce the adversary to come to the table, to make concessions, to accept an agreement that meets their interests and needs, and to live up to that agreement. Third parties, too, exercise influence in conflict situations by backing one or the other party, mediating between them, or maneuvering to protect their own interests.

The typical influence process in international conflict relies on a mixture of threats and inducements, although the balance between negative and positive incentives varies considerably from case to case. Political analysts and decision makers often rely heavily, if not exclusively, on the use and threat of force to exert influence on adversaries. Thus, the U.S.–Soviet relationship during the Cold War was framed largely in terms of an elaborate theory of deterrence—a form of influence designed to keep the other side from doing what you do not want it to do. In other conflict relationships, the emphasis may be on compellence—a form of influence designed to make the other side do what you want it to do. Such coercive strategies are part of the repertoire of influence processes in all domains of social life, but they entail serious costs and risks, and their effects may be severely limited. For example, they are likely to be reciprocated by the other side and thus lead to escalation of the conflict, and they are unlikely to change behavior to which the other is committed.

Thus, the effective exercise of influence in international conflict requires broadening the repertoire of influence strategies, at least to the extent of combining "carrots and sticks"—of supplementing the negative incentives that typically dominate international conflict relationships with positive incentives (see, for example, Baldwin 1971 and Kriesberg 1981, 1982). Positive incentives may take the form of economic benefits, sharing essential resources, international approval, integration in regional or global institutions, or a general reduction in the level of tension. They are particularly effective if they meet the other's interests or respond to the other's security concerns that are at the heart of the conflict, and if they are part of a concerted strategy that invites reciprocation. An example of an approach based on the systematic use of positive incentives is Osgood's (1962) GRIT (Graduated and Reciprocated Initiatives in Tension Reduction) strategy. In his 1977 trip to Jerusalem, Egyptian president Anwar Sadat used a variant of this strategy by undertaking a unilateral initiative based on the expectation (partly prenegotiated) of Israeli reciprocation (Kelman 1985). But unlike the GRIT strategy, which starts with small concessions and gradually builds on them, Sadat's strategy in effect started at the end: "He made a massive, fundamental concession by accepting the basic principles of Israel's position . . . in the anticipation that negotiations would fill in the intervening steps" (Kelman 1985, 216). GRIT, the Sadat initiative, and other strategies based on positive incentives have the potential of transforming a conflict into a new relationship in which both parties' needs and interests are met and continuing differences are resolved by peaceful means.

The view of influence as a multifaceted process emphasizes positive inducements as a useful complement to the negative inducements that predominate in international conflict—as a strategy that often entails smaller short-term risks and greater long-term benefits than the use or threat of force. But it goes further: It also provides a framework for identifying the *types* of positive inducements that are most likely to be effective. Effective use of positive incentives requires more than offering the other party whatever rewards, promises, or confidence-building measures seem most readily available. It requires actions that address the fundamental needs and fears of the other party. Thus, the key to an effective influence strategy based on the exchange of positive incentives is *responsiveness* to the other's concerns. The parties influence each other by actively exploring ways in which they can help meet each other's needs and allay each other's fears. Responsiveness also implies sensitivity to the other's constraints. It requires that both parties explore ways to help each other overcome the constraints within their respective societies against taking the actions that each wants the other to take. Responsiveness to the other's needs and fears is a fairly common form of influence in normal social relations. It is not, however, a strategy that parties in conflict are normally inclined to use, since it requires them to explore and carry out actions designed to benefit the adversary.

The advantage of a strategy of responsiveness is that it alerts parties to ways of exerting influence on the other through their own actions—through positive steps (not threats) that are within their own capacity to take. The process is greatly facilitated by communication between the parties to identify actions that are politically feasible and perhaps not even especially costly to one party, but are likely to have an impact on the other. Ultimately, the effectiveness of a strategy of responsiveness depends on careful adherence to the principle of reciprocity. One-sided responsiveness cannot sustain itself for long.

A key element in an influence strategy based on responsiveness is *mutual reassurance*, which is particularly critical in any effort to resolve an existential conflict. For example, how can the parties to such a conflict be induced to come to the negotiating table and, once there, to make the concessions necessary to reach an agreement? Since they are afraid that negotiations and concessions might jeopardize their national existence, mutual reassurance is a major motivating force—along with a mutually hurting stalemate and mutual enticements.

Negative incentives clearly play a significant role. The negotiation literature suggests that parties are often driven to the table by a mutually hurting stalemate, which makes negotiations more attractive than continuing the conflict (Zartman and Berman 1982; Touval and Zartman 1985, 16). Thus, one way of inducing an adversary to negotiate is to make the conflict more painful through the use of threats, military pressure, or other coercive means. But reliance on such negative incentives has many liabilities: It may push the parties to the table, but does not necessarily make for productive negotiations once they get there; and it may reduce the likelihood of achieving an agreement that is mutually satisfactory and desirable. Therefore, negative incentives must at least be complemented by positive ones through what Zartman has called "mutual enticement" (see, for example, Zartman and Aurik 1991).

But parties engaged in existential conflicts are afraid to move to the negotiating table and make concessions even when the status quo has become increasingly painful and they recognize that a negotiated agreement is in their interest. They worry that negotiations may lead to ever more costly concessions that will ultimately jeopardize their security, their national identity, and their very existence. To advance the negotiating process under such circumstances, it is at least as important to reduce the parties' fears as it is to increase their pain.

Mutual reassurance can take the form of acknowledgments, symbolic gestures, or confidence-building measures. To be maximally effective, such steps need to address the other's central needs and fears as directly as possible. When President Sadat spoke to the Israeli Knesset during his dramatic visit to Jerusalem in November 1977, he acknowledged that in the past Egypt had rejected Israel, refused to meet with Israelis, refused to exchange greetings. By clearly acknowledging the past hostility and thus validating the Israelis' own experiences, he greatly enhanced the credibility of the change in course that he was announcing. These remarks helped to reassure the Israeli public that his offer was sincere and not just a trick to extract concessions that would weaken Israel's position in the continuing confrontation.

At the opening of this visit, Sadat offered a symbolic gesture that had an electrifying effect on Israelis: As he stepped off the plane, he engaged in a round of cordial handshakes with the Israeli officials who had come to greet him. The refusal of Arab officials to shake the hands of their Israeli counterparts had been profoundly disturbing to Israelis throughout the years of the conflict. It symbolized Arab denial of Israel's legitimacy and the very humanity of its people. Sadat's gesture spoke directly to this deep hurt and signaled the beginning of a new relationship.

Confidence-building measures may consist of any acts that respond to the other's demands or accrue to the other's benefit. Again, however, they are particularly effective when they address major grievances and demonstrate sensitivity to the other's fundamental concerns. Thus, for example, the closing of military installations and withdrawal of Israeli troops anywhere in the occupied territories—despite their limited scope—are concrete indicators to Palestinians that the peace process might ultimately lead to an end to the occupation and thus reassure them that their leaders have not embarked on a course that threatens their national aspirations.

Acknowledgments often have a powerful psychological impact in opening the way to negotiation and accommodation, even though they are verbal statements that may not be immediately translated into concrete actions. "Acknowledgment" in this context refers to a party's public acceptance or confirmation of the other party's view of its status, its experience, its reality. Thus, one party may acknowledge the other's humanity, nationhood, national rights, suffering, grievances, interpretation of its history, authentic links to disputed lands, or commitment to peace. Such acknowledgments do not constitute acceptance of the other's position or accession to its claims, but at least they serve to recognize that there is some legitimacy to these positions and claims and some basis for them in the other's experience. Acknowledgments have such a potentially powerful impact because the history of a conflict is often marked by the systematic denial of the other's experience, authenticity, legitimacy, and even membership in the human family. These denials create profound fear and insecurity, because they undermine the very foundations of the other's claim to nationhood and challenge the other's right to national existence. Acknowledgment of what was heretofore denied is thus an important source of reassurance to the recipients, because it signals that the other side, having accepted the legitimacy of their claims, may indeed be ready to negotiate an agreement that addresses their fundamental concerns. Under these circumstances, the parties are likely to feel safer about entering negotiations, despite the risks and uncertainties, and to make significant concessions. A good example of this kind of acknowledgment was Israel's and the Palestine Liberation Organization's (PLO) mutual recognition in the September 1993 Oslo Accords, which helped create the breakthrough in Israeli-Palestinian negotiations.

Apart from persuading the parties that their fundamental concerns will be addressed in the negotiations, acknowledgments may play a more subtle role in reassuring them that it is now safe to end the conflict even if it requires major concessions. Acknowledgements do so insofar as they confirm the parties' "national narratives." A central element of the Palestinian narrative, for example, is that the establishment of Israel constituted a profound injustice to the Palestinian people, who were displaced, dispossessed, dispersed, and deprived of their society and their future. An Israeli acknowledgment of that injustice, by confirming the Palestinians' national narrative, might allow them to let go of the conflict and accept a compromise solution even though it would not fully remove the injustice they feel. Ultimately, the acknowledgment would vindicate the Palestinians' view of history, thus providing a justification for accepting a pragmatic approach so they can end the struggle and go on with their lives. By contrast, a central element of the Israeli national narrative holds that the establishment of Israel was an act of historical justice that enabled the Jewish people to return to its ancestral homeland after centuries of dispersion and persecution. A Palestinian acknowledgment of the Jewish people's historic roots in the land, by confirming the Israelis' national narrative, might enable them to let go of their claim to exclusive ownership of the land and accept a formula for sharing it with the Palestinians. Again, the acknowledgment would vindicate their view of history and thus provide a justification for accepting the reality of the Palestinian presence and putting an end to the conflict.

In sum, acknowledgments provide reassurance at the levels of both security and identity. By signaling acceptance of the other's legitimacy, each party reassures the other that negotiations and concessions no longer constitute mortal threats to its security and national existence. By confirming the other's national narrative, each reassures the other that a compromise does not represent an abandonment of its identity, which is articulated by its national narrative.

Acknowledgments with the capacity to reassure the other are difficult to formulate because national narratives of the conflicting parties typically clash. In confirming the narrative of the other, each party risks undermining its own narrative. Therefore, the parties often need to "negotiate" their acknowledgments with each other (perhaps in the context of a problem-solving workshop)—that is, to engage in a joint process of formulating statements that will reassure the recipient without threatening the issuer (Kelman 1992b). The effectiveness of other forms of mutual reassurance, such as symbolic gestures and confidence-building measures, may be similarly enhanced if they are generated through such an informal "negotiation" process, in which the impact on the recipient and the constraints of the issuer can be considered jointly and balanced. A critical criterion for the maximal effectiveness of acknowledgments, gestures, and confidence-building measures is careful adherence to the principle of reciprocity. Reassuring the other is rarely cost-free; the reassurance involves some concession—or at least is perceived to do so—and it often generates some domestic criticism. Thus, it is important that reassurance occur in a context in which the initiator receives a visible return. Reciprocity itself is a source of mutual reassurance in that it signals to the parties that their concessions will not simply be pocketed by the other, but are likely to advance their own interests.

An influence strategy based on responsiveness to each other's needs and fears and the resulting search for ways of reassuring and benefiting each other has important advantages from a long-term point of view. It does not merely elicit specific desired behaviors from the other party, but it can contribute to a creative redefinition of the conflict, joint discovery of mutually satisfactory solutions, and transformation of the relationship between the parties. In terms of my earlier distinction among three processes of social influence (Kelman 1961; Kelman and Hamilton 1989; see also Rubin 1989), a strategy of mutual responsiveness is likely to have an impact that goes beyond *compliance*, inducing changes at the level of *identification* and potentially at the level of *internalization*.

Positive incentives per se have an advantage over negative incentives in that they create an atmosphere more conducive to negotiation and provide greater opportunities for building a new relationship. But if promises, rewards, and confidence-building measures are offered randomly—essentially as "bribes"—without reference to the recipient's underlying needs and fears, they are likely to induce change only at the level of compliance (that is, a relatively unstable change in public behavior without accompanying changes in private beliefs).

On the other hand, if positive incentives are used as part of a systematic strategy of responsiveness and reciprocity, they help develop a working trust and a valued relationship between the parties. The relationship becomes an incentive in its own right, in that the parties will be inclined to live up to each other's expectations in order to maintain and extend their new relationship. In this case, the resulting influence can be said to be at the level of identification: The parties are likely to change not only their public behavior, but also their private beliefs—at least as long as the relationship remains salient.

As parties develop a relationship based on responsiveness and reciprocity, they become better able to approach their conflict as a shared dilemma that requires joint efforts at analysis and problem solving. A joint problem-solving approach is conducive to agreements that are inherently satisfactory to the parties because they meet their fundamental needs, and that are lasting because they create a sense of ownership and commitment. The negotiation and implementation of such agreements can be characterized as changes at the level of internalization: changes in behavior and beliefs that are congruent with the parties' own values and are relatively stable and enduring. The gradual transformation of the parties' relationship, which makes these changes possible, itself becomes a key element of the mutually satisfactory and stable (that is, "internalized") outcome of a successful negotiation.

Conflict as an Interactive Process with an Escalatory, Self-Perpetuating Dynamic

Conflict is an interactive process, in which the parties change as they act and react in relation to each other. In intense conflict relationships, the natural course of the interaction tends to reinforce and deepen the conflict, rather than reduce and resolve it. The interaction is governed by a set of norms and guided by a set of images that create an escalatory, self-perpetuating dynamic. This dynamic can be reversed through skillful diplomacy, imaginative leadership, third-party intervention, and institutionalized mechanisms for managing and resolving conflict. But in the absence of such deliberate efforts, the spontaneous interaction between the parties is likely to increase distrust, hostility, and the sense of grievance.

The needs and fears of parties engaged in intense conflict impose perceptual and cognitive constraints on their processing of new information, with the resulting tendency to underestimate the occurrence and the possibility of change. In normal human relations, social interaction is the way in which people determine what the other needs and expects, assess the occurrence and possibility of change in these needs and expectations, and adjust their own behavior accordingly. By accommodating to each other's needs and expectations, both participants are able to advance the achievement of their respective goals. An essential feature of social interaction is the effort to take account of the other's purposes, perceptions, intentions, and expectations by implicitly taking the role of the other on the assumption that the other has a mind like one's own, with similar kinds of purposes, perceptions, intentions, and expectations. In intense conflict relationships, this ability to take the role of the other is severely impaired. Dehumanization of the enemy makes it even more difficult to acknowledge and gain access to the other's perspective.

The inaccessibility of the other's perspective contributes significantly to some of the psychological barriers to conflict resolution described by Ross and Ward (1995). The dynamics of conflict interaction tend to entrench the parties firmly in their own perspectives on history and justice. Conflicting parties have particularly strong tendencies to find evidence that confirms their negative images of each other and to resist evidence that counters these images. Thus, interaction not only fails to contribute to a revision of the enemy image, but actually helps to reinforce and perpetuate it. The combination of demonic enemy images and virtuous self-images leads to the formation of mirror images (see, for example, Bronfenbrenner 1961and White 1965), which greatly contributes to the escalatory dynamic of conflict interaction, as exemplified by the classical pattern of an arms race. When one side increases its arms and takes other actions that it considers defensive, the other interprets these steps as preparation for aggression and proceeds to increase its arms—presumably in defense against the other's intended aggression. The first side, however, interprets these steps in turn as preparation for aggression and further increases its arms, which further persuades the second party of the other's aggressive intentions—and thus a conflict spiral is set into motion. Interaction guided by such mirror images of enemy and self create self-fulfilling prophecies by inducing the parties to engage in the hostile actions they expect from one another.

Self-fulfilling prophecies are also generated by the conflict norms that typically govern the interaction between parties engaged in an intense conflict. Expressions in word and action of hostility and distrust toward the enemy are not just spontaneous manifestations of the conflict, but are normatively

prescribed behaviors. Both leaders and publics operate under norms that require them to be militant and unyielding vis-à-vis the other side, accuse the
other of misdeeds, remain suspicious of their intentions, and deny all justice
to their cause. Political leaders assume that their public's evaluation of them
depends on their adherence to these norms and may go out of their way to
avoid appearing weak or gullible. These tendencies are reflected in the leaders' tactical and strategic decisions, the way they approach negotiations with
the other side, their public pronouncements, and, ultimately, the way they
educate their own publics. For the publics, in turn, adherence to these norms
is often taken as an indication of group loyalty; those who acknowledge that
there may be some justice on the other side or propose a conciliatory posture
may expose themselves to accusations of treason or at least naiveté. In short,
the discourse in deep-rooted conflicts is marked by mutual delegitimization
and dehumanization. Interaction governed by this set of norms—at the micro and the macro levels—contributes to escalation and perpetuation of the
conflict. Parties that systematically treat each other with hostility and distrust are likely to become increasingly hateful and untrustworthy.

The dynamics of conflict interaction carry a high probability that opportunities for conflict resolution will be missed. As realities change in the
international, regional, or domestic environment, the parties in a long-
standing conflict may well become amenable to compromise. There may
be possibilities for resolving the conflict in ways that are mutually satisfactory—or at least preferable to continuing the struggle. But parties caught
up in the conflict dynamics, whose interaction is shaped by the norms and
images rooted in the history of the conflict, are systematically constrained
in their capacity to respond to the occurrence and possibility of change.
The nature of their interaction makes it difficult to communicate the
changes that have occurred on their own side or to notice the changes on
the other side, and to explore the possibilities for change that would serve
both sides' interests. Conflict resolution efforts, therefore, require promotion of a different kind of interaction, capable of reversing the escalatory
and self-perpetuating dynamics of conflict: an interaction conducive to sharing perspectives, differentiating enemy images, and developing a language
of mutual reassurance and a new discourse based on the norms of responsiveness and reciprocity.

The remainder of this chapter discusses in somewhat greater detail the
social-psychological processes that contribute to the escalation and perpetuation of international conflict, and concludes with a comment on how
these processes might be reversed in the interest of conflict resolution.

SOCIAL-PSYCHOLOGICAL PROCESSES PROMOTING CONFLICT

The four propositions about the nature of international conflict discussed so far—especially the view of conflict as a process driven by collective needs and fears—suggest the important role of social-psychological factors in generating conflict. Social-psychological analysis can be particularly helpful, however, in explaining why and how, once a conflict has started, powerful forces are set into motion that promote the escalation and perpetuation of that conflict. The role of social-psychological processes in creating or intensifying barriers to conflict resolution is most apparent in deep-rooted conflicts over identity and security. By the same token, social-psychological analysis, in helping to identify and understand these barriers, can also suggest ways of overcoming them.

The discussion of social-psychological factors that promote international and ethnic conflict will focus on two sets of processes that were introduced in the preceding section: *normative* processes and *perceptual* processes. The term "normative" is used to refer to social processes that provide expectations, support, and pressure to hold on to the conflict, affirm it, and engage in conflictive behavior. The term "perceptual" is used to refer to cognitive processes that help to interpret and organize conflict-related information, particularly information bearing on the image of the enemy and each party's self-image in relation to the conflict. Normative and perceptual processes are clearly interrelated. As we shall see, for example, the normatively prescribed behavior in a conflict relationship is heavily influenced by the image of the enemy; and the enemy image, in turn, is itself normatively prescribed. Nevertheless, these two sets of processes are conceptually separable and provide a convenient basis for organizing the discussion of social-psychological processes. What both sets of processes have in common is that they create a dynamic that inhibits the perception and occurrence of change: Despite changing circumstances and interests, parties engaged in an intense conflict tend to underestimate the degree to which change has taken place and further change is possible, and to act in ways that reduce the likelihood of change in their relationship.

The normative and perceptual processes that promote conflict can best be understood in the context of the four propositions about the nature of international conflict presented in the first part of the chapter:

- First, conflict norms and images are rooted in the collective needs and fears that drive the conflict.

- Second, given its intersocietal nature, conflict is shaped by the norms and images at the level of both the political leadership and the general public, and by the mutual effect of these two levels on each other.
- Third, conflict norms and images severely limit the range and character of influence processes employed by the parties.
- Finally, and most directly, it is the conflict norms and images on both sides that create the escalatory, self-perpetuating dynamic that characterizes conflict interaction.

Normative Processes

A variety of interaction processes occurring at the mass and elite levels within societies engaged in conflict play an important role in the evolving course of the conflict: formation of collective moods, mobilization of group loyalties, decision-making processes, negotiation and bargaining processes, and processes of structural and psychological commitment. All these processes are governed by a set of powerful social norms that, in an intense conflict relationship, typically encourage actions and attitudes conducive to the generation, escalation, and perpetuation of conflict, and inhibit the perception and occurrence of change in the direction of tension reduction and conflict resolution.

Formation of Collective Moods. Public opinion on issues relating to a protracted conflict (and on foreign policy issues generally) is marked by shifts in collective mood. At different times, the general mood may be characterized by optimism or pessimism, defiance or resignation, anger or conciliation. Moods may shift dramatically in response to major events. Thus, for example, within the Israeli public, the assassination of Prime Minister Rabin in November 1995 created, along with the national shock and mourning, a mood of determination to continue the peace process that had cost the prime minister his life. Several months later, in February and March 1996, the series of deadly bombings in Jerusalem and Tel Aviv shifted the public mood in Israel to one of widespread wariness about the course of the peace process. Such moods have a significant effect on political leaders' sense of how far they can go in the pursuit of peace, or what they must do to demonstrate their continued commitment to pursue the conflict.

Periodic shifts in collective mood underscore the general role of public opinion as both a resource and a constraint for political leaders in the foreign policy process. Public opinion may work both ways: Public support can be a valuable resource in the leaders' pursuit of an aggressive policy as well as in their search for peaceful alternatives. Similarly, public opposition or skepticism may constrain leaders from taking hostile initiatives as well as from making conciliatory moves toward the enemy. In an intense, protracted conflict, however, the prevailing norms are more likely to encourage leaders to choose hostile actions over conciliatory ones. Leaders find it easier to mobilize public support for escalatory than de-escalatory steps; in fact, according to the conventional wisdom, leaders at times initiate external aggression in order to distract the public from internal failures and boost their popular support. By the same token, leaders are more constrained in the pursuit of conciliatory policies than in the pursuit of aggressive policies—or at least they believe they are. The relationship between leadership and public opinion is often circular: Decision makers play an important role in shaping public opinion about a conflict, framing the issues, and defining the limits of acceptable action. Public opinion then takes on a life of its own, and at some future time, when the leaders contemplate a change in policy, they feel constrained by the very views they previously helped shape. When they pronounce, rightly or wrongly, that "our public will never accept" this or that action, they may well be referring to actions that they themselves had publicly declared unacceptable earlier.

Apart from transitory moods, certain pervasive states of consciousness underlie public opinion in a society engulfed in a deep-rooted conflict. These states of consciousness reflect the existential concerns and the central national narratives that are widely shared within the population. In the Israeli-Palestinian conflict, for example, an underlying theme in both peoples' national consciousness is a profound concern, rooted in their respective historical experiences, about survival of the group and loss of the homeland. At the heart of Israelis' strong emphasis on security is their experience of rejection by their neighbors, who have regarded the establishment of Israel as an illegitimate intrusion of outsiders into the region—in contrast to the Israeli narrative of returning to their ancestral homeland after centuries of exile. The resulting sense of vulnerability is magnified by the Jewish historical memories of exclusion and persecution, culminating in the Holocaust. At the heart of Palestinians' strong emphasis on independent statehood is their experience of displacement, dispossession, dispersion, and occupation, and the resulting sense that they have been stripped not only of their homeland but of their identity as a people. The historical trauma at the center of Palestinian consciousness is *al-naqba* (the catastrophe), the Palestinians' term for the war of 1948 and its consequences for their society.

In most intense, protracted conflicts—for example, in the former Yugoslavia, Northern Ireland, and the Middle East—historical traumas serve as the points of reference for current events. There is no question that ambitious, often ruthless, nationalist leaders manipulate memories in order to whip up public support for their projects. But the fact remains that these memories—and the associated sense of injustice, abandonment, and vulnerability—are part of the people's consciousness and available for manipulation. Moreover, although political leaders may be cynical in using these public sentiments for their own purposes, they generally share the existential concerns that underlie pervasive states of national consciousness. Differences between leaders and publics—and, for that matter, between hawks and doves—diminish in importance when threats to group survival and identity are touched off.

The effect of such collective moods is to bring to the fore powerful social norms that support escalatory actions and inhibit moves toward compromise and accommodation. When fundamental concerns about survival and identity are tapped, national leaders are more prone to resort to hostile speech and action, and, if necessary, to go to war in defense of what they see as their society's threatened values and way of life. And they do so in the full expectation that the public will support them, despite the risks entailed. By contrast, these pervasive moods—especially when aroused by dramatic events, such as bombings or expulsions—inhibit the readiness to take risks for peace. This tendency appears consistent with the proposition derived from prospect theory that people are more reluctant to take risks to achieve gains than to avoid losses (see Levy 1992). Pervasive existential concerns within a society create a strong inclination to remain vigilant, distrust the enemy, and avoid any action that might weaken the nation's defenses. When these existential concerns are at issue, the prevailing norms support extreme caution. Political leaders, the general public, and even the political opposition reinforce one another in adhering to the old, established formulas. Change itself comes to be seen as dangerous; there is great reluctance to experiment with the nation's very existence.

Beyond contributing to escalation and inhibiting change in the direction of conflict resolution, the activation of collective fears about national survival and identity may lead to the extremes of violence and hostility that have marked some of this era's recent ethnic conflicts. Unscrupulous and fanatical leaders, taking advantage of opportunities to expand their power and fulfill their nationalist ambitions—such as the opportunity presented to Serbian leaders with the breakup of Yugoslavia—may manipulate collective memories of humiliation and revive old fears (and manufacture new ones) to instigate and justify hostile acts, which may set an escalatory process into motion. With active incitement by the leadership, a new set of norms takes over, whereby members of the other group—including former neighbors—come to be seen as the reincarnation of historic enemies who are planning to dominate one's own group, destroy its way of life, and annihilate its members. Harassing, expelling, and killing them thus come to be seen as justified acts of self-defense and patriotic duty. Small steps, even the silence of bystanders who may not approve of what is happening but are not prepared to take an active stand against the conflict norms that have taken hold, may initiate a continuum of destruction (Staub 1989) that ends with the kind of ethnic cleansing and genocide witnessed in Bosnia and elsewhere. Such actions are planned and orchestrated by political leaders who believe—or persuade themselves, along with their citizenry, to believe—that they are saving their people from imminent destruction, and they are carried out at various levels of command, with varying mixtures of motivation: obedience to authority, conformity to social pressures, and immersion in the collective sense of threat to national and personal survival and hostility against the purported source of that threat.

Mobilization of Group Loyalties. Public support, as already noted, is an essential resource for political leaders engaged in a conflict relationship. Leaders need assurance that the public is prepared to accept the costs and risks that their policies will inevitably entail. Furthermore, assurance of public support enhances the credibility of the threats and promises they issue to the other side. The primary means of gaining public support is the mobilization of group loyalties.

The arousal of nationalist and patriotic sentiments is a powerful tool in mobilizing public support. The display of national symbols evokes a strong emotional reaction, developed in the course of early and continuing socialization, which often translates into automatic endorsement of the policies and actions the leadership defines as necessary. When leaders invoke national security and national survival as the issues at stake in the conflict, people are often prepared to make enormous sacrifices that cannot be entirely understood in terms of rational calculations of costs and benefits.

The nation generates such powerful identifications and loyalties because it brings together two central psychological dispositions: the needs for self-protection and self-transcendence (Kelman 1969, 1997).

In principle, group loyalties should be just as available to mobilize support for policies that entail risks for the sake of peace as for aggressive policies that entail risks of war. In practice, however, the dynamics of intense conflict generally favor efforts to mobilize support for intransigent, hostile actions. An appeal to defend the nation against an imminent attack is more compelling than an appeal to seize a promising opportunity. This phenomenon represents a special case of the central observation of prospect theory: Where the expected utilities are equal, people tend to be risk-acceptant to avoid losses and risk-averse to achieve gains (see Farnham 1992 and Levy 1992). Also, an appeal to defend the nation against imminent attack elicits almost unanimous response among members of the population. Even doves are not immune to such appeals in the short run, although they may believe that conciliatory policies are more conducive to national security and survival in the long run. On the other hand, an appeal to take advantage of an opportunity for peace holds no attraction to that segment of the population that equates peace with surrender. Furthermore, proposals for aggressive actions can more easily rely on the vocabulary of nationalism, which characteristically marks off the in-group from the out-group to the detriment of the latter. Proposals for conciliatory actions, even if they are in one's own interest, may offend nationalist thinking simply because they are seen as extending some benefits to the enemy or acknowledging a degree of justice in the enemy's positions.

A central element of group loyalty is adherence to the group's norms. In an intense conflict relationship, these norms call for a militant, unyielding, uncompromising, and suspicious attitude toward the enemy. There is a special taboo against any position that implies that the enemy may not be as implacable as had been assumed or may be undergoing change. Those who take such positions expose themselves to the charge that they are being naive, if not treasonous, weakening national unity and resolve, and opening the way to surrender. Militancy and intransigence become the measures of loyalty. Those most militant and unyielding become the reference points against which all positions are evaluated. Hence, particularly in situations of perceived national crisis, the militants exercise disproportionate power and often exercise a veto over official actions and policies. They impose severe constraints on the ability of leaders to explore peaceful options. Even the society's dovish elements are constrained and cautious in their analyses and proposals, lest they expose themselves to the accusations of endangering national security and survival.

When national security and survival are seen to be at stake in a society, there are strong pressures to conform to the dominant conflict norms. Dissent is considered an act of disloyalty under these circumstances and is often penalized by exclusion, rejection, and ostracism. To dissent at a time of national crisis is seen as tantamount to excluding oneself from the group, to separating one's fate from that of fellow members—a cardinal sin in the nationalist doctrine. One of the dualities of nationalism is the readiness to accept fellow nationals unconditionally, as long as they identify themselves as part of the group, but to reject them totally if they are seen as separating themselves from the group. The resulting inhibition of dissent on matters that touch on national security and survival may create a state of pluralistic ignorance that further intensifies conformity: Since people with reservations about the dominant policy are reluctant to speak out, and those who do speak out are quickly marginalized, potential dissenters are discouraged from expressing their views because they see themselves as a tiny minority confronting a near-unanimous consensus.

In sum, processes of group loyalty in a conflict situation create barriers to change in the relationship. The criteria by which loyalty is measured, the disproportionate power of the militant elements in setting the national agenda, and the suppression of dissent undermine the exploration of peaceful alternatives and reduce the options for conflict resolution. The militants on the two sides reinforce each other by creating self-fulfilling prophecies—a phenomenon to be described more fully in the discussion of perceptual processes below. Each confirms the other's worst expectations and creates realities that extend and intensify the conflict.

Decision-making Processes. In a conflict situation, decision makers tend to be inhibited in the search for alternatives and the exploration of new possibilities, particularly when they are operating in an atmosphere of crisis.

A major source of reluctance to explore new options are the domestic constraints under which decision makers labor. In view of the political divisions within their society, they are constantly looking over their shoulders to make sure they are not opening themselves up to disabling attacks from the opposition. In an intense conflict situation, adherence to the conflict norms tends to be seen as the safest course of action. For reasons already discussed, decision makers are likely to see themselves most vulnerable if their policies and actions move toward compromise or even communication with the adversary. Since hawkish opposition elements are often effective in appropriating the definition of group loyalty and national security and are able to appeal to the collective memories and fears of wide segments of the population, they tend to exercise stronger constraints on policy than do dovish opposition elements. Cautious decision makers assume that they are less vulnerable domestically if they stay with the conflict's status quo, adhere to a discourse of hostility and distrust vis-à-vis the other side, or threaten escalatory actions than if they take steps toward accommodation and compromise.

The search for alternatives and the exploration of new options in response to changing realities are further inhibited by institutionalized rigidities in the decision-making apparatus. Decision makers and decision-making bureaucracies operate within a certain framework of assumptions about the choices available to them, the effectiveness of different strategies, and the expectations of different constituencies; such assumptions are rarely questioned and therefore reduce the range of options that are likely to be considered. In long-standing conflicts, these decision-making frameworks are shaped by the prevailing conflict norms. Thus, decision makers may take it for granted, for example, that the two parties' interests are inherently incompatible, that the other side responds only to force, or that their own public demands a militant posture. Operating under unquestioned assumptions of this kind, they are unlikely to recognize the occurrence and possibility of change and to consider policies aimed at resolving the conflict.

Furthermore, decision-making bureaucracies tend to operate with certain established procedures and technologies; the actions they consider are those that they are equipped to carry out. In conflict situations, the discourse, skills, and technology for pursuing the conflict are much more readily available than those geared toward resolving it. The prime example is the military establishment, which has the weapons systems, personnel, and operational plans in place and is ready to go into action when the need arises. Decision makers are, therefore, more inclined to resort to military options at moments of crisis than to less developed and untried alternatives.

Finally, the micro-processes of action and interaction in crisis decision making inhibit the exploration of new options. At the level of individual decision makers, the stress they inevitably experience in situations of crisis—when consequential decisions have to be made under severe time pressures—has the effect of limiting the number of alternatives they consider and impelling them to settle quickly on the dominant response. In intense conflicts, the dominant response, dictated by the habits and norms of the conflict, is likely to be aggressive and escalatory. At the level of decision-making groups, crisis decision making often leads to what Janis (1982) has called "groupthink" processes. In order to maintain the cohesiveness of the group, the members studiously avoid any actions that might break the evolving consensus. Thus, they are reluctant to raise questions, offer criticisms, and propose different approaches or alternative solutions to the problem. The group's members reinforce each other in affirming the correctness and righteousness of the course of action on which their deliberations are converging. The decision-making process under these circumstances is much more likely to produce policies and actions that perpetuate and escalate the conflict than innovative ideas for conflict resolution.

Negotiation and Bargaining Processes. Negotiation is possible only when both parties define the situation, at least at some level, as a win-win, mixed-motive game. To engage in the process, each must be able to conceive of some outcome that would be better than the status quo. Thus, negotiation is based on the parties' recognition that they have both competitive and cooperative goals. They are competing in that each is trying to maximize interests that are—or at least are perceived to be—incompatible with the other's interests; but they must cooperate in order to continue the "game" and eventually achieve an agreement that advances both their interests. Even in a narrow bargaining process that focuses strictly on the distribution of fixed, limited resources, the parties have a common interest in consummating the exchange. They must cooperate in devising an outcome that gives each party enough to make the agreement worth its while.

Win-win solutions are particularly difficult to attain in protracted identity conflicts. Depending on the circumstances, a mutually satisfactory outcome might be devised by fractionating the conflict (Fisher 1964), which may help the parties move gradually toward an overall settlement by first achieving agreements on a series of less contentious issues; transcending the conflict as they focus on superordinate goals that can be achieved only through joint efforts (Sherif 1958); or redefining the conflict and reframing the issues in ways that make them amenable to solutions that address the needs and fears of both parties (Kelman 1996). Ultimately, success in negotiating a win-win solution depends on mutual responsiveness, as described in the earlier discussion of influence processes. In effect, while pursuing its own interests, each party must actively seek out ways in which the adversary can also win and appear to be winning. But this is precisely the kind of effort that is discouraged by the conflict norms; the approach to negotiation is dominated by zero-sum thinking. Success in how much one's own side is winning and appears to be winning is often measured by how much the other side is losing and appears to be losing.

At the micro-level, negotiators around the table serve as instructed representatives. In an intense conflict, they evaluate their performance by the forcefulness with which they present their own case and by their effectiveness in warding off pressures to compromise. They are not in a listening mode; they are unlikely to pay attention to what the other side needs and how they could help the other side achieve its goals. Indeed, to do so would violate the conflict norms and might subject the negotiators to criticism from their own constituencies and particularly from the domestic opposition that they are "soft" on the enemy and selling out the national cause. Nor are they likely to present their own positions in ways that convey what they need and how the other side can help them achieve it. The interaction does not usually allow the parties to learn something new or gain a better understanding of the other's perspective. Rather, it tends to confirm old images and to keep the conflict alive. Clearly, it does not contribute to the search for ways in which each party can help the other make valuable and visible gains. Such a search is further undermined by public reports on the progress of negotiations. To appeal to its own constituencies, each side may stress how much it is winning—at the other side's expense. Such pronouncements impose further burdens on the continuing negotiations. In this respect, secret negotiations have a considerable advantage, although their disadvantage is that they usually offer no opportunity to prepare the public for the changes in the relationship that are being negotiated.

At the macro-level, the overall strategy for negotiations is often marked by zero-sum thinking. Even when the parties recognize their common interest in negotiating certain specific issues, they tend to keep an eye on how the negotiations may affect their relative power advantage. They want to make sure that, at the end of the day, their own position will be strengthened and the adversary's will be weakened. Such strategic considerations may undermine the purpose of the negotiations. A strategy that weakens one's negotiating partners may reduce both their incentive for concluding an agreement and their ability to mobilize their own public's support for whatever agreement is negotiated. It is a strategy that limits the other's opportunity to make valuable or visible gains.

As a description of international negotiations in general, the picture presented here is exaggerated, to be sure. Skilled and experienced negotiators know that if the process is to succeed, the other side must achieve substantial and visible gains and its leadership must be strengthened. But the norms governing political behavior in long-standing conflicts strongly encourage zero-sum thinking, which equates the enemy's loss with one's own gain. As a result, even when the parties have concluded that negotiations are in their own best interest, their actions inside and outside of the negotiating room often undermine the process, causing delays, setbacks, and repeated failures.

Processes of Structural and Psychological Commitment. Conflict creates certain structural and psychological commitments, which then take on a life of their own (see Pruitt and Gahagan 1974 and Rubin, Pruitt, and Kim 1994). The most obvious sources of commitment to the conflict and its perpetuation are the vested interests in the status quo. A conflict of long standing and significance to a society—such as that in Northern Ireland (see George 1996)—inevitably becomes a focal point for the lives of various individuals, groups, and organizations within that society. They benefit in a variety of ways from the existence and prosecution of the conflict; ending it threatens to deprive them of profit, power, status, or raison d'être. Such vested interests can be found, for example, in the armaments industry, the military establishment, paramilitary and guerrilla organizations, defense-related research laboratories, and political groups organized to pursue the conflict. A vested interest in maintaining the conflict may also develop, to different degrees, in individuals whose careers are built around the conflict, including political leaders who have played a prominent role in pursuing the struggle and "conflict professionals"—scholars, writers, and journalists who have specialized in chronicling, analyzing, and perhaps even resolving the conflict.

There is another source of commitment that is based not on a vested interest in maintaining the conflict as such, but on an interest in forestalling a compromise solution. Two rather different examples can be cited from the Israeli-Palestinian case. Israeli settlers in the occupied territories generally have been opposed to the peace process because they are convinced that a negotiated agreement would spell the end of their settlement project. Many Palestinians in the refugee camps in Lebanon and Syria have opposed the current peace process because they see it as leading to an agreement that will not address their particular needs and grievances.

Vested interests do not necessarily manifest themselves in a direct, calculated way. There are, of course, those who deliberately undermine efforts at conflict resolution because they do not want to give up the power and privilege that depend on continuation of the status quo (although even they may persuade themselves that they are acting for the good of the nation). In many cases, however, the effects of vested interests are indirect and subtle. People's commitment to the perpetuation of the conflict may motivate their interpretation of ambiguous realities and their choice among uncertain alternatives. Thus, they may be predisposed to dismiss changes or possibilities of change on the other side that might make negotiations promising, and they may be risk-averse in evaluating initiatives for peace but risk-acceptant in their support for aggressive policies that might lead to war.

Vested interests and similar structural commitments to the conflict are bolstered by psychological commitments. People involved in a long-standing and deep-rooted conflict tend to develop a worldview that includes the conflict as a central component. Elements of this worldview may be passed on from one generation to the next, and attitudes and beliefs about the conflict may become firmly embedded in the entire structure of one's thinking and feeling. In this way, people become committed to the continuation of the conflict because ending it would jeopardize their entire worldview; it would force them to revise the way they think and feel about significant aspects of their national and personal lives. The resistance to change may be particularly pronounced among intellectuals, who have more elaborate cognitive structures in which their views of the conflict are embedded. Thus, changing their views of the conflict would have wider ramifications for them.

The image of the enemy is often a particularly important part of the worldview of people engaged in an intense conflict; it has implications for their national identity, their view of their own society, and their interpretation of history. Thus, for Palestinians to revise their view of Israelis as Western intruders in the Middle East who will eventually leave just as the Crusaders did, or for Israelis to revise their view of Palestinians as implacable enemies committed to the destruction of Israel, raises many troublesome issues about their own past, present, and future. This is one of the reasons images of the enemy are highly resistant to change and contribute to the escalatory and self-perpetuating dynamic of conflict.

Perceptual Processes

Perceptual and cognitive processes play a major role in the escalation and perpetuation of conflict, and create barriers to redefining and resolving the conflict despite changing realities and interests. Two perceptual processes that characterize mutual images of parties in conflict can account for this effect: the formation of mirror images and the resistance of images to contradictory information. When both parties, in mirror-image fashion, perceive the enemy as harboring hostile intentions in the face of their own vulnerability, their interaction produces a self-fulfilling dynamic; under these circumstances, it is difficult to discover common and complementary interests. Further, conflict-based interactions—within and between the parties—inhibit the perception and the occurrence of change in the other, and thus the opportunity to revise the enemy image. These two processes will be discussed in the remainder of this section.

Formation of Mirror Images. Social psychologists writing about U.S.–Soviet relations (Bronfenbrenner 1961 and White 1965) first noted the phenomenon of mirror image formation as a characteristic of many conflict relationships. Both parties tend to develop parallel images of self and other, except with the value reversed; that is, the two parties have similarly positive self-images and similarly negative enemy images. The core content of mirror images is basically captured by the good-bad dimension: Each side sees itself as good and peaceful, arming only for defensive reasons and fully prepared to engage in open give-and-take and compromise. The enemy, by contrast, is seen as evil and hostile, arming for aggressive reasons and responsive only to the language of force.

A typical corollary of the good-bad images in protracted conflicts is the view that the other side's aggressiveness is inherent in its nature: in their ideology (for example, Zionism or PLO nationalism), in their system (for example, capitalist imperialism or communist expansionism), in their religion, or in their national character. On the other hand, if one's own side ever displays aggressiveness, it is entirely reactive and defensive. In the language of attribution theory, the tendency on both sides is to explain the enemy's aggressive behavior in dispositional terms and one's own in situational terms (see Jones and Nisbett 1971). To perceive the enemy's evil action as inherent in its nature is tantamount to demonization and dehumanization of the other, with all of the dangerous consequences thereof. Once a group perceived as threatening one's own welfare is excluded from the human family, almost any action against it—including expulsion, dispossession, torture, rape, genocide, and ethnic cleansing in its various forms—comes to be seen as necessary and justified (see Kelman 1973).

Another common corollary of the good-bad image—one that derives from the virtuous self-image—is the assumption on each side that the enemy knows very well we are not threatening them. Our own basic decency and peacefulness, and the provocation to which we have been subjected, are so obvious to us that they must also be obvious to the other side (see the discussion of naive realism in Ross and Ward 1995). Thus, the assumption is that they see us as we see *ourselves*—when in fact they see us as we see *them*. As we shall see, this feature of the mirror image process contributes significantly to the escalatory dynamic of conflict interaction.

Another, though less common element of the mirror image is the "evil-ruler" image, which White (1965, 1968) has described in the context of U.S.–Soviet relations. A distinction is made between mass and elite levels on the "enemy's" side: The people are basically decent but have been misled, brainwashed, or intimidated by their rulers. By contrast, there is complete harmony between rulers and citizens on "our" side. A related element, often found in mirror images—as, for example, in the Israeli-Palestinian case—is the view that, in contrast to the genuine unity on one's own side, the enemy's unity is artificial and sustained only by its leaders' keeping the conflict alive.

Apart from such generic features of mirror images, which arise from the dynamics of intergroup conflict across the board, mirror images in any given case may reflect the dynamics of the specific conflict. Thus, a central feature of the Israeli-Palestinian conflict over the years has been mutual denial of the other's national identity, accompanied by efforts to delegitimize the other's national movement and claim to nationhood (see Kelman 1978, 1987). Other mirror images that have characterized the Israeli-Palestinian and other intense ethnic conflicts (such as those in Bosnia and Northern Ireland) are

- Mutual fear of national and personal annihilation, anchored in the view that the project of destroying one's group is inherent in and central to the other's ideology
- A mutual sense of victimization by the other side, accompanied by a tendency to assimilate the images of the enemy to the image of the historical enemy and the current experience of victimization to the collective memories of past experiences
- A mutual view of the enemy as a source of the negative components of one's own identity, such as the sense of humiliation and vulnerability

While mirror images are an important and central feature of the dynamics of conflict, the concept requires several qualifications, particularly since it is often taken to imply that conflicts are necessarily symmetrical—an idea vehemently rejected by the parties engaged in conflict. The mirror image concept implies that *certain* symmetries in the parties' reactions arise from the very nature of conflict interaction, and that it is important to understand them because of their role in escalating the conflict. There is no assumption, however, that *all* images of self and enemy are mirror images. In the Israeli-Palestinian conflict, for example, both sides agree that Israel is the more powerful party in this particular conflict (although Israelis point out that their conflict has been not only with the Palestinians but with the entire Arab world). Furthermore, there is no assumption that the images on the two sides are equally inaccurate. Clearly, the mirror image concept implies that there is some distortion, since the two views of reality are diametrical opposites and thus cannot both be completely right. It is also presumed that there is probably some distortion on each side because both sides' perceptions are affected by the conflict dynamics. This does not mean, however, that both sides manifest equal degrees of distortion.

A third qualification is that the mirror image concept does not imply empirical symmetry between the two sides. There is no assumption that the historical experiences or the current situations of the two sides are comparable on all or even the most important dimensions. To take one important dimension as an example, many conflicts are marked by asymmetries in power between the parties, which have significant effects on the parties' perceptions of the conflict (Rouhana and Fiske 1995). Finally, the mirror image concept does not imply moral equivalence in the positions of the two parties. To note the symmetry in the two sides' perceptions of their own moral superiority is not to postulate moral symmetry in their claims or their actions. Thus, for example, one can point to many mirror images in the relationship between Serbs and Muslims in Bosnia and still make the moral judgment that it is the Serbs who are guilty of genocide.

With these qualifications in mind, one can trace the common tendency among parties in conflict to form mirror images to the dynamics of the conflict relationship itself. Since each party is engaged in the conflict and subject to similar forces generated by that engagement, parallelism in some of their images is bound to develop. Parallel images arise out of the motivational and cognitive contexts in which parties in conflict generally operate: Motivationally, each side is concerned with "looking good" when blame for the conflict events is being apportioned; political leaders, therefore, feel a strong need to persuade themselves, their own people, the rest of the world, and future historians that the blame rests with the enemy—that their own cause is just and their own actions have been entirely defensive in nature. Cognitively, each side views the conflict from its own perspective and—painfully aware of its own needs, fears, historical traumas, grievances, suspicions, and political constraints—is convinced that it is acting defensively and with the best intentions. Furthermore, each side assumes that this is so self-evident that it must be equally clear to the enemy; signs of hostility from the enemy must therefore be due to its aggressive intent.

When both sides are motivated to deflect blame from themselves and convinced that their own good intentions are as clear to the other as to themselves, mirror images are formed. Mirror images increase the danger of escalation, as illustrated in the earlier discussion of arms races. They produce a spiraling effect because each side interprets any hostile action by the other as an indication of aggressive intent against which it must defend itself, and its own reactions—whose defensive nature, it assumes, should be obvious to the enemy—are taken as signs of aggressive intent by the other. The effect of mirror images is accentuated insofar as the enemy's ideology or national character is perceived to be inherently aggressive and expansionist, since this essentialist view provides a stable framework for explaining the other's behavior. In addition to their escalatory effect, mirror images tend to make conflicts more intractable because the sharp contrast between the innocent self and the aggressive other makes it difficult to break out of a zero-sum conception of the conflict.

However, the concept of mirror images may be a useful tool in conflict resolution. Under the proper circumstances—such as those that problem-solving workshops try to create—the parties may gradually come to recognize the conflict-induced parallelisms in their views. The first and relatively easy step is to discover that one's own actions are perceived differently by the other side than they are by oneself. This, in turn, can open one up to the possibility that the reverse may be true: that one's perceptions of the other's actions may be different from the other's self-perceptions. Thus, the parties may gain access to each other's perspective and insight into the effects that such two-directional differences in perception can have on the course of the conflict. Such discoveries may encourage the parties to focus on the need for mutual reassurance about each other's intentions and set a de-escalatory process in motion.

Resistance of Images to Contradictory Information. Conflict images are highly resistant to new information that challenges their validity. The persistence of such images inhibits the perception of change and the expectation of future change that might create possibilities for conflict resolution and thus helps to perpetuate the conflict.

A great deal of social-psychological theorizing and research has addressed the general phenomenon of the persistence of attitudes and beliefs in the face of new information that, from an outside point of view, is clearly contradictory—information that should at least call the existing attitudes into question but is somehow neutralized or ignored. This is not to say that attitudes never change; indeed, there is considerable evidence that individuals' and societies' attitudes constantly change—sometimes gradually, sometimes drastically—in response to new events and experiences. But change always faces some resistance: The continuing struggle between forces for stability and forces for change is one of the hallmarks of attitudes. Resistance is motivated in the sense that people tend to hold on to their attitudes because those attitudes perform certain important functions for them. Beyond that, however, resistances are built into the very functioning of attitudes: Since attitudes help shape our experiences and the way new information is organized, they play a role in creating the conditions for their own confirmation and for avoiding disconfirmation. Research has focused on several types of mechanisms that account for resistance to contradictory information: selectivity, consistency, attribution, and the self-fulfilling prophecy.

The concepts of selective exposure, selective perception, and selective recall all point to the fact that our attitudes help determine the kind of information that is available to us. Our political attitudes, for example, determine the organizations we join, the meetings we attend, and the publications we receive. Consequently, we are more likely to be exposed to information that confirms our views than to information that contradicts them. We also tend to seek out confirmatory information because we enjoy it more, trust it more, and find it more useful—for example, to support our view in subsequent discussions. Furthermore, we are more likely to perceive the information to which we are exposed in a way that is congruent with our initial attitudes, because these attitudes create expectations for what we will find and provide a framework for making sense of it. Finally, we are more likely to remember confirmatory information because we have a preexisting framework into which it can be fit and because we are more likely to find it useful. These selection processes also operate in interpersonal and intergroup relations. We are less likely to communicate with people whom we dislike; as a result we have less opportunity to make new observations that might conceivably lead to a revision in our attitudes. Similarly, our initial attitudes—sometimes based on first impressions or group labels—create expectations that affect our subsequent observations and provide a framework for how we perceive the person's behavior and what we recall about it.

Cognitive consistency has received a great deal of attention in experimental social psychology. Among the different models explored in numerous studies, the two most influential ones have been Heider's (1958) theory of cognitive balance and Festinger's (1957) theory of cognitive dissonance. The general assumption of the various consistency models is that inconsistency between different cognitive elements (for example, between feelings and beliefs about an object, between our attitudes and our actions, or between our attitudes and the attitudes of important others) is an uncomfortable psychological state. It creates tension, which we seek to reduce by whatever means are most readily available to restore consistency.

The role of consistency mechanisms in reaction to new information is rather complex. Inconsistent information is often an important instigator of change in attitudes and behavior, provided the information is compelling and challenging and situational forces motivate the person to seek out new information. At other times, however, consistency mechanisms serve to reinforce selective exposure, perception, and recall: People screen out information that is incongruent with their existing attitudes and beliefs and thus maintain cognitive consistency. This is especially likely to happen when the existing attitudes are strongly held and have wide ramifications—as is the case with enemy images.

Attribution theory continues to be a central focus for research on social cognition. This theory addresses the ways in which people explain their own and others' behavior—how they assess the causes of behavior. One of the key distinctions in the field has been between dispositional and situational attributions: The perceived cause of a particular action may be placed in the actor's character or underlying nature, or in situational forces (Jones and Nisbett 1971). When observing the behavior of others, people have a strong tendency to make dispositional attributions—to commit what has been called "the fundamental attribution error" (Ross 1977). On the other hand, when explaining the causes of their own behavior, people are much more likely to make situational attributions, because they are aware of the many pressures and constraints that affect their behavior at any given time and place. As it turns out, however, in both interpersonal and international relations, these attributional tendencies depend on the nature of the actor and the action. When people explain their own behavior or that of friends and allies, they tend to make dispositional attributions for positive acts and situational attributions for negative acts; when they explain the behavior of enemies, they are inclined to do the reverse (Heradstveit 1981). Thus, attribution mechanisms, again, promote confirmation of the original enemy image. Hostile actions are attributed dispositionally and thus provide further evidence of the enemy's inherently aggressive, implacable character. Conciliatory actions are explained away as reactions to situational forces—as tactical maneuvers, responses to external pressure, or temporary adjustments to a position of weakness—and therefore require no revision of the original image.

The concept of the self-fulfilling prophecy refers to the effect of expectations about another person or group on the other's actual behavior. Our expectations are communicated, perhaps subtly and unconsciously, in the way we approach others in the course of interaction. In doing so, we often create conditions that cause others to behave in line with our expectations—to take on the roles in which we have cast them (Weinstein and Deutschberger 1963). For example, a party that enters negotiations with the expectation that the other side will be unyielding may be particularly tough in its own demeanor and present proposals that the other is bound to reject, thus living up to the original expectations and confirming the original attitudes. When the interaction between conflicting parties is characterized by mirror images and mutual expectations of unprovoked hostility, it produces self-fulfilling prophecies that escalate the conflict, as described earlier.

The mechanisms that account for resistance to disconfirming information—selectivity, consistency, attribution, and self-fulfilling prophecy—are particularly powerful in a conflict relationship for several reasons. First, images of the enemy and conflict-related self-images are central aspects of the national consensus. The earlier discussion of the normative processes that operate in a society engaged in an intense conflict pointed to the strong social pressures toward maintaining uniformity of opinion, especially in a crisis atmosphere. These pressures, as we have seen, prevail in both small decision-making groups and the larger society. Softening the image of the enemy breaks the consensus and invites accusations of disloyalty. The militant elements resist a revision of the enemy image because they see it as weakening the national resolve, lowering defenses, and signaling a readiness for hazardous compromise. Their objections may have a broad appeal because of the widely shared notion that the risks of underestimating the enemy's hostility are more dangerous than the risks of overestimating it (and thus underestimating the opportunities for peace); only the former invokes the charge of disloyalty. In sum, the mechanisms of resistance to disconfirming information are reinforced by normative pressures in a conflict situation.

Second, enemy images are especially resistant to disconfirmation because, in a conflict relationship, the opportunities for taking the perspective of the other side are limited, and the capacity for doing so is impaired. In normal social interaction, participants' mutual attitudes often change in response to new information they acquire and/or evaluate by temporarily assuming each other's perspective. However, interaction among parties in conflict— if it occurs at all—is governed by the conflict norms. Under these circumstances, the empathy required for taking the other's perspective is difficult to achieve and is, in fact, frowned upon. As a result, a party's analysis of its enemy's society is dominated by that party's own perspective. In the Arab-Israeli case, for example, the parties tend to overestimate how much each knows about the other's intentions and concerns: Parties' estimates of what the other knows are based on what they themselves know (an important source of the escalatory effect of mirror images, as noted earlier). Other consequences of looking at the other primarily from one's own perspective are

- The inability to differentiate among various strata and segments of the other society and a tendency to categorize it in terms of one's own concerns (for example, pro-PLO versus anti-PLO Palestinians, Zionist versus anti-Zionist Israelis) rather than the society's internal dynamics

- A self-centered view of the other sides' opposition, equating them with supporters of one's own cause (which is bound to lead to disappointment once one discovers that even the dovish opposition elements have not switched sides)

- A self-centered view of the other's ideology that considers the destruction of one's own national existence as the entire meaning and sole purpose of the other side's national movement

These and similar failures to take account of the other's perspective reduce the impact of potentially new information. Lacking the appropriate context, the parties may not notice or adequately appreciate the varieties, changes, and signs of flexibility in the other side's views.

Third, the resistance of enemy images to disconfirmation is magnified by strong beliefs concerning the unchangeability of the enemy. Such beliefs are typically part of the mirror image, which regards the enemy's hostility as inherent in its ideology and character (that is, the mirror image attributes such hostility to dispositional causes). Thus, for many years, both Israelis and Palestinians insisted that there had been no real change in the enemy's position, only tactical maneuvers; many still maintain that view today. One reason for underestimating the amount of change on the other side is that the two parties use different anchors in assessing movement. The side taking a given action measures the amount of change it represents in terms of how far it has moved from its original position; the other side measures it in terms of how close it has come to its own position. Thus, in the Palestinian view, the 1974 decision of the Palestine National Council to accept a "national authority" on any part of Palestine that is liberated represented a major change—one that was bitterly contested and divided the movement, since it was seen as a step toward a two-state solution. Israelis, however, saw no significance in this move because it was still a long way from recognizing Israel and ending the armed struggle. Not only do parties in conflict—starting from different reference points—find it difficult to perceive change in the enemy, but they often believe that there will not and cannot be any change in the enemy's position. They give greater credence to history and formal documents than to the ongoing and evolving political process. They therefore consider it dangerous or even treasonous to propose that the enemy has changed or will change and see no way to exert influence and encourage change other than by force—"the only language the enemy understands." Such a set of beliefs is not easily penetrated by new information suggesting that there has been change in the enemy camp and that further changes are in the offing.

Despite all the reasons why conflict images are particularly resistant to contradictory information, they are not immutable. Social-psychological evidence suggests that they can change, and historical evidence shows that they do change. The challenge for scholars and practitioners of international conflict resolution is to devise the means to overcome their resistance to change.

CONCLUSION

Social-psychological analysis can contribute significantly to the study of international relations by providing some handles for conceptualizing change in the world system and in the relationships among its various components. To be sure, there are powerful forces—historical, geopolitical, structural, and institutional—that lend stability and continuity to the interests of nation-states and their alliances, and hence to the conflicts that result from the defense or advancement of these interests. Indeed, as the preceding section has argued, social-psychological processes contribute in their own way to the resistance to change characteristic of international conflict by entrapping the parties in a pattern of interaction with an escalatory, self-perpetuating dynamic. Nevertheless, despite the forces that continually feed conflicts and keep them alive, international conflict is largely a dynamic phenomenon. The relationships between nations have always been changing, but in recent decades change has become more rapid and all-encompassing. Technological, demographic, economic, and environmental factors have contributed to the creation of new interests, new alliances, new actors, and new institutions at the national, international, and global levels. These changing circumstances represent many possibilities for generating new conflicts—but also for resolving old conflicts.

By focusing on the social-psychological dimensions, one can often gain insight into the causes and impact of change and the ways of promoting change at the level of the national and international systems, precisely because it becomes possible to approach these systemic processes from the perspective of a different level of analysis. The psychological processes by which decision makers and political elites define national interests and frame the issues in conflict, by which publics develop a collective readiness for pursuing either war or peace, and by which both leaders and publics on the two sides in interaction with each other create an atmosphere and discourse conducive to mutual hostility or mutual accommodation illuminate the precise ways in which changes in public policy and state action may be resisted, facilitated, or deliberately induced. The motivations, perceptions, and emotions characterizing the behavior and interaction of individual actors at any given time are, of course, heavily determined by the necessities and opportunities created by events and changes at the macro-level. But analysis of these micro-level processes in turn provides a lever for understanding and predicting when and how change at the macro-level is likely to occur and what kind of change it is likely to be, and for creating the conditions that promote change in the direction of conflict resolution.

Creating these conditions requires changes in the habitual ways of thinking, acting, and interacting in any given conflict and, indeed, in the international system as a whole: promoting changes in collective consciousness that center around a shared vision of a peaceful world; redefining the criteria for group loyalty; counteracting the pressures that make militancy and aggressive posturing the politically "safest" course for decision makers to follow; moving from zero-sum thinking to a win-win approach in negotiation and bargaining; creating structural and psychological commitments to a peaceful, cooperative relationship; breaking the conflict spirals initiated by mirror images; and changing communication patterns to allow new information to challenge old assumptions. Promoting such changes is the task of diplomacy in all its varieties, of public education, and of institutional development. It is certainly not an easy task, but the possibilities for change are always present, given the dynamic character of international conflict.

Conflict resolution efforts must be geared toward discovering the possibilities for change, identifying the conditions for change, and overcoming the resistance to change. Such an approach to conflict resolution calls for best-case analyses and an attitude of strategic optimism (Kelman 1978, 1979)

> not because of an unrealistic denial of malignant trends, but as part of a deliberate strategy to promote change by actively searching for and accentuating whatever realistic possibilities for peaceful resolution of the conflict might be on the horizon. Optimism, in this sense, is part of a strategy designed to create self-fulfilling prophecies of a positive nature, balancing the self-fulfilling prophecies of escalation created by the pessimistic expectations and the worst-case scenarios often favored by more traditional analysts (Kelman 1992a, 89).

The barriers to conflict resolution are strengthened by the escalatory, self-perpetuating dynamic that characterizes the interaction between conflicting parties. To overcome these barriers requires the promotion of a different kind of interaction, one that is capable of reversing this conflict dynamic. At the micro-level, problem-solving workshops and similar approaches to conflict resolution can contribute to this objective by encouraging the parties to penetrate each other's perspective, to differentiate their image of the enemy, to develop a de-escalatory language and ideas for mutual reassurance, and to engage in joint problem solving designed to generate ideas for resolving the conflict that are responsive to the fundamental needs and fears of both sides. At the macro-level, reversal of the conflict dynamic depends on the establishment of a new discourse among the parties, characterized by a shift in emphasis from power politics and threat of coercion to mutual responsiveness, reciprocity, and openness to a new relationship.

REFERENCES

Baldwin, David. 1971. "The Power of Positive Sanctions." *World Politics* 24 (October): 19–38.

Bronfenbrenner, Urie. 1961. "The Mirror Image in Soviet-American Relations: A Social Psychologist's Report." *Journal of Social Issues* 17 (3): 45–56.

Burton, John W. 1969. *Conflict and Communication. The Use of Controlled Communication in International Relations.* London: Macmillan.

———. 1979. *Deviance, Terrorism, and War: The Process of Solving Unsolved Social and Political Problems.* New York: St. Martin's Press.

———. 1984. *Global Conflict: The Domestic Sources of International Crisis.* Brighton, Sussex: Wheatsheaf.

———. 1988. "Conflict Resolution as a Function of Human Needs." In *The Power of Human Needs in World Society,* ed. Roger A. Coate and Jerel A. Rosati. Boulder, Colo.: Lynne Rienner.

Druckman, Daniel, and P. Terrence Hopmann. 1989. "Behavioral Aspects of Negotiations on Mutual Security." In *Behavior, Society, and Nuclear War.* Vol. 1. Edited by Philip E. Tetlock, Jo L. Husbands, Robert Jervis, Paul C. Stern, and Charles Tilly: New York: Oxford University Press.

Farnham, Barbara, ed. 1992. "Special Issue: Prospect Theory and Political Psychology." *Political Psychology* 13 (2): 167–329.

Festinger, Leon. 1957. *A Theory of Cognitive Dissonance.* Stanford, Calif.: Stanford University Press.

Fischhoff, Baruch. 1991. "Nuclear Decisions: Cognitive Limits to the Thinkable." In *Behavior, Society, and Nuclear War.* Vol. 2. Edited by Philip E. Tetlock, Jo L. Husbands, Robert Jervis, Paul C. Stern, and Charles Tilly. New York: Oxford University Press.

Fisher, Roger. 1964. "Fractionating Conflict." In *International Conflict and Behavioral Science,* ed. Roger Fisher. New York: Basic Books.

Fisher, Ronald J. 1983. "Third-Party Consultation as a Method of Intergroup Conflict Resolution: A Review of Studies." *Journal of Conflict Resolution* 27 (2): 301–34.

———. 1989. "Prenegotiation Problem-Solving Discussions: Enhancing the Potential for Successful Negotiations." In *Getting to the Table: The Processes of International Prenegotiation,* ed. Janice Gross Stein. Baltimore: Johns Hopkins University Press.

George, Terry. 1996. "Lost Without War in Northern Ireland." *New York Times,* July 17.

Heider, Fritz. 1958. *The Psychology of Interpersonal Relations.* New York: Wiley.

Heradstveit, Daniel. 1981. *The Arab-Israeli Conflict: Psychological Obstacles to Peace.* 2d ed. Oslo: Universitetsforlaget.

Holsti, Ole R. 1989. "Crisis Decision Making." In *Behavior, Society, and Nuclear War.* Vol. 1. Edited by Philip E. Tetlock, Jo L. Husbands, Robert Jervis, Paul C. Stern, and Charles Tilly. New York: Oxford University Press.

Holt, Robert R., and Brett Silverstein, eds. 1989. "The Image of the Enemy: U.S. Views of the Soviet Union." *Journal of Social Issues* 45 (2): 1–175.

Janis, Irving L. 1982. *Groupthink.* 2d ed. Boston: Houghton Mifflin.

Jones, Edward E., and Richard E. Nisbett. 1971. "The Actor and the Observer: Divergent Perceptions of the Causes of Behavior." In *Attribution: Perceiving the Causes of Behavior,* ed. Edward E. Jones, et al. Morristown, N.J.: General Learning Press.

Kelman, Herbert C. 1961. "Processes of Opinion Change." *Public Opinion Quarterly* 25 (Spring): 57–78.

———. 1969. "Patterns of Personal Involvement in the National System: A Social-Psychological Analysis of Political Legitimacy." In *International Politics and Foreign Policy: A Reader in Research and Theory.* Rev. ed. Edited by James N. Rosenau: New York: Free Press.

———. 1973. "Violence Without Moral Restraint: Reflections on the Dehumanization of Victims and Victimness." *Journal of Social Issues* 29 (4): 25-61.

———. 1978. "Israelis and Palestinians: Psychological Prerequisites for Mutual Acceptance." *International Security* 3 (1): 162–86.

———. 1979. "An Interactional Approach to Conflict Resolution and Its Application to Israeli-Palestinian Relations." *International Interactions* 6 (2): 99–122.

———. 1985. "Overcoming the Psychological Barrier: An Analysis of the Egyptian-Israeli Peace Process." *Negotiation Journal* 1 (3): 213–34.

———. 1986. "Interactive Problem Solving: A Social-Psychological Approach to Conflict Resolution." In *Dialogue toward Interfaith Understanding,* ed. William Klassen.Tantur/Jerusalem: Ecumenical Institute for Theological Research.

———. 1987. "The Political Psychology of the Israeli-Palestinian Conflict: How Can We Overcome the Barriers to a Negotiated Solution?" *Political Psychology* 8 (3): 347–63.

———. 1991. "A Behavioral Science Perspective on the Study of War and Peace." In *Perspectives on Behavioral Science: The Colorado Lectures,* ed. Richard Jessor. Boulder, Colo.: Westview.

———. 1992a. "Informal Mediation by the Scholar/Practitioner." In *Mediation in International Relations: Multiple Approaches to Conflict Management,* ed. Jacob Bercovitch and Jeffrey Z. Rubin. New York: St. Martin's Press.

———. 1992b. "Acknowledging the Other's Nationhood: How to Create a Momentum for the Israeli-Palestinian Negotiations." *Journal of Palestine Studies* 22 (1): 18–38.

———. 1993. "Coalitions Across Conflict Lines: The Interplay of Conflicts Within and Between the Israeli and Palestinian Communities." In *Conflict Between People and Groups,* ed. Stephen Worchel and Jeffry A. Simpson. Chicago: Nelson-Hall.

———. 1996. "Negotiation as Interactive Problem Solving." *International Negotiation: A Journal of Theory and Practice* 1 (1): 99–123.

———. 1997. "Nationalism, Patriotism, and National Identity: Social-Psychological Dimensions." In *Patriotism in the Lives of Individuals and Nations,* ed. Daniel Bar-Tal and Ervin Staub. Chicago: Nelson-Hall.

————, ed. 1965. *International Behavior: A Social-Psychological Analysis.* New York: Holt, Rinehart & Winston.

Kelman, Herbert C., and Alfred H. Bloom. 1973. "Assumptive Frameworks in International Politics." In *Handbook of Political Psychology,* ed. Jeanne Nickell Knutson. San Francisco: Jossey-Bass.

Kelman, Herbert C., and V. Lee Hamilton. 1989. *Crimes of Obedience.* New Haven: Yale University Press.

Kriesberg, Louis. 1981. "Non-Coercive Inducements in U.S.–Soviet Conflicts: Ending the Occupation of Austria and Nuclear Weapons Tests." *Journal of Military and Political Sociology* 9 (Spring): 1–16.

————. 1982. "Non-Coercive Inducements in International Conflict." In *Alternative Methods for International Security,* ed. Carolyn M. Stephenson. Lanham, Md.: University Press of America.

Levy, Jack S. 1992. "Prospect Theory and International Relations: Theoretical Applications and Analytical Problems." *Political Psychology* 13 (2): 283–310.

Osgood, Charles E. 1962. *An Alternative to War or Surrender.* Urbana: University of Illinois Press.

Pruitt, Dean G., and James P. Gahagan. 1974. "Campus Crisis: The Search for Power." In *Perspectives on Social Power,* ed. James T. Tedeschi. Chicago: Aldine.

Ross, Lee. 1977. "The Intuitive Psychologist and His Shortcomings: Distortions in the Attribution Process." In *Advances in Experimental Social Psychology.* Vol. 10. Edited by L. Berkowitz. New York: Academic Press.

Ross, Lee, and Andrew Ward. 1995. "Psychological Barriers to Dispute Resolution." In *Advances in Experimental Social Psychology.* Vol. 27. Edited by Mark P. Zanna. New York: Academic Press.

Rouhana, Nadim N., and Susan T. Fiske. 1995. "Perception of Power, Threat, and Conflict Intensity in Asymmetric Intergroup Conflict." *Journal of Conflict Resolution* 39 (1): 49–81.

Rouhana, Nadim N., and Herbert C. Kelman. 1994. "Promoting Joint Thinking in International Conflicts: An Israeli-Palestinian Continuing Workshop." *Journal of Social Issues* 50 (1): 157–78.

Rubin, Jeffrey Z. 1989. "Some Wise and Mistaken Assumptions about Conflict and Negotiation." *Journal of Social Issues* 45 (2): 195–209.

Rubin, Jeffrey Z., Dean G. Pruitt, and Sung Hee Kim. 1994. *Social Conflict: Escalation, Stalemate, and Settlement.* 2d ed. New York: McGraw-Hill.

Russett, Bruce. 1989. "Democracy, Public Opinion, and Nuclear Weapons." In *Behavior, Society, and Nuclear War.* Vol. 1. Edited by Philip E. Tetlock, Jo L. Husbands, Robert Jervis, Paul C. Stern, and Charles Tilly. New York : Oxford University Press.

Saunders, Harold H. 1988. "The Arab-Israeli Conflict in a Global Perspective." In *Restructuring American Foreign Policy,* ed. John D. Steinbruner. Washington, D.C.: Brookings Institution.

Sherif, Muzafer. 1958. "Superordinate Goals in the Reduction of Intergroup Conflict." *American Journal of Sociology* 63 (4): 349–56.

Staub, Ervin. 1989. *The Roots of Evil: The Origins of Genocide and Other Group Violence.* New York: Cambridge University Press.

Stein, Janice Gross. 1991. "Deterrence and Reassurance." In *Behavior, Society, and Nuclear War.* Vol. 2. Edited by Philip E. Tetlock, Jo L. Husbands, Robert Jervis, Paul C. Stern, and Charles Tilly. New York: Oxford University Press.

Tetlock, Philip E. In press. "Social Psychology and World Politics." In *Handbook of Social Psychology.* 4th ed. Edited by Daniel Gilbert, Susan T. Fiske, and Gardner Lindzey. New York: McGraw-Hill.

Touval, Saadia, and I. William Zartman, eds. 1985. *International Mediation in Theory and Practice.* Boulder, Colo.: Westview.

Weinstein, Eugene A., and Paul Deutschberger. 1963. "Some Dimensions of Altercasting." *Sociometry* 26 (4): 454–66.

White, Ralph K. 1965. "Images in the Context of International Conflict: Soviet Perceptions of the U.S. and the U.S.S.R." In *International Behavior: A Social-Psychological Analysis,* ed. Herbert C. Kelman. New York: Holt, Rinehart & Winston.

———. 1968. *Nobody Wanted War: Misperception in Vietnam and Other Wars.* New York: Doubleday.

———. 1984. *Fearful Warriors: A Psychological Profile of U.S.-Soviet Relations.* New York: Free Press.

Zartman, I. William, and Johannes Aurik. 1991. "Power Strategies in De-Escalation." In *Timing the De-escalation of International Conflicts,* ed. Louis Kriesberg and Stuart J. Thorson. Syracuse, N.Y.: Syracuse University Press.

Zartman, I.William, and Maureen R. Berman, (1982). *The Practical Negotiator.* New Haven: Yale University Press.

7

INTERACTIVE CONFLICT RESOLUTION

Ronald J. Fisher

Interactive conflict resolution (ICR) involves problem-solving discussions between unofficial representatives of groups or states engaged in violent protracted conflict. Since 1965, various academic-based initiatives have sought to increase mutual understanding and encourage movement toward the resolution of many destructive intercommunal and international conflicts. The analysis of the conflict and the development of alternative solutions or directions toward resolution are facilitated by a skilled and impartial team of scholar-practitioners who organize and manage the discussions. Objectives have ranged from simple education in terms of increased understanding and improved attitudes, to shared realizations about the sources and nature of the conflict, to the joint generation of creative solutions that can and have been put into operation (Fisher 1993a, 1996).

This chapter reviews various applications of ICR, from seminal contributions to ongoing initiatives at both the international and intercommunal levels. Major contributions to a theory of practice are identified before the present state of the field is briefly assessed. The chapter concludes with challenges that ICR must meet to attain its unique potential in contributing to the resolution of international conflict.

While ICR is a multidisciplinary effort, the method is rooted primarily in social-psychological assumptions about international disputes. Conflict is generally seen to be a mix of objective interests and subjective factors, the latter having greater influence as the conflict intensifies. Thus subjective aspects—such as misperceptions, negative attitudes, unwitting commitments, and miscommunication—need to be addressed, as must the relationship issues—such as mistrust, win-lose orientations, and unrecognized basic needs—to which they contribute. Although ICR is initially directed toward changes in individuals, it recognizes that these changes must be transferred and integrated into policy formulation and decision making at the political level for conflict de-escalation to be influenced. It is therefore assumed that conflict systems, like social systems, comprise interacting individuals and that influence processes move both ways. Thus, the more influential and representative the individual participants in ICR workshops are, the greater the potential impact on the political process and policymaking.

Some workshops are primarily educational; that is, they focus on changing individual perceptions, attitudes, and ideas. Others are more political, concerned with transferring these changes via influential participants to decision-making bodies. Many interventions combine both these aspects (Kelman 1986). Foltz (1977) has distinguished process-promoting workshops from problem-solving ones: The former provide participants with new knowledge and abilities that they can take back so they can function more effectively in their conflict-torn societies; the latter facilitate a better understanding of the differences between the parties, a distinction between negotiable and immutable issues, and an examination of creative and even radical solutions.

These distinctions relate to an understanding of the major functions that workshops can perform in the wider conflict resolution process:

- *Prenegotiation*, in which the workshop helps the parties examine the barriers to negotiation, including relationship issues, creating conditions conducive to negotiations, and developing actions to promote negotiations (Fisher 1989; Kelman 1982)
- *Paranegotiation*, in which a continuing workshop provides a parallel track to official negotiations where unofficial representatives can examine obstacles in the negotiating process, formulate shared principles underlying negotiations, analyze particularly thorny issues, and consider future topics that are not yet on the table (Kelman 1993b)
- *Peacebuilding*, in which workshop interactions among antagonists occur at different levels in various sectors (e.g., education, business, media) and focus on ways of de-escalating the conflict and planning joint

activities to improve the relationship (Fisher 1993b). In a postsettlement phase, ICR can continue to play a peacebuilding role by helping to reestablish cooperation among past enemies so that reconciliation and reconstruction go hand in hand.

ICR assumes that dialogue and problem solving between adversaries are most likely to be brought about through the efforts of a trusted, knowledgeable, skilled intermediary. Thus, one variant is termed "third-party consultation" to emphasize the facilitative and diagnostic role of the scholar-practitioners who manage the sessions (Fisher 1972, 1990). The third party improves communication using a range of human relations skills and encourages analysis of the conflict by providing a variety of relevant concepts from the study of conflict. The participants are thereby invited to engage in a common analysis of their situation before exploring the joint development of creative ideas for its improvement. The method further assumes that only authentic and effective face-to-face interaction among the parties themselves can lead to the de-escalation and resolution of destructive, intractable conflicts. The ultimate goals are deep understanding, mutual recognition and respect, and jointly acceptable and sustainable solutions— in sum, an improved relationship between the parties.

ICR is an unofficial approach that is not seen as a replacement for official diplomatic and governmental activities, but as a complement to them. The rationale is to provide an informal, low-risk, noncommittal, and neutral forum in which unofficial representatives of the parties may engage in exploratory analysis and creative problem solving, free from the usual constraints of official policy and public scrutiny. But ICR is more than simple citizen-to-citizen contact, since the delegates are often selected with the approval of official decision makers and are chosen in part for their ability to influence policy.

As a form of third-party intervention, ICR or "consultation" needs to be distinguished from other intermediary activities, including conciliation, mediation, and arbitration and adjudication (Fisher and Keashly 1988). Whereas the more established methods generally accept an adversarial and/ or judgmental approach to settling the substantive issues in a conflict, ICR (and some forms of conciliation and mediation) attempt to induce an analytical and collaborative reorientation of the parties, which may ultimately transform their relationship in the conflict—and thus the conflict itself— into a more positive social reality. ICR may thus play a useful premediation role by reducing the negative effects of subjective factors so that other third parties can more effectively address the substantive elements of the conflict (Fisher and Keashly 1991).

ICR's focus has generally been on complex and destructive conflicts between communal identity groups defined in racial, religious, cultural, linguistic, or ethnic terms. Azar (1983, 1990) coined the term "protracted social conflict" to denote seemingly irresolvable and hostile interactions with sporadic outbreaks of violence that are based on communal and ethnic cleavages rooted in the denial of fundamental human needs for individual and social development. These needs include security; the establishment, maintenance, and recognition of a distinct identity; effective participation in social and political decision making; and the promotion of distributive justice to overcome inequality. In a similar vein, Burton (1987) uses the term "deep-rooted conflict" to refer to differences that are based not on interests that can be negotiated, but on underlying needs that cannot be compromised—needs that, paradoxically, are not in short supply. Such conflicts tend to occur in situations of profound and pervasive social inequality, where needs for identity and participation are frustrated; and they are most violent where communities or nations resort to extraordinary means to mobilize their members in the cause of preserving their culture and values. Thus, the primary foci for ICR scholar-practitioners have been on the world's seemingly intractable conflicts, from Cyprus to Northern Ireland, from Sri Lanka to Afghanistan, from Lebanon to the Horn of Africa, and from Cambodia to the Middle East.

REVIEW OF APPLICATIONS

Initiatives in Interactive Conflict Resolution

The creation of ICR is attributed to the work of John Burton and his colleagues at University College London, who arranged informal but officially sanctioned discussions with high-level representatives of factions and countries engaged in violent conflict. Burton, an Australian diplomat turned academic, was able to use his connections and practical understanding of diplomacy in combination with his nontraditional approach to international relations to create a unique methodology for conflict-resolution activities (Burton 1969). Burton's idea of a third-party panel of social scientists established the use of skilled and impartial facilitators who controlled communication to foster an open and supportive climate for the representatives to examine their perceptions, analyze the conflict, and create innovative directions toward resolution. The rationale came partly from an understanding of small-group dynamics provided by colleagues like Anthony de Reuck (1974), who had experience in facilitating multinational problem-solving discussions.

The escalating conflict among Indonesia, Malaysia, and Singapore, which defied continued attempts at mediation in the early to mid-1960s, was the Burton group's first focus. Delegates from the three countries were invited to London for a five-day workshop, followed by a series of briefer sessions over the next six months. After some initial confusion, the workshop moved toward correcting mutual misperceptions, redefining the conflict, reassessing the costs of the parties' objectives, and envisaging new policy options (de Reuck 1974). The parties re-established diplomatic relations and developed the overall understanding and framework that was represented in the 1966 Manila Peace Agreement.

On the crest of this success, Burton and his colleagues moved on to address the deadlocked intercommunal conflict in the Republic of Cyprus. Representatives from the Greek and Turkish Cypriot communities met in London with Burton's group for five days of discussions in late 1966 at a point when UN mediation had broken down. The two sides shared their perceptions of the political situation on the island, considered new directions for resolving the conflict, and developed fresh insights. As judged by follow-up contacts, these discussions in part led to a resumption of the UN-sponsored negotiations (Mitchell 1981). Thus, the London group saw both initiatives having an important influence on international conflict resolution.

Also during the mid-1960s, American social psychologist Leonard Doob sought to explore whether the analytical basis of modern social science had anything to offer the world of practice in terms of addressing destructive conflicts. Doob and his colleagues organized workshops, based largely on human-relations training models (see Shaffer and Galinsky 1974), which brought together influential members of parties engaged in violent conflicts, specifically in the Horn of Africa and Northern Ireland (Doob 1970; Doob and Foltz 1973). A two-week workshop with participants from Ethiopia, Somalia, and Kenya held in 1969 met with some success in applying sensitivity training and other workshop methods, but was unable to achieve a consensus or have any apparent influence on the conflict. A ten-day workshop with Catholic and Protestant community leaders from Belfast in 1971 employed the Tavistock method and other exercises, and had considerable impact on the participants in both positive and negative terms. In fact, an acrimonious conflict emerged among members of the organizing team over the workshop's appropriateness and outcomes, covering the workshop with a cloud of confusion and concern to this day. Doob attempted to intervene in the Cyprus conflict, but his plans for a workshop were cut short by an Athens-sponsored coup and a military intervention by Turkey in 1974, and a series of discussions in 1985 was terminated by authorities of one of the Cypriot communities (Doob 1974, 1987).

Herbert Kelman, an American social psychologist with interests in international relations, was a member of the third-party panel for Burton's Cyprus workshop. Kelman's encounter with Burton's work led him to conclude that this social-psychological approach to international conflict resolution was potentially useful (Kelman 1993b). His initial comparison of the Burton and Doob approaches helped prepare the way for a 1971 prototype workshop, codesigned with Canadian social psychologist Stephen Cohen, on the Israeli-Palestinian conflict (Kelman 1972; Cohen et al. 1977). Subsequently, Kelman and his colleagues have organized more than thirty workshops with Palestinian and Israeli representatives, contributing positively to the political discourse between the two communities and to the peace process in general (Kelman 1979, 1986, 1993a, 1995). The typical workshop begins with separate preworkshop sessions with each side to allow the third party to understand each side's concerns and build familiarity within each national team. The workshop proper starts with participants expressing their views of the conflict and their central concerns (needs and fears) about it, followed by an exploration of the overall shape of a mutually acceptable solution. The workshop ends with a discussion of the constraints hindering movement toward resolution and how to overcome them. Over time, Kelman's workshops have been tailored to ongoing relations in the region and have involved representatives of increasing political influence.

Edward Azar, an American political scientist of Lebanese origin, was a third-party member in one of Kelman's early workshops and later teamed up with Cohen to make further contributions to peace in the Middle East. Azar and Cohen served as facilitators for discussions beginning in 1976 and culminating in a two-day problem-solving workshop in 1979 with Egyptian and Israeli intellectuals that covered a number of the conflict's central issues. Combined with in-depth interviews with decision makers, this experience enabled Cohen and Azar (1981) to provide a social-psychological description and evaluation of the peace process that culminated in the peace treaty between Israel and Egypt. In 1985, Azar invited Burton to help launch the Center for International Development and Conflict Management at the University of Maryland. In addition to studies in conflict and development, the center began specializing in a conflict-resolution method Azar termed "problem-solving forums."

Azar drew on the work of Burton, Doob, Kelman, and others in developing the forum model, which he saw as the most appropriate applied intervention for addressing protracted social conflicts (Azar 1990). The forum uses a panel of third-party facilitators to help create an analytical, nonadversarial environment in which representatives of the groups in conflict can discuss identity-related needs and explore the alternatives necessary to achieve a breakthrough from intractable conflict to peace. Azar, Burton, and their colleagues carried out a series of problem-solving forums during the early to mid-1980s, focusing on three apparently intractable conflicts:

- Three forums addressed the conflict between Argentina and the United Kingdom over the Falkland/Malvinas Islands, which led to military confrontation in 1982. Influential representatives, including parliamentarians from both countries, searched for directions toward mutually agreeable definitions of sovereignty over the disputed islands. The meetings produced a set of principles that balanced the question of sovereignty with that of self-determination. The principles served as a basis for negotiations, carrying over into official meetings between the parties, but without any apparent effects (Little and Mitchell 1989).

- Two forums were held on the civil war in Lebanon, bringing together representatives nominated by the country's various religious and political leaders. The first meeting produced a consensual agreement on an integrated and independent Lebanon, while the second worked on principles for a united country and established an ongoing network that produced the 1988 National Covenant Document that was integrated into the 1989 Taif Accords bringing peace to Lebanon.

- In 1985, a forum on the conflict in Sri Lanka brought together Tamil and Sinhalese influentials. This session resulted in joint realizations about the conflict and a commitment to develop tension-reducing measures to address it. The forum was followed by two briefer seminars in 1986 and 1987.

Unfortunately, Azar had to discontinue his work in the late 1980s because of ill health. Following his untimely death in 1991, no further forums have been held, although the center continues to sponsor other activities in international conflict resolution.

Continuing Contributions to Theory and Practice

Many individuals have contributed to ICR in theory and practice. Since it is impossible to acknowledge them all in this brief overview, the following sections highlight the work of a select number of scholar-practitioners who have contributed to both.

Christopher Mitchell, a British specialist on international relations, was an original member of Burton's group and served as a panel member in the Cyprus meetings (Mitchell 1966). Along with A. J. R. Groom, de Reuck, and others, he helped Burton found the Centre for the Analysis of Conflict (CAC) in London in 1965, which proposed to conduct research on conflict and offer reconciliation services to various parties. Mitchell (1973) was a staunch defender of the new methodology, countering a slate of criticisms raised by Yalem (1971). Mitchell served as a primary field worker, attempting to arrange further problem-solving sessions on various destructive international conflicts, and was a panel member in a workshop involving trade unionists from Northern Ireland, of which no report has been published. In 1978, the CAC moved to the University of Kent at Canterbury with Groom and Burton as codirectors. Following Burton's departure for the United States in 1982, the CAC continued as a forum for research, engaging in no direct problem-solving applications until a recent, successful project on the Moldova conflict, whose results have yet to be published. In 1989, the CAC was reorganized as the Centre for Conflict Analysis to recognize the incorporation of a new generation of scholars whose interests focus on international mediation as well as problem solving.

On the basis of his varied experiences, Mitchell (1981) argues for a subjective approach to understanding conflict, which underlies the need for a shift from traditional, often ineffective third-party methods to that of problem solving. He proposes the development of "third-party consultancy" as a means of providing professional services to parties in a voluntary and nondirective manner so that all sides can gain through innovative solutions. Mitchell (1981) counters criticisms that the problem-solving approach is impractical, ineffective, and untestable, and maintains that there are no a priori reasons to preclude its further development. However, he does conclude that strenuous efforts will be required to convince decision makers and policy specialists of the new methodology's potential.

In the early 1980s, Mitchell took part in the initiatives organized by Azar and Burton at the University of Maryland and coedited a collection of papers on the Falklands/Malvinas conflict in the wake of the Maryland workshops (Little and Mitchell 1989). In the late 1980s, he joined Burton at George Mason University, where both contributed to the continuing development of the Institute for Conflict Analysis and Resolution (ICAR), initially established in 1981 by the late Bryant Wedge and his colleagues to train professional practitioners in conflict management (Wedge and Sandole 1982). As a result, ICAR has become the major center for promulgating the problem-solving approach to complex and persistent conflicts in a multifaceted fashion, offering a master's degree and the world's first interdisciplinary doctoral program in conflict analysis and resolution. An innovative aspect of ICAR is its Applied Theory and Practice Program (formerly the Conflict Clinic, founded by the late James Laue), which engages in various interventions and involves graduate students through working groups and practicums. Internationally, ICAR has worked on several protracted conflicts, including that in Northern Ireland and Spain's Basque conflict, although no reports have been published.

Herbert Kelman has used his academic base at Harvard's Center for International Affairs to make a continuing contribution to the peace process in the Israeli-Palestinian conflict. Kelman's workshops have involved influentials of increasingly greater stature over more than twenty years, beginning with graduate students and young professionals, and moving to academics, parliamentarians, former government officials, policy advisors, and political activists. Kelman (1979) casts this work as a program of action research that integrates efforts at conflict analysis and resolution with opportunities to learn about the Middle East conflict and international conflict in general. Action research was created in part by Kurt Lewin, a founder of applied social psychology, and typically involves a social scientist collaborating with a group of people experiencing a problem (such as a conflict) to collect data on the problem, develop interventions to deal with the problem, and evaluate the interventions through further data collection (Fisher 1982). In Kelman's program, workshops are the unique action component (intervention), but they are combined with various other activities, including contacting and interviewing decision makers and policy advisors, training third-party panel members, and developing detailed policy analyses of the conflict. Kelman (1986) emphasizes how the action component requires a research context to provide rationale and legitimacy, and how the research aspect requires action to learn about and contribute to the resolution of the conflict.

Over time, Kelman (1978, 1982) came to see his work as helping to identify the psychological prerequisites for mutual acceptance of the parties in a conflict and to create the conditions for negotiations. Thus, the workshop approach became primarily a prenegotiation process between Palestinians and Israelis that helped create the psychological and political conditions for negotiations, particularly a mutual recognition of each other's identity and rights and a differentiated rather than monolithic image of the adversary (Kelman 1987). Kelman (1991) has consistently maintained that problem-solving workshops are not a substitute for official negotiations but can help prepare the way for, supplement, and feed into negotiations by helping to create an atmosphere of mutual reassurance and giving parties an opportunity to explore elements of a solution that can be fed into the formal negotiation process.

One unique aspect of Kelman's contributions is an ongoing series of policy analyses of the Israeli-Palestinian conflict based on his workshop and related experiences. He has articulated the psychological prerequisites for mutual acceptance, portrayed prenegotiation as a series of successive approximations toward mutual reassurance, and identified ways of overcoming barriers to a negotiated solution (Kelman 1978, 1982, 1987). In this way, he has provided a powerful and balanced statement of the directions required to move toward settlement and resolution, which are reflected whenever movement occurs in the Israeli-Palestinian peace process.

In 1990, Kelman and Nadim Rouhana, based at Boston College, initiated a continuing workshop in which the same high-level influentials participate in an ongoing series of sessions tailored to developments in the conflict itself (Kelman 1992; Rouhana and Kelman 1994). Kelman and Rouhana were joined on the third-party panel by Christopher Mitchell and Harold Saunders (the latter now at the Kettering Foundation). The continuing workshop design has the unique potential of developing joint ideas on an iterative basis and building pronegotiation coalitions across the lines of the conflict (Kelman 1993b). The advent of formal peace talks in 1991 required a reformulation of the continuing workshop toward paranegotiation, exploring obstacles to progress and helping create a supportive political climate. The breakthrough of the Norwegian-sponsored back-channel talks of 1993 affirmed many of the principles that Kelman saw as essential for progress in negotiations. The continuing workshop has been superseded by a joint working group that meets regularly with third-party facilitation to explore particularly difficult political issues in preparation for the final-status negotiations (Kelman 1995). A number of the negotiators and advisors on both sides in both the formal talks and the back-channel meetings have participated in Kelman's workshops. Their participation is just one tangible indicator of how the work has helped build a network of influentials who have contributed to a constructive political dialogue and to the emerging conditions for peace in the Middle East.

Recently, Kelman and his associates formalized their longtime working group as the Program in International Conflict Analysis and Resolution

(PICAR) at Harvard University, which is devoted to understanding protracted intergroup conflict and the processes for resolving it. In particular, PICAR works on developing interactive problem-solving approaches; the Israeli-Palestinian conflict is its primary focus. Other efforts have centered on Northern Ireland, racially diverse communities in the United States, and indigenous communities in Canada.

This chapter's author has also made a continuing contribution to ICR over the years by developing the approach of "third-party consultation," a term coined by Richard Walton (1969) to describe interpersonal "peacemaking" among corporate executives. An initial review (Fisher 1972) drew on the work of Burton (1969) and Doob (1970) but was also informed by the intergroup methodology of Blake, Shepard, and Mouton (1964). A later review focused on intergroup interventions in a number of spheres, including organizational, community, and international (Fisher 1983). This assessment identified limitations in both guiding theory and evaluative research, and therefore cautioned against premature conclusions of effectiveness. A review focusing exclusively on intercommunal and international interventions introduced the broader concept of interactive conflict resolution and cautioned that the field needs to address a number of critical issues for its continued development (Fisher 1993a). This author's comprehensive treatment of ICR provides an overview of its history, its current expressions, and its potential as a major method of conflict analysis and resolution (Fisher 1996).

The initial focus of this work was on intergroup conflict in community settings (Fisher 1976; Fisher and White 1976a, 1976b). Moving to the international level, a pilot workshop was organized in 1976, bringing together representatives of the Indian and Pakistani communities in Canada to discuss the conflict between their two countries. The workshop resulted in more positive—and more complex—intergroup attitudes among participants and provided an analysis of the conflict's major issues. Content analyses of the tape-recorded discussions documented the problem-solving process and the facilitative role of the third-party consultants (Fisher 1980). In 1984, the domain of international conflict resolution in Canada acquired an institutional base with the establishment of the Canadian Institute for International Peace and Security (CIIPS), which organized a series of seminars focusing on the protracted conflict on Cyprus (LaFreniere and Mitchell 1990; Salem 1992).

During 1989–91, a follow-up project was organized, using conflict analysis workshops to bring together influential Greek and Turkish Cypriots. The first event in 1990 included Turkish and Greek Cypriots living in Canada who maintained close ties with Cyprus and in some cases had connections with decision makers on the island. The session engendered intense dialogue, with some new realizations on both sides and some consensus on the nature of a renewed relationship to help resolve the conflict (Fisher 1991). A second, four-day, workshop was held in England in 1991, bringing together influential unofficial representatives from the two communities on the island. The agenda covered the underlying fears and needs of the two communities, the assurances and acknowledgments required to address them, the principles and qualities of a renewed relationship, potential peacebuilding activities, and ways of overcoming the barriers to them (Fisher 1992). The agenda was influenced by the work of Herbert Kelman, who was a member of the third-party panels, along with Fisher, Mitchell, Groom, and Brian Mandell. Evaluations indicating high levels of satisfaction and usefulness were reported to the leadership of the two communities. Also, participants subsequently were able to undertake a number of concrete peacebuilding activities, including bicommunal art exhibits, cross-community visits by business leaders, and creation of a joint committee to foster intercommunal contact.

CIIPS was abolished in 1992, but two workshops were held on the island in 1993 with alternate funding and the assistance of the UN peacekeeping force. These workshops brought together influential specialists in education from the two communities to focus on their field as a potential confidence-building activity. Following an analysis of issues, fears, and needs, the participants discussed the role of education in sustaining the conflict and its possible role as a peacebuilding mechanism for de-escalating the conflict and rebuilding the intercommunal relationship. Joining the two third-party panels were Louise Diamond, Loraleigh Keashly, Christopher Mitchell, and Jay Rothman. Subsequently, two bicommunal planning meetings were held, in which workshop graduates formed mixed task forces to develop and implement specific projects (Fisher 1994). These efforts were frustrated by an intense media campaign by Greek Cypriot nationalists against all forms of intercommunal interaction, particularly a North American-based training program in conflict resolution. This attack was ultimately countered by both official and unofficial efforts, and the peacebuilding movement emerged stronger than before. Unfortunately, funding for further conflict analysis workshops has not been forthcoming; however, follow-up interviews have been conducted with all participants.

Most of the primary contributors to ICR are academics who have developed their own interests in unofficial diplomacy. Saunders is one of a small number of diplomats, along with John McDonald and Joseph Montville, who have moved in the other direction, from official diplomatic work to unofficial conflict resolution efforts. Saunders served on the National Security Council in the White House and then in various roles with the State Department. He was involved in the Kissinger shuttle diplomacy efforts in the Middle East and in the Carter mediation team that brought about the Camp David accords and the Egyptian-Israeli peace treaty. On the unofficial side, Saunders was on the third-party panel in an early 1980s workshop involving Egyptians, Israelis, and Palestinians organized by the American Psychiatric Association (Julius 1991; Montville 1987). However, Saunders made his most extensive contributions through his role in the Dartmouth Conference, sponsored in the United States by the Kettering Foundation, and in the Soviet Union by the Soviet Peace Committee and the Institute of USA/Canada Affairs.

Since 1960, the Dartmouth Conference has annually invited Soviet (now Russian) and U.S. influentials, primarily foreign policy specialists, to an unofficial, policy-relevant, citizen-to-citizen dialogue on relations between the two countries (Saunders 1991; Stewart 1987). In 1981, two task forces were set up, one on arms control and one on regional conflicts, which Saunders was asked to co-chair along with a Soviet counterpart (Chufrin and Saunders 1993; Saunders 1991). Over the course of more than ten years and twenty biannual meetings, the task force analyzed and developed a conceptual framework for addressing difficult regional situations—Afghanistan, the Middle East, Central America—and shared its insights with official decision makers. Discussions also focused on the overall relationship between the superpowers as reflected in their interaction over regional conflicts. Analyses of interests were used to probe the motivations behind each side's actions and to understand more deeply how each side viewed the other. In the late 1980s, a number of the Soviet participants served as policy advisors to Gorbachev, and many of the principles and approaches articulated in the Soviet leader's "new political thinking" had part of their genesis in the Dartmouth discussions (Chufrin and Saunders 1993). Saunders and his colleagues attribute part of the success of the Dartmouth task force to the mutual ownership of the process, including the co-chairing of sessions as a balanced third party.

Saunders, as director of international affairs at the Kettering Foundation, is now applying the process to other conflicts. He and colleague Randa Slim are organizing a series of dialogue sessions with representatives of the factions involved in the Tajikistan conflict (Saunders and Slim 1994; Slim

1995). In these sessions, a third-party team of three Americans is joined by three Russian colleagues who are also graduates of the Dartmouth experience. The dialogue was initiated in 1993, bringing together representatives of the various factions and regions, and has continued meeting about every two months. Representation is roughly divided between government supporters and members of the opposition. When formal negotiations were started in 1994 under UN auspices, some dialogue participants became formal delegates. According to Saunders and Slim (1994), the dialogue process made a number of useful contributions to the initiation of negotiations and then turned its attention to future concerns. Most recently, the dialogue developed a memorandum on national reconciliation in Tajikistan and has worked hard to adapt to the country's changing political conditions (Slim 1995). It is clear that this work is at the cutting edge of developments in ICR.

Intercommunal Dialogues

Many applications of ICR deal not with highly influential representatives but simply with interested members of the groups or individual citizens of the countries involved, members of their diaspora communities in other countries, or others associated with their cause. These interventions are generally concerned not so much with directly influencing policy processes as with instituting dialogue and increasing understanding among the wider publics, which may eventually affect policy.

Given the significance of the Middle East conflict and ICR's development primarily in the United States, it is not surprising that a number of interventions pertain to the Arab-Israeli conflict and have often involved Jewish Americans as organizers and/or facilitators. Illustrations of dialogue projects focusing on this conflict will be briefly described before various other examples are considered. The sampling of the field's diversity provided here is illustrative rather than representative, since many dialogue interventions are likely to go unreported.

An early example of applying sensitivity training supplemented by other exercises in a mixed group of Israeli Jews and Arabs is provided by Lakin, Lomranz, and Lieberman (1969). The objectives of improving communication and reducing intergroup suspicion were assessed with a variety of techniques, which generally indicated mildly positive outcomes. A number of problem-solving workshops bringing together Arabs and Jews living in Israel have been carried out by Levi and Benjamin (1976) following a systematic and iterative task model of conflict resolution. Although many "mine fields" must be dealt with in the process, participants generally make progress and in one workshop agreed on a mutually acceptable peace plan (Benjamin and Levi 1979). More recently, based on his innovative work in prenegotiation, Rothman (1991, 1993) implemented a problem-solving intervention, bringing together Jews and Arabs living in Jerusalem to explore and promote functional cooperation between the two communities in such areas as economic development, education, and safety. Facilitated seminars were used to engage participants in a joint analysis of the problems and to produce cooperative solutions and recommendations. Participants from the two groups developed implementation plans and co-authored policy papers.

In the United States, a number of dialogue sessions have been organized between Jewish and Arab Americans who identify with the conflict in the Middle East. Reena Bernards has coordinated a dialogue project bringing together American Jewish and Palestinian women in positions of leadership who represent mainstream organizations in their respective communities. Reports on three workshops held during 1989–91 indicate a challenging and useful process in which the two groups explored the major issues in the Israel-Palestinian conflict, identified areas of agreement and disagreement, and created options for the future of the region. A working relationship between the groups was established, proposals for separate and joint actions to promote peace were developed, and a joint coordinating committee was formed to oversee activities, including two joint trips to Israel and the occupied territories. In a similar vein, a team from Kelman's program at Harvard facilitated a series of meetings involving a mixed Arab-Israeli political group (Hicks et al. 1995). A variety of difficult issues was discussed, and the participants came to realize the basic hopes and ultimate fears on both sides, thus building a stronger base for their joint political actions. Hicks and her colleagues also provide a candid analysis of the process within the third-party team, which is valuable for educating others about the challenges of ICR (Hicks et al. 1995).

Louis Kriesberg and Richard Schwartz at Syracuse University have played a central role for more than a decade in helping to organize the Syracuse Area Middle East Dialogue (SAMED). This grassroots initiative, beginning with a core group of Jews, Palestinians, and interested Americans, produced a consensus statement on the Israeli-Palestinian conflict through numerous interactions. Subsequently, SAMED initiated contacts with other dialogue groups, leading to the formation of a national coalition to share support and influence U.S. policy on the Middle East. Schwartz (1989) concludes that grassroots reconciliatory dialogue across adversarial lines can be successful in creating mutual understanding and generating ideas that help counteract the influence of pressure groups working to block concilia-tory policies.

Dialogue and problem-solving forums of various kinds have been applied to a variety of conflicts around the world over the past three decades. Again, many of these meetings, such as those organized by the Society of Friends or the International Peace Academy, are not publicly reported because of the sensitivity of the situation and concern over risks to the participants. In one early example, American sociologist A. Paul Hare describes a private intervention in the escalating political conflict on the island nation of Curaçao (Hare, Carney, and Osview 1977). Following preliminary inter-views with informal leaders on the two sides, Hare identified important issues in economic development and governance, and organized a series of joint seminars in which impartial experts provided their input into mutual problem solving. The impending crisis was defused over time, and develop-ment work was undertaken to address the conflict's underlying issues.

A similar intervention at a different point in a conflict was a workshop on Cambodian reconstruction held in 1991 and chaired by Peter Wallensteen (1991), founder of the Department of Peace and Conflict Re-search at Uppsala University. During a critical period in the peace process, the workshop brought together mostly Cambodian experts and influentials, from both inside Cambodia and abroad, with outside development experts to discuss in a nonpolitical forum the strategies necessary for reconstruc-tion. After exploring various aspirations and images for the country's fu-ture, participants discussed strategies to move from the current reality to the desired future and then worked on proposals in key development sec-tors, such as agriculture, health, and education. The sessions rebuilt trust among participants from various factions and stimulated ongoing dialogue within the Cambodian community.

An intervention focusing on the question of national unity in Canada provides a unique example of a dialogue process that was sponsored by and reported in a national newsmagazine (*Maclean's* 1991). The publisher en-gaged Roger Fisher and two colleagues from his Conflict Management Group to facilitate a weekend workshop to bring together participants from all parts of Canada representing important clusters of conflicting opinions on national issues—the primary one being the separation of the province of Quebec. The consultants facilitated the sharing of concerns and the de-velopment of strategies for action on major problems, using a single-text procedure to guide the participants toward producing a mutually accept-able set of suggestions for the country's future. A follow-up workshop six months later produced a restatement of shared Canadian values and a com-promise formula for renewed federalism (*Maclean's* 1992). The outcomes were communicated to politicians involved in the ongoing process of con-stitutional reform, which unfortunately failed in a national referendum some months later.

The development of a structured dialogue process and its application to various intergroup and international conflicts form part of the work of the Center for Psychology and Social Change affiliated with Harvard Medical School. The center's projects on facilitating dialogue have adapted tech-niques of family systems therapy to promote dialogue between groups with differing ideologies or cultures whose intergroup perceptions are distorted by hostility. One example is a 1987 workshop in which participants from forty countries, primarily Americans, Soviets, and citizens of countries al-lied with each superpower, exchanged and clarified their assumptions about one another (Chasin and Herzig 1988). The exchange resulted in a wide range of useful confrontations and realizations on all sides. Similar tech-niques have been applied in workshop formats to a variety of intergroup cleavages, including whites and Asians in Australia, peace activists and defense analysts in the United States, and more recently, supporters and opponents of abortion rights (Chasin and Herzig 1993).

A final example comes from an application of the decision seminar, de-veloped by Harold Lasswell, to the question of postwar governance in Af-ghanistan (Willard and Norchi 1993). Conducted in 1990, this seminar involved a diverse group of influential Afghan refugees in Pakistan who represented a range of political and other affiliations. The American semi-nar leaders provided input on a number of topics, including the tasks of decision making, basic values and human rights, and an interactive ap-proach to problem solving. The participants applied these concepts to the Afghan situation through seminar-wide and small-group discussions. The seminar provided a unique opportunity for a diverse group of Afghan influentials to engage in mutual inquiry to clarify their common interest in the postwar governance of their country.

CONTRIBUTIONS TO A THEORY OF PRACTICE

ICR is not a body of strategies and activities based on a set of lofty ideals, hidden assumptions, and unspoken principles. It is a field of professional practice with a value base and a conceptual rationale that underlie a social technology of conflict analysis and resolution. A number of contributors have articulated an understanding of this practice, thus adding to a body of theory that is related and somewhat cumulative. However, there has been no comprehensive distillation of the various pieces into a widely accepted model; thus, there is no single statement of the essential principles and techniques of the method. This section serves only to draw attention to the various contributions.

Burton, the field's intellectual pioneer, produced his first practice model of "controlled communication" through inductive theorizing based on the Malaysia-Indonesia and Cyprus workshops (Burton 1969). This model stressed the role of the third party in creating a nonthreatening, analytical atmosphere in which the parties could mutually examine their misperceptions about the conflict and each other, and then jointly explore functional avenues toward resolution. According to Burton (1969), successful re-perception enables the parties to understand the subjective elements of their conflict and thus paves the way for developing broad directions toward resolution and, ultimately, successful negotiations on administrative arrangements to manage the objective differences. The problem-solving aspect of the method was emphasized by de Reuck (1974), who saw parallels between the conflict analysis workshops and other small-group problem-solving sessions. As noted above, Mitchell (1981) provided a broad treatment of the consultant's role, situating the method in the domain of peacemaking and inducing from various applications a positive and yet realistic assessment of its potential. Groom (1986), another member of the initial London group, presented a concise statement of problem solving in international relations that identified many common features of the method and adapted it to the international level.

For his part, Burton continued to grapple with the nature of the approach and its place within the political system. He came to see the basis of "deep-rooted conflict" not so much in the subjective difficulties of dealing with differences as in the pursuit of fundamental human needs that are irrepressible and non-negotiable, such as the needs for identity, security, and distributive justice (e.g., Burton 1985). Concurrently, he articulated a systematic process to analyze deeper motivations and explore the means to address basic needs (Burton 1987). This *Handbook* provides an explicit, although somewhat rigid, statement of the "rules" for facilitated conflict resolution and the professional and ethical obligations of facilitators. A wider context for the method is found in a four-volume series in which

Burton (1990) details the case for problem solving—not just for conflict resolution but for conflict "provention," where the sources of conflict are removed through the promotion of environmental conditions that create collaborative relationships. Thus, Burton (1992) sees conflict resolution not simply as a method for dealing with specific cases, but as a new approach to political decision making that is based on human needs and requires institutions to embody problem solving rather than adversarial procedures. This thinking requires all institutions to constantly reassess the relevance of their assumptions, goals, and procedures, and for conflict resolution to be incorporated into all aspects of their functioning (Burton 1992).

Doob's contributions to a theory of practice are apparently less well known, but are nonetheless significant. He discusses the major components (goals, participants, methods, and so forth) involved in unofficial interventions in destructive conflicts and concludes that the work is useful although highly risky (Doob 1975). Doob (1976) considers the question of evaluating interventions in detail and concludes that the complexities of the process make assessment an immense challenge. In his broader work on the pursuit of peace, Doob (1981) considers the unique role of unofficial diplomacy and notes the potential of workshops as a prelude to negotiations. In a comprehensive treatment of intervention, which includes intermediary activities in situations of two-party conflict, Doob (1993) covers important considerations in the planning, selection, timing, implementation, and evaluation of interventions. Thus, Doob's cumulative contributions have provided useful input for the conceptual basis underlying the social technology of interactive conflict resolution.

Kelman has made major ongoing contributions to the conceptual underpinnings of the problem-solving approach, not the least of which is his promotion of the term "problem-solving workshop" to emphasize its experiential, participatory nature and the process of problem-solving, distinguishing it from human relations training (Kelman 1972). According to this approach, the discussions are facilitated by social scientists serving as special third parties who induce norms of respectful and sustained analysis rather than debate and accusation (Kelman and Cohen 1976, 1979, 1986). In addition, the third party provides observations on the process to improve communication as well as problem-solving and provides theory-based interventions to increase understanding of the conflict and the participants' interactions, which often mirror the conflict. According to Kelman (1979), the power of the method lies in its social-psychological nature, which emphasizes the centrality of social interaction in conflict processes, and the simultaneous

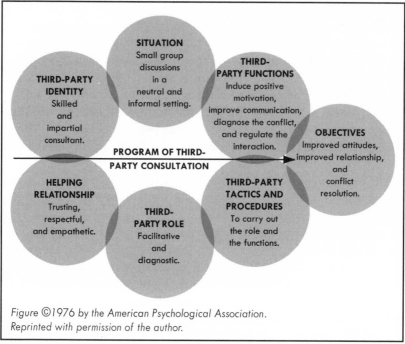

Figure ©1976 by the American Psychological Association.
Reprinted with permission of the author.

Figure 7.1. A Model of Third-Party Consultation. This generic model of third-party consultation specifies the essential components of ICR practice and their integration.

interplay of individual and institutional factors in intergroup conflict. Social-psychological assumptions consider international conflict as occurring between societies rather than states. Thus, conflict must be addressed through face-to-face interactions of the parties, which result in new realizations and, eventually, a transformation in their relationship (Kelman 1992).

Fisher (1972, 1983) was the first to review and integrate a variety of applications and develop a generic model of third-party consultation that specifies the essential components of ICR practice. As shown in Figure 7.1, the model includes the identity and role of the third party, the setting, the core strategies and related tactics, and the objectives of the method (Fisher 1976). In terms of identity, the third party must be a skilled and impartial intermediary who can facilitate productive confrontation and is not seen by either party as biased. At the international level, the intervenor typically is a team of conflict resolution specialists with unofficial status and a national or group identification that is neutral or at least balanced. The team needs skills in human relations, group processes, and problem solving as well as knowledge about conflict processes in the context of the international system. A working knowledge of the conflict in question is essential, although a high degree of substantive knowledge can bias the team toward preconceived solutions, thus inhibiting the problem-solving process. The team's identity lays the basis for a respectful, understanding, and trusting relationship between the third party and the parties to the conflict, which is characterized as a helping or consulting relationship. Given that the approach operates from a base of low power, it is primarily through a combination of expertise and rapport with the parties that the intervenor has influence.

The social structure of the method is expressed in the third-party role and the situation. The role (i.e., appropriate pattern of behavior) of the consultant is primarily facilitative and diagnostic and somewhat parallels that of mediator; yet its emphasis and focus differs in that it is designed to facilitate creative problem solving on the basic relationship, rather than a negotiated settlement on specific issues (Fisher 1983; Fisher and Keashly 1988). The consultant works to diagnose the conflict in direct and open interaction with the representatives of the parties, using substantive knowledge of conflict processes and skills of group facilitation. In contrast, mediators often work around relationship issues such as hatred and mistrust, assuming that an acceptable settlement will ultimately take care of such problems. The situation embodies the essential physical and social arrangements in which the consultant arranges the problem-solving discussions, typically following a workshop format. The informal meetings are usually held in secluded yet accessible locations on neutral territory. The agendas for the group sessions themselves must be flexible and yet directed at key aspects of the conflict. The rationale for the role and situation is to enable the parties to focus directly on the nature of their conflict, mutually understand its deeper elements, and jointly search for ways to de-escalate and resolve it.

The core strategies of the method are captured in the four functions of (a) inducing mutual positive motivation for problem solving, (b) improving the openness and accuracy of communication, (c) diagnosing the issues and processes of the conflict, and (d) regulating the interaction through the sequence of joint problem solving. Of course, these strategies must be operationalized through specific behaviors, referred to as tactics and procedures, which the third party implements when appropriate. Motivation, for example, can be increased by emphasizing the costs of nonresolution, communication is aided by skills such as paraphrasing or empathy, diagnosis is induced by drawing concepts from conflict theory into the discussions, and regulation is assisted by balancing the time allotted to the parties for discussion and moving problem solving from differentiation to integration when appropriate. Procedures refer to broader, structured activities in which participants engage in order to increase mutual understanding or joint problem solving. For example, to induce greater motivation and provide direction, the conflict's two sides might be asked to independently develop their images of an ideal future relationship, which are then shared and discussed.

All previous components of the model are directed toward a set of objectives, the priority of which varies with different interventions. At a minimum, the third party looks for positive changes in attitudes among the participants, in the sense that they now have a more realistic (i.e., accurate and complex) and favorable predisposition toward the other side. Concurrently, the orientation of participants toward the interparty relationship should shift from adversarial and destructive to cooperative and constructive, and the potential for these changes should be transferred to the relationship itself. Finally, the intervention should produce innovative proposals for peacebuilding or conflict resolution that have been jointly created and are mutually supported.

The critical issue facing ICR, however, is whether any of these changes, assuming they occur, can be transferred back to the political decision-making venues of the parties. No clearly articulated model of transfer exists, and only impressionistic evidence for such effects can be found (Fisher 1996). Nonetheless, the model depicted in Figure 7.1 has guided practice and been evaluated in terms of interaction process, participant outcomes, and unique effects on attitudinal and relationship variables in comparison to mediation (e.g., Fisher 1980, 1990; Fisher and White 1976a; Keashly, Fisher, and Grant 1993).

A different, yet related, model describes needed preparation, nature of the interaction, identity of participants, competency and role of the facilitators, and manner of follow-up (Azar 1990). Rothman, one of Azar's student associates, has gone on to produce groundbreaking work in the area of prenegotiation, developing a systematic model based on the problem-solving approach that includes the stages of framing the issues, inventing integrative options, and structuring the process and substance of negotiations (Rothman 1992). The model has been used for training diplomats and complements a wider framework for moving ethnic conflict from confrontation to cooperation through dialogue and problem solving, illustrated by its application to conflicts in the Middle East.

Based on his Dartmouth experience, Saunders has come to emphasize the concept of relationship for understanding and improving the international system and has articulated a framework for public, intercommunal problem solving (Saunders 1992). Building on this framework, Chufrin and Saunders (1993) describe the Dartmouth work in terms of a "public peace process" consisting of five stages whereby adversaries can analyze their relationship and develop new ways of thinking and acting together. Saunders's work is compatible with previous thinking about unofficial diplomacy (e.g., Berman and Johnson 1977) and in particular with Joseph Montville's (1987) concept of Track Two diplomacy, which denotes unofficial, informal interaction directed toward conflict resolution among members of adversarial groups or nations.

John McDonald has been a primary contributor to Track Two thinking (e.g., McDonald and Bendahmane 1987). After initially expanding the distinction to five tracks, he collaborated with Louise Diamond to produce a typology consisting of nine tracks of interaction. In Diamond and McDonald's conceptualization of multitrack diplomacy, track one is official government-to-government interaction, whereas tracks two through nine are various unofficial activities that contribute to international peacebuilding and peacemaking (Diamond and McDonald 1991; McDonald 1991). Track two involves nongovernmental activities by professionals in conflict resolution, roughly corresponding to ICR. Tracks three through nine involve various unofficial actors' (individuals, groups, organizations) interaction in different sectors of international society such as business, research, training and education, peace and environmental activism, religion, and the media and public opinion. This typology highlights the potential power of unofficial processes for transforming situations of destructive conflict into peaceful and cooperative relations.

ASSESSING THE STATE OF THE FIELD

One review of third-party consultation efforts (Fisher 1983) concluded that the realm of practice demonstrates potential, but the underlying theory is rudimentary and supporting research lacks rigor and sophistication. Unfortunately, not much has changed in ICR since the time of that review, although some positive developments have occurred.

With respect to theory, most models are inductive descriptions of core components of practice, with some prescriptive guidelines for interventions. The need to move from this normative theory to a scientific or predictive theory still exists (Hill 1982). Most conceptualizations of the method are static pictures of practice, rather than dynamic representations of the links and flow among components and outcomes. Thus, we still need a comprehensive and systematic theory that captures the static and dynamic complexity of the method and serves as a basis for practice and a guide for research (Fisher 1983).

Each major approach has its strengths and limitations. Burton's innovative thinking was in part based on the experiences of the first workshops and developed alongside his pluralist, systems approach to international relations that called for a paradigm shift in the discipline (Banks 1984; Burton 1968). At the same time, his rules of practice (Burton 1987) can be seen as overly restrictive and lacking adequate explanation (Warfield 1988). Doob's adaptation of group training methods to social intervention in destructive conflicts, while creative, resulted in controversies severe enough to call into question its basic approach (Fisher 1996). Among the pioneers, Kelman's work stands as the most impressive—carefully crafted interventions with a solid conceptual base carried out over the long term with ongoing connections to the complexity of the conflict. Azar's contribution is a succinct statement of the problem-solving method wedded to the characteristics of protracted social conflict. However, in terms of a theory of practice, his model adds little to previous work. In substantive terms, the same can be said of Fisher's model, although it may stand as the most systematic and comprehensive statement of the essence of the method, as articulated by a variety of other contributors. Saunders's approach gains strength because it is consistently sensitive to the processes of policymaking that must be understood and influenced if ICR interventions are to have any utility.

Among the trends in theory development is the growing contribution of scholar-practitioners who are primarily diplomats to descriptions of practice, increasing the richness and validity of ICR theory. In addition to Montville's and McDonald's concepts of Track Two and multitrack diplomacy, Saunders's articulation of a public, intercommunal problem-solving process is most useful. A second trend is the continual broadening of the scope of theory. Burton's own view shifted from one primarily directed to the subjective aspects of particular conflicts to one of seeing conflict analysis and resolution as grounded in a concept of basic human needs and as an essential element in decision making at all levels of society.

Mitchell (1993) considers how problem-solving exercises are useful for developing theory about conflict and its resolution, and identifies different types or domains of theory that are necessary to fully understand problem solving and its outcomes. Micro-level theories posit relations among aspects of the practice (e.g., third-party functions) and their impact on individual perceptions, attitudes, expectations, and so on. Macro-level theories deal with the sources and dynamics of social conflict and are used in workshops to stimulate analysis and help produce useful outputs in terms of proposals, and such. Meso-level theories involve hypotheses about the design and outcomes of workshops in relation to characteristics of the particular conflict in question. As Mitchell notes, the ultimate goal for the ICR community is to discover how ICR can be adapted to the stages of a conflict and coordinated with other methods of conflict management to be maximally effective in particular situations.

Research remains the weakest link in the theory-research-practice loop (Fisher 1983, 1996). Case-study analysis continues to be the predominant form of documentation, and many projects go unpublished. While these descriptions provide a richness for understanding specific interventions, they do not yield a rigorous evaluation of workshop processes or outcomes, nor do they provide a base for meta-analyses. Quantitative measures having adequate psychometric properties in before-and-after or control-group designs would enable inferences about immediate effectiveness to be drawn. Longitudinal field research in the wider community is necessary to assess transfer effects to political decision making where appropriate. Measuring and tracking process variables in relation to both short- and long-term outcomes would allow for the study of theoretical relationships and the development of more scientific models. Thus, the potential for useful research is extremely high.

Unfortunately, as is the case with any third-party intervention, a number of factors render research evaluations of ICR, especially on transfer effects, highly problematic (Keashly and Fisher 1996). Professional intervenors guarantee anonymity and confidentiality and are therefore opposed to follow-up evaluations that might identify participants and place them at risk. In addition, a concern about interfering with the practice side of the work prevents many third parties from collecting systematic research data, either during or after interventions. For intervenors who want to assess outcomes, a daunting array of methodological and practical constraints present themselves. A simple pre/postevaluation of a workshop is a major research effort in itself, and many practitioners do not have the time or money to complete one. Long-term evaluations of transfer effects would require an even larger-scale effort, involving multiple methods (interviews, observation, content analysis) and would in some cases run into restrictions on access to sensitive information. Finally, even if data on political effects were collected, placing and evaluating the contribution of an ICR intervention within the complexity of multiple factors that affect policymaking would be an immense and uncertain task. Clearly, the research side of the enterprise has a long way to go and would face limitations even if more resources were available.

The practice of ICR creates the most satisfaction and optimism. Applications continue to grow in number and variety, addressing an expanding range of complex and intense conflicts. Fisher (1996) reviews more than seventy-five interventions from the past three decades, most of which claim positive results. The method has been successfully operationalized in numerous contexts, has generally had positive effects on participants' perceptions and attitudes, and has resulted in concrete forms of interparty cooperation. In addition, a number of politically focused interventions have apparently had useful inputs and effects on the wider interaction that contributed to conflict de-escalation and resolution. At the same time, the number of documented cases is relatively small, especially when one considers the seriousness of the problem. One important development is the move to continuing workshops, such as in the work of Kelman and Saunders and their colleagues, which can make a sustained contribution to conflict analysis and management by complementing other methods, such as negotiation or mediation. On the whole, ICR can be seen as a promising social technology to help address protracted social conflicts.

CHALLENGES FOR THE FIELD

To fulfill its rich potential, ICR must overcome a number of challenges (Fisher 1993a, 1996). The degree of applicability of this individually focused, small-group method to the complex, power-driven, and relatively anarchical realm of global politics remains a concern. While there may be no a priori reasons for dismissing ICR's applicability, there is a need to develop and test theoretically sophisticated models of linkage to political processes. Kelman's ongoing articulation of workshop outcomes in relation to political processes, and his policy analyses based in large part on workshop interaction, are good examples of movement in this direction.

The question of effectiveness needs to be addressed through the increased operationalization of high-quality demonstration research projects that are systematically and rigorously evaluated and that do not compromise ethics. However, because some funders and decision makers question applicability, they will not provide the resources and support to assess effectiveness in a more sophisticated manner, thus trapping the method in a perplexing Catch-22. In addition, increased applications require skilled professionals with assured support and a secure and flexible institutional base.

Although growing, the pool of available, well-trained talent in ICR is small and needs to be nurtured. Interdisciplinary, doctoral-level training programs for scholar-practitioners, following an apprenticeship model, are required. This training must stress the linkages among theory, research, and practice, and must place a high premium on ethical considerations. While there are a few bright lights, such as George Mason University's ICAR and Harvard's PICAR, adequate training is not generally available; thus, the concern remains that well-meaning but naive practitioners are marketing their services to enthusiastic but uninformed, and ultimately disappointed, clients.

The low funding level is a central concern for ICR, especially in comparison with the money available to more traditional methods of studying and improving international security. Even senior practitioners often have to scramble from one grant to the next, making it virtually impossible to mount continuous programs for maximal effect. Those new to the field have trouble acquiring enough funding to mount adequately powerful interventions, which predetermines their ineffectiveness. This situation is created in part because of a particular further set of Catch-22s that trouble funders and applicants (Fisher 1993a). For example, funders appear reluctant to support the large amount of necessary preintervention work, and yet without it, projects may be inappropriate or misguided. Also, funders often want detailed action plans from the intervenor or public commitments from the parties, both of which are incompatible with the adaptable and unofficial nature of the enterprise. Therefore, a clear need exists for dialogue between funders and applicants. However, the need for such communication largely goes unaddressed despite some good intentions on both sides.

The final issue is the need for strong institutional bases to support ICR. The pioneers in the field tended to be academics who blended the unpredictable requirements of the work into the constant demands and limited resources of a faculty member's role. Many requests for interventions have been declined because of a lack of funding and an inflexible and unsupportive institutional base. A solid institutional foundation for ICR would generally provide greater flexibility, credibility, and consistency of practice; more resources for research and theorizing; and a stronger base for training. While the disadvantages of such institutionalization need to be considered, the ideal base would appear to be a university-affiliated, nonprofit, interdisciplinary center for research and practice in which scholar-practitioners at different levels of competence could interact on agendas of professional development.

The challenges facing ICR can also be partly addressed through a movement toward professionalization focusing on educational and associational activities; regulatory mechanisms would best be left to a later stage of development. Thus, current activities toward forming an international network of scholar-practitioners in ICR should be encouraged. Through various kinds of developmental activities, the field should eventually find its useful and legitimate place in the domain of international conflict management and resolution.

The point here is that ICR in some form is essential if the world is to shift from power-coercive and adversarial approaches to ways of dealing with conflict in an effective and multifaceted fashion. The social technology that ICR brings to the field is uniquely designed to enable parties to diagnose their dilemma more fully and jointly, create flexible options for de-escalation and resolution, and develop mutually collaborative actions that address their basic needs. This technology in some ways parallels approaches being developed to address complex, multiparty policy and environmental disputes, which have been advanced by individuals like James Laue, Thomas Scott, and Barbara Gray. The bottom line is finding mutually beneficial ways to solve problems and collaborate rather than compete and attack. Nothing inherent in the international system should preclude this change as a necessary element in the social evolution of humankind.

REFERENCES

Azar, Edward E. 1983. "The Theory of Protracted Social Conflict and the Challenge of Transforming Conflict Situations." *Monograph Series in World Affairs* 20, M2:81–99.

———. 1990. *The Management of Protracted Social Conflict.* Hampshire, U.K.: Dartmouth Publishing.

Banks, Michael, ed. 1984. *Conflict in World Society: A New Perspective on International Relations.* New York: St. Martin's Press.

Benjamin, A. J., and A. M. Levi. 1979. "Process Minefields in Intergroup Conflict Resolution: The Sdot Yam Workshop." *Journal of Applied Behavioral Science* 15 (4): 507–19.

Berman, Maureen R., and Joseph E. Johnson, eds. 1977. *Unofficial Diplomats.* New York: Columbia University Press.

Blake, Robert R., Herbert A. Shepard, and Jane S. Mouton. 1964. *Managing Intergroup Conflict in Industry*. Houston: Gulf.

Burton, John W. 1968. *Systems, States, Diplomacy, and Rules*. London: Cambridge University Press.

————. 1969. *Conflict and Communication: The Use of Controlled Communication in International Relations*. London: Macmillan.

————. 1985. "The Facilitation of International Conflict Resolution." *Research in Social Movements, Conflicts, and Change* 8:33–45

————. 1987. *Resolving Deep-Rooted Conflict: A Handbook*. Lanham, Md.: University Press of America.

————. 1990. *Conflict: Resolution and Provention*. New York: St. Martin's Press.

————. 1992. "Conflict Prevention as a Political System." Paper presented at George Mason University, Institute for Conflict Analysis and Resolution, June, Fairfax, Virginia.

Chasin, Richard, and Margaret Herzig. 1988. "Correcting Misperceptions in Soviet-American Relations." *Journal of Humanistic Psychology* 28 (Summer): 88–97.

————. 1993. "Creating Systemic Interventions for the Sociopolitical Arena." In *The Global Family Therapist: Integrating the Personal, Professional, and Political*, ed. B. Berger Gould and D. Hilleboe DeMuth. Boston: Allyn and Bacon.

Chufrin, Gennadi I., and Harold H. Saunders, 1993. "A Public Peace Process." *Negotiation Journal* 9 (2): 155–77.

Cohen, Stephen P., and Edward E. Azar. 1981. "From War to Peace: The Transition between Egypt and Israel." *Journal of Conflict Resolution* 25 (1): 87–114.

Cohen, Stephen P., et al. 1977. "Evolving Intergroup Techniques for Conflict Resolution: An Israeli-Palestinian Workshop." *Journal of Social Issues* 33 (Winter): 165–89.

de Reuck, Anthony V. S. 1974. "Controlled Communication: Rationale and Dynamics." *The Human Context* 6 (Spring): 64–80.

Diamond, Louise, and John McDonald. 1991. *Multi-Track Diplomacy: A Systems Guide and Analysis*. Grinnell, Iowa: Iowa Peace Institute.

Doob, Leonard W., ed. 1970. *Resolving Conflict in Africa: The Fermeda Workshop*. New Haven: Yale University Press.

————. 1974. "A Cyprus Workshop: An Exercise in Intervention Methodology." *Journal of Social Psychology* 94 (December): 161–78.

————. 1975. "Unofficial Intervention in Destructive Social Conflicts." In *Cross-Cultural Perspectives on Learning*, ed. Richard W. Brislin, Stephen Bochner, and Walter J. Lonner. New York: Wiley.

————. 1976. "Evaluating Interventions: An Instance of Academic Anarchy." In *Aboriginal Cognition: Retrospect and Prospect*, ed. G. E. Kearney and D. W. McElwain. Canberra: Australian Institute of Aboriginal Studies.

————. 1981. *The Pursuit of Peace.* Westport, Conn.: Greenwood Press.

————. 1987. "Adieu to Private Intervention in Political Conflicts?" *International Journal of Group Tensions* 17 (1): 15–27.

————. 1993. *Intervention: Guides and Perils.* New Haven: Yale University Press.

Doob, Leonard W., and William J. Foltz. 1973. "The Belfast Workshop: An Application of Group Tensions to a Destructive Conflict." *Journal of Conflict Resolution* 17 (3): 489–512

Fisher, Ronald J. 1972. "Third-Party Consultation: A Method for the Study and Resolution of Conflict." *Journal of Conflict Resolution* 16 (1): 67–94.

————. 1976. "Third-Party Consultation: A Skill for Professional Psychologists in Community Practice." *Professional Psychology* 7 (3): 344–51.

————. 1980. "A Third-Party Consultation Workshop on the India-Pakistan Conflict." *Journal of Social Psychology* 112 (2): 191–206.

————. 1982. *Social Psychology: An Applied Approach.* New York: St. Martin's Press.

————. 1983. "Third-Party Consultation as a Method of Conflict Resolution: A Review of Studies." *Journal of Conflict Resolution* 27 (2): 301–34.

————. 1989. "Prenegotiation Problem-Solving Discussions: Enhancing the Potential for Successful Negotiations." *International Journal* 64 (Spring): 442–74.

————. 1990. *The Social Psychology of Intergroup and International Conflict Resolution.* New York: Springer-Verlag.

————. 1991. *Conflict Analysis Workshop on Cyprus: Final Workshop Report.* Ottawa: Canadian Institute for International Peace and Security.

————. 1992. *Peacebuilding for Cyprus: Report on a Conflict Analysis Workshop, June 1991.* Ottawa: Canadian Institute for International Peace and Security.

————. 1993a. "Developing the Field of Interactive Conflict Resolution: Issues in Training, Funding, and Institutionalization." *Political Psychology* 14 (1): 123–38.

————. 1993b. "The Potential for Peacebuilding: Forging a Bridge from Peacekeeping to Peacemaking." *Peace and Change* 18 (3): 247–66.

————. 1994. *Education and Peacebuilding in Cyprus: A Report on Two Conflict Analysis Workshops.* Saskatoon, Sask.: University of Saskatchewan.

————. 1996. *Interactive Conflict Resolution.* Syracuse, N.Y.: Syracuse University Press.

Fisher, Ronald J., and Loraleigh Keashly. 1988. "Third-Party Interventions in Intergroup Conflict: Consultation Is Not Mediation." *Negotiation Journal* 4 (4): 381–93.

————. 1991. "The Potential Complementarity of Mediation and Consultation within a Contingency Model of Third Party Intervention." *Journal of Peace Research* 28 (1): 29–42.

Fisher, Ronald J., and James H. White. 1976a. "Reducing Tensions between Neighborhood Housing Groups: A Pilot Study in Third-Party Consultation." *International Journal of Group Tensions* 6 (1–2): 41–52.

———. 1976b. "Intergroup Conflicts Resolved by Outside Consultants." *Journal of the Community Development Society* 7 (Spring): 88–98.

Foltz, William J. 1977. "Two Forms of Unofficial Conflict Intervention: The Problem-Solving and Process-Promoting Workshops." In *Unofficial Diplomats*, ed. Maureen R. Berman and Joseph E. Johnson. New York: Columbia University Press.

Groom, A. J. R. 1986. "Problem Solving in International Relations." In *International Conflict Resolution: Theory and Practice*, ed. Edward E. Azar and John W. Burton. Brighton, U.K.: Wheatsheaf.

Hare, A. Paul, Frank Carney, and Fred Osview. 1977. "Youth Responds to Crisis: Curaçao." In *Liberation without Violence*, ed. A. Paul Hare and Herbert H. Blumberg. London: Rex Collings.

Hicks, Donna, et al. 1995. "Addressing Intergroup Conflict by Integrating and Realigning Identity: An Arab-Israeli Workshop." In *Group Process and Political Dynamics*, ed. Mark F. Ettin, Jay W. Fidler, and Bertram D. Cohen. Madison, Conn.: International Universities Press.

Hill, Barbara J. 1982. "An Analysis of Conflict Resolution Techniques: From Problem-Solving Workshops to Theory." *Journal of Conflict Resolution* 26: 109–38.

Julius, Demetrios A. 1991. "The Practice of Track Two Diplomacy in the Arab-Israeli Conferences." In *Unofficial Diplomacy at Work*. Vol. 2 of *The Psychodynamics of International Relationships*, ed. Vamik D. Volkan, Joseph V. Montville, and Demetrios A. Julius. Lexington, Mass.: Lexington Books.

Keashly, Loraleigh, Ronald J. Fisher, and Peter R. Grant. 1993. "The Comparative Utility of Third Party Consultation and Mediation within a Complex Simulation of Intergroup Conflict." *Human Relations* 46 (3): 371–93.

Keashly, Loraleigh, and Ronald J. Fisher. 1996. "A Contingency Perspective on Conflict Interventions: Theoretical and Practical Considerations." In *Resolving International Conflicts: The Theory and Practice of Mediation*, ed. Jacob Bercovitch. Boulder, Colo.: Lynne Rienner.

Kelman, Herbert C. 1972. "The Problem-Solving Workshop in Conflict Resolution." In *Communication in International Politics*, ed. Richard L. Merritt. Urbana: University of Illinois Press.

———. 1978. "Israelis and Palestinians: Psychological Prerequisites for Mutual Acceptance." *International Security* 3 (Summer): 162–86.

———. 1979. "An Interactional Approach to Conflict Resolution and Its Applications to Israeli-Palestinian Relations." *International Interactions* 6 (2): 99–122.

———. 1982. "Creating the Conditions for Israeli-Palestinian Negotiations." *Journal of Conflict Resolution* 26 (1): 39–75.

————. 1986. "Interactive Problem Solving: A Social-Psychological Approach to Conflict Resolution." In *Dialogue toward Interfaith Understanding*, ed. William Klassen. Jerusalem: Ecumenical Institute for Theological Research.

————. 1987. "The Political Psychology of the Israeli-Palestinian Conflict: How Can We Overcome the Barriers to a Negotiated Solution?" *Political Psychology* 8 (3): 347–63.

————. 1991. "Interactive Problem Solving: The Uses and Limits of a Therapeutic Model for the Resolution of International Conflicts." In *Unofficial Diplomacy at Work.* Vol. 2 of *The Psychodynamics of International Relationships*, ed. Vamik D. Volkan, Joseph V. Montville, and Demetrios A. Julius. Lexington, Mass.: Lexington Books.

————. 1992. "Informal Mediation by the Scholar-Practitioner." In *Mediation in International Relations: Multiple Approaches to Conflict Management*, ed. Jacob Bercovitch and Jeffrey Z. Rubin. New York: St. Martin's Press.

————. 1993a. "Coalitions across Conflict Lines: The Interplay of Conflicts within and between the Israeli and Palestinian Communities." In *Conflict between People and Peoples*, ed. Jeffry Simpson and Stephen Worchel. Chicago: Nelson-Hall.

————. 1993b. "Social-Psychological Approaches to Peacemaking in the Middle East." Invited address to the Third Symposium on the Contributions of Psychology to Peace, Randolph-Macon College, August 16, Ashland, Virginia.

————. 1995. "Contributions of an Unofficial Conflict Resolution Effort to the Israeli-Palestinian Breakthrough." *Negotiation Journal* 11 (1): 19–27.

Kelman, Herbert C., and Stephen P. Cohen. 1976. "The Problem-Solving Workshop: A Social-Psychological Contribution to the Resolution of International Conflict." *Journal of Peace Research* 13 (2): 79–90.

————. 1979. "Reduction of International Conflict: An Interactional Approach." In *The Social Psychology of Intergroup Relations*, ed. William G. Austin and Stephen Worchel. Monterey, Calif.: Brooks/Cole.

————. 1986. "Resolution of International Conflict: An Interactional Approach." In *The Social Psychology of Intergroup Relations.* 2d ed. Edited by Stephen Worchel and William G. Austin. Chicago: Nelson-Hall.

LaFreniere, Francois, and Robert Mitchell. 1990. *Cyprus: Visions for the Future.* Working Paper No. 21. Ottawa: Canadian Institute for International Peace and Security.

Lakin, Martin, Jack Lomranz, and Morton A. Lieberman. 1969. *Arab and Jew in Israel: A Case Study in a Human Relations Approach to Conflict.* Washington, D.C.: NTL Institute.

Levi, A. M., and A. Benjamin. 1976. "Jews and Arabs Rehearse Geneva: A Model of Conflict Resolution." *Human Relations* 29 (11): 1035–44.

Little, Walter, and Christopher R. Mitchell. 1989. "The Maryland Workshops." In *In the Aftermath: Anglo-Argentine Relations since the War for the Falklands/Malvinas*

Islands, ed. Walter Little and Christopher R. Mitchell. College Park, Md.: Center for International Development and Conflict Management, University of Maryland.

Maclean's. 1991. "The People's Verdict: How Canadians Can Agree on Their Future." July 1, 10–76.

———. 1992. "An Action Plan for Canada." January 6, 8–45.

McDonald, John W. 1991. "Further Exploration of Track Two Diplomacy." In *Timing the De-Escalation of International Conflict*, ed. Louis Kriesberg. Syracuse, N.Y.: Syracuse University Press.

McDonald, John W., and Diane B. Bendahmane, eds. 1987. *Conflict Resolution: Track Two Diplomacy*. Washington, D.C.: Foreign Service Institute.

Mitchell, Christopher R. 1966. *Cyprus Report*. London: Centre for the Analysis of Conflict.

———. 1973. "Conflict Resolution and Controlled Communication: Some Further Comments." *Journal of Peace Research* 10 (1–2): 123–32.

———. 1981. *Peacemaking and the Consultant's Role*. Westmead, U.K.: Gower.

———. 1993. "Problem Solving Exercises and Theories of Conflict Resolution." In *Conflict Resolution Theory and Practice: Integration and Application*, ed. Dennis J. D. Sandole and Hugo van der Merwe. Manchester, U.K.: Manchester University Press.

Montville, Joseph V. 1987. "The Arrow and the Olive Branch: The Case for Track Two Diplomacy." In *Conflict Resolution: Track Two Diplomacy*, ed. John W. McDonald and Diane B. Bendahmane. Washington, D.C.: Foreign Service Institute.

Rothman, Jay. 1991. "Negotiation as Consolidation: Prenegotiation in the Israeli-Palestinian Conflict." *The Jerusalem Journal of International Relations* 13 (1): 22–44.

———. 1992. *From Confrontation to Cooperation: Resolving Ethnic and Regional Conflict*. Newbury Park, Calif.: Sage.

———. 1993. "Defining and Evaluating Success and Failure in an Action-Research Conflict-Resolution Project with Israelis and Palestinians." Paper presented at the Annual Scientific Meeting of the International Society of Political Psychology, July 4–8, Cambridge, Mass.

Rouhana, Nadim N., and Herbert C. Kelman. 1994. "Promoting Joint Thinking in International Conflict: An Israeli-Palestinian Continuing Workshop." *Journal of Social Issues* 50 (Spring): 157–78.

Salem, Norman, ed. 1992. *Cyprus: A Regional Conflict and Its Resolution*. London: Macmillan.

Saunders, Harold H. 1991. "Officials and Citizens in International Relationships: The Dartmouth Conference." In *Unofficial Diplomacy at Work*. Vol. 2 of *The Psychodynamics of International Relationships*, ed. Vamik D. Volkan, Joseph V. Montville, and Demetrios A. Julius. Lexington, Mass.: Lexington Books.

————. 1992. "Thinking in Stages: A Framework for Public Intercommunal Problem Solving from Experience in the Dartmouth Conference Regional Conflicts Task Force, 1982–1992." Paper presented at the Annual Meeting of the International Society of Political Psychology, July 4–8, San Francisco.

Saunders, Harold H., and Randa Slim. 1994. "Dialogue to Change Conflictual Relationships: The Tajikistani Dialogue." Paper presented at the Annual Scientific Meeting of the International Society of Political Psychology, July 12–15, Santiago, Spain.

Schwartz, Richard D. 1989. "Arab-Jewish Dialogue in the United States: Toward Track II Tractability." In *Intractable Conflicts and Their Transformation*, ed. Louis Kriesberg, Terrell A. Northrup, and Stuart J. Thorson. Syracuse, N.Y.: Syracuse University Press.

Shaffer, John B. P., and M. David Galinsky. 1974. *Models of Group Therapy and Sensitivity Training*. Englewood Cliffs, N.J.: Prentice-Hall.

Slim, Randa M. 1995. "A Framework for Managing Conflict in Divided Societies: The Tajikistan Case Study." Paper presented at the Annual Scientific Meeting of the International Society of Political Psychology, July 5–9, Washington, D.C.

Stewart, Philip D. 1987. "The Dartmouth Conference: U.S.-USSR Relations." In *Conflict Resolution: Track Two Diplomacy*, ed. John W. McDonald and Diane B. Bendahmane. Washington, D.C.: Foreign Service Institute.

Wallensteen, Peter 1991. "Report from the Workshop Chairman." Cambodian Workshop on Reconstruction and Development, Penang, Malaysia, August 18–25, 1991. Penang, Malaysia: Unit for Peace Research and Education, School of Social Sciences, University Science Malaysia.

Walton, Richard E. 1969. *Interpersonal Peacemaking: Confrontations and Third-Party Consultation*. Reading, Mass.: Addison-Wesley.

Warfield, John N. 1988. "Do as I Say: A Review Essay of John W. Burton's *Resolving Deep-Rooted Conflict: A Handbook*." *International Journal of Group Tensions* 18: 228–36.

Wedge, Bryant, and Dennis Sandole. 1982. "Conflict Management: A New Venture into Professionalization." *Peace and Change* 8 (Summer): 129–38.

Willard, Andrew R., and Charles H. Norchi. 1993. "The Decision Seminar as an Instrument of Power and Enlightenment." *Political Psychology* 14 (4): 575–606.

Yalem, Ronald J. 1971. "Controlled Communication and Conflict Resolution." *Journal of Peace Research* 8:263–72.

8

RELIGION AND PEACEBUILDING

Cynthia Sampson

INTRODUCTION

The religious sector may well be the most rapidly expanding in the field of international conflict analysis and transformation today. Religious actors have already made many notable contributions to peacebuilding. What for decades was the untold, unnoticed story behind the news—the undocumented history of religiously motivated peacemaking and reconciliation efforts—has now begun to grab the attention of scholars, journalists, diplomats, various governmental and nongovernmental agencies, and funding organizations as these efforts have become more numerous, more visible, and more needed. The record to date but hints at the much greater potential inherent in a more systematic and coordinated mobilization of the resources and capacities of religious communities for conflict transformation and peacebuilding. Religious involvement in peacemaking initiatives, which previously occurred sporadically, episodically, sometimes almost by happenstance, is giving way to institutional commitments by certain denominations and ecumenical or multireligious bodies to prepare and equip themselves for more proactive peacebuilding roles.

Growing numbers of religious actors of many sorts—laypersons, individual religious leaders, denominational structures, ad hoc commissions and delegations, and interdenominational and multireligious bodies—have been involved in a range of peacebuilding efforts over the past couple of decades. Their activities have included education for peace, reconciliation, and democracy; advocacy for nonviolent socio-political change; conflict resolution; election monitoring; and trauma healing and reconciliation. In addition, many of the relief and development nongovernmental organizations (NGOs) operating in conflict zones, and now being heralded as the "new conflict managers" (a major theme of the 1994 "Managing Chaos" conference, sponsored by the United States Institute of Peace), operate from a religious affiliation and resource base.

This chapter differs from others in this volume in that its focus is not on one particular approach to conflict intervention, but rather on a particular category of actor. It provides an overview of a diverse array of peacebuilding roles performed by a wide variety of actors, with a religious impetus serving as the common thread. In describing and situating this multiplicity of roles and actors, the chapter also makes use of a broader conceptual framework than that of conflict resolution and peacemaking. The proper framework for understanding the motivations, activities, and potentials of religious actors is that of conflict transformation and peacebuilding.

Why Religion and Why Now?

What accounts for the increasing salience of religion and religiously motivated approaches in post-Cold War conflicts? To begin with, religion is often an important defining characteristic of communities in conflict, whether they be Croats, Serbs, and Muslims in Bosnia; Armenians and Azerbaijanis in the Caucasus; Hindus and Muslims in India; or Catholics and Protestants in Northern Ireland. Despite their appearance as religious conflicts, these and similar conflicts often have more to do, initially, with how religion defines a people and a culture than with religious doctrine. Once religious passions are aroused, however, they tend to be fiercely prosecuted.

The politicization of religion in conflicts is often facilitated by contradictions found in sacred texts and other doctrinal sources of religions as they relate to war and peace (Vendley and Little 1994; Gopin 1996). Most religions, for example, have two distinctly contrasting cultures: the "holy war" and the "peaceable kingdom" (Boulding 1986). Ambiguities in religious teachings have found parallels in social behavior. Even within religio-cultural traditions that have a relatively clear mandate for peacemaking, the record of action is likely to be mixed. Indeed, one sign of how tenacious religious conflicts can be is that religiously motivated peacemaking efforts to date have had their greatest impact in conflicts in which religion is not an important defining characteristic.(See, for example, the seven case studies in Johnston and Sampson 1994. A notable exception was the successful mediation of Sudanese peace talks in 1972 by religious figures, discussed later in this chapter.)

Many religions nonetheless possess social and moral characteristics that give them the potential to act as constructive forces for peace and conflict transformation. Dispersed throughout societies, religious communities are often organized at the national and international levels, representing significant potential channels for communication and action. Religious traditions establish ethical visions that can summon those who believe in them to powerful forms of committed action. Many religions provide moral warrants for resistance against unjust conditions, including those that give rise to conflict, and thus provide an impetus for adherents to take responsibility for preventing, ameliorating, or resolving conflicts nonviolently (World Conference on Religion and Peace n.d.[1992]). In societies in which the government is widely viewed as illegitimate, or centralized authority has broken down altogether, organized religion may be the only institution retaining some measure of credibility, trust, and moral authority among the population at large. Perhaps most significant to peacebuilding, religious actors who are indigenous to conflict situations are long-term players who come from and work with the peoples and groups in the conflict throughout its life cycle.

Given the nature of conflict in today's world, the social and moral resources of religious communities are particularly relevant as potential resources for conflict resolution and healing. Not only are religious communities located in and on all sides of contemporary conflicts, but

> the primary arena of church activity and faith—that of the spiritual, emotional, and relational well-being of people—lies at the heart of contemporary conflict. . . . [W]here neighbor fears neighbor and blood is shed by each, the emotive, perceptual, social-psychological, and spiritual dimensions are core, not peripheral, concerns (Lederach 1993, 11-12).

While conflict management techniques designed to end hostilities and separate the parties might be adequate in conflicts between states, in internal conflicts, where antagonists living in close proximity serve as constant reminders of the bitter fighting and atrocities that have occurred, it is necessary to move beyond conflict management to reconciliation and healing in order to arrest the recurring cycles of violence and revenge and restore the torn fabric of human relationships and community. Until recently, these processes have tended to fall outside the purview of traditional diplomacy and have tended to be viewed as soft or naive by the secular social science field of conflict resolution (Assefa 1993b).

Indeed, some aspects of peacebuilding are best understood using concepts and approaches found in religion. In particular, the processes associated with reconciliation—confession, repentance, forgiveness, mercy, and conversion based on self-reflection and acceptance of personal responsibility—have emerged from religious, not secular, contexts (Assefa 1994, 1993a; Hamlin 1991). Many religiously motivated peacemakers have a natural predisposition to working on reconciliation—the restoration of relationships—as well as personal and social transformation (Sampson 1987; Nhat Hanh 1987b; Kraybill 1988; Assefa 1993a; Sivaraksa n.d.[1994]; Lederach forthcoming). Moreover, it is easier for religious figures to talk about repentance and forgiveness—and they are more likely to be viewed as the legitimate actors to do so—than many secular leaders, for whom such talk does not come naturally or whose motives might be questioned (Assefa 1993b).

Conceptual Framework

Building peace in a fractured world at the close of the twentieth century involves a broad range of functions and tasks designed to transform social conflict and construct the conditions and infrastructure necessary to support a dynamic, sustainable peace (Curle 1971; Laue and Cormick 1978; Kraybill 1980; Mitchell 1993; Lederach 1995, forthcoming). Although the majority of religious actors to date have not been formally schooled in the concepts and theories of conflict resolution, two particularly active religious practitioners have contributed to the development of theory by reflecting on their peacebuilding experiences. These contributions provide a framework for understanding the broader body of work in the religious sector, particularly as it relates to the relationship and interplay of two distinct but interdependent conflict intervention roles: advocate and intermediary.

In an early conceptual work, Quaker conciliator Adam Curle identified "peacemaking approaches appropriate for different sorts or stages of conflict" (1971, 186). A key variable in determining the approach, according to Curle, was the distribution of power between the adversaries. In a situation of balance, where the adversaries are roughly equal in terms of resources and capabilities, conciliation and negotiation could be applied to end an open conflict and reach a settlement. In a situation of imbalance, however, education is needed to increase awareness of the structural inequities. With higher awareness, confrontation can be employed as necessary to reduce the imbalance and enable the weaker party(ies) to negotiate on the basis of greater equality. Curle saw this restructuring of the relationship as essential to achieving the ultimate goal of stable, peaceful relations.

Mennonite conciliator John Paul Lederach builds on Curle's work in describing conflict as a progression and elaborating the roles that emerge in the transformation of conflict from violent and destructive to constructive and peaceful manifestations (see Figure 8.1). Lederach notes that, according to this framework, "education, advocacy, and mediation share the goal of change and restructuring unpeaceful relationships. . . . They share the vision of justice, of substantive and procedural change. . . ." The roles do differ, however. "Advocacy, for example, chooses to stand by one side for justice's sake. Mediation chooses to stand in connection to all sides for justice's sake" (Lederach 1995, 14–15). Yet Lederach sees these roles as mutually supportive and dependent:

> Negotiation becomes possible when the needs and interests of all those involved and affected by the conflict are legitimated and articulated. This process happens most often through confrontation and advocacy. . . . On the other hand, restructuring the relationship toward increased equality and justice does not emanate automatically from confrontation. . . . Mediation can and should facilitate the articulation of legitimate needs and interests of all concerned into fair, practical, and mutually acceptable solutions.
>
> . . . [T]he former [advocacy] is experienced as increasing conflict and the latter [mediation] as reducing conflict, creating the impression of incompat-ibility. This framework, however, suggests the inverse: that the longer-term progression of conflict toward justice and peaceful relations must integrate and view these activities as necessary and mutually interdependent in the pursuit of just change and peaceful transformation (Lederach 1995, 14–15).

Moreover, the interplay of these two roles in the experience of several religious actors in conflict situations would seem to defy the conventional wisdom that advocacy and intermediary roles are mutually exclusive and therefore cannot be performed by the same individual, or at least not concurrently. In both South Africa and the former East Germany (both discussed below), certain church leaders moved in and out of advocacy and mediation roles, the latter taking the form of an insider/partial third party (Wehr and Lederach 1991, 90–91). The mediators were clearly aligned with groups that were challenging repressive regimes, but it was precisely their position of trust and connectedness with the opposition that made it possible for them to serve as third parties in those contexts.

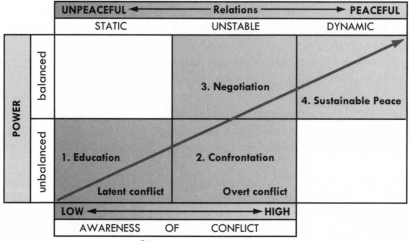

Figure from Lederach (1995). ©1995 by Syracuse University Press. Reprinted with permission.

Figure 8.1. The Progression of Conflict. Appropriate roles for advocates and intermediaries in a conflict transformation process can be seen in the graphic representation of a conflict progression above. Advocates have a role to play at a conflict's earliest stages (lower left) in educating the less powerful about the prospects of changing the static conflict system's power imbalance. Advocates are also active during the phase when the weaker party confronts the more powerful party (lower middle) to have its grievances acknowledged and to gain more power. Once the distribution of power becomes more balanced and parties can negotiate on a roughly equal basis (upper middle), mediation can be employed to assist the parties in finding ways of ending hostilities and redressing grievances. Peace becomes sustainable if the settlement succeeds in maintaining the parties in a dynamic, balanced relationship (upper right).

Several key points should be emphasized with regard to advocacy in the religious sector. The first is that the type of advocacy prescribed by these two practitioners (both members of historic peace churches), illustrated in the cases below, is nonviolent activism. Moreover, advocacy by religious actors tends to be oriented more to defending human rights and empowering disenfranchised parties than to taking sides on the substantive issues in the conflict, even though such advocacy may end up favoring one side. In fact, several types of roles discussed below—truth-teller, observer, and educator—although conceived as neutral by the religious actor, may be perceived as partisan by the dominant power in the conflict whose actions are being spotlighted. (For more on the interrelationship of advocacy and mediation in the religious sector, see Sampson forthcoming.)

In addition to a predisposition toward empowering weak parties to restructure the conflictual relationship, as noted earlier, many religiously motivated peacemakers naturally gravitate toward the work of reconciliation. Here again the focus is on relationship (Sampson forthcoming)—the restoration of relationship and community severed by war and dislocation. These two aspects of conflict transformation seek to restore or build conditions that can help achieve and sustain peace. They are, in short, peacebuilding dimensions, and they are appropriate at every stage of conflict transformation, not only in the period following a peace accord.

Thus, peacebuilding, as used in this chapter, spans a continuum of activity from conflict prevention, through the establishment of a just social order and healthy civil society, to conflict transformation. Throughout the various stages of conflict (latent, confrontation, negotiation, and postconflict), transformation may involve education, advocacy, conflict resolution, reconciliation, rehabilitation, reconstruction, and development.

Religion is a pervasive social institution. As such, religious actors potentially can be—and in some cases already are—active in the full range of peacebuilding activities within a process of conflict transformation, operating at different levels of society and from different levels of organization within the religious community. To gain a better understanding of the range of actors and activities in the religious sector, several actor typologies are used in this chapter:

- *type of religious affiliation* (single denomination or religion, interdenominational body within a religious tradition, multireligious body, or spiritually motivated nondenominational organization)
- *organizational structure of the religious actor* (individual layperson or cleric; religious institution, body, or ad hoc grouping)
- *organizational level* (local, subnational, national, regional, or international).

Finally, as an overarching organizing framework, the case examples are grouped according to four broad categories of conflict intervention roles: advocate, intermediary, observer, and educator. Religiously motivated advocates are primarily concerned with empowering the weaker party(ies) in a conflict situation, restructuring relationships, and transforming unjust social structures. Intermediaries devote themselves to the task of peacemaking, focusing their efforts on bringing the parties together to resolve their differences and reach a settlement. Observers offer themselves as a physical and moral presence in a setting of conflict, in hopes of preventing violence and transforming the conflict dynamics. Educators lay the ground-work for conflict transformation by conveying to others—whether in the classroom, the training seminar, or experientially—the knowledge and skills of conflict transformation and peacebuilding. In practice, the roles most associated with—but not restricted to—the different stages of conflict are advocate during the confrontation stage; intermediary during the negotia-tion stage; observer during the confrontation, negotiation, and postconflict stages; and educator during the entire conflict progression, including the latent stage—before a conflict has come to full awareness and has become manifest in society.

In the following survey, each of the four roles is illustrated with a num-ber of site-specific examples of conflict interventions by religiously moti-vated actors. Next comes a more generic look at the body of work of cer-tain institutional actors—religious communities or spiritually motivated groups that have worked over a sustained period across role categories. These actors include the Roman Catholic Church, Society of Friends (Quakers), Mennonites, Moral Re-Armament, Engaged Buddhists, and the Nairobi Peace Initiative. The chapter then provides a more detailed sketch of South Africa as a case of significant social and political transformation to illus-trate the multiplicity of religious actors that may be involved in a conflict's progression over time. The chapter concludes with a look at the emerging trends in and future directions of the religious sector. What follows should be viewed not as an exhaustive survey but, rather, as suggestive of a larger body of experience yet to be acknowledged, documented, and better un-derstood through more systematic research and analysis.

ROLES PLAYED BY RELIGIOUS ACTORS

Advocates

Moving beyond Curle's (1971) typology noted above, Laue and Cormick (1978) identified two partisan conflict-intervention roles: the activist, who is closely aligned with the powerless or nonestablishment party, and the advocate, who supports the goals of one conflict party but is not directly affiliated with that party and therefore can promote its cause to opponents and to the wider community. The dichotomy is useful for distinguishing the functions of internal and external religious actors in several cases in which the conflict is national in scope and involves massive social change.

Internal religious actors, and particularly those representing institutional religion, are integral to the society and may play critical activist roles as catalysts for change. External religious actors, as in the cases of South Africa and Rhodesia/Zimbabwe, play the role of advocate in promoting the cause of the proponents of change beyond national borders, serving to help internationalize the conflict and bring to bear on the ruling regime the pressures of world opinion and of powerful state and multilateral actors. However, given that both the internal activist and external advocate are essentially partisan roles, they are treated together in this chapter under the common heading of "advocate."

A further subset within the advocate role is that of "truth-teller" (Kraybill 1994), which involves raising a voice of moral outrage against what are seen as systemic injustices or wrongful acts committed by a party to the conflict. Truth-telling is not intended to be an act of taking sides in the conflict, although it is likely to be perceived as such by the party whose actions are being exposed. In any case, it is distinctly an act of moral advocacy on the part of the religious actor.

When a moral message serves to mobilize mass action, or when the moral messenger backs its words with effective leadership of its own, the religious actor can become a significant catalyst for change. In the examples that follow, it is institutional religion that functions in this way; for example, the church (or churches) in predominantly Christian societies or the *sangha* (the religious order of monks) in predominantly Buddhist societies, which represents a substantial portion of the population and possesses moral legitimacy as well as temporal power, or at least the capacity to reach and mobilize adherents and others throughout the society.

Truth-Telling and the Transition from Rhodesia to Zimbabwe. A significant example of truth-telling to both a nation and the world was that of the Roman Catholic Church during the war of independence in Rhodesia (Linden 1980; Kraybill 1994, 212–222). Through a long-distance liaison between two Catholic institutions—the Justice and Peace Commission (JPC) in Rhodesia and the London-based Catholic Institute for International Relations (CIIR)—the church was active from 1975 until the war ended in 1979 in exposing wartime atrocities committed by the Rhodesian security forces. As government censorship tightened, the church became virtually the only reliable source of information about life in the war zones, often through the accounts of deported missionaries and church workers (some eighteen Catholics were expelled by the government for speaking out). The JPC and CIIR also lobbied the British and other Western governments, arguing against both accepting the compromise Internal Settlement government and lifting sanctions against Rhodesia. Rhodesia's Catholic bishops issued ten pastoral statements between 1961 and 1980, calling for racial justice and principled behavior on the part of the combatants. Catholic bodies also challenged the liberation fronts on several occasions, deploring both publicly and privately reported atrocities by guerrilla forces.

In 1977, recognizing an impasse in the war and the devastation of the country's economy and social welfare, the JPC and Catholic hierarchy shifted to active, high-level peace-process advocacy, in hopes of getting the parties to the bargaining table. In a final initiative just months before a negotiated settlement would end the war, the JPC enlisted the pope to urgently pressure five Western governments to intervene in an attempt to stop the suffering.

Pronouncements and "People Power": The Catholic Church in the Philippines.
The world was held spellbound in February 1986, as two million Filipinos massed in Manila to provide a cordon of protection around soldiers rebelling against the repressive and corrupt regime of Ferdinand Marcos. Many of these citizens responded to a call by Cardinal Jaime Sin, the archbishop of Manila, "to all the children of God" to protect "our idealist friends" (Wooster 1994, 163; Wise and Cardel 1991).

The Second Vatican Council of 1962 and subsequent papal encyclicals stressed that efforts to eradicate injustice and economic inequality were integral to preaching the Gospel. From the imposition of martial law in the Philippines in 1972, the Catholic Church led the religious opposition to the Marcos regime. Through frequent pastoral letters, the church was able to reach parishes throughout the country with calls for the defense of human rights, social justice, and rejection of violence, and with increasingly direct attacks against the Marcos regime's repression, corruption, and economic mismanagement (Wooster 1994, 159–66). Many priests and nuns served as monitors in the election that Marcos fraudulently claimed as a victory over Corazon Aquino and that was subsequently denounced in a Bishops Conference declaration that the regime had lost its mandate to govern (International Observer Delegation 1986, 19–20). As the four-day "People Power" revolution unfolded, the Catholic-owned Radio Veritas was instrumental in mobilizing the popular defense of the military that proved decisive in expelling Marcos nonviolently and bringing Aquino to power (Wooster 1994, 163).

Turning East Germany Around. During *die Wende* (the turnaround), East Germany's nonviolent revolution of 1989–90, the churches, particularly the Evangelische Kirche, played a central role in the overthrow of the communist system. Initially providing support, meeting space, and protection from harassment to the independent peace movement, in 1988 the church became more actively involved in protesting government actions, defending human rights, and holding prayer services that became the rallying points for mass demonstrations. As tensions heightened, and especially with the fall of the regime of Erich Honecker, the church's role in East Germany became a blend of continued activism on the one hand, and facilitation of dialogue between protesters and the government and security forces on the other. Many individual church leaders were instrumental in moderating roundtables that formed at the national and local levels to allow for popular participation in establishing a new political order, and that served in some locations as de facto governments during the turbulent transition to democracy and unification with West Germany (Steele 1994).

Society's "Conscience" in Vietnam. Political protest by Vietnamese Buddhist monks was emblazoned in the global consciousness during the Vietnam War with images of monks, in lotus meditation position, committing the act of self-immolation. Monks play an important role as the conscience of Vietnamese society; their selfless acts reflect a Buddhist understanding of humility and service (Barr 1994).

More recent acts of self-immolation by a monk in 1994 and a layperson in a sacred Buddhist pagoda in 1993 have been taken by Vietnamese sympathizers and international human rights groups as extreme statements of protest against the repressive policies of the ruling communist regime. The 1993 self-immolation led to what was probably the largest antigovernment demonstration in Vietnam since the communists took control and reunified the country in 1976. Other Buddhist-led protests were reported in 1993 and 1994 (Barr 1994).

With free-market reforms and relaxed restrictions on some religious organizations have come greater repression and imprisonment of religious activists with political agendas, especially the Unified Buddhist Church of Vietnam (UBCV). The church played a central role in the Vietnamese antiwar movement of the 1960s and 1970s and has been banned since 1981. The UBCV has been campaigning for reinstatement; however, its petitions are accompanied by underground statements calling for religious freedom, sweeping democratic reforms, and an end to the Communist Party's monopoly on power

(Barr 1994). Reportedly, dozens of monks have been arrested, and both Amnesty International and Human Rights Watch/Asia have charged the government with political repression of Buddhists (Barr 1995).

A "Subtle Protest" in Burma. In the closed country of Burma (Myanmar), the *sangha* is the only nationally organized institution other than the army. More than 90 percent of the population is Buddhist. Monks hold strong moral authority, enjoying popular support for their asceticism, and monasteries have often served as both launching pads for mass protests and sanctuaries for political outlaws (Jones 1989a). For five weeks in 1988, during the country's brief period of prodemocracy protests just before the army's imposition of martial law, hundreds of thousands of protesters led by Buddhist monks took over Burma's second-largest city of Mandalay, home to some 260 monasteries and 100,000 monks. Upon the imposition of martial law, hundreds of monks and lay people were arrested, and many others fled or went underground (Jones 1989a). One year later and still under martial law, thousands of monks, lacquer begging bowls in hand, walked single file past Mandalay's military installations in a "subtle protest" of silent defiance, marking the anniversary of the start of massive killings of prodemocracy protesters (Jones 1989c). Four years later, all protest by monks had apparently been silenced (Bradley 1994).

Intermediaries

Intermediary roles played by religious actors have included fact finding, good offices, peace-process advocacy, facilitation, conciliation, and mediation, usually in some combination. Religious actors have mediated high-level peace talks and have also been active nonofficially at all levels of peacemaking in advocating for a negotiated settlement and trying to improve the climate and prospects for peace. Their means of entry into conflict situations and their methodologies have varied widely, including the particular characteristic that would outwardly distinguish them most from secular counterparts: the degree to which explicit religiousness is or is not expressed during the peace process.

Peacemaking in Sudan, Then and Now. In 1972, peace talks between the government of Sudan and rebels from the country's southern insurgency, the Southern Sudan Liberation Movement, ended the civil war between the two sides and brought a decade of peace to the war-ravaged country. The negotiations—which featured prayers and sermons as part of the proceedings and produced tears of remorse among Muslim and Christian generals alike—

were successfully mediated by a three-man team: Reverend Burgess Carr, secretary-general of the All-Africa Conference of Churches (AACC); Leopoldo Niilus, director of the World Council of Churches' (WCC) Commission of the Churches on International Affairs; and Kodwo Ankrah, WCC refugee secretary (Assefa 1987). The WCC/AACC delegation's access to the Khartoum government came through a meeting called to discuss aid, although the members went prepared to provide their good offices, an offer that was readily accepted (Rees 1977). Also influential in gaining the government's confidence was a WCC-commissioned report on the background and issues of the conflict, which was considered knowledgeable, fair, and objective.

The 1972 agreement gradually eroded over the following decade because of problems with its implementation. It was finally abrogated in 1983, when the Sudanese government imposed Islamic *sharia* law over the entire country, including the non-Muslim south. Civil war again broke out between the northern and southern regions. After eight years of fighting, a split occurred in the leadership of the south's Sudanese People's Liberation Army and interfactional fighting ensued. Concerned about the impact on civilians of this conflict within a conflict, and aware that without southern unity peace with the north could not be achieved, the National Council of Churches of Kenya, the Kenyan Catholic Secretariat, and the largely church-supported Nairobi Peace Initiative decided to back a 1991 mediation attempt by a group of church leaders from southern Sudan. Significant agreement was reached on a number of contentious issues, but the process broke down in 1992, followed by further splintering of the southern insurgency movement (Assefa 1993c).

Conciliation in Nicaragua. In Nicaragua, a process of negotiations between the Sandinista government and a coalition of exiled Indian groups from the country's east coast was mediated by a Conciliation Commission of religious figures, which brokered a preliminary agreement between the two sides in 1988 (Nichols 1994). Commission members included a minister, Andy Shogreen, and three other representatives of the Moravian Church (the predominant denomination in the country's east coast provinces); a Baptist pastor and director of an ecumenical relief and development agency, Gustavo Parajon; and an American Mennonite, John Paul Lederach, who served as a conflict resolution consultant. The agreement apparently opened the way for a substantial number of Indian refugees living in exile to return to Nicaragua (Nichols 1994, 82).

Although subsequent rounds of talks failed to resolve the remaining issues at the time, a final agreement was brokered by former U.S. president Jimmy Carter in 1989 on a trip to arrange for monitoring of the upcoming Nicaraguan election, thus opening the way for the remaining Indian leaders to return and participate in the elections. That agreement was signed in a Moravian church on the east coast, with the Conciliation Commission members present (Lederach 1989).

Peacemaking in the Punjab. Jainism, a religion of India that dates from the sixth century B.C., was the earliest historical expression of *ahimsa*, the philosophy of nonviolence. For adherents living a life of strict asceticism, absolute nonviolence is considered the highest virtue (Sharma 1990). Mahavira, an early Jain reformer, is said to have instructed his followers not to preach Jainism but to "go from village to village and maintain peace among mankind" (*Free Press Journal, Sunday Press,* May 24, 1987, as cited in Hall 1987, 4).

One recent example of the religion's active embrace of nonviolence is the work of a Jain monk, Acharya Sushil Kumar, who was active in Hindu-Sikh conciliation in the Indian state of Punjab. In 1987, Kumar opened channels of communication and mediated between the government of India and Sikh militants who had been occupying the Golden Temple at Amritsar in the Punjab since 1984. Before each of his meetings in the temple, the monk was successful in securing the withdrawal of the heavily armed Indian police guard, which had encircled the shrine continuously for three years. Some of the most militant Sikh leaders participated in the meetings. The dialogue produced a four-point peace plan, which faltered, apparently owing to the lack of support from the Punjab state government (*Patriot* 1987; *Siddhachalam Newsletter* 1987; Hall 1987).

In 1988, Kumar arranged a meeting for Sikh leaders from the Punjab to try to settle their differences, but the meeting was canceled when one of the leaders was assassinated. However, Kumar's final initiative, an appeal to the central government for the release of imprisoned priests from the Golden Temple, met with success (*Siddhachalam Newsletter* 1988).

Observers

In a conflict situation, the observer provides a watchful, compelling physical presence that is intended to discourage violence, corruption, human rights violations, or other behavior deemed threatening and undesirable. Far from being passive, religiously motivated observers have, for example, actively monitored and verified—and even ensured—the legitimacy of elections.

In the observer's more activist form of providing a presence, civilian peacekeeping groups, or "peace teams," have positioned themselves between sides in active conflict situations—becoming a "living wall," as Gandhi termed it—to stop the violence and transform the conflict dynamics (Schirch 1995, 2). In this form, civilian peacekeeping involves taking an impartial stance toward all parties. Or, in situations where parties are not easily separated or violence is perpetrated primarily by one party against another, intercessionary peacekeeping may be used to deter violence, either through accompanying individuals or groups believed to be in danger or by maintaining a presence in a threatened community (Schirch 1995, 21–26).

Election Monitoring in Zambia. In Zambia, a predominantly Christian country, the churches played a central role in carrying out the 1991 national election. About a month before the election, the churches pulled out of a national coalition of NGOs after they lost confidence that the coalition could ensure a free and fair election. Then, using the infrastructures of three denominational networks working in close cooperation—a Protestant evangelical association, the national council of churches, and the Catholic Bishops Conference—the churches recruited, trained, and deployed monitors for three thousand polling sites (Vendley 1995). Several months earlier, in a political impasse with President Kenneth Kaunda's government, the Movement for Multiparty Democracy, the party of the leading presidential contender (and soon-to-be-elected-president), Frederick Chiluba, threatened to boycott the election. The two men agreed to meet in the Anglican cathedral in Lusaka. Their meeting, set within a shared faith context and begun with prayer, resulted in a redrafting of the constitution that opened the way for the elections to proceed (Carter 1994, vi).

Civilian Peacekeeping in Central America. Two religiously motivated groups currently involved in ongoing civilian peacekeeping work have been active primarily in Central America. Witness for Peace (WFP), an ecumenical organization formed in the early 1980s, has provided a nonviolent presence in Nicaragua, Guatemala, El Salvador, Mexico, Haiti, South Africa, and the Middle East. Its principal engagement was in Nicaragua, where more than four thousand North Americans from various religious traditions visited for periods of several weeks to more than a year between 1983 and 1991. WFP's primary objective was activist in nature: to change U.S. foreign policy in the region. Members' activities in Nicaragua included living among and working with the Nicaraguan people, and reporting on Nicaraguan living conditions upon their return home, documenting human rights violations, fostering dialogue and reconciliation, documenting the conflict and peace initiatives, and providing nonviolence training (Schirch 1995, 84–86).

Christian Peacemaker Teams (CPT) sponsored by the Mennonites and the Church of the Brethren have pursued nonviolent direct action as human rights monitors since 1986, focusing attention on issues of violence and militarism in Iraq, Palestine, Israel, and Haiti, as well as in the United States and Canada (Christian Peacemaker Teams n.d.[1994]; Charles 1994, 20–21). CPT sees its role as proclaiming the Gospel of repentance, salvation, and reconciliation, and its mandate as a new dimension of the churches' ongoing peace and justice ministries. CPT's most sustained involvement has been in Haiti, where since 1993 it has been active in accompaniment—providing a protective presence for community leaders and communities in danger—and in documenting human rights abuses (Schirch 1995, 86–87).

Educators

Education and training play a role during each stage of conflict transformation, whether to sensitize a society to inequities in the system; to foster an understanding of and build the skills of advocacy, conflict resolution, democracy, or living with diversity; or to promote healing and reconciliation. The key to this activity is the dimension of preparation—of teaching or in some way providing a learning experience for others from a position one step removed from direct involvement in conflict intervention.

Nonviolence Training. Three religiously motivated actors have been particularly active in the area of nonviolence training. Continuing the legacy of the grandfather of all modern nonviolence movements, the Gandhi Peace Foundation, headquartered in Delhi with thirty-three field centers across India, conducts research, field work, and educational programs on the nonviolent alternative in conflict situations and in relation to nature and the environment (Gandhi Peace Foundation n.d.[1992]).

The International Fellowship of Reconciliation, founded in 1919 in the Netherlands, is represented on every continent through a network of organizations, branches, and affiliated groups of people working for active nonviolence from a faith perspective. In 1992, it established a Nonviolence Education and Training Project as a grassroots movement to train people in peace and social change movements and to develop cross-cultural and interfaith training resources (Nonviolence Education and Training Project n.d.[1994]).

Nonviolence International (NI) was founded by Mubarak Awad, a Palestinian Christian who was schooled in Quaker and Mennonite beliefs, trained in the techniques of Gandhi, and further inspired by the work of Martin Luther King, Jr. (Ingram 1990, 28–53). Headquartered in Washington, D.C., NI provides training in nonviolent action; coordinates international teams; provides legal support to activists and campaigns; and cooperates internationally with other programs, including resource centers in Moscow, Bangkok, Jerusalem, and Johannesburg (Nonviolence International 1995).

Learning Communities in Northern Ireland. In Northern Ireland, where the Catholic and Protestant communities have historically lived, worshipped, and even been educated separately, one of the faith-based responses to the conflict has been the emergence of "intentional communities of reconciliation" (Morrow and Wilson 1994, 23). These communities provide a chance for experiential learning so that their members may "rediscover each other as human beings" (Morrow n.d.[1994], 4). Best known among them is the ecumenical Corrymeela Community, founded in 1965, whose direct work with local community groups is supported by an all-age residential program (Morrow n.d. [1994]; Morrow and Wilson 1994, 23). Other examples are the Cornerstone and Curragh communities in Belfast, which work with community development programs; the Columbanus Community, which offers courses in ecumenics; and the Rostrevor Centre, which specializes in renewal and healing. Most people in these communities are "dispersed" members, who live and work outside the communities but join together through them for work on particular projects (Morrow and Wilson 1994).

Preparing People for Peace in Mozambique. The Christian Council of Mozambique (CCM), an ecumenical body of Protestant churches, launched its Preparing People for Peace Program in 1991 (Brubaker 1993)—a year before peace came to that country—to begin to prepare for the transition a population that had known almost thirty years of war. CCM's Peace and Reconciliation Commission, under the leadership of Anglican Bishop Dinis Sengulane, had been active during the conflict in bringing the warring sides together. Now it turned its attention to the pressing needs of building peace and resettling a massively dislocated population. The program proceeded in two phases. The first was a five-week training seminar held in Maputo for

CCM and church representatives (including those from non-CCM churches) from all ten provinces, using material on the Bible as an instrument of peace and including sessions on conflict resolution and the "three r's" (reconciliation, repatriation, and rehabilitation), public health, the family, child development, trauma treatment, nonviolence, human rights, the Mozambican Constitution, disarmament, and amnesty. The second phase consisted of two-week training seminars in the provinces, delivered by the people trained in Maputo, for church and district representatives (Brubaker 1993).

INSTITUTIONAL ACTORS

This section focuses on the work of religious communities and other institutional actors that have been engaged in peacebuilding over many years and in diverse roles.

Roman Catholic Church

At the international level, Pope John Paul II officially mediated the process leading to the signing of a 1984 treaty that ended a century-old border dispute between Chile and Argentina over the Beagle Channel (Princen 1987; 1992a, 133–85). The day-to-day mediation process took more than six years to reach an agreement and was conducted by a team of clerics headed by Cardinal Antonio Samore, a career Vatican diplomat. However, the mediation was leveraged by messages from the pontiff and occasional audiences with him for the negotiators. The Vatican attributed its success largely to the pope's moral authority as the spiritual sovereign of the two Catholic nations. The church was able to make demands on the parties no other third party could have made; for example, the pope couched his urgings for reconciliation in religious terms, and the Vatican periodically called on local parishes to pray for peace (Princen 1987, 348–50).

A regional-level peacebuilding program on the African continent was proposed in late 1994 by a group of nine Catholic bishops participating in the "African Church as Peacemaker" colloquium at Duquesne University in Pittsburgh, Pennsylvania. The group unanimously proposed to the Symposium of Episcopal Conferences of Africa and Madagascar (SECAM), the association of all of Africa's subregional and national bishops conferences, to establish a unit to "monitor, promote, and coordinate the ever-growing efforts of our local churches at peacemaking and peacebuilding," and actively pursue collaboration with ecumenical and multireligious bodies working in these areas (Proposal for Action 1994). At the time of this writing, preliminary steps were under way on the part of the SECAM leadership to formulate a response to the bishops' proposal.

In teamwork that spanned international, national, and local levels of the Roman Catholic Church, Mozambican Archbishop Jaime Goncalves and the predominantly Catholic lay Community of Sant'Egidio—supported by encouragement and strategically applied pressure from the Vatican— played a prominent mediation role in two years of peace talks that ended Mozambique's civil war in 1990 (United States Institute of Peace 1993; Schneidman 1993; Hume 1994; Goncalves 1994). Sant'Egidio is headquartered in a sixteenth-century former Carmelite convent in Rome, where ten rounds of peace talks were held from 1990 to 1992, and has communities in several Italian cities and thirteen other countries (Community of Sant'Egidio n.d.[1993]). Joining Archbishop Goncalves on the mediation team were two Sant'Egidio representatives: Andrea Riccardi, its founder and leader, and Don Mateo Zuppi, a parish priest in Rome. (A fourth team member, Mario Raffaelli, represented the Italian government.)

In 1994–95, Sant'Egidio was again active in mediation, this time between Algerian political opposition parties. In talks held at the community's Rome headquarters in September and again in January, eight opposition leaders, several of them bitter rivals, reached agreement on a proposal to the government to end the political violence that was taking hundreds of lives each week in Algeria (Drozdiak 1995; Pierre and Quandt 1995).

Mediation by national-level Catholic figures has occurred in Nicaragua by Cardinal Obando y Bravo, head of the Nicaraguan National Reconciliation Commission (Wehr and Lederach 1991, 90–91; Larmer 1988); in Guatemala by Bishop Rudolfo Quezada, head of the Guatemalan National Reconciliation Commission (*Washington Post* 1992); in Panama by Archbishop Marcos McGrath (Germani 1988); and in El Salvador by Archbishop Arturo Rivera y Damas.

Five Francophone African states—Congo, Zaire, Benin, Burundi, and Rwanda—have turned to national-level Catholic figures to head national constitutional conferences. In Zaire, Archbishop Monsengwo Pasinya served as president of the High Council of the Republic, a broad-based, national legislative conference formed as part of that country's abortive transition to multiparty democracy, and also as a mediator between opposition groups and Zairian president Mobutu Sese Seko (Richburg 1993; Reuters News Service 1993). In Congo, Archbishop Ernest Nkombo presided at sessions of the Supreme Council of the Republic, a 153-member legislative body established in 1991 to govern for twelve months and organize elections for the following year (*Africa News* 1991; Shiner 1992). In Benin, Archbishop Isidore de Souza served as president of a national conference that prepared the country's transition from Marxist dictatorship to democracy (de Souza 1994; *Washington Post* 1993).

At the local level, in the Mexican state of Chiapas, Bishop Samuel Ruiz was accepted by the Mexican government and Mayan Indian rebels (*zapatistas*) to mediate their conflict, even though the bishop, who was outspoken in denouncing human rights abuses against the Mayans, had been accused earlier by the government of fomenting the unrest that led to the rebels' 1994 armed uprising (Robberson 1994; Scott 1994a, 1994b). Ten days of negotiations, held in a sixteenth-century Chiapas cathedral, produced an agreement on reforms that ended the violence, although tensions continued and a new outbreak threatened by year's end. In 1995, the government again agreed to a *zapatista* demand for a Catholic mediator for peace talks, this time in the form of a Church-supported mediation commission (LaFranchi 1995).

Society of Friends

Until recently, virtually the only case literature of religiously motivated peacemaking activity concerned the intermediary work of the Society of Friends, or Quakers, between India and Pakistan in 1965 (Yarrow 1977, 1978); in Nigeria during the Biafran war (Yarrow 1978; Princen 1992a; Sampson 1994); during the war of independence in Rhodesia (Kraybill 1994); in Sri Lanka (Princen 1992b); and personal accounts or reflections of experienced Quaker conciliators involved in these initiatives (Curle 1971, 1981, 1986a, 1986b, 1990, 1995; Warren 1987) or in the Middle East (Bolling 1977, 1987; Jackson 1983; Bailey 1979, 1993).

One of the historic peace churches, the Society of Friends has traditionally coupled its refusal to fight with efforts to "bind up the wounds of the victims of war" through war-relief activities that date from the mid-1850s (Bailey 1993, 37–61). Quakers have also historically pursued advocacy— referred to as "speaking truth to power"—at the local, national, and international levels on behalf of the peaceful settlement of disputes and over a wide variety of issues, including disarmament and human rights (Bailey 1993, 65–75, 122–26). Quaker humanitarian and conciliation efforts are motivated by a belief of "that of God in every one" (Curle 1981, 5), which imbues its adherents with a deep respect for all those involved in a conflict and a desire to relieve the suffering it creates on all sides.

Quakers have fostered a distinctive intermediary role—a blend of conciliation and mediation—that characterizes much of their work (Bailey 1993). These religious actors capitalize on the "power of the powerless" in doing for parties—at little risk to them—what they cannot do on their own (Princen 1992b). Often initiated through a fact-finding process of seeking to gain a sympathetic, yet balanced, understanding of each party's perspective ("balanced partiality," [Yarrow 1977]), Quaker involvement typically evolves quickly into a good offices function of carrying messages among the parties. Working in teams of two or three, the Quakers move at the highest levels of decision making, interacting with heads of state or high officials in governments, liberation movements, and international organizations. Their access at this level often has been facilitated by the leaders' prior exposure to Quaker humanitarian programs, conferences for diplomats, or other service activities (Yarrow 1978; Sampson 1994; Kraybill 1994).

In carrying messages for parties in conflict, the Quaker conciliator is not simply a passive messenger but an active participant in the peace process who tries to remove obstacles to a negotiated settlement by reducing suspicions, misperceptions, and fears (Curle 1990, 61). Sometimes this role evolves into mediation, when teams become involved in conveying or themselves proposing the substantive terms of a possible settlement. Quakers actively engage in peace-process advocacy and often work in support of other intermediaries and initiatives in the course of an extended peace process (Yarrow 1978; Sampson 1994; Kraybill 1994).

Another area of Quaker intermediary work is in reconciliation, which involves a long-term, open-ended effort to build bridges of understanding between peoples (Bailey 1993, 126–32). Reconciliation takes two principal forms. One is the work of Quaker international affairs representatives stationed on the ground in areas of conflict, such as that between East and West Germany during the 1960s (Yarrow 1977, 51–143; Warren 1987) or in the Middle East (Young 1987). The other form is convening and facilitating informal, off-the-record meetings that bring parties face to face in nonofficial settings, for example, Russians and Americans during the Cold War, Jews and Arabs, Indians and Pakistanis in the Kashmir dispute, and Greeks and Turks in the conflict over Cyprus (Bailey 1979).

Mennonites

Rooted in the traditional Anabaptist values of nonviolence, social justice, and reconciliation, Mennonite peacebuilding has evolved a distinctive orientation and form that builds on seventy-five years of direct involvement in international relief and development work by the Mennonite Central Committee (MCC) (Eastern Mennonite University 1994). The denomination's commitment to peacebuilding is evidenced by its distinction of providing the highest level of institutionalized activity in the religious sector to date.

Although conciliation had been an MCC concern over the decades, its proactive pursuit of peace-related activity began with the formation of the MCC Peace Section in 1960 (Driedger and Kraybill 1994). Next came the founding of the Pennsylvania-based Mennonite Conciliation Service in 1978, one of the earliest entries in the nascent North American alternative dispute resolution field, under the direction of Ron Kraybill. In the mid-1980s, acting on the growing recognition of the links between relief, development, and conciliation work in settings of protracted conflict, MCC began to formulate specific conciliation assignments in its international programs (e.g., community-level conflict resolution training in Central America) (Eastern Mennonite University 1994). Finally, in 1990 it established the International Conciliation Service (ICS), under the direction of John Paul Lederach, to strengthen the peacebuilding capacities of overseas volunteers, churches, and local "partner" organizations (e.g., local NGOs) through consultancy, training, and occasional direct mediation services. ICS has been a resource in some forty countries in Africa, Asia, Europe, the Middle East, and Latin America (Eastern Mennonite University 1994).

Mennonite international work is characterized by the long-term commitment to and presence in a region (for example, more than two decades in South Africa and fifteen years in Northern Ireland); a selective focus on working with the poor and the most disadvantaged (for example, ethnic minorities, women, rural inhabitants, or Christians in some settings); a preference for strengthening and supporting existing initiatives, rather than starting new ones; an emphasis on relationship-building without a further agenda; and an emphasis on diverse forms of service that reflect different contexts (Herr et al. 1995). Other principles include: "loving the enemy" by directing humanitarian assistance to countries with pariah status (e.g., North Vietnam during the Vietnam War) and a commitment to the universality of the church, which is expressed through a preference for joining efforts with local churches rather than governments or other NGOs (Herr et al. 1995). Because of their long tradition of experience on the ground in situations of protracted conflict, Mennonite practitioners have pioneered "elicitive" approaches that tailor conflict resolution training and practice to fit particular cultural contexts (Lederach 1995).

In a distinctive blend of third-party facilitation and training, Mennonite Barry Hart, seconded by the Mennonite Board of Missions to the indigenous Christian Health Association of Liberia, developed and conducted some fifty trauma healing and reconciliation workshops across Liberia in 1992–93, involving some fifteen hundred health workers, traditional leaders and representatives of ethnic groups, and representatives of civic groups. The week-long sessions combined group work on grief and mourning with training in prejudice reduction, problem solving, and conflict resolution, and ended with ceremonies of forgiveness and repentance and rituals of remembering the dead—all set in a Christian context of songs, scriptural readings, and biblical stories (Hart 1993, 1995; Hart and Gbaba 1993). At least as many workshops have been conducted since 1993 by Liberian trainers. In 1994, Hart and others from MCC initiated similar trauma healing work with Rwandan Hutu refugees in Tanzanian camps (Brubaker 1994; Hart 1995); in 1995–96, Hart pursued similar work in the former Yugoslavia through the Health Reach program of McMaster University in Ontario.

The establishment of a new master's degree program in conflict transformation and an associated Institute for Peacebuilding at Eastern Mennonite University in Harrisonburg, Virginia, further underscores the growing Mennonite involvement in the practical and theoretical dimensions of conciliation (Charles 1994, 21). With programs targeted principally at religious communities and NGO personnel involved in developing peacebuilding programs in settings of protracted conflict, it also illustrates the denomination's distinctive niche in the field.

Moral Re-Armament

Founded at Oxford University in the 1920s by Frank Buchman, an American Lutheran minister (Lean 1985), Moral Re-Armament (MRA) is non-denominational in approach, interreligious in participation, and is today organized in some forty countries as a loosely structured global network. MRA's work is founded on a spiritual philosophy that stresses moral regeneration and personal transformation as a precursor to reconciliation in relationships, peacemaking, and constructive social change. The MRA approach involves seeking God's guidance in all aspects of daily living and striving to live according to four absolute moral standards: honesty, purity, unselfishness, and love. It strongly emphasizes personal responsibility and the role of repentance and forgiveness in relationships, whether personal, intergroup, or international (Piguet 1985; Hamlin 1992).

Large international assemblies have long been an important vehicle for advancing MRA's ideas. Since its opening in 1946, the MRA conference center in Caux, Switzerland, has been a venue for meetings of people from different sides of conflicts, as have other MRA centers around the world. Caux was an important site for Franco-German reconciliation following World War II (Luttwak 1994), and also provided a venue for a 1969 meeting of Austrian and Italian political figures to discuss the two countries' dispute of more than two decades over the South Tyrol (Henderson 1992).

Aspects of MRA involvement during Rhodesia's war of independence illustrate the broad range of approaches that characterize the group's work. Such involvement included a major international conference attended by more than a thousand participants in Salisbury; a confession of guilt at the conference from Alec Smith, an MRA worker and son of the prime minister, for his complicity in the country's oppressive white-minority rule, and his expressed personal commitment to work for a solution; visits by individuals from other countries and different walks of life whose personal stories of moral regeneration and change were deemed to have parable-like relevance for those enmeshed in the Rhodesian conflict; the promotion of reconciliation among key individuals in the society by involving them in conferences at Caux, regional meetings in Africa, small gatherings in Rhodesia, and one-on-one encounters; the facilitation of moral discourse with public figures; provision of personal support to members of negotiating teams during peace talks; and attempts to reach the larger society with a moral message through publications, newspaper ads, open meetings, and MRA educational films (Kraybill 1994, 222–233).

Engaged Buddhism

Adherents of the generally introspective tradition of Buddhism have tended to pursue social action and conflict resolution under the rubric of "engaged Buddhism" (Kraft 1988). The philosophy was developed in the 1960s by the Vietnamese monk Thich Nhat Hanh, who founded the Tiep Hien order in Vietnam as a Buddhist center for political action, as well as a school to train young adults in social action to relieve the human suffering on both sides during the Vietnam War (Nhat Hanh 1987a; Perry n.d.[1989]; Ingram 1990,74–97).

The social activism of engaged Buddhism is based on the fundamental Buddhist precept that meaningful outward change cannot occur without inner transformation. It holds that peace work begins with an inner process of "being peace," which then proceeds outward to all parts of an individual's personal, social, and political life (Nhat Hanh 1987a). Two key tenets constitute Nhat Hanh's peace framework. The first is *nondualism*, which rejects the categories of "them" and "us" in favor of the "we" of a common humanity united against a common enemy of hatred, ignorance, and violence. The second tenet is *interbeing*, which stresses the interconnectedness of everything and the interwoven nature of relationships (Nhat Hanh 1987a, 1988; Perry n.d.[1989]).

Elaborating on these themes, Sulak Sivaraksa, a founder of the International Network of Engaged Buddhists (INEB), writes that the causes of conflict are essentially spiritual and psychological. Thus, critical self-awareness is key to bringing out an individual's anger, greed, or delusion. The task in Buddhism, then, is "to find ways in which the destructive cycle of greed, hate, and delusion may be transformed into that of renunciation, compassion, and wisdom" (Sivaraksa n.d.[1994], 5).

The rest of this section highlights the manifestations of engaged Buddhism found within the stages of conflict transformation: latent, confrontation, negotiation, and postconflict. Though not exclusively falling within the educator role, most activity by engaged Buddhists is within the realm of preparing others for action; promoting awareness through symbolic action; or creating a learning environment, whether a program or a spontaneous event, that teaches people the skills of peaceful interaction, peacemaking, and reconciliation through joint participation. The first example discussed below, the Sarvodaya Shramadana Movement of Sri Lanka, actually dates from before the concept of engaged Buddhism was articulated by Thich Nhat Hanh, and it continues today.

Sri Lanka, currently recognized as a deeply divided society, has experienced almost continuous ethno-religious violence since 1983 between the politically dominant Sinhalese Buddhist majority and the minority Tamil Hindu community (Little 1994). Since 1958, long before the fissures in Sri Lankan society had erupted into open warfare—and therefore during the latent conflict stage—the Sarvodaya Shramadana Movement has applied a model of social transformation through people-centered development at the grassroots level (Ariyaratne 1989, 170–71; Macy 1985). Headed by A. T. Ariyaratne, a devout Buddhist who was also inspired by Gandhi (a Hindu), Sarvodaya Shramadana means literally "the awakening of all in society by the mutual sharing of one's time, thought, and energy" (Ariyaratne n.d.[1979], 23–43). Spiritual and cultural patterns of Sri Lankan life, including meditation, devotional songs, and traditional customs, have played a major role in Sarvodaya development programs, as have morality, self-discipline, and service to the community (Perera and Ariyaratne 1989, 3). Currently organized in almost one-third of all Sri Lankan villages, Sarvodaya Shramadana has sought not only to attack the causes of poverty and disease—themselves contributors to conflict—but also to build bridges of collaboration across Sinhalese and Tamil communities. Once communal violence between the two communities did break out (the confrontation stage), Ariyaratne, a well-known figure throughout Sri Lankan society, organized peace meetings and seminars around the country and led a number of peace marches and meditations for peace (Liyanage 1988).

INEB has conducted training in a variety of conflict situations, including programs in nonviolence, mediation, and reconciliation for exiled Burmese prodemocracy students living in camps along the Burmese-Thai border (in confrontation with Burma's military dictatorship) (Sivaraksa n.d.[1994]). INEB and Quakers have collaborated on training workshops in mediation and reconciliation and in nonviolent approaches to democratization for people from Cambodia, Sri Lanka, Burma (Myanmar), Nepal, India, and Thailand (Sivaraksa n.d. [1994]). The INEB-Quaker collaboration has been fostered by the minimal role of doctrinal beliefs in the two traditions and the shared emphasis on the quality of goodness and sacredness in every human being (Sivaraksa n.d. [1994]). One British Quaker has written a handbook on mediation for Buddhist peacemakers (McConnell 1995) and has used this method in conjunction with the work of INEB and other groups in Thailand, between Thais and non-Thais who are mostly Buddhist.

The work of the supreme patriarch of Cambodian Buddhists, Maha Ghosananda, and the Cambodian Mission for Peace, which he leads, began in 1979 with reconciliation and cultural restoration work in refugee camps, including some controlled by the Khmer Rouge (confrontation stage). (Ghosananda himself lost his entire family to the killing fields of the Khmer Rouge [Channer 1994].) That year, his Interreligious Mission for Peace attracted religious leaders from around the world in support of this work (Pond 1995). Ghosananda and a small band of colleagues attended every round of Cambodian peace talks (negotiation stage) to serve as a spiritual presence, meditate, and conduct symbolic rituals of unity (Pond 1995).

Following the peace accord (postconflict reconstruction stage), the Cambodian Mission for Peace was again active in the refugee camps, this time reintroducing Buddhism to the victims of the country's political strife. (Nearly all of Cambodia's 80,000 to 100,000 monks had been killed or died of starvation during the Khmer Rouge period [Jones 1989b].) Ghosananda's organization ordained new monks and trained them in Buddhism and the skills of democracy, human rights, nonviolence, and conflict resolution (Cambodian Mission for Peace 1989). Then, during the three weeks leading up to the national election in May 1993, Ghosananda led a 350-kilometer, cross-country *dhamma yietra* (peace march) through war-torn provinces and regions controlled by the Khmer Rouge. Beginning with some four hundred Buddhist monks, nuns, and lay people, the numbers of the *dhamma yietra* swelled to more than three thousand by the time it reached the capital city of Phnom Penh. Even though the the city was gripped with fear of violent clashes, the marchers held silent meditations for peace at various monuments. Meditations, ceremonies, and peace festivities continued in the days following the election (Kim Teng Nhem 1993, 34–41). Since 1992, the Mission for Peace has involved thousands of youths in its Cambodian Volunteers for Community Development program, and a Cambodian Peace Institute is currently being planned (Cambodian Mission for Peace 1994).

Thich Nhat Hanh himself, who for decades has lived in exile in France, has been active in postconflict reconciliation work among Vietnamese refugee communities in the United States, Australia, and France, as well as among Vietnam veterans. A 1989 retreat held in California for U.S. veterans—in his view, the "other" victims of the war, along with Vietnamese civilians and soldiers—featured talks by Nhat Hanh; long periods of silence; periods of sitting, walking, and tea meditations; and a reconciliation dinner with Vietnamese participants (Perry n.d.[1989]).

Nairobi Peace Initiative

The Nairobi Peace Initiative (NPI) of Kenya, under the direction of Hizkias Assefa since 1990, has actively engaged religious bodies and their leaders in peacebuilding activities across the African continent. Although not a religious organization, NPI incorporates a spiritual dimension in its processes and works within the nexus of theological and social science approaches to peace and peacemaking methodologies. Since 1990, NPI has been engaged in Track Two conciliation and mediation work at the political level in the civil wars in Mozambique, Sudan, Liberia, Burundi, and Rwanda. It has also worked at the grassroots level in these countries, as well as in Kenya, Ghana, and Ethiopia, on peacemaking and reconciliation with churches and church-related organizations (Assefa 1995).

Often working in collaboration with the All-Africa Conference of Churches (Protestant), NPI has also provided conflict resolution training

and facilitated interaction as peacebuilding strategies in societies torn by
conflict (Lusophone Consultation 1990; Miller 1993). In 1993 the two
groups, together with the Association of Member Episcopal Conferences
in Eastern Africa (Roman Catholic), convened a conference of religious
representatives on "The Role of Religious Leaders in Peacemaking and Social Change in Africa." Its purpose was to generate ideas and alternative
approaches to social change processes based on deeply held moral and ethical values emanating from Africa's various religious traditions (Wachira
and Mpaayei 1993).

A CONSTELLATION OF ACTORS: THE CASE OF SOUTH AFRICA

The multiplicity of religious actors that participated in South Africa's transformation from apartheid to majority democratic rule illustrates the myriad
types of religious actors existing at the societal and international levels that
can contribute to social change and peacebuilding. While admittedly a difficult undertaking, constructing a map of all possible religious actors in a
religiously diverse society might be aided by looking at the multiple inter-
sections of three typologies:

- *the organizational structure of the religious actor*, be it an individual member of the laity or clergy, an institution (church, mosque, synagogue,
  temple), an established body (a collective entity, such as a youth group
  or a federation), or an ad hoc body (such as a commission, delegation,
  or gathering)
- *the religious or spiritual base of the religious actor*, be it a single religious
  denomination or tradition, an interdenominational body within a single
  tradition, a multireligious body working across religions, or a nondenominational body comprising people who operate from a religious or spiritual motivation
- *the organizational level represented by the religious actor*, be it local,
  subnational, national, regional, or international.

South Africa's struggle includes more than twenty such types of actors.
This list is incomplete, to be sure. Indeed, the cursory review of individual
action, provided for illustrative purposes only, does not do credit to the
large number of spiritually impelled and courageous individuals at all levels
of South African society who actively opposed apartheid at great personal
risk. Suffice it to say that beginning with the period of confrontation and
struggle against apartheid, religious actors of many sorts have been involved,

some more deeply than others, and some whose role has evolved through the transition to the present postconflict phase.

Looking first at the level of individual action, many laypersons at the local church level repudiated the pro-apartheid position of the Dutch Reformed Church (DRC), and numerous local clergy were defrocked for their opposition to apartheid. Within the Islamic community, arrests and detentions of individual Muslims occurred in numbers out of proportion to their share of the population (Esack 1994).

Among the most prominent national denominational leaders who took courageous stances were Anglican Archbishop Desmond Tutu, whose championing of nonviolent resistance won him the Nobel Prize in 1984 and who has also at times served as a mediator (Ingram 1990, 272–84; Tutu 1994); Rev. Allan Boesak, the colored leader of the Dutch Reformed Mission Church and president of the World Alliance of Reformed Churches (Claiborne 1989); and Beyers Naude, an influential DRC minister who forsook his position by repudiating the church's role in sanctifying apartheid and founded the Christian Institute for Nonracial Christianity, the first religious institution established to criticize and act against apartheid (Johnston 1994, 186–93). Other prominent national religious leaders included Reverend Frank Chikane, general secretary of the South African Council of Churches (Claiborne 1989), and Michael Cassidy, a Christian evangelist and head of African Enterprise (Lean 1995).

Also working at the level of individual action was Methodist Bishop Stanley Mogoba. During the 1991–94 transition period leading to the national election, Mogoba chaired the National Peace Committee, a body charged with overseeing implementation of the National Peace Accord, to which key political parties agreed as a response to the violence that threatened to engulf the country. As part of this process, many pastors (denominational leaders working at local and regional levels) were deeply involved in peace committees as chairs, organizers of committee activities, mediators, and violence monitors (Kraybill 1995).

Finally, in a dramatic feat that may have saved the national election in 1994 and prevented an outbreak of violence, Professor Washington Okumu, a former Kenyan diplomat and layperson acting internationally, brokered the agreement among Zulu Chief Mangosuthu Buthelezi, African National Congress (ANC) leader Nelson Mandela, and then-president F. W. de Klerk that brought Buthelezi's Inkatha Freedom Party into the election in the final hour. Okumu and Buthelezi had met twenty years earlier at a White House prayer meeting (Keller 1994; Lean 1995; Henderson 1995).

At the institutional level, many white churches, both local and national denominational institutions, opposed apartheid. At the Rosettenville Conference in 1949, the first national interdenominational gathering following the National Party's victory in 1948, the English-speaking churches came out in clear opposition to apartheid. In time, as other groups opposed to apartheid were effectively nullified through banning and arrests, churches assumed the leadership in the defense of human rights and became virtually the only place where anti-apartheid activists could meet for discussion and to organize protests (Johnston 1994, 190). Within the DRC, the Cape Province Synod, a subnational denominational body, broke ranks with the church on apartheid, as did one of the DRC "daughter" churches, the colored Dutch Reformed Mission Church, a national denominational institution (Johnston 1994, 192). The Muslim youth organization Call of Islam, a national denominational body, was the most visible organization through which Islamic resistance to apartheid was galvanized (Esack 1994).

The South African Council of Churches, a national interdenominational body, took strong and sometimes confrontational stances against the government. Its 1968 "Message to the People of South Africa" underscored the incongruity between the teachings of Christianity and the concepts of apartheid (Johnston 1994, 191–200). The evangelical Christian group African Enterprise, a continental or regional interdenominational body, worked at building bridges across the lines of division in South African society. In 1992, it began a series of weekend retreats for political leaders across the political spectrum, not all of them Christians (Lean 1995). The National Initiative for Reconciliation, a national ad hoc interdenominational body, was initiated at a 1994 conference attended by church leaders and theologians from a wide range of denominations. Its "Statement of Affirmation" rejected apartheid but avoided further social analysis and criticism. Immediately following this statement came the publication by 153 predominantly black church leaders and theologians of the Kairos Document, a theological critique calling for decisive action against apartheid (Winkler 1986; Johnston 1994). At the Rustenburg Conference of 1990, the largest national interdenominational gathering of black and white South African churches in history, representatives of ninety-seven denominations and forty organizations endorsed a declaration confessing responsibility for the wrongs perpetrated by apartheid (Johnston 1994, 199; Battersby 1990). In the country's first national nonracial election, in 1994, the Ecumenical Monitoring Programme in South Africa, a national ad hoc interdenominational body organized by the South African Council of Churches (SACC) and the Catholic Bishops Conference played an active role.

Christian and Muslim individuals and bodies were not the only religious actors involved in the anti-apartheid struggle. The South African chapter of the World Conference on Religion and Peace (WCRP-SA), a national multireligious body, was founded as a result of the Interfaith Colloquium on Apartheid, an international multireligious gathering held in London in 1984 (Lubbe 1994, 2–8). Active in promoting interfaith dialogue and co-operation, WCRP-SA held prayer and protest meetings in various parts of the country; in 1987, it held a consultation with the ANC in Zambia on "Religion in a Post-Apartheid South Africa"; and in 1988, it waged a campaign against the racial municipal elections. National denominational bodies representing seven religious traditions, which actively associate with WCRP-SA, include the South African Catholic Bishops Conference, South African Hindu Maha Sabha, South African Tamil Federation, Jewish Board of Deputies, Jews for Social Justice, Call of Islam, Muslim Judicial Council, Spiritual Assembly of Baha'is, Pretoria Buddhist Group, Sikh Council of South Africa, and the Federation of Indigenous Churches in South Africa, in addition to the interdenominational SACC (Lubbe 1994, 2–8). Prompted by the 1990 Johannesburg National Interfaith Conference, a national multireligious gathering, WCRP-SA took up the issue of religious freedom during the transition period as its contribution to South African democracy (Lubbe 1994, 2–8). Since late 1994, at the request of the National Truth and Reconciliation Commission, it has worked to coordinate religious participation in the commission's work.

At the global level, two international interdenominational bodies were active as advocates on behalf of the anti-apartheid struggle. The World Council of Churches (WCC) held a consultation to protest apartheid in 1960, began to provide humanitarian support to the liberation movements in 1970, called on its members to press for comprehensive sanctions against South Africa in 1985, and organized a 1987 conference in Zambia for SACC representatives and exiled members of the ANC (Johnston 1994, 190–91, 195, 196). The World Alliance of Reformed Churches, a grouping of some 150 Reformed, Presbyterian, and Congregational churches, declared apartheid a heresy in 1987, suspended two proapartheid Afrikaans-language churches, and elected Allan Boesak its president (Johnston 1994, 192). Dating from the 1960s, the International Fellowship of Reconciliation, an international nondenominational body, was the group that worked in the most systematic manner to advocate the concept of nonviolent struggle (see, for example, Wink 1987). The Vatican, an international denominational institution, also denounced apartheid, and Pope John Paul II, an international denominational leader, added his voice to the call for strict sanctions (Johnston 1994).

CONCLUSIONS AND FUTURE TRENDS

What future trends are suggested by this survey and recent developments?

First, institutional moves within some religious communities suggest an increasingly intentional and systematic approach to peacebuilding. The Mennonite Central Committee, for example, in addition to increasing the number of its specific conciliation-related assignments, is beginning to reassess its ongoing development programs for ways to incorporate more explicit peacebuilding dimensions. The new Conflict Transformation Program at Eastern Mennonite University represents a faith-based institutional commitment to developing the peacebuilding field, and a chief constituency of the program is the religious sector. Clergy; other representatives of denominational, and interfaith ecumenical, bodies; and staff from religiously affiliated humanitarian agencies attend the program's Summer Peacebuilding Institute in significant numbers.

Duquesne University, a Catholic institution that hosted the "African Church as Peacemaker" colloquium, has launched a Conflict Resolution and Peace Studies program, under the direction of William Headley, CSSp, as part of its Graduate Center for Social and Public Policy. The first nine fellowships in this new program were awarded to scholars from each of the nine countries represented by the bishops at the 1994 colloquium.

Second, the interreligious sphere is also adopting a more intentional approach to peacebuilding. The World Conference on Religion and Peace/International, which since its founding in 1974 has pursued a holistic peace agenda in the areas of disarmament, development, human rights, conflict resolution, refugees, and children (Jack 1993), launched a major new program on religion and peacebuilding in 1994. Capitalizing on the body's strengths as a global association of world religions, the program builds on the premises that multireligious efforts can often be more powerful than those of a religious community acting alone, and that cooperation across religions can promote tolerance and an understanding of pluralism in circumstances where religion is a divisive factor in conflict (World Conference on Religion and Peace n.d. [1992]). A broad program of research and publication, training, and site-specific peacebuilding initiatives to explicitly engage the "meaning structures"—the moral and spiritual resources—of religions, in addition to their social structures, is in the early stages of implementation.

Third, beyond the efforts rooted in specific religious communities, religious actors are being targeted as a critical constituency to be trained and mobilized for peacebuilding, as witnessed in the work of the Nairobi Peace Initiative or the Mozambican Preparing People for Peace Program, described above. Other examples abound. In South Africa in 1991–93, for example, the Empowering for Reconciliation with Justice project, using Christian trainers and operating with the endorsement of church leaders, trained some five hundred local, regional, and national leaders, about half of whom came from the religious community, in conflict resolution skills (Kraybill 1995). In 1995 and 1996, Croatia, Serbia, and Bosnia-Herzegovina were sites for conflict-resolution training workshops for religious representatives, conducted by the Religion and Conflict Resolution Program of the Center for Strategic and International Studies, a think tank based in Washington, D.C.

Fourth, a number of religiously affiliated NGOs working in relief and development are seeking consultation and training at their headquarters and for field workers in conflict transformation and peacebuilding. The U.S.-based Catholic Relief Services has incorporated conflict transformation into its official mandate. Other examples include World Vision, Church World Service, and Lutheran World Relief. The World Conference on Religion and Peace has assisted in creating an Interreligious Development Action Committee as part of its Religion and Peacebuilding Program. Composed of major humanitarian agencies from the Islamic, Christian Orthodox, Catholic, and Protestant communities, the committee is planning a joint project in Bosnia (Steinfels 1995).

Fifth, because religious actors live and work in regions experiencing the most horrific conflicts and are able to draw on the special spiritual and institutional resources of their communities, a growing area of specialization is likely to be in healing and reconciliation—providing spiritual, pastoral, and psychological support to people who are emotionally and psychologically traumatized by war, violence, and torture. Examples in addition to those cited above (Liberia, Rwanda, and the former Yugoslavia) are programs for women who are victims of rape, also in the former Yugoslavia, and the Trauma Centre in Cape Town, South Africa (Raiser 1994, 8).

Sixth, in particularly difficult conflict situations, the above trends come together, amounting to a significant degree and multiplicity of religious engagement. In the former Yugoslavia, for example, a partial listing of internal and external religiously motivated actors working in fact finding, consultation, facilitation of interreligious dialogue, conflict resolution, nonviolence training, trauma healing, and so forth, includes the Center for the Promotion of Interreligious Dialogue, Justice, and Peace (Sarajevo); the Franciscans (Bosnia); Christian Information Service (Zagreb); Peace and Justice Institute of the Evangelical Theological Faculty (Osijek, Croatia); Conference of European Churches; World Council of Churches; International Fellowship of Reconciliation; Pax Christi; World Conference on Religion and Peace; Mennonites, Quakers, and Methodists; Council of Churches for Britain and Ireland; Conflict Resolution Training Committee of the University of Bradford (United Kingdom); Religion and Conflict Resolution Program of the Center for Strategic and International Studies (Washington, D.C.); International Orthodox Christian Charities (Baltimore); Appeal of Conscience Foundation (New York); and Catholic Relief Services (Baltimore). This list (based on Steele 1995) does not include religiously affiliated NGOs working on humanitarian assistance.

Seventh, there is a proliferation of proposals for ecumenically based citizens' services for peace, justice, and reconciliation (for example, the proposal made by the Justice, Peace, and the Integrity of Creation program of the World Council of Churches), signaling a growing desire, even determination, on the part of concerned individuals to become more personally and actively engaged in securing peace nonviolently. Possible functions of such programs include early warning for conflict prevention by indigenous religious actors, conflict monitoring, and conflict resolution (Raiser 1994, 8).

Germany's major political parties and NGOs have drafted a number of proposals for a Civilian Peace Service (CPS). One proposal from the Evangelical Church in Berlin-Brandenburg would offer the peace service as an alternative to military service for young male draftees and would also include women and members of other distinct social groups. Financed by the government but managed by NGOs and religious groups active in peace, development, and human rights work, the fields of action for the CPS would include security partnership at the local level (such as overcoming enmity toward foreigners); out-of-country deployment (for example, conflict resolution, peace-settlement and election monitoring); international refugee work (for example, prevention, accompaniment, return); and social defense (that is, resistance against armed threats to democracy) (Evangelical Church in Berlin-Brandenburg 1994).

Eighth, a final intriguing development is that of citizens holding dialogues across the planet by way of religious "conferences" on the Internet.

Participants converse within and across denominations and religions—sometimes angrily, but nonetheless newly engaging many people not used to such interreligious communication (Beer 1995).

What does all of this add up to for conflict transformation and peacebuilding? For one thing, it necessarily implies a pluralism of actors, roles, and methodologies in the religious sector. The sheer diversity of possible actors within, outside, or across religious communities is clear. The roles that religious actors define or develop for themselves, too, are necessarily manifold, for they are a function of various temporal factors, among them size, organizational level, and organizational structure of the religious actor; base of operation (inside or outside the conflict setting); degree of power and/or moral authority in the society; history of past programs (humanitarian, educational, and so on); and familiarity with the conflict parties or level of recognition in the society at large.

At least as important in shaping these roles, however, are the moral and spiritual—the theological and philosophical—resources motivating and informing the work of religiously motivated practitioners. These resources affect the way a given religious actor defines the fundamental problem in the conflict—what is wrong and what needs changing, be it structural, spiritual, moral, or psychological. The way the problem is defined shapes the way an intervention is conceived, its goals, and the methodologies and activities chosen to achieve the goals. Although religious actors are increasingly pursuing training in specific skill areas (active nonviolence, conflict resolution, trauma healing, and reconciliation), because of the inherent differences in the meaning structures of religious communities, it is likely that broad methodological diversity in the overall character of religiously motivated interventions in conflict situations will continue.

If active engagement and pluralism on the part of religious actors are here to stay, then other conclusions certainly follow: that the time has come to identify, encourage, develop, mobilize, and empower the special resources and potentials of religious actors for constructive conflict transformation—and to coordinate their contributions as integral to the larger peacebuilding enterprise.

ACKNOWLEDGMENTS

I wish to acknowledge William Vendley, secretary-general of the World Conference on Religion and Peace (WCRP), for his insights into the nature of religion and its potential role in conflict transformation and peacebuilding and the very helpful comments on an early draft of this chapter from Christopher Mitchell, William Headley, Marc Gopin, Kevin Clements, Ron Kraybill, and John Paul Lederach. I also wish to acknowledge the support of WCRP and, through it, the Rockefeller Foundation during the writing of this chapter.

REFERENCES

Ariyaratne, A. T. n.d.[1979]. *Collected Works.* Vol. I. Netherlands: n.p.

———. 1989. *Collected Works.* Vol. IV. Moratuwa, Sri Lanka: Vishva Lekha.

Africa News. 1991. "Bits and Pieces: Church and State." Summer.

Assefa, Hizkias. 1987. *Mediation of Civil Wars: Approaches and Strategies—The Sudan Conflict.* Boulder, Colo.: Westview.

———. 1993a. *Peace and Reconciliation as a Paradigm.* Nairobi, Kenya: Nairobi Peace Initiative.

———. 1993b. "On Healing and Reconciliation: A Dialogue." In *Pilgrim Voices: Citizens as Peacemakers,* ed. Garcia. Manila: Ateneo de Manila University Press.

———. 1993c. "The Sudan: Peacemaking in a Conflict within a Conflict." In *Pilgrim Voices: Citizens as Peacemakers,* ed. Garcia. Manila: Ateneo de Manila University Press.

———. 1994. "Relevance of Religion to Peacemaking." Paper presented at the sixth world assembly of the World Conference on Religion and Peace, November 5, Riva del Garda, Italy.

———. 1995. Interview, Harrisonburg, Virginia, February 17.

Bailey, S. 1979. "The Christian Vocation of Reconciliation." *Crucible: The Journal of the Board of Social Responsibility of the General Synod of the Church of England* (July-September): reprint.

———. 1993. *Peace Is a Process.* London: Quaker Home Service and Woodbrooke College.

Barr, C. W. 1994. "In Vietnam Monks Lead Protest to Repression." *Christian Science Monitor,* November 21.

———. 1995. "Vietnam's Monks Lead in Battle for Freedom." *Christian Science Monitor,* March 28.

Battersby, J. 1990. "South Africa's Churches Move Toward Conciliation." *Christian Science Monitor,* November 13.

Beer, Michael. 1995. Telephone interview. January 25. (Mr. Beer works with Nonviolence International in Washington, D.C.)

Berman, Maureen R., and Joseph E. Johnson, eds. 1977. *Unofficial Diplomats.* New York: Columbia University Press.

Bolling, L. 1977. "Quaker Work in the Middle East Following the June 1967 War." In *Unofficial Diplomats*, ed. Maureen R. Berman and Joseph E. Johnson. New York: Columbia University Press.

———. 1987. "Strengths and Weaknesses of Track Two: A Personal Account." In *Conflict Resolution: Track Two Diplomacy*, ed. John W. McDonald, Jr. and Diane B. Bendahmane. Washington, D.C.: Foreign Service Institute.

Boulding, Elise. 1986. "Two Cultures of Religion as Obstacles to Peace." *Zygon* 21 (December): 501–18.

Bradley, Barbara. 1994. "Under Burmese Junta, Tourists' Dollars Rule." *Christian Science Monitor*, December 29.

Brubaker, Alta. 1993. "Preparing People for Peace: Program of Work by the Peace and Reconciliation Committee of the Christian Council of Mozambique." Report to the Mennonite Central Committee, Nampula, Mozambique, March 18.

Brubaker, David. 1994. "Report on Healing/Reconciliation Assignment to Tanzania, Rwanda, Kenya (September, 1994)." Mennonite Central Committee, Akron, Pennsylvania.

Cambodian Mission for Peace. 1989. Press Release. May 12. Bangkok, Thailand.

———. 1994. "The Cambodian Mission for Peace: Description of Strategic Program Development." May 10.

Carter, Jimmy. 1994. Foreword to *Religion, The Missing Dimension of Statecraft*, ed. Douglas Johnston and Cynthia Sampson. New York: Oxford University Press.

Channer, Alan. 1994. "Cambodia's Nobel Nominee." *For a Change* 7 (October/November): 12–13.

Charles, J. Robert. 1994. *Mennonite International Peacemaking During and After the Cold War*. Occasional Paper No. 21. Akron, Penn.: Mennonite Central Committee.

Christian Peacemaker Teams. n.d.[1994]. "Christian Peacemaker Teams." Informational brochure of Mennonite, Church of the Brethren, and General Conference Mennonite churches. Chicago.

Claiborne, William. 1989. "De Klerk, Tutu Group to Meet." *Washington Post*, October 7.

Community of Sant'Egidio. n.d.[1993]. "Community of Sant'Egidio." Informational brochure. Rome.

Curle, Adam. 1971. *Making Peace*. London: Tavistock Press.

———. 1981. *True Justice: Quaker Peace Makers and Peace Making*. London: Quaker Home Service.

———. 1986a. *In the Middle: Non-official Mediation in Violent Situations*. New York: St. Martin's Press.

———. 1986b. "Mediation: Steps on the Long Road to Negotiated Settlement of Conflicts." *Transnational Perspectives* 12 (1): 5–7.

――. 1990. *Tools for Transformation: A Personal Study.* Stroud, U.K.: Hawthorn Press.

――. 1995. *Another Way: Positive Response to Contemporary Violence.* Oxford: Jon Carpenter Publishing.

de Souza, Isidore. 1994. "African Churches as Peacemakers." Presentation made at the African Church as Peacemaker Colloquium, October 2–6, Duquesne University, Pittsburgh, Pennsylvania.

Driedger, Leo, and Donald B. Kraybill. 1994. *Mennonite Peacemaking: From Quietism to Activism.* Scottdale, Penn.: Herald Press.

Drozdiak, William. 1995. "Algerian Parties Unite in Call for Peace Talks." *Washington Post,* January 14.

Eastern Mennonite University. 1994. "Prospectus: Conflict Analysis and Transformation Program," Harrisonburg, Virginia.

Esack, Maulana Faried. 1994. Presentation made at the Magaliesburg Consultation of the World Conference on Religion and Peace, August 8, Magaliesburg, South Africa.

Evangelical Church in Berlin-Brandenburg. 1994. "Civilian Peace Service." Declaration by the Executive. Evangelische Akademie, Berlin–Brandenburg, Berlin. Hans Sinn, trans. July 8.

Gandhi Peace Foundation. n.d.[1992]. "Gandhi Peace Foundation." Informational brochure. Delhi, India.

Germani, Clara. 1988. "Panama's Reluctant Church: Conservative Catholic Clergy Uneasy in Political Role." *Christian Science Monitor,* April 12.

Goncalves, Jaime. 1994. Presentation made at the African Church as Peacemaker Colloquium, October 2–6, Duquesne University, Pittsburgh, Pennsylvania.

Gopin, Marc. 1996. "Religion, Violence and Conflict Resolution." *Peace and Change* 22 (January): 1–31.

Hall, Mitchell. 1987. "In the Lion's Mouth: The Non-violent Mission of Acharya Muni Sushil Kumarji Maharaj." Unpublished manuscript. Warren, Vermont.

Hamlin, Bryan. 1991. "The Role of Religiously Motivated Peacemakers in International and Intercommunal Conflict." Paper presented at the National Conference on Peacemaking and Conflict Resolution, June 3–8, Charlotte, North Carolina.

――. 1992. *Forgiveness in International Affairs.* Salem, Ore.: Grosvenor Books.

Hart, Barry. 1993. *Trauma Healing and Reconciliation Training Manual: A Handbook for Trainers and Trainees.* Monrovia, Liberia: Christian Health Association of Liberia.

――. 1995. Telephone interview, January 28.

Hart, Barry, and Joe Gbaba. 1993. *UNICEF Training Manual of Conflict Resolution, Reconciliation, and Peace.* Monrovia, Liberia: UNICEF.

Henderson, Michael. 1992. "South Tyrol's Example." *Christian Science Monitor*, July 1.

———. 1995. "Africa's Quiet Peace-Maker." *For a Change* 8 (June/July): 13.

Herr, J. Robert, Ann Martin, Albert Widjaja, and Wilma Bailey. 1995. "Burma Report." Mennonite Central Committee, Akron, Pennsylvania.

Hume, Cameron. 1994. *Ending Mozambique's War: The Role of Mediation and Good Offices.* Washington, D.C.: United States Institute of Peace Press.

Ingram, Catherine. 1990. *In the Footsteps of Gandhi: Interviews with Spiritual Social Activists.* Berkeley, Calif.: Parallax Press.

International Observer Delegation. 1986. "A Path to Democratic Renewal: A Report of the February 7 Presidential Election in the Philippines." Washington, D.C.: National Democratic Institute for International Affairs.

Jack, Homer. 1993. *WCRP: A History of the World Conference on Religion and Peace.* New York: World Conference on Religion and Peace.

Jackson, Elmore. 1983. *Middle East Mission.* New York: W.W. Norton.

Johnston, Douglas. 1994. "The Churches and Apartheid in South Africa." In *Religion, The Missing Dimension of Statecraft*, ed. Douglas Johnston and Cynthia Sampson. New York: Oxford University Press.

Johnston, Douglas, and Cynthia Sampson, eds. 1994. *Religion, The Missing Dimension of Statecraft.* New York: Oxford University Press.

Jones, Clayton. 1989a. "Mending Broken Burma." *World Monitor* (August): 44–51.

———. 1989b. "Preaching Peace to Khmer Rouge." *Christian Science Monitor*, May 25.

———. 1989c. "Monks March in Subtle Protest." *Christian Science Monitor*, August 14.

Keller, Bill. 1994. "Zulu Party Ends Boycott of Vote in South Africa." *New York Times*, April 20.

Kim Teng Nhem. 1993. "Walking Slowly Towards Peace in Cambodia." In *Pilgrim Voices*, ed. Edward Garcia. Manila: Ateneo de Manila University Press.

Kraft, Kenneth. 1988. "Engaged Buddhism: An Introduction." In *The Path of Compassion: Writings on Socially Engaged Buddhism*, ed. Fred Eppsteiner. Berkeley, Calif.: Parallax Press.

Kraybill, Ronald. S. 1980. *Repairing the Breach: Ministering in Community Conflict.* Akron, Penn.: Mennonite Central Committee.

———. 1988. "From Head to Heart: The Cycle of Reconciliation." *Conciliation Quarterly* 7 (Fall): 2–3, 8.

———. 1994. "Transition from Rhodesia to Zimbabwe: The Role of Religious Actors." In *Religion, The Missing Dimension of Statecraft*, ed. Douglas Johnston and Cynthia Sampson. New York: Oxford University Press.

———. 1995. Interview, Harrisonburg, Virginia. February 13. (Ronald Kraybill worked for the Centre for Conflict Resolution [formerly Centre for Intergroup Studies] in Cape Town, South Africa, 1989–95.)

LaFranchi, Howard. 1995. "How a Year Changed Chiapas." *Christian Science Monitor*, January 3.

Larmer, Brook. 1988. "Cardinal Throws the Contras a Lifeline: Mediator's Plan Gives Rebels New Negotiating Power." *Christian Science Monitor* (Weekly International Edition), February 29–March 6.

Laue, James, and Gerald Cormick. 1978. "The Ethics of Intervention in Community Disputes." In *The Ethics of Social Intervention*, ed. Gordon Bermant, Herbert C. Kelman, and Donald P. Warwick. Washington, D.C.: Halsted Press.

Lean, Garth. 1983. *Frank Buchman: A Life*. London: Constable and Company.

Lean, Mary. 1995. "Did God Intervene in South Africa?" *For a Change* 8 (June/July): 10–11.

Lederach, John Paul. 1989. Interview, Washington, D.C., June 13.

———. 1993. "Pacifism in Contemporary Conflict: A Christian Perspective." Paper presented at the United States Institute of Peace symposium on "Religious Perspectives on Pacifism," July 28, Washington, D.C.

———. 1995. *Preparing for Peace: Conflict Transformation Across Cultures*. Syracuse, N.Y.: Syracuse University Press.

———. Forthcoming. *Building Peace: Sustainable Reconciliation in Divided Societies*. Washington, D.C.: United States Institute of Peace Press.

Linden, Ian. 1980. *The Catholic Church and the Struggle for Zimbabwe*. London: Longman.

Little, David. 1994. *Sri Lanka: The Invention of Enmity*. Washington, D.C.: United States Institute of Peace Press.

Liyanage, Gunadasa. 1988. *Revolution Under the Breadfruit Tree*. Nugegoda, Sri Lanka: Sinha Publishers.

Lubbe, Gerrie. 1994. *A Decade of Interfaith Dialogue*. Johannesburg: South African Chapter of the World Conference on Religion and Peace.

Lusophone Consultation. 1990. "Peace and Reconciliation in Angola and Mozambique." Communique from participants. Limuru, Kenya, September 20–27.

Luttwak, Edward. 1994. "Franco-German Reconciliation: The Overlooked Role of the Moral Re-Armament Movement." In *Religion, The Missing Dimension of Statecraft*, ed. Douglas Johnston and Cynthia Sampson. New York: Oxford University Press.

Macy, Joanna. 1985. "In Indra's Net: Sarvodaya and Our Mutual Efforts for Peace." In *The Path of Compassion: Writings on Socially Engaged Buddhism*, ed. Fred Eppsteiner. Berkeley, Calif.: Parallax Press.

McConnell, John A. 1995. *Mindful Mediation: A Handbook for Buddhist Peacemakers*. Bangkok: Buddhist Research Center, Mahachula Buddhist University.

Miller, Harold F. 1993. *Peace and Reconciliation in Africa: A Preliminary Survey of Ecumenical Perspectives and Initiatives*. Occasional Paper No. 19. Akron, Penn.: Mennonite Central Committee.

Mitchell, Christopher. 1993. "The Process and Stages of Mediation: Two Sudanese Cases." In *Making War and Waging Peace: Foreign Intervention in Africa*, ed. David R. Smock. Washington, D.C.: U.S. Institute of Peace Press.

Morrow, John. n.d.[1994]. "The Corrymeela Community." Informational brochure. Belfast, Northern Ireland.

Morrow, Duncan, and Derick Wilson. 1994. "Churches and Chaos in Northern Ireland: From Religion and Conflict to Freedom in Faith?" Paper prepared for a consultation of the World Conference on Religion and Peace, September 6–11, Bellagio, Italy.

Nichols, Bruce. 1994. "Religious Conciliation between the Sandinistas and the East Coast Indians of Nicaragua." In *Religion, The Missing Dimension of Statecraft*, ed. Douglas Johnston and Cynthia Sampson. New York: Oxford University Press.

Nhat Hanh, Thich. 1987a. *Being Peace*. Berkeley, Calif.: Parallax Press.

———. 1987b. "Seven Steps to Reconciliation." *Fellowship* (July/August): 4–5.

———. 1988. *The Heart of Understanding*. Berkeley, Calif.: Parallax Press.

Nonviolence Education and Training Program. n.d.[1994]. "The Nonviolence Education and Training Program." Informational brochure of the International Fellowship of Reconciliation, Alkmaar, Netherlands.

Nonviolence International. 1995. "Nonviolence International." Informational brochure, Washington, D.C.

Patriot (New Delhi). 1987. "Punjab Talks Gaining Momentum," May 9.

Perera, D.A., and A.T. Ariyaratne. 1989. "Sarvodaya as a Movement." Occasional Paper. Moratuwa, Sri Lanka: Sarvodaya Shramadana.

Perry, Patricia Hunt. n.d.[1989]. "Opening the Cone and Harvesting the Seeds: Thich Nhat Hanh, Buddhism, and the Peace Movement." Unpublished paper. Ramapo College of New Jersey, Mahwah, New Jersey.

Pierre, Andrew J., and William B. Quandt. 1995. "The 'Contract' With Algeria: One Last Chance for the West to Help Stop the Civil War." *Washington Post*, January 22.

Piguet, Jacqueline. 1985. *For the Love of Tomorrow: The Story of Irene Laure*. London: Grosvenor Books.

Pond, Peter. 1995. Telephone interview, February 8. (Mr. Pond works with the Cambodian Mission for Peace from his home in Providence, Rhode Island.)

Princen, Thomas. 1987. "International Mediation—The View from the Vatican: Lessons from Mediating the Beagle Channel Dispute." *Negotiation Journal* 3 (4): 347–66.

———. 1992a. *Intermediaries in International Conflict.* Princeton: Princeton University Press.

———. 1992b. "Quiet Peacemaking in a Civil War." In *When Talk Works: Profiles of Mediators,* ed. Deborah M. Kolb and Associates. San Francisco: Jossey-Bass.

Proposal for Action. 1994. African Church as Peacemaker Colloquium, October 2–6, Duquesne University, Pittsburgh, Pennsylvania.

Raiser, Konrad. 1994. "Peace on Earth: New Visions and New Praxis." Address presented at the Corrymeela Consultation on Non-Violent Approaches to Conflict Resolution, June 2, Bally Castle, County Antrim, Northern Ireland.

Rees, Elfan. 1977. "Exercises in Private Diplomacy: Selected Activities of the Commission of the Churches on International Affairs." In *Unofficial Diplomats,* ed. Maureen R. Berman and Joseph E. Johnson. New York: Columbia University Press.

Reuters News Service. 1993. "Zaire's Ruler Returns after Trip to France." *Washington Post,* February 28.

Richburg, Keith. 1993. "Mobutu Clings to Power in Violence-Torn Zaire." *Washington Post,* February 23.

Robberson, Tod. 1994. "Mexico Says Catholic Church Fomented Peasant Rebellion." *Washington Post,* January 1.

Sampson, Cynthia. 1987. "A Study of the International Conciliation Work of Religious Figures." Harvard University Program on Negotiation, Working Paper Series 87-6. Cambridge, Mass.

———. 1994. "To Make Real the Bond Between Us All: Quaker Conciliation During the Nigerian Civil War." In *Religion, The Missing Dimension of Statecraft,* ed. Douglas Johnston and Cynthia Sampson. New York: Oxford University Press.

———. Forthcoming. "The Impact of Social Action as a Path to Peacemaking for Religious Practitioners." In *Conflict Resolution and Social Justice,* ed. R. Rubenstein and F. Blechman.

Sampson, Cynthia, and John Paul Lederach, eds. Forthcoming. *From the Ground Up: Mennonite Contributions to International Peacebuilding.*

Schirch, Lisa. 1995. *Conflict Intervention by Civilian Peace Teams.* Uppsala, Sweden: Life and Peace Institute.

Schneidman, Whitney W. 1993. "Conflict Resolution in Mozambique." In *Making War and Waging Peace: Foreign Intervention in Africa,* ed. David R. Smock. Washington, D.C.: United States Institute of Peace Press.

Scott, David Clark. 1994a. "Mexico Bishop at Center of Crisis." *Christian Science Monitor*, January 24.

———. 1994b. "Rebels Win Rights for Indians, Spur Ballot Reforms for Mexico." *Christian Science Monitor*, March 4.

Sharma, I. C. 1990. "The Ethics in Eastern Philosophy and Religion." In *Nonviolence in Theory and Practice*, ed. Robert L. Holmes. Belmont, Calif.: Wadsworth Publishing Company.

Shiner, Cindy. 1992. "Congo Takes Faltering First Steps Toward Democracy." *Africa News*. July 6–19.

Siddhachalam Newsletter. 1987. "Guruji's Peace Mission in Punjab." July.

Siddhachalam Newsletter. 1988. "Punjab." June.

Sivaraksa, Sulak. n.d.[1994]. "Buddhism and Peace: A Buddhist Approach to Mediation and Reconciliation." Paper presented at the Sixth World Assembly of the World Conference on Religion and Peace, Riva del Garda, Italy, November 5.

Steele, David. 1994. "At the Front Lines of the Revolution: East Germany's Churches Give Sanctuary and Succor to the Purveyors of Change." In *Religion, The Missing Dimension of Statecraft*, ed. Douglas Johnston and Cynthia Sampson. New York: Oxford University Press.

———. 1995. Telephone interview, January 10. (Dr. Steele works with the Religion and Conflict Resolution Program of the Center for Strategic and International Studies, Washington, D.C.)

Steinfels, Peter. 1995. "Two World Conferences and Two Very Different Roles for Religion: One Quiet, the Other Noisy." *New York Times*, March 18.

Tutu, Desmond. 1994. *The Rainbow People of God: The Making of a Peaceful Revolution*. New York: Doubleday.

United States Institute of Peace. 1993. "Conflict and Conflict Resolution in Mozambique." Report from a conference on "Discussions from Dialogues on Conflict Resolution," July 13–15, 1992, Washington, D.C.

Vendley, William F. 1995. Telephone interview, February 8.

Vendley, William, and David Little. 1994. "Implications for Religious Community." In *Religion, The Missing Dimension of Statecraft*, ed. Douglas Johnston and Cynthia Sampson. New York: Oxford University Press.

Wachira, George, and Florence Mpaayei. 1993. *Report of the Symposium on the Role of Religious Leaders in Peacemaking and Social Change in Africa*. Nyeri, Kenya, July 18–23. Nairobi: Nairobi Peace Initiative.

Warren, Roland L. 1987. "American Friends Service Committee Mediation Efforts in Germany and Korea." In *Conflict Resolution: Track Two Diplomacy*, ed. John W. McDonald, Jr. and Diane B. Bendahmane. Washington, D.C.: Foreign Service Institute.

Washington Post. 1992. "Guatemalans Find Limited Accord in Peace Talks," August 9.

——. 1993. "Pope Touring Africa," February 4.

Wehr, Paul, and John Paul Lederach. 1991. "Mediating Conflict in Central America." *Journal of Peace Research* 28 (February): 85–98.

Wink, Walter. 1987. *Violence and Nonviolence in South Africa: Jesus' Third Way.* Philadelphia: New Society Publishers.

Winkler, Renate. 1986. "Recent Church Initiatives for Peace and Justice in South Africa." Centre for Intergroup Studies, Cape Town, South Africa. Mimeograph.

Wise, Gordon, and Alice Cardel. 1991. "The Cardinal and the Revolution." *For a Change* 4 (April): 12–13.

Wooster, Henry. 1994. "Faith at the Ramparts: The Philippine Catholic Church and the 1986 Revolution." In *Religion, The Missing Dimension of Statecraft,* ed. Douglas Johnston and Cynthia Sampson. New York: Oxford University Press.

World Conference on Religion and Peace. n.d.[1992]. *World Conference on Religion and Peace.* New York: WCRP/International.

Yarrow, C. H. 1977. "Quaker Efforts toward Reconciliation in the India-Pakistan War of 1965." In *Unofficial Diplomats,* ed. M.R. Berman and J.E. Johnson. New York: Columbia University Press.

——. 1978. *Quaker Experiences in International Conciliation.* New Haven: Yale University Press.

Young, Ronald. 1987. Interview, Cambridge, Massachusetts. (Mr. Young served as a Quaker International Affairs Representative in the Middle East, 1982–85.)

PART THREE

PRACTITIONERS

9

A DIPLOMAT'S VIEW

Cameron R. Hume

The experience of the last half-decade has brought a shift away from the traditional view of international conflict and its resolution. First, the direct role of major powers—both former colonial powers and the superpowers— is decreasing. These states have a narrow view of their interests abroad and therefore a diminished will to act. They have not withdrawn from world affairs, but they are searching for collective means to influence events.

Second, the prohibition against foreign intervention in a state's domestic affairs has eroded. Since so many conflicts today are internal, it could not be otherwise. Some interventions, such as assistance to Haiti to conduct national elections, train a police force, and build a judiciary, reinforce state sovereignty; others, such as Operation Provide Comfort in northern Iraq, derogate from state sovereignty. Nonetheless, claims for exceptions to this prohibition should be treated with extreme caution.

Third, because diplomats prefer to act collectively, they rely on the UN Security Council to coordinate actions and to secure maximum international legitimacy for interventions. They often turn to the UN secretary-general to implement policy. During the Cold War, the UN role in security matters was limited to problems in the Third World, but Washington and

---

The views expressed are the author's own and do not necessarily represent those of the U.S. Department of State.

Moscow have now invited the United Nations to assist in conflicts as close to home as Haiti and Georgia, respectively.

Diplomats now use experimental approaches that combine several conflict-resolution measures, including the following:

- *An enhanced role for the UN secretary-general.* This position has unique legitimacy for acting on behalf of the international community, especially when providing third-party good offices, facilitation, or mediation to sustain a dialogue between parties. Secretary-General Boutros Boutros-Ghali expanded his ability to act by maintaining political agents (Special Representatives) in crisis areas; small diplomatic coalitions (Friends of the Secretary-General) provide advice and support to bolster his influence.

- *States acting in concert.* Regional arrangements, such as the Organization of American States (OAS) and the Organization of African Unity (OAU), now collaborate with UN operations. Ad hoc coalitions of states have filled gaps between inaction and UN peacekeeping in places like Somalia and Haiti.

- *UN-sanctioned enforcement measures.* Before 1990, the Security Council had adopted enforcement measures in only two cases: the arms embargo against South Africa and the trade embargo against Southern Rhodesia. Since then, it has adopted sanctions against Iraq, Libya, the former Yugoslavia and its successor states, Somalia, Liberia, Rwanda, parts of Angola, and Haiti. It has authorized coalitions of willing states to take all necessary measures to enforce its resolutions, in the first instance to reverse Iraq's invasion of Kuwait. In Somalia and Bosnia, it authorized UN peacekeeping forces to enforce their own mandates, even when doing so would require the use of force. It established international tribunals to consider charges of crimes against humanity in the former Yugoslavia and Rwanda.

- *Assistance for the civilian authority.* When there has been an agreement with local authorities, starting with Namibia in 1989, the United Nations has helped states to exercise their basic political powers. It conducted or monitored elections in Haiti, El Salvador, South Africa, Cambodia, Mozambique, and Angola. It has monitored or trained police, organized national armies, and established judicial systems.

Because the UN Security Council has become the key forum for sorting out diplomatic approaches to so many conflicts, it is a natural place to start this analysis. We then turn to Africa, the states of the former Soviet Union, and the former Yugoslavia to see how these approaches have been applied.

EXPERIMENTAL AND PRACTICAL APPROACHES: THE SECURITY COUNCIL

As a member of the U.S. delegation to the UN Security Council, I now frequently encounter two questions: To what use can you put the Security Council, and when should you use it?

The Security Council is diplomacy's emergency room. Cases that lack urgency or that can be treated elsewhere are not admitted. The remaining cases threaten international peace and security and risk the use of force. These are the Security Council's business.

The historic change in world politics in the last half-decade has meant a change in the council's agenda as well. Before 1989, it met most frequently because of the Arab-Israeli conflict; the next most acute cases were in southern Africa. In the years since, southern Africa has been removed from the agenda, with the exception of the current peacekeeping operation in Angola. The Arab-Israeli conflict remains, but the main action is in the Israeli-Palestinian dialogue and the various regional working groups for the Middle East peace process. Today, conflicts in Africa, ex-Yugoslavia, and the former Soviet Union dominate the agenda.

Within the council, a shift in leadership has accompanied the shift in agenda. Ten years ago, the nonaligned caucus initiated almost all meetings and sponsored all resolutions on the Arab-Israeli conflict and southern Africa. This is no longer the case. Many resolutions are drafted initially by other council members (such as the Contact Group on ex-Yugoslavia) or by the council president acting on behalf of all members. The Security Council's five permanent members (China, France, Russia, the United Kingdom, and the United States) exercise leadership on issues involving sanctions or the use of force.

Now the council meets more frequently, and the tone is different. Most meetings in the past consisted of debates, often lasting several sessions, during which ambassadors, many of whom were not members of the council, recorded the views of their governments. A resolution might or might not be adopted. Now the council infrequently meets for extended debates. With the exception of parties to a conflict, nonmembers rarely speak, and members normally speak only to explain their votes. Today the council is less a forum for debate and more a decision-making body.

Most work of the council is done through informal consultations of the whole, open only to members of the council and selected secretariat officials. Here members exchange views on reports submitted by the secretary-general, ask the secretariat for updates, receive briefings from key officials, negotiate decisions to be made by the council, and prepare for formal meetings. The atmosphere is collegial.

In addition, members consult among themselves prior to informal consultations. For example, the permanent members consult on issues such as reform of the UN Charter or disarmament. The nonaligned caucus determines positions to be represented by the group's monthly spokesperson. The Contact Group (France, Germany, Russia, the United Kingdom, the United States and—in New York—Italy) negotiate a group position before every council meeting on ex-Yugoslavia. Comparable groups, at times including nonmembers of the council, influence the council on such issues as Haiti, Somalia, Western Sahara, Georgia, and Afghanistan.

The increased importance of the council's work has stimulated proposals for reform, the most fundamental of which would expand the fifteen-member council by adding an as yet undetermined number of permanent and nonpermanent members. For its part, the council has taken steps to expedite its work methods and to keep nonmembers of the council informed: The agenda for informal consultations is now published in advance, members holding the council's rotating presidency provide briefings on a regular basis, and governments that contribute troops to a peacekeeping operation are consulted before the council makes decisions on these operations. Change continues toward a more open, action-oriented council.

Ever since Iraq's invasion of Kuwait, the range of council activity has expanded dramatically. For the first time, it has dispatched members on several fact-finding missions to crisis areas, including Angola, Bosnia, Somalia, Rwanda, Burundi, and Western Sahara. In addition to arms and trade embargoes, it has instituted a border demarcation, a disarmament program, cooperation with NATO in the use of force, and international tribunals. Short of constituting and using a force under its own command to end a threat to peace and security, the council has now made use of all the authority granted it by the UN Charter.

The Security Council is a political and legislative forum. Negotiations within the council typically involve decision-making issues and matters of process, leaving substantive negotiations with a particular conflict's parties up to the secretary-general. The council acts by granting authority for the secretary-general to act on its behalf or by conferring legitimacy on actions by states. Given the myriad of forms for diplomacy today, the council plays an invaluable role as a clearinghouse for many diplomatic initiatives.

IMPARTIAL THIRD PARTIES IN AFRICA

Conflicts in Africa, formerly viewed as a consequence of great power rivalry, are now considered essentially internal conflicts. Local protagonists must play the primary role in resolving these conflicts.

Efforts to use the channels of diplomacy for peacemaking initiatives in the region have been on a collective rather than unilateral basis, with Secretary-General Boutros-Ghali often in the lead. Instruments of intervention have been purposely impartial: special representatives of the secretary-general, peacekeeping forces, human rights monitors, humanitarian-assistance operations, support for elections, arms embargoes, and commissions of inquiry or international tribunals. Nongovernmental organizations (NGOs) have made special contributions. Coordinating such efforts with states in the region and with major powers is a prerequisite for progress. In many cases, a special representative of the secretary-general is the person who seems the most able to combine the various components of intervention into a coherent approach.

Although UN secretaries-general have always sent representatives on official missions, Boutros-Ghali has greatly expanded this practice. Special representatives derive their authority from the secretary-general, they are bound by the UN Charter and the resolutions of the Security Council, and they must be impartial. Most, like Lakhdar Brahimi, are former diplomats; others, like Aldo Ajello, are career international civil servants. Real talent, as always, is in short supply. Unlike ambassadors, special representatives do not promote the interests of a sovereign state but help the secretary-general accomplish the goals of the United Nations. Boutros-Ghali used special representatives to maintain a watching brief, manage programs designed to forestall conflict, negotiate comprehensive agreements, and direct peacekeeping operations.

In January 1995, Boutros-Ghali informed the Security Council that he had decided to send Berhanu Dinka of Ethiopia as special envoy to Sierra Leone, a country suffering from the consequences of a local insurgency and the spillover effects of the civil war in neighboring Liberia. Dinka would report on the situation and explore opportunities to resolve the conflict. As initial steps, he established contact with the government, UN agency representatives, well-informed members of the diplomatic corps, and, after a year of attempts, with representatives of the insurgency. Special represen-tatives generally seek contact with representatives of humanitarian-relief agencies, such as the International Committee of the Red Cross, NGOs, and local churches, especially if they have been active in areas controlled by insurgents.

Such a presence is only in the embryonic stage. In neighboring Liberia, the secretary-general maintains a special representative, assisted by mili-tary and civilian officials. Since September 1993, this small peacekeeping operation has been charged with monitoring the situation and assisting in the peace process managed by the Economic Community of West African States (ECOWAS), whose peacekeeping force tries to maintain a cease-fire and to provide essential security, at least in urban areas along the coast. Following agreement in late 1995 among the parties in the Liberian con-flict, the ECOWAS peacekeeping force received a new mandate to assist with demobilization of forces and preparation for elections. Despite the dif-ferent circumstances and size of operations in Sierra Leone and Liberia, the secretary-general's special representatives play a similar role: to be thor-oughly engaged in the situation, to coordinate with other actors on the ground, and to seek ways of resolving the conflict.

Until October 1995, Amadou Ould Abdallah, special representative in Burundi, showed to what extent an individual endowed with special acu-men and initiative can develop this role. The risks of violent conflict in Burundi are great. In this country, UN human rights monitors reinforce the special representative. The OAU has military observers in the field. The UN High Commissioner for Refugees (UNHCR) provides assistance to refugees from neighboring Rwanda. Ould Abdallah worked out his own modus operandi, meeting regularly with leaders from all parties but making his independence and impartiality evident; he made judicious use of the media to emphasize his views to a wider audience. For example, after the presidents of Rwanda and Burundi were killed when their plane was shot down, Ould Abdallah maintained a vigil of radio broadcasts to keep the country calm. Throughout his mission, he insisted that the parties main-tain a dialogue as the alternative to more violence.

The secretary-general, following his trip to Burundi in July 1995, set up an independent Commission of Inquiry into the assassination of President Melchior Ndadaye in October 1993 and the massacres that ensued. The commission operates separately from the special representative, but they are both working to improve the prospects for political dialogue. Although no group of donor states has been formally constituted with the specific aim of supporting peace efforts in Burundi, consultations to this effect have taken place among members of the Rwanda Operational Support Group, which was set up in November 1994 to encourage and coordinate efforts to help improve conditions inside Rwanda.

The secretary-general's special representative for Angola, Alioune Blondin Beye, former foreign minister of Mali, has worked within a more specific framework. Beye undertook the task of putting back on track the Angolan peace process, which collapsed when Uniao Nacional para a Independencia Total de Angola (UNITA) leader Jonas Savimbi withdrew because of his dissatisfaction with the first round of voting in September 1992. Despite initial UNITA victories in the ensuing fighting, government forces achieved a dominant position within two years. During this time, Beye maintained a difficult dialogue between the parties that was aimed at repairing the peace process.

Beye's mediation was sustained by resources from the United Nations and support from outside governments. The United Nations Angola Verification Mission (UNAVEM) II peacekeeping force was reduced to a few hundred military observers, enough to keep tabs on events, monitor local cessations of hostilities when possible, and coordinate with humanitarian-relief agencies. Governments in the region used their influence with both sides, and Zambia hosted marathon talks to relaunch the peace process. From farther afield, the "troika" countries (Portugal, Russia, and the United States) that brokered the 1991 Bicesse Accords between the government and UNITA sent envoys to support Beye.

Beye's successful mediation led to a new agreement between the conflict's parties and to a new UN operation, UNAVEM III. This operation stayed on track throughout the first year of implementation, but the lack of progress toward disarmament and the residue of distrust threaten the desired outcome.

Special representatives have maximum clout when they direct large peacekeeping operations. In October 1992, Boutros-Ghali named Aldo Ajello to head the UN peacekeeping operation in Mozambique. Ajello soon found that the comprehensive peace accords negotiated in Rome with the assistance of the Community of Sant'Egidio (an Italian religion-based NGO) needed modification. The implementation timetable had to be extended by up to two years; it took almost six months to build up the peacekeeping force to its authorized strength. Right from the beginning, Ajello knew he would have to play two major roles—one as the chief executive officer of the UN operation, and the other as the mediator in charge of convincing the parties to accept pragmatic modifications to the Rome agreement.

In his role as mediator, Ajello would have to persuade the parties to modify their expectations for implementing the peace agreement while maintaining their commitment to peace. Such a task required good political skills. Unlike a situation in which two private parties need to modify a mutually binding contract, no court could decide the Mozambique case. Nor were there any arrangements for dispute settlement, such as those frequently included in state treaties and other international legal agreements. Since the Resistencia Nacional Mocambicana (RENAMO) lacked technical experience, Ajello would have to serve as both coach and referee.

The Mozambique operation had a significant civilian component. In the course of the negotiations, the RENAMO insurgents accepted the theoretical authority of the government, but they required practical assurance that this authority would be exercised fairly. The United Nations provided this assurance through its election assistance unit, which helped to ensure that the elections were organized properly and conducted fairly. Although RENAMO's leader threatened at one point to withdraw from the elections, a timely intervention by Ajello, with broad international support, kept RENAMO in the game. The United Nations also provided a unit of police monitors, who advised in the reform of the national police force and monitored police performance during the period of the peacekeeping mandate. Election assistance and police monitors are often the key components of peacekeeping operations in internal conflicts.

Ajello emphasized the importance of acting not for the UN bureaucracy, but for the international community. Shortly after his arrival he instituted regular Monday meetings with ambassadors of major donor countries—France, Italy, Portugal, the United Kingdom, and the United States—all of which had already been involved in the Rome negotiations. He held parallel sessions with ambassadors from countries in the region—Botswana, Malawi, Kenya, Zimbabwe, and South Africa—which had in different ways already supported the peace process. Ajello's coordination ensured that governments with influence would operate on the same factual assessments, making joint action more likely.

Special representatives must be impartial among the parties to a conflict; committed to dialogue as an alternative to force; and able to coordinate efforts to this end made by governments, international organizations, humanitarian-relief agencies, and NGOs.

REGIONAL ARRANGEMENTS: CENTRAL ASIA AND THE CAUCASUS

Perhaps the one diplomatic approach that has been explored and developed the most in recent years has been the use of a select group of countries to conduct or, at times, support an effort at conflict resolution. Regional organizations, such as the OAU, have undertaken various conflict-resolution tasks; ad hoc coalitions, such as the multinational force led by the United States in Haiti, have performed peacekeeping functions; and NATO was in charge of the peacekeeping operation in Bosnia. The challenge in such efforts is to ensure sufficient cohesive participation by states that have an ability to influence the parties in conflict, so that their power can be consistently exerted toward a solution. They can act directly or in support of a negotiating process conducted by the UN secretary-general.

Diplomats insist that lasting solutions are realistic solutions. As one enduring example, diplomats are inclined to accommodate the interests of a major power when a conflict takes place in its own region. Such a power is likely to have relations with one or more of the protagonists to the conflict, the capacity to project force into the area of conflict, and the determination to stick with an operation until it reaches a successful conclusion. When the Soviet Union dissolved into separate independent states, Russia was, by all standards, the major regional power. Because the involvement of major powers in a conflict increases the risk of its escalation, diplomats want to construct controlled circumstances.

International law does not countenance special norms permitting major powers to intervene in conflicts throughout their regions. The inherent right of self-defense may apply more frequently when the conflict is near home, as may the right of collective security from the besieged state's perspective. When a state confronts an internal conflict, no other state has a right or obligation to act as policeman.

Article 52 of the UN Charter recognizes the role of regional arrangements. This provision certainly includes such formally constituted organizations as the OAU, the OAS, NATO, and the Organization for Security and Cooperation in Europe (OSCE). Such recognition becomes more ambiguous with other organizations such as the League of Arab States, which excludes some states in its region, and the Commonwealth of Independent States (CIS), whose legitimacy as an organization of equal states is not universally acknowledged. The status of informal, ad hoc groupings has yet to be determined.

The case of Haiti demonstrates several such arrangements. In the early stages of the country's political crisis, the OAS was an equal partner with the United Nations in addressing the crisis; the International Civilian Verification Mission, a jointly managed group of human rights monitors, is concrete evidence of this partnership. Second, Canada, France, the United

States, and Venezuela constituted a group of states supporting the secretary-general's efforts. Finally, in the summer of 1994, the United States organized a coalition of states constituting a multinational force that entered Haiti a few months later. This case demonstrates how to arrange for such a UN peacekeeping deployment to succeed a multinational force: The transition was planned months in advance; the rotation of troops was phased to ensure continuity at all times; and the United States, which had led the multinational force, stayed on as the largest troop contributor.

The cases of Nagorno-Karabakh (for which operations are only in the planning stage), Georgia, and Tajikistan also demonstrate approaches involving regional arrangements. Here the peacekeeping operations fielded by the United Nations and the countries in the region have been concurrent, not consecutive. While the United Nations, the OSCE, and Moscow all encourage negotiations between the parties, Moscow has taken the lead in providing troops for the main peacekeeping operations in Georgia and Tajikistan; the UN operations are small. How can the international community sanction a major power's intervention but restrain how that major power intervenes?

Various regional groups have active programs aimed at resolving conflicts in the former Soviet Union. The OSCE traces its origins back to the 1975 Helsinki Conference, which reaffirmed the borders of postwar Europe but boosted human rights issues as an engine for change. In 1992, it promulgated standards for peacekeeping in Europe, and since then it has prepared to mount a peacekeeping operation in Nagorno-Karabakh, whose members include all European states, Canada, and the United States.

Shortly after the collapse of the Soviet Union, Russia gradually brought together the other Soviet republics that had recently gained independence (except for the three Baltic states) to form the CIS. The idea behind the new regional organization was to fill the gap created by the transformation of the Soviet Army into a Russian defense force and by the organization of separate armed forces in the newly independent states. Moscow is concerned about the security situation in these neighboring countries, and the CIS could be a vehicle for Moscow to project Russian power under a collective regional umbrella.

Ad hoc groups also support mediation between the parties in a conflict. Nine OSCE members constituted the "Minsk Group" to facilitate negotiations over the future of Nagorno-Karabakh. Britain, France, Russia, Germany, and the United States constitute both the "Friends of Georgia" and the "Friends of Tajikistan," which were formed to support the secretary-general's mediation. The goal of both groups is to bring a consistent position to bear on the parties in these countries' conflicts; acting together, strength is multiplied. While the effort in these cases is ad hoc, the effect roughly equals the strength that a unanimous Security Council mandate can give to diplomatic efforts by the secretary-general.

Nagorno-Karabakh, a predominantly Armenian enclave inside Azerbaijan, was the first of these areas to receive international attention. The Minsk Group, led by its Western and Russian co-chairs, achieved a diminution in the level of fighting. The OSCE has planned a peacekeeping operation in the area, to be conducted with assistance from the United Nations; Russia would be the largest troop contributor. In contrast, the negotiations involving Baku, Yerevan, and Stepanakert (the capital of Nagorno-Karabakh) have stalled. Fear and animosity divide the parties; differences in approach among members of the Minsk Group, especially between Moscow and Western capitals, have not helped. Although Boutros-Ghali has held talks with both sides and flirted with the idea of a greater UN role, so far the United Nations has kept to the sidelines.

The Abkhazian minority in Georgia has waged a separatist battle for years against the central government for control of its own region. There is no international support for the minority's own independent state, but Abkhaz forces, initially supported by the Russian military, expelled ethnic Georgians from the region and established control. The Russians then brokered a cease-fire and an agreement for a CIS peacekeeping force made up of Russian troops; the situation on the ground has since been frozen in place. UN involvement started with humanitarian assistance provided by UNHCR. In 1993, the secretary-general appointed Eduard Brunner, the Swiss ambassador in Paris, as special envoy for the purpose of facilitating a dialogue between Abkhaz and Georgian leaders. Shortly thereafter, the Security Council approved the establishment of a small peacekeeping force to monitor the situation, to assist with refugee resettlement arrangements, and to keep an eye on the CIS force. No decisive progress has been made.

Tajikistan, where an Islamic insurgency is waging war against the Moscow-imposed regime, offers an interesting comparison. CIS forces, again predominantly Russian, patrol the border with Afghanistan and monitor a cease-fire. The United Nations has the lead on negotiations. Ramiro Piriz-Ballon, a Uruguayan diplomat who is the special representative of the secretary-general, has conducted four rounds of talks with the parties. A small but effective peacekeeping operation buttresses his role by dispatching monitoring teams to investigate incidents and to observe the CIS force. The

•

"Friends" group and periodic resolutions of the Security Council provide political support. The peacekeeping operation was designed primarily to meet the needs of the mediation, thus strengthening the political effort. The force in Georgia has a broader mandate, but it has been a less effective adjunct to the mediation.

These approaches are all works in progress. A few elements are repeated in each case: an effort by Moscow to play a privileged role in dealing with conflicts in the former Soviet republics; deployment of Russian forces as peacekeepers; a UN or OSCE role in directing or monitoring the peacekeepers; an international mediation or negotiating forum; and an ad hoc group of governments that supports the negotiations. Until one of the efforts is crowned with success, it is too early to affirm that this pattern constitutes the right approach.

SANCTIONS AND THE USE OF FORCE IN THE FORMER YUGOSLAVIA

The international response to the crisis in ex-Yugoslavia includes the largest UN peacekeeping operation ever, the largest NATO operation ever, and perhaps the most complex matrix of negotiating tracks ever. Out of this experience four questions stand out.

1. How can sanctions be used? The sanctions imposed by the Security Council have several purposes:

   • The arms embargo imposed on all ex-Yugoslav states in September 1991 was designed to reduce the level of fighting. However, the immediate result of the embargo was to strengthen the power of the Serbs vis-à-vis the other parties, since the predominantly Serb Yugoslav National Army was one of the most heavily armed in Europe and much of its weaponry was produced domestically. This advantage has gradually diminished. Both Bosnia and Croatia circumvented the embargo, and Croatia in particular acquired major weapons systems. The result of the arms embargo has not matched its intentions.

   • The comprehensive economic embargo imposed on Serbia in March 1993 was intended to dissuade Belgrade from supporting the Bosnian Serb party. Such support did indeed diminish, in conjunction with a growing rift between Belgrade's Slobodan Milosevic and the Bosnian Serbs' Radovan Karadzic. The European Union (EU) dispatched monitors to encourage compliance with the embargo, which inflicted real, but not decisive, damage to the Serbian economy.

- Belgrade imposed its own sanctions against the Bosnian Serbs in August 1994, following the latter's failure to accept the territorial proposal made by the Contact Group. In response, the Security Council suspended a number of sanctions against Belgrade: the bans on air travel, cultural exchanges, and sporting events. An independent monitoring mission under the authority of the co-chairs of the International Conference on the Former Yugoslavia (ICFY) then certified Belgrade's compliance. These sanctions reduced Bosnian Serb access to supplies in Serbia.

- Targeted sanctions were imposed in August 1994 by the Security Council. These stiffer sanctions on the Bosnian Serbs prohibited financial transfers and international travel by key Bosnian Serb leaders. They have not, in fact, traveled abroad since.

Sanctions are a blunt instrument of persuasion, and their greatest impact is typically delayed. The UN machinery for managing sanctions is cumbersome, and it has proven difficult to change a sanctions regime once it has been established. In this case, the arms embargo hampered the Bosnian government's exercise of its right to self-defense. Later, Belgrade's desire to have comprehensive sanctions lifted eventually led to a breakthrough in negotiations.

2. How can the use of force be restricted? The Security Council experimented with several arrangements in Bosnia:

- *The no-fly zone.* In March 1992, the Security Council prohibited unauthorized flights over Bosnia in order to prevent the Bosnian Serb military from using its aircraft against the Bosnian forces. NATO organized Operation Deny Flight to enforce the regime. There were frequent unauthorized flights, and NATO planes responded by shooting down Bosnian Serb aircraft in October 1993 and May 1995.

- *Heavy-weapons exclusion zones.* Following the February 1994 mortar attack on a market square in Sarajevo, NATO declared that both sides must withdraw heavy weapons from within a twenty-kilometer radius centered on Sarajevo or consign the weapons to storage sites controlled by UN peacekeepers. NATO adopted a similar regime for the Bosnian Muslim "safe area" of Gorazde. After several attacks to eliminate individual weapons, NATO planes struck at Bosnian Serb artillery sites on May 29, 1995. The Bosnian Serbs responded by taking the UN peacekeepers hostage. NATO's air attacks in August 1995 were intended to persuade the Bosnian Serbs to remove all heavy weapons from the Sarajevo area.

- *Safe areas*. In the midst of a Bosnian Serb attack on Srebrenica in March 1993, the Security Council designated the Bosnian Muslim enclaves of Bihac, Gorazde, Sarajevo, Srebrenica, Tuzla, and Zepa as "safe areas" that were to be off-limits to offensive military activity. The secretary-general told the council he needed an additional 36,000 troops to manage the safe-area arrangements; the council authorized 7,000. The UN troops were not expected to defend the safe areas; it was hoped that their presence would restrain both sides. The United Nations, the Bosnian government, and the Bosnian Serbs never agreed on detailed arrangements for the safe areas. Following Bosnian Serb attacks in June and July 1995, the safe areas of Srebrenica and Zepa fell, but the world reaction to the ensuing atrocities and genocide contributed to the pressure that produced the Dayton Accords in November 1995.

It is difficult to get parties to respect arrangements that prohibit some uses of force while permitting others. The "safe-area" arrangements did not work when compliance depended only on the good will of the parties. Experience validates the commonsense expectation that respect for such arrangements requires a credible threat by an outside authority to use force.

3. How can force be used in conjunction with peacekeeping? Dag Hammarskjold once said that a UN peacekeeping mandate could not require the initiative in the use of force. Other UN officials assert that peacekeepers may use force only in self-defense. Because peacekeeping is often joined with a UN mediation, officials oppose any action, including the use of force, that might jeopardize the impartiality required for mediation. To the contrary, critics of the United Nations argue that force should be used to save the organization's credibility, and they can now support their arguments by citing the breakthrough in negotiations after the August–September 1995 NATO assault against Bosnian Serbs.

A sovereign state, by definition, has the right to use force. As an organization of states, the United Nations has neither the inherent right nor innate capacity to use force. It can do so only if states provide equipment and troops and authorize them to be given the initiative in the use of force. Such decisions are not made easily.

The "dual key" procedure was the standard for deciding on the use of air power in Bosnia. The secretary-general, or his delegated authority, had to confirm the request from his military commander that air power be used;

the NATO secretary-general, who takes his guidance from the North Atlantic Council, had to concur in order for NATO commanders to respond. Arrangements were made for NATO to provide close air support to protect a UN peacekeeping unit under attack, enforce the heavy-weapons exclusion zones around Gorazde and Sarajevo, and assist the UN Protection Force in its mandate to monitor the safe areas. NATO enforced the no-fly zone without the involvement of the UN chain of command.

The final UN initiative was to establish a Rapid Reaction Force to make armed responses to threats against the peacekeeping mission in Bosnia. Its members wore their own militaries' battle gear, not the UN's blue helmets; but a UN peacekeeping force traditionally operates with the consent of the parties, assumes a permissive environment, avoids surprises, and uses minimum force. The experience with the Rapid Reaction Force did not conclusively prove that a UN force could be successfully bolstered by a military force designed to operate without the consent of at least one party, in a hostile environment, using surprise, and employing any force needed to obtain its objective.

In a different sector, the council deployed Nordic and U.S. troops to Macedonia. Although this sector has been quiet, the presence of U.S. forces at the border with Serbia constitutes a severe warning against invasion. At times, the threat of force is persuasive.

However history judges the experience of the United Nations in the former Yugoslavia, it will confirm the impediments to the use of force by the international organization. This is one function sovereign states retain.

4. How can multiform negotiations be conducted? The contacts involving the parties were myriad—direct and indirect, formal and informal, bilateral and multilateral. This mix of negotiations was unique. How can such activity be organized so that it is not conducted at cross-purposes? The main approaches included the following:

- *The regional approach.* In 1990, the European Community (now the European Union) began negotiations to produce a plan for Bosnia. The main EU negotiators have included José Cutileiro, Peter Carrington, David Owen, and Carl Bildt, a former prime minister of Sweden. The EU took other important steps, including the decision in December 1991 that led to the recognition of Croatia, the Badinter Report on criteria for recognizing the independence of the former Yugoslav republics, and assistance for monitoring sanctions against Serbia. In addition, EU members pursued separate bilateral contacts with the conflict's parties.

- *The UN approach.* In 1991, UN Secretary-General Perez de Cuellar appointed Cyrus Vance to secure the end of fighting in Croatia. Vance obtained agreement for a cease-fire and the withdrawal of the Yugoslav National Army, the deployment of a UN peacekeeping force, the establishment of separation zones between Croatian forces and territory held by local Serb forces, and disarmament of the local Serbs. When Vance resigned, Boutros-Ghali appointed Thorvald Stoltenberg in his place. Vance retained his role as UN mediator in the dispute between Greece and the Former Yugoslav Republic of Macedonia. Yasushi Akashi directed UN operations in the region, with a French general as overall theater force commander and a British general as commander for Bosnia. On any issue, several UN approaches could be taken.

- *The conference approach.* In 1991, the United Nations and the EU convened the International Conference on the Former Yugoslavia in London. The co-chairs were the representatives of the United Nations and the EU at the time, Vance and Carrington. Subcommittees worked through the political and technical issues of Yugoslavia's dissolution. ICFY monitored compliance with inter-Serbian sanctions.

- *The Contact Group approach.* In response to a Franco-German initiative, the United States joined a Contact Group of five countries (France, Germany, Russia, the United Kingdom, and the United States) in February 1994. In July 1994, the Contact Group presented to the conflict's parties a territorial proposal that allocated 51 percent of Bosnia's territory to the Bosnian government and 49 percent to the Bosnian Serbs. Finally, U.S. Assistant Secretary of State Richard Holbrooke secured the agreement of all parties to talks in November 1995 in Dayton, Ohio. The result of these talks was a peace agreement. All Contact Group members were present in Dayton, and all supported the outcome. During earlier periods, the Contact Group members had at times demonstrated their capacities for independent action.

- *The key representative approach.* In 1994, the Zagreb Four (Z-4) prepared a plan to reintegrate into Croatia land controlled by Croatian Serbs. The Z-4 included the Russian and U.S. ambassadors, the German ambassador (also representing the EU), and a UN representative. Neither side accepted this plan, but it became the framework for the Basic Agreement of November 12, which, in turn, was the basis for a new UN operation.

Although it is still early to judge the contribution made by any one approach, this exact mixture could not be replicated. Because this is a world of dispersed authority, diplomats need to understand better how to manage complex negotiations.

FURTHER AVENUES

In an era of extremely complex world politics, statesmen need open minds regarding alternative avenues for resolving conflicts. Throughout the Cold War, annual conferences brought together U.S. and Soviet citizens to discuss relations between their countries. Despite recurrent Arab-Israeli wars, academics, journalists, and civic leaders built bridges between Israelis and Palestinians. And, even during the worst years of apartheid, courageous Africans and Afrikaners dispelled the sense of tragedy facing their own country. The diplomacy of conflict resolution often needs the leaven of experiment and private initiative.

Voting is one mechanism that diplomats are resorting to increasingly in their efforts to resolve conflicts; a plebiscite can decide a disputed but decisive issue for the future of those involved. Such a vote is planned to decide whether the Western Sahara will be part of Morocco or a sovereign state. Since the 1990 elections in Namibia, the United Nations has helped to conduct elections in Nicaragua, El Salvador, Haiti, Angola, Mozambique, South Africa, and Cambodia. The OSCE was charged with assisting the elections in Bosnia that were called for in the Dayton agreement. Many NGOs have helped to monitor the conduct of elections, such as the vote for the representatives in the Palestinian Authority in 1996. In the field of diplomacy, elections are a growth industry.

An equally significant departure is the establishment of separate international tribunals with authority to try crimes against humanity arising out of the fighting in the former Yugoslavia and Rwanda. Events will determine the impact of these tribunals on resolving the conflicts during which these heinous crimes were committed. The intent is to dissuade such crimes by adjudicating the personal responsibility of the perpetrators. Justice should help to cement the peace.

CHALLENGES AHEAD

With decolonization and the Cold War in the past, managing conflicts means going back to the basics. The spread of internal conflicts makes it harder for diplomats to get leverage over a situation by manipulating the international connections of a conflict's parties. Today's perspective on conflict and change requires closer examination of the grievances, emphasis on the needs of the protagonists, and fewer panoramas taken from the view-point of the major powers.

Multilateral diplomacy does not have all the means for addressing many of today's conflicts. After all, diplomacy is the conduct of relations among sovereign states that is governed by doctrine and practice developed over several centuries. For example, one rule bars interference in the internal affairs of a state; an honored practice is to respect the formal equality of all states. Trying to launch a peace process between a recognized government and an insurgency requires a more flexible approach, one that opens contacts with the parties but postpones any judgment as to status. At times nondiplomats, such as church leaders, academics, or former officials, may be in a better position to act.

We need to bring the protagonists into a dialogue. Whether they are in conflict over dividing a state or deciding who rules, dialogue is essential. In either case, as neighbors in different states or as competitors for power within one state, dialogue is just as essential for managing tomorrow's change as it is for resolving today's conflict.

We also need to create a common vision. Dialogue must serve to change the way protagonists see their options. Antagonistic, mutually exclusive views of the future must yield to a common vision. It is precisely this sort of change that is transforming southern African and Arab-Israeli relations.

Finally, we need to coordinate multiple efforts. Because many of today's conflicts involve practically every institution of a society, the struggle for peace often engenders multiple efforts. Coordination and a coherent strategy are needed both to avoid efforts that work at cross-purposes and to move the protagonists toward a common goal. Leadership can come from various sources: the United Nations has been a frequent focal point for this coordination; neighboring states and major powers need to pull together.

10

AN NGO PERSPECTIVE

Andrew S. Natsios

Nongovernmental organizations (NGOs) have become all the rage in post–Cold War diplomacy, with their less critical advocates making unstudied and exaggerated claims about their capabilities. In the search for tools to supplement what appear to be increasingly insufficient diplomatic interventions in the new types of conflicts around the world, the international community has grasped the NGO alternative with promiscuous enthusiasm. What it does not realize is that NGOs have weaknesses like any other actor in conflict resolution. They also have strengths that more traditional players do not have, strengths that could prove useful in the chaotic conditions of the post–Cold War world. A more sober view of the value of the NGO contribution to conflict resolution should consider both factors and avoid creating unachievable expectations. To be sure, NGOs can help in a variety of peacemaking scenarios. They are a unique and underused instrument of conflict resolution, but they have significant limitations as well, which, if ignored or left unexamined, could prove disappointing at best and disastrous at worst.

NGOs are unlike one another in more ways than they are similar. They represent a type of institution so varied and broadly defined that making generalizations about them is difficult without dividing them into more manageable categories. In this chapter, I attempt to describe the arcane distinctions among NGOs that limit their promise as instruments of conflict resolution. I also discuss their strengths and weaknesses, including their suitability as impartial mediators, and then review their performance in some specific case studies.

THE RISE OF NEW ACTORS

NGOs have achieved a certain prominence as major actors in the global arena, largely in connection with the international community's response to the state of "complex emergencies" that have come to define conflict in the post-Soviet era. By definition, complex emergencies involve the destruction of the economy, including the currency and banking system; the collapse of food security; the dislocation of a large portion of the civilian population; and the erosion or complete failure of the apparatus of government itself, including its criminal justice and public safety functions. These complex emergencies are made even deadlier by the sudden appearance of marauding clans, regional factions, or paramilitary groups, whose competition for power in the absence of state authority complicates humanitarian-relief efforts.

Two peculiar characteristics of conflict in the post–Cold War order have encouraged policymakers to turn to NGOs to provide not only traditional humanitarian aid but also conflict resolution and reconciliation interventions.

First, during the Cold War, the intervention of the two superpowers in a conflict tended to concentrate power in the leadership of a particular government or rebel movement. By dispensing a variety of benefits, they discouraged rival factions from operating simultaneously on either side of the conflict. Benefiting from superpower involvement meant choosing sides, not creating a third or fourth side; the United States and the Soviet Union simply would not abide a half-dozen factions in any given conflict. This tendency to limit the number of sides to a conflict made negotiations much simpler and, therefore, more prone to successful outcomes. It is an iron law of probability that in these types of conflicts, the greater the number of discernible sides with independent power bases, the more remote the possibility of success at the negotiating table. The breakdown of central authority and the rise of numerous centers of power is surely one reason why some policymakers are turning to NGOs with deep roots in the community and at the lowest level of social organization as sources of indigenous authority that might act as mediators among warring factions. In the case of societies whose government has entirely collapsed, NGOs and religious institutions may be the only sources of authority that have any influence.

In all complex humanitarian emergencies, the intricate mosaic of public and private institutions that make up the social order collapses, as the elites who lead and run these institutions are killed or traumatized, flee the country, or migrate to refugee camps, where they are separated from the communities and institutions they once led. The sudden collapse of this network of traditional elites and the rise of warlords to take their places reduces the utility of traditional diplomacy as a tool of conflict resolution. Diplomats, through both training and experience, are accustomed to dealing with other diplomats and traditional elites, the very people who have lost their authority in the midst of chaos. The new interest in NGOs reflects the search for some viable institution in the absence of any other levers of influence during these complex emergencies.

The decentralization of conflict has manifested itself not only on the side of the contestants but among the humanitarian-relief providers as well. An array of humanitarian-relief actors have provided the infrastructure and organization to care for the casualties of these new types of conflicts: four voluntary agencies of the United Nations—the UN High Commissioner for Refugees (UNHCR), the UN Children's Fund (UNICEF), the World Food Program, and the UN Development Program—and international organizations, such as the International Committee of the Red Cross (ICRC) and the International Organization for Migration. Add to this the donor-country foreign aid offices, donor-country diplomats, and military forces (usually joined together as a multinational force under the UN banner) and you have a complex response system that makes the design and execution of a coherent strategy difficult, if not impossible. In the past, except for a handful of NGOs, these institutions were usually not involved in the international response to conflict, so negotiators used whatever techniques seemed appropriate to try to resolve a conflict, with little regard for the few humanitarian-relief actors on the scene.

These other outside actors, which are now an integral part of the international response to conflict situations, can have profound effects on the conflict, sometimes unintentionally, adding numerous complications to the negotiating process. Sometimes these other actors can diminish the violence of the conflict and contribute to the peace process by the manner in which they conduct their relief interventions, quite apart from any mediation role they may have. These new actors may also exacerbate the conflict with thoughtless interventions. Despite assertions to the contrary, their relief work is seldom neutral, even though such putative neutrality is a fundamental principle in the humanitarian-relief community. It is nearly impossible to work in these conflicts without affecting them for better or worse. Negotiators may work toward political settlements ignorant of these other actors' ability to influence the course of the conflict, but they do so at their own risk.

Mary Anderson has suggested in a recent essay several ways humanitarian-relief agencies can exacerbate conflicts. While I would dispute some of her analysis, a good deal of it sadly rings true in my own experience. She argues that "introducing resources into a resource-scarce environment where there is conflict usually increases competition and suspicion among warring parties." In some cases, relief resources can distort the local economy, distortions that improve the well-being of some groups and diminish that of others, thereby encouraging conflict. By providing humanitarian assistance to people in revolt against oppressive governments, humanitarian-relief organizations may be inadvertently prolonging the conflict by strengthening their resolve when they would otherwise give up or agree to a negotiated settlement. Anderson's argument supports the proposition that relief is seldom neutral, however much humanitarian-relief organizations may try to make it so. In any analysis of NGO work in conflicts, these unintended but pernicious consequences of humanitarian assistance must be considered (Anderson 1996).

A second reason for the new interest in NGOs as mediators stems from the absence of discipline not just among but within these diffuse centers of power. We are seeing the egalitarian imperative being played out in the collapsing hierarchies of the military units (regular and irregular) and political movements involved in conflicts: Factional leaders and warlords no longer exercise the same degree of control over their own forces that they did under the older centralized model. Conflicts are being driven by followers more than leaders. Indeed, in some conflicts warlords become prisoners of their own militias. This phenomenon has played itself out in both Somalia and Liberia. General Aidid in Somalia and Charles Taylor in Liberia were frequently not in control of their own militia forces (which were undisciplined, untrained, and unmotivated by anything other than access to plunder), but instead were controlled by them. In both cases the young men just out of the bush who comprised the warlord militias had dramatically improved their standard of living, their political power, and their stature overnight as they learned to use a gun and joined what amounted to a gang disguised as a political movement. There is little motivation for these young men to give up what they have taken by consenting to a negotiated end to their perquisites.

This situation has profound implications for the conflict-resolution discipline in contemporary conflicts: Factional leaders may be negotiating with little if any real authority, since whatever is agreed to may be unenforceable. If power in a stable political system is sometimes described as fluid, it usually exists in a gaseous state during complex emergencies—unpredictable from day to day, unmanageable, and unfathomable when warlords themselves hesitate to act for fear of their lives. Mediation presupposes that factional leaders sitting at the negotiating table possess the requisite authority to ensure the terms of a settlement are carried out. In complex emergencies, such presumptions are usually unfounded.

This deterioration of hierarchical control in conflicts has also given mass media an even more important influence on the course of events than in the past. In totalitarian regimes, the state uses the media to mobilize mass support for its objectives. Hitler whipped up anti-Semitism to ensure public silence during the Nazi regime's genocide against the Jews; Stalin pursued a similar strategy against the *kulaks* who opposed his forced collectivization of private farms. In both cases, the state did the dirty work. In some complex emergencies, political leaders use the media to enlist the public in carrying out their policies. Hate radio in Rwanda whipped up anti-Tutsi hysteria, which led to a killing rampage executed with brutal efficiency by Hutus themselves. Citizens of both Nazi Germany and the Soviet Union could blame the state for the genocides in their respective countries, but Rwanda's hate radio—in a psychotic, maniacal way—recruited the mass citizenry of the country to be genocidal killers. In essence, genocide has been democratized, making negotiations between the two sides difficult, if not impossible, since the entire society has been implicated in the killings. Replacing bad leaders or intransigent negotiators does not expunge the guilt of the entire society. Several NGOs have attempted to counteract the malevolent influence of hate media by broadcasting conflict-resolution radio programming to reduce tension, an innovative technique that is covered in more detail in the case studies.

THE PROBLEM OF IMPLEMENTATION

Implementation has long been recognized as one of the principal problems in public policy; so it is in peacemaking as well, though this is perhaps not as widely recognized. During complex emergencies, NGOs are often the only organizations with the operational capability to perform some of the tasks essential to the implementation of the peace process. They serve in this capacity as much by default as by choice, since government services and private markets typically have been destroyed or seriously impaired. When diplomatic delegations or the media travel to the scene of these conflicts, they often accompany the ICRC or other NGOs. This is especially true where there are no peacekeeping contingents. NGOs have been called upon after a conflict is over to conduct demining operations; demobilize soldiers; resettle refugees and displaced persons; provide public services such as water, sanitation, and shelter repair and construction; encourage agricultural rehabilitation to achieve food security; manage health clinics; and undertake numerous other activities designed to promote reconciliation.

Conflict resolution can be undone in the implementation stage, as operational problems occur that undermine carefully drawn political agreements. Compared with conventional conflicts, the operational problems in implementing a complex emergency's peace agreement increase exponentially; in these circumstances, doing even simple things becomes quite complicated, even untenable. What may appear to diplomats or negotiators to be easily executed agreements in a mediated settlement become insurmountable obstacles to peace at the implementation stage.

In the implementation of the second Angolan peace agreement, the demobilization and resettlement of soldiers is being carried out primarily by NGOs because of the failure of the United Nations and the Angolan government to perform this function after the first peace accord. The first Angolan peace agreement, signed in December 1991, which the United States played a major role in mediating, collapsed during the implementation process for a variety of reasons. The agreement called for demobilization centers, to which troops from both sides of the conflict could come to be disarmed, have their families fed and cared for, and finally be resettled. Neither the Angolan government bureaucracy charged with implementing this provision of the agreement nor the UN agencies in Angola that were supposed to assist them were able to carry out their duties for these demobilization centers under the peace agreement. Soldiers arrived with their families only to find that no food, shelter, medical care, water, or sanitation were available. In order to keep soldiers of the Uniao Nacional para a Independencia Total de Angola (UNITA) safely away from populated areas, the Angolan government designated remote areas with no airstrips or roads as demobilization sites. UNITA soldiers were not provided for at all, and the government troops were supported inadequately. An underfed army under any circumstances is dangerous; with the fragile political conditions in Angola at the time, it could have been catastrophic had the U.S. government not intervened. This intervention, conducted through NGOs, had to provide rations to the UN monitors assigned to each of the demobilization sites, since the UN logistical system in the country was dysfunctional even for its own staff. Diplomats tend to focus on what they know best—political agreements, power-sharing arrangements, elections, and coalition governments. The logistics of demobilization are not in the lexicon of most mediators, so they are not factored into the negotiating process as a potential pitfall. This increases the dependence on NGOs as the implementing agents of peace accords.

THE STRENGTHS AND WEAKNESSES OF NGOs AS MEDIATORS

This chapter suggests that the evolving international system in the post–Cold War period will demand expanded roles for nonstate actors—particularly NGOs—roles they neither founded nor were structured to perform. That NGOs seem to be assuming the mantle of traditional diplomacy in their roles during complex emergencies stems from their unique characteristics as institutions; from their size, variety, and capabilities; and from the very nature of conflict itself in the post–Cold War world. What are the unique characteristics, strengths, and weaknesses of NGOs that make them attractive alternative instruments for carrying out conflict-resolution initiatives?

The conceptual and philosophical framework in which NGOs undertake development work profoundly affects their ability to assume the functions and responsibilities of international conflict resolution. The work of most NGOs falls within the rubric of what is called community development, an approach to the alleviation of poverty guided by several abiding principles: (a) people at the grassroots level know best what their problems are and how to deal with them (with some outside support); (b) solutions to local problems that do not have the support and "ownership" of the community will ultimately fail; (c) people's attitudes and values have a profound effect on how successful they are in dealing with their problems, and therefore, working with them over a long period of time to change these attitudes is the only way to ensure solutions are sustainable over the long term; and (d) the indigenous culture and authority structure of the community should be respected and not undermined.

NGOs carry on their work at the very lowest level of social order, the rural village and city neighborhood. Their highly participatory system of decision making and program management, while time-consuming and laborious, does tend to engage the energy and commitment of the community. This approach to development creates loyalty and trust between NGOs and the communities in which they work, and this can serve an important purpose in conflict resolution. Ironically, the limitation of the NGO as conflict mediator issues from its strength: its intimate connection to the communities it serves and to their leaders, cultures, values, and sensitivities. This intimate connection to the community sometimes distorts an NGO's understanding of what is happening in the country as a whole, given the human tendency to generalize based on one's own immediate conditions and circumstances, however unrepresentative those circumstances may be; local conditions in one area are sometimes not representative of those in a region or the country as a whole.

Perhaps the most serious weakness of NGOs as actors in conflict resolution stems from their proliferation and autonomy. While some of the accounts of the burgeoning numbers of NGOs working in complex emergencies are exaggerated, there is indisputably a large number of them. In most of the more visible conflicts, such as Rwanda in the immediate aftermath of the 1994 genocide, as many as one hundred NGOs claimed to have a presence. In reality, perhaps thirty to forty NGOs provided sustained services of sufficient extent and quality to have an impact on the situation; even at this more modest number, there were too many to create and execute a coherent countrywide program of any kind. The proliferation of NGOs, combined with their (sometimes compulsive) tendency to guard their autonomy from one another, from donor governments, and from the UN system, create serious problems for diplomats and policymakers alike who look to NGOs to carry out conflict-resolution interventions. Other than each NGO's own internal decision-making process, no authority exists to determine which NGO should undertake an intervention; how competent or well prepared it is to do the work; where and among whom it will undertake the conflict-resolution activities; and, perhaps most disturbingly, what exact program of activities it should undertake. If humanitarian-relief interventions are any guide, NGO work in conflict-resolution activities may well result in contradictory approaches. Government officials in Africa have repeatedly complained to me that NGOs in close geographic proximity carry out activities that conflict with one another, causing serious problems in the communities. In one country, a provincial governor told me of two NGOs distributing food in the aftermath of a war in two neighboring communities: one NGO insisted no one would get food (unless they were disabled or too weak to work) without participating in food-for-work projects;

the other NGO distributed food freely, with no work requirement attached. This created serious political and morale problems when the villagers from the two communities relayed their experiences to each other. So few NGOs are actively involved in conflict resolution at this point that such coordination, tactical, and programming problems have not yet been publicized. But they are likely to—the situation is changing rapidly.

What kinds of NGOs are there and how might they perform conflict resolution activities? NGOs can be divided into distinct categories: development versus relief, government-funded versus those that accept no public-sector grants, operational versus policy and advocacy, religious versus secular, indigenous versus international, and commodity-based versus skills-transfer- and development-based. Most larger NGOs do not fall easily into any one or even two categories, and yet these distinctions do provide some basis for analyzing how an NGO might approach conflict resolution as a discipline.

Perhaps half the NGOs that work in conflicts do relief work exclusively, while the other half do both relief and development work. Work in complex emergencies is not easy, and a number of NGOs have chosen to focus on development work in areas that are poor but comparatively stable and free of these types of conflicts. The larger development NGOs that do work in complex-emergency areas have the added advantage of drawing on their experiences with development programs they established in the countries prior to the onset of the conflict. This experience provides them not only with a familiarity with the culture, ethnic groups, and development problems of the country, but with an indigenous staff base as well.

A few NGOs, many of which come out of a faith-based tradition, have focused on conflict resolution as a discrete discipline that requires specific programmatic interventions. The Quakers' American Friends Service Committee (AFS) and the Mennonite Central Committee (MCC), the NGOs of what are called the "peace churches," have historically led the NGO community in conflict resolution in both the development of theory and program implementation (Lederach forthcoming). These NGOs, whose sponsoring churches have a long history of theological aversion to the use of military force, might make difficult partners where coordination with UN peacekeeping forces is essential, particularly when their mandate falls under Chapter VII of the UN Charter.

This weakness can also be a strength, however. If mediators with no formal connection to any government (MCC and AFS accept no public-sector funding) and an aversion to all forms of military force are what the particular situation demands, these peace-church NGOs may be well positioned to intervene. Faith-based NGOs with deep roots in indigenous religious institutions can use those connections to their advantage in working on conflict resolution efforts. For example, Catholic Relief Services can speak easily and quickly to the Vatican or the Roman Catholic hierarchy in any country in which they work. While the Carter Center is not directly connected to a specific church, Jimmy Carter's evangelical Protestant faith animates his mediation work. Several religion-based NGOs, including World Vision and Catholic Relief Services, are now undertaking major reviews of their potential role as conflict mediators. While religion, particularly in its social and economic manifestations, may be a source of peacemaking and conflict resolution, some conflicts have grown out of religious differences, which political leaders have sometimes exacerbated for their own purposes. Placing religious NGOs into conflicts as mediators where the faith tradition they represent is seen as the source of the conflict by one or more of the parties would obviously be an unwise practice.

NGOs that design their relief interventions with a heavy development component would be, I suspect, much more effective in conflict resolution than those that focus on logistics and the distribution of commodities; the former tend to consider the longer term consequences of their actions and better understand the complexities of each conflict. Since the 1985–88 Ethiopian famine, a watershed event for most of the major NGOs that do relief work, a quiet revolution has taken place in doctrine and practice in the connection between relief and development. Traditional commodity-driven and logistically based relief efforts devoted little programmatic, economic, or developmental thought to the outcomes of the relief effort beyond pushing down death rates and saving lives.

As a matter of policy, most NGOs now try to integrate development components into their relief interventions, particularly NGOs that receive a high proportion of their total funding from government grants. These NGOs might serve as better partners to complement the diplomacy of a Western government engaged in conflict resolution because they are more comfortable and familiar with the protocols and sensitivities of official diplomacy than NGOs that have a policy of not accepting public-sector funding. Some NGOs get the great bulk of their resources from government grants, some as high as 70 to 80 percent. These NGOs are sometimes unfairly seen at the field level as an extension of U.S. policy or that of another Western government, rather than as entirely independent actors. If distance from Western governments is a useful attribute in an NGO mediator, NGOs that accept little public-sector funding and have few official ties to governments may be a better choice to undertake conflict-resolution activities.

How NGOs are organized and governed affects their work. They have four basic models for organizing themselves internationally. First, all began with and some still have their headquarters based entirely in one country, though they work in many countries (e.g., the International Rescue Committee and the International Medical Corps). Second, some have entirely autonomous national chapters with independent field organizations, each reporting back to the home offices; this means several offices of the same organization may work independently of one another in the same country (e.g., Save the Children and Oxfam). Third, some have all their national offices pool their collective funds in a central bank and spend them through a single worldwide field organization that is indigenously staffed and managed (e.g., World Vision International and the International Federation of Red Cross and Red Crescent Societies). A variation is a hybrid of the second and third models, in which each national headquarters has its own field organization but is assigned to specific emergencies by a central international organization; thus, the organizations are not competing with each other in the same country (CARE operates this way). Finally, others work only through indigenous local NGOs that are not part of their organizational structure; they have no independent operational capacity in the field outside of these indigenous partner agencies (e.g., the Church World Service).

Each model has its own strengths and weaknesses. The first model tends to be the fastest in operations and decision making and the least bureaucratic. The second model tends to be the most flexible, internally competitive, and, at times, organizationally contentious. The third tends to have deep community roots and the capacity to aggregate large amounts of money rapidly for a particular relief program; however, it also has a tendency to act slowly. The fourth model consists of NGOs that have the deepest community roots but no field staff that they can direct to a particular emergency, contributing to a lack of flexibility and quality control in these organizations.

International NGOs (those that work in more than one country) that are "internationalized," having independent fundraising offices and boards of directors in more than one country, have several important capabilities with implications for conflict resolution. These NGOs can and do draw on the diplomatic capital, media attention, and public opinion of their home countries. For example, although originally an American organization, CARE now has chapters in Great Britain, Germany, Canada, and Australia, with prominent public figures on their boards of directors and staffs. The former prime minister of Australia, Malcolm Fraser, is the president of CARE International and can command instant media attention and access to the highest levels of Western governments. This international reach allows some internationalized NGOs to issue one consistent policy position regarding a particular conflict to a number of Western countries simultaneously, an advantage governments do not have.

NGOs are all governed by boards of directors that tend to reflect the particular culture, history, and mandates of the organization. The board of directors of the International Medical Corps, an American NGO that specializes in providing emergency medical care during conflicts, is dominated by the medical professionals who founded it. Catholic bishops serve as the board of directors for Catholic Relief Services.

Since most NGOs raise money among members of a particular segment of the public by design, they must keep the interests of their constituency in mind as they carry out their missions; otherwise, their financial survival will be imperiled. If the institutional constituency or fundraising base of an NGO has an ideological (or ethnic, or religious) predisposition against one party or another in a conflict, the organization's usefulness as a neutral mediator is compromised. For example, a particular NGO may call for the prosecution of war criminals among the Serbian and Hutu elites in its policy statements on Bosnia or Rwanda, a position that may well make sense but renders the NGO unacceptable as a mediator in the conflict. If an NGO's conflict-resolution efforts in a complex emergency annoy its constituency in a country in which it raises money (should its work become public), its role may be so circumscribed and hesitant that it may become largely ineffective. Some NGOs have political, religious, and ideological agendas, though they might call them by other names, which limit the type of conflict-resolution work they might undertake.

CAN NGOs BE IMPARTIAL MEDIATORS?

Some of the interest in NGOs as mediators stems from their presumed neutrality. This is a tenuous presumption. Some NGOs have long taken the view that relief is seldom neutral and have designed their programs with an understanding of their political implications. They make no claims to impartiality or neutrality; indeed, they argue that such claims are inherently specious. Much of the controversy over neutrality arose from the Biafran civil war in the late 1960s, where a group of medical doctors led by Dr.

Bernard Kouchner walked off their jobs with the ICRC in protest of the organization's adherence to the neutrality principle. Kouchner, who later founded two French NGOs, including Doctors without Borders (Médecins sans Frontières), argued that humanitarian-relief organizations could not be neutral in the face of genocide or other atrocities. Even though the conditions surrounding complex emergencies border on total anarchy, everyone is not always equally guilty or innocent in such conflicts, a fact that must be considered in designing relief interventions. The Red Cross organization, particularly the ICRC, takes a very different view and has long insisted on absolute neutrality and nonpartisanship in its relief interventions in conflicts. Its credo is simple and straightforward: People should be served based on their need, not their politics. The problem, of course, is that if the humanitarian need is heavily concentrated on one side of the conflict, an organization can understandably be accused of supporting that side in administering theoretically neutral humanitarian assistance.

These philosophical positions have been put to the test in the refugee camps in Goma, Zaire, where nearly one million Hutu refugees have been helped by NGOs, UNHCR, and the Red Cross. In these camps, at least a hundred thousand Hutu soldiers and militia members were training and arming themselves to return to Rwanda to take back their land and control of their country from the Tutsis they attempted to exterminate in genocidal massacres in 1994. In December 1994, a couple of dozen NGOs withdrew from active work in these camps because they knew that relief agencies were, in effect, acting as the quartermaster for the Hutu militias that were likely to engage in more killings as soon as they were militarily prepared. Rwanda's Tutsi-dominated government does not regard as neutral the remaining humanitarian agencies that continue to feed and provision their enemies. The NGOs that remain in the Hutu camps, despite their philosophical neutrality and efforts to be evenhanded, may be unsuitable to act as mediators in any way, since one side views them as partisan (indeed, both sides may see them as partisan). For NGOs to perform a conflict-resolution role, they must not only act in a genuinely neutral way, but they must also be perceived as neutral by the parties to the conflict. NGOs cannot always make either claim convincingly.

The hiring practices of indigenous NGO staff can profoundly, but subtly, affect the perception of neutrality, as can the geographic location of programs in a particular country. If NGOs hire from one tribal, ethnic, or religious group, or locate their programs in one tribal or ethnic area but not another, the neglected or aggrieved groups may read into these decisions of

geography and staffing prejudicial sentiments that compromise the neutrality of the NGO. With a few exceptions, such as the International Rescue Committee and the International Orthodox Christian Charities, few
international NGOs have chosen to work in Serb-held areas of the former
Yugoslavia or to hire ethnic Serb staff, while dozens are working in the
Bosnian Muslim areas with mostly ethnic Croat or Muslim (or mixed par-
entage) staff members. This has led to the overall perception of NGOs as
pro-Muslim among Bosnian Muslims themselves and certainly among the
Serbs. In addition, many NGOs offer significantly higher salaries than those
available in the host country's public sector. This practice often leads the
country's "best and brightest" to abandon public service for the NGOs,
thereby adding another complication to the perception of NGOs, their roles,
and their agendas.

NGOs are the best early warning system for impending conflict, long
before it reaches the more visible, violent stage. Most major international
NGOs have information-management systems at their central headquarters, processing daily field reports on what is happening in a particular conflict or relief operation. Taken together, these reports comprise an underused
but rich source of early-warning information on the conditions surrounding potential conflicts all over the world. Increasingly, the State Department, the U.S. Agency for International Development (USAID), and the
National Security Council are using this independent source of information to confirm or correct official reporting. If an NGO's field reports on an
impending conflict or its advocacy efforts in Western capitals become
known in the country in which it is operating, it endangers both its staff
and its very presence in the country. Under these circumstances, an NGO
can hardly play a neutral role.

By the very nature of their work, NGOs in many Third World countries
perform many of the functions of government conducted solely by the public sector in Western countries. If one were to list the functions of the typical municipal government in the United States and compare them with
the functions NGOs perform in the developing world, the comparison would
show an astonishing degree of coincidence. NGOs work with communities
to build and maintain roads, schools, health clinics, agricultural extension
services, community-owned forests, and water and sanitation systems. They
perform these functions sometimes with the cooperation of national governments and sometimes without it. Even when they work cooperatively,
there is always a level of tension, an understandable resentment of well-
equipped NGOs by government employees who have no vehicles, no

equipment, anemic budgets, untrained staffs, and poor salaries that are irregularly paid by their own governments. This tension intensifies as the institutions of government in an unstable country become more and more dysfunctional and NGOs find themselves virtually replacing the government in terms of providing public services. The more tenuous a faltering government's hold on power is, the greater the level of tension in dealing with NGOs; government officials at first regard the organizations as competitors and then, in the final stages of the relationship, as a threat to their very survival. Thus, government officials may not regard NGOs as neutral mediators at all.

The presence of international NGOs in conflicts tends to restrain the commission of atrocities and human rights abuses and thus serves a preventive function. Writers such as Francis Deng, Larry Minear, and Tom Weiss have noted the restraining influence an outside presence can have on the parties to a conflict (Minear 1991; Weiss and Minear 1993). Rebel groups and governments alike do not wish to have their human rights abuses seen by Western NGO workers, who may pass along their observations to their own countries' governments and news organizations, causing the perpetrators enormous political problems. Adverse publicity can lead to their defeat in propaganda wars, which are sometimes more important than tactical victories on the battlefield. This consequence of an NGO's presence, however, is peripheral to its work: Few, if any, humanitarian-relief NGOs I know of have deliberately chosen to do relief or rehabilitation work in a conflict in order to reduce the incidence of human rights abuses. For most NGOs, this is an unintended, though admirable, consequence of their work. The problem with this subsidiary role, of course, is that it places NGO workers at risk, when one side sees them as an impediment to committing atrocities. This has happened in Sudan and Burundi, where relief workers have been systematically killed or their NGOs expelled from the country by parties to the conflict who do not want them watching and possibly reporting their abusive behavior.

One NGO cannot simultaneously perform the four functions that these organizations are increasingly being asked to fulfill: monitoring human rights abuses, acting as neutral mediators among warring factions in a conflict-resolution role, providing humanitarian relief, and influencing foreign policy decisions in Western capitals on these conflicts. It may be possible to perform some of these functions well, but it is nearly impossible to coordinate efforts in all four of these very different disciplines so that they are performed well and do not conflict with one another. Policymakers need to determine which role is of paramount importance before they encourage NGOs to undertake activities in these areas. Since NGO activities do, to some degree, follow funding sources, public-sector grants can influence the choice of mediation interventions in a particular conflict situation.

HOW NGOs APPROACH INTERNATIONAL CONFLICT RESOLUTION

The NGO approach to international conflict resolution takes several diverse forms:

- by employing some of the traditional conflict-resolution models described in this book, including bargaining and negotiation, third-party mediation, and faith-based reconciliation (I am not aware of any cases where NGOs have used methods of arbitration and adjudication in conflict resolution);
- by attempting to address the fundamental economic, social, and political inequities in host countries, which some NGOs believe are at the root of most conflicts;
- by creating neutral forums at which contestants can safely meet to open informal lines of communication, share their experiences of personal anguish during the conflict, and discuss approaches to reducing the tensions;
- through mass education campaigns to provide the citizens of the countries in conflict with impartial information, thereby counteracting propaganda disseminated by factional leaders who seek to exacerbate animosities; and
- through economic interventions to employ young men in constructive work to reduce the likelihood of their recruitment into military or paramilitary groups, and through efforts to create incentives for the indigenous merchant class to become advocates of peace.

Much NGO conflict-resolution work does not follow any analytically developed approach; rather, it usually consists of the practical need for people working in the midst of conflict to deal with its devastating consequences. Many of the most masterly NGO practitioners in the recent past might not even identify what they have done as conflict resolution in any formal sense.

Several NGOs are engaged in conflict-resolution programming in Burundi, among them the Appeal to Conscience, Refugees International, the Search for Common Ground (associated with the Soros Foundation), and the National Democratic Institute. Drawing from the working papers and program-planning documents of these organizations, their activities include radio broadcasts on interethnic harmony and reconciliation; retreats for civic leaders from both the Tutsi and Hutu communities; the production and distribution to public schools of educational material on peace, tolerance, and nonviolent dispute resolution; the creation of a national truth commission to investigate and expose human rights abuses, including the writing of a modern history of Burundi to which prominent Tutsi and Hutu leaders can mutually subscribe; the strengthening of the traditional village elder system; and the encouragement of business enterprises with joint Hutu and Tutsi participation. The programs do not actually resolve anything per se, nor do they settle the political disputes that manifest themselves in mass violence. However, these activities provide a setting for conflict resolution to take place or attack the proximate causes of the conflict by rearranging the incentives of various segments of society to support the resolution of the conflict rather than its continuation.

The civic retreats for Hutu and Tutsi leaders begin with participants sharing personal accounts of how the violence has affected them and their families, with the hope that this sharing of pain will provide some common experience upon which the sessions can proceed. These retreats are essentially a form of group therapy, using the psychodynamic approach developed by Joseph Montville, which I will describe later. While it is not formally an NGO, the Center for Strategic and International Studies (CSIS) has conducted a series of seminars for Muslim, Roman Catholic, and Orthodox leaders in Bosnia using this same interactive prescription with great success (Steele 1995). It is instructive to note that these examples of NGO conflict-resolution activities in Burundi and Bosnia are not taken from the work of the larger relief and development NGOs, but from advocacy, research, and policy organizations, which are not traditionally viewed as operational. Certainly part of the reason is that operational humanitarian-relief NGOs have been stretched to their limits because of the explosion of complex emergencies in the post-Soviet era, and they have been reluctant to initiate new programs.

Operational NGO managers use bargaining and negotiation more widely in civil wars than any other form of conflict resolution, for no other reason than that the chaos of war requires it. In these cases, NGOs do not set as their objective the resolution of the conflict, but, rather, hope to place constraints on the activities of the conflicting parties as they affect noncombatants, specifically with respect to lifesaving relief interventions for people who no longer have the ability to cope with the chaos of war. In this case, an NGO negotiates with the conflicting parties to ensure the protection of relief commodities in their areas of control. In any conflict, all sides use whatever resources they can find to pursue their military and political objectives, including attempts to divert relief resources. These re-sources, whether they be food aid, trucks, or tents and blankets stolen from humanitarian-relief agencies, are used to buy more weapons, purchase or guarantee the loyalty of other factions or ethnic groups, and pay troops their wages. NGOs know the consequences of surrendering to this con-stant pressure to divert resources. If they agree once, the contestants will be back for more. If donors find out, the NGOs will be censured or disci-plined. NGOs negotiate and bargain constantly with military and para-military commanders to get relief commodities through conflict lines to those most in need. In general, the basis for such negotiations is the prin-ciple that relief distributions are based on humanitarian need.

NGOs do have some tools at their disposal: appeals to powerful donor governments (like the United States or the European Union) that the conflict's parties either respect or fear, threats to expose the contestants to the international media, and warnings to the contestants that diversions will cause donor governments to terminate relief programs altogether. Per-haps the most developed form of negotiation in these circumstances was regularly undertaken by the ICRC in Somalia, where the chaotic security conditions required not only that the contestants not divert relief resources, but that clan elders and militias protect these resources from attacks by rival clans or organized bands of looters. The ICRC did this skillfully under difficult circumstances but at heavy cost: It had to turn over a portion of the commodities to the clans and warlords for their own distribution. The ICRC used the threat of terminating the relief effort in a given area as countervailing pressure to protect the relief resources if the demands be-came too egregious or if the conflict over relief commodities became vio-lent. The ICRC suspended its normally irrevocable principle of avoiding cooperation with military forces in its relief operations in order to protect its relief convoys. The chaos in Somalia became so bad and the negotiating position of humanitarian agencies so tenuous that military force became the only viable alternative.

Some forms of conflict resolution take place at the village level, with NGOs acting as the organizing force behind the forums where this work occurs. One such example in Ethiopia illustrates the role of NGOs in this process. World Vision had been working for nearly a decade in the country's Omo Sheleko region, in the southern part of the country. In early 1994, a tribal dispute broke out in the province, which turned ugly and threatened to deteriorate into violence. The conflict arose because one of the smaller tribes in the province announced its intention to redraw the provincial borders so that it could be joined with the rest of its tribe in the neighboring province in anticipation of national elections. The dominant tribe in Omo Sheleko strongly opposed this move and clashed with a smaller tribe over the issue. The tribal elders concerned with the deteriorating situation asked World Vision to convene a meeting of the elders' council that World Vision had helped to establish as the principal decision-making body for its projects in the province; it is noteworthy that provincial government officials were not asked to get involved in the mediation process. The World Vision council had been formed in 1985; its members were elected in each village in the province and met regularly in a meeting hall especially constructed for that purpose. When World Vision staff created the council, two tribes in the province had requested that separate tribal councils be established so that they would not have to deal with each other. World Vision explained that both the projects and the decision making had to cut across tribal lines or else it would leave and do its work elsewhere. The elders reluctantly agreed to the multiethnic council and, over the course of a decade, began not only to work together but to trust each other as well.

The logical forum for the resolution of this particular border dispute was the World Vision elders' council. After lengthy debates and some World Vision mediation, the council agreed to hold a referendum in the villages of the province's breakaway region and ask people to vote on which province they wished to be part of. The results were accepted by both sides as binding. Once the decision by the tribal leaders was made, the provincial government was asked to administer the referendum. This forum was not formal third-party mediation, as World Vision staff played a subordinate, even peripheral, role in the discussions and acted more as a convenor than a mediator. The critical decision in this instance took place in 1985, when World Vision insisted on a multitribal forum for making decisions on the NGO's projects, because this successful outcome probably would not have occurred without it. Conflict resolution took place through an NGO governing body that had not been established for that purpose but was effective nevertheless. The NGO involvement in settling the immediate political dispute was peripheral; its real work had already been done in creating the elders' council and giving it practical work to do.

STRUCTURAL INTERVENTIONS BY NGOs

Much of the recent NGO work in conflict resolution has taken a deliberately programmatic approach, with which some traditional diplomatic practitioners may be unfamiliar—if not uncomfortable. This approach attempts
to attack the root causes of a conflict, or at least alter the conflict's incentive structure, so that some actors supporting the violence will instead support peace and stability. This program-oriented approach stems from the
nature of NGOs as organizations: They focus on defined tasks and the personnel (budgetary, managerial, and project-planning) they must have to
carry out their activities.

NGO relief and development work focuses on its sustainability (Will
the program continue after the NGO has withdrawn its external support?),
on transferring skills through training, on tangible activities (Exactly what
did the NGO use the funding to do?), and on attempting to change behavior or provide services with the active participation of people at the community level. NGOs approach conflict resolution as they approach relief
and development, using an analytical construct called the "logframe" (logical framework), which breaks down a program into objectives, tasks, activities, and measurable indicators of success. An objective might well employ several different conflict-resolution techniques in the form of tasks
and activities designed to reach the objective. This technique has allowed
NGOs to use a high degree of analytical rigor in their development work,
thereby reducing the risk of unintended consequences and pernicious outcomes in their programs. It is also the approach that many NGOs must use
to get public-sector funding from USAID and other donor agencies for their
conflict-resolution activities. Even when they are using private funding for
these activities, they revert to their organizational bias: NGO executives
who must approve these conflict-resolution programs think in terms of tasks
and activities, so their staffs write project proposals that will attract the
support of their superiors by employing familiar models of analysis.

While a comprehensive review of the causes of conflict would carry us
well beyond the focus of this chapter, some NGO efforts at conflict resolution that use the programmatic approach described above have focused on
the more proximate causes of conflict. This requires some comment. During the chaotic period following the collapse of the Barre regime in Somalia, NGOs carried out efforts to provide humanitarian relief to the large
population movements brought on by drought and mass violence. This relief effort involved the distribution of food aid to at-risk populations. (Displaced and refugee populations are at a much greater risk of disease and

starvation once they leave their home villages.) As the clan conflict grew more and more violent, chaotic, roving bands of young men—some associated with clan militias, some not—preyed on the food conveys of the NGOs; a large portion of the food aid was being looted before it could be distributed to the needy.

In August 1992, USAID's Office of Foreign Disaster Assistance (OFDA) dispatched Fred Cuny (later assassinated in Chechnya) to report on what might be done to deal with the insecurity that was complicating the relief effort. Cuny's insightful analysis found that members of the country's merchant class were encouraging the violence and the looting, since the regular sources of agricultural goods for their markets had been destroyed by the drought and clan conflict. Cuny reasoned that if the merchants returned to their traditional role as defenders of law and order, essential conditions for the conduct of commerce, they might put pressure on clan leaders to restrain the violence destroying the country. This perspective was shared by some of the NGOs working in the country (CARE, the International Rescue Committee, and the UN-sponsored World Food Program), which OFDA encouraged to implement a monetization strategy to sell food aid to these merchants on a regular basis at prices that would simultaneously eliminate their need for looted food (for which they paid wildly fluctuating prices) and end their dependence on militia leaders to conduct the looting. (Militia commanders were using the merchants' payments to buy more weapons and expand their militias.)

Cuny also used this approach in Sri Lanka's civil war, where the same conditions prevailed: The merchants were encouraging the violence and the looting because it was the only source of commodities for their markets. Once USAID and other donors began a monetization program with merchant participation, the merchants began putting heavy pressure on the government and rebels alike to settle the war, since it was interfering with commerce. In the case of Somalia, it took a year and a half after the monetization program began before the merchant class organized itself across clan lines and began putting pressure on the warring clans, particularly in Mogadishu; merchants also focused their efforts on attempts to take over the city's port and run it in a businesslike fashion to import goods for their markets. Somalia and Sri Lanka are case studies in the deliberate use of economics in the service of conflict resolution by USAID and NGOs (Natsios 1996).

A second joint initiative between OFDA and NGOs was an effort to create a large number of jobs, which would get people off the street, keep them busy with constructive work, help them provide for their own support, and improve the long-term prospects for food security in Somalia. Save the Children, U.S. (with a grant from OFDA) employed twelve thousand farmers in the first half of 1992 in the lower Shebelle valley to reconstruct hundreds of miles of irrigation canals that had fallen into disrepair; the workers were paid daily according to the number of ditches dug. The consequence of the project was that agricultural production, which had suffered a massive decline in the preceding several years, was restored and in some areas actually increased above any previous levels. The result was a dramatic drop in imported food aid and the employment of a large number of able-bodied people. The repair of the irrigation ditches made marginal farmland productive again so that farmers could return to plant crops and support themselves.

THE RELIGIOUS DIMENSION: RECONCILIATION

The growing role of religious institutions and faith-based NGOs in conflict resolution was the subject of a recent book, *Religion, The Missing Dimension of Statecraft*, written under the aegis of CSIS. The book's coeditor, Cynthia Sampson, provides a comprehensive survey of religion-based modalities of conflict resolution in an earlier chapter of this collection. For the purposes of this essay, one crucial element of this emerging approach should be emphasized. Religion adds a new dimension to the discussion of conflict resolution in that it introduces the notion of reconciliation, a concept at the root of the Judeo-Christian tradition as well as elements of Hindu, Islamic, and Buddhist teaching (Johnston and Sampson 1994, 266–81). Reconciliation as a theological construct suggests that the broken relationships that led to and perpetuate a conflict can be repaired, and a constructive relationship can be established among the parties in conflict.

The religious dimension of conflict resolution is not a discrete model, but a framework in which any of the models—negotiation, mediation, or interactive conflict resolution—can apply. Indeed, one could argue that the religious framework enhances the effectiveness of these other models. We can see the application of this theological framework in several recent conflicts, where church and other religion-based organizations intervened in ways that do not exactly fit the traditional models described in this book.

In April 1994 a plane carrying the presidents of Rwanda and Burundi was shot down as it approached the Kigali airport, touching off a wave of killings that were launched by extremist elements in the Rwandan government opposed to a peace agreement between the Tutsi rebel movement and the Hutu-dominated government. These massacres threatened to spread into neighboring Burundi, which is divided along similar ethnic lines and had already experienced a wave of massacres in the fall of 1993. The Burundi Bible Society, a fairly well-known Christian organization, asked the government to allow the broadcast of religious music and appeals for peace over national radio in order to calm the public, given the spreading social panic over what was happening in Rwanda. The Burundian government ordered that ten hours of airtime be reserved each day for these broadcasts in the hope that they might have some salutary effect. In the broadcasts, the Bible Society asked people to go to their churches and pray for peace, quoting Biblical scriptures on peace, reconciliation, and forgiveness.

There is some anecdotal evidence that people did go to their churches in large numbers, though no systematic data have been collected on this response. Burundi did not experience the massive bloodletting that swept across Rwanda, but other factors unrelated to these broadcasts certainly played a role in preventing bloodshed; it is difficult to determine the actual effect of each factor individually. Despite these efforts, violence had returned to Burundi by the spring of 1995. The broadcasts and other measures may have restrained people for a short time, but over the longer term the country's unresolved political instability and seething ethnic hatred between the Tutsis and the Hutus had violently reasserted themselves.

The case of Burundi does not fit comfortably into any of the conflict-resolution models presented in this book: It displays some, but not all, of the characteristics of third-party mediation. One side refused to bargain or negotiate with the other side. No interaction occurred between the two sides, either directly or indirectly through a third party, except perhaps vicariously, as they listened to the radio broadcasts of church leaders. No set of disputes was addressed in any negotiation. The Burundi Bible Society acted as a neutral third party, but it did not mediate anything. The role of the broadcasts was preventive; it simply appealed to the religious convictions of the listeners to restrain their anger and their fears. Nevertheless, it seems to have worked—at least for a while.

Joseph Montville, a senior program official for CSIS (the sponsoring publisher of the aforementioned book), has developed an approach to conflict resolution based on an interesting fusion of modern psychiatry and Christian tradition, which served as the basis for some of the NGO conflict-resolution projects in Burundi and Bosnia mentioned in the preceding section. Montville's approach includes efforts to set up a national process for writing a common history of the conflict, since he has noted the wide disparity in the accounts given by each side. National truth commissions are an integral part of this effort: Members of each party to the conflict recount their personal experiences of pain and suffering during the conflict so the other sides can acknowledge and take responsibility for the harm they have done and ask forgiveness; the aggrieved side accepts the apology. Montville argues that some effort must be made toward bringing to justice those actually guilty of the most egregious atrocities as part of the reconciliation process. Much of this process is now taking place through indigenous and international NGO-managed workshops and seminars (Montville 1993).

Conflict-resolution interventions in this case focused only on national elites—specifically, the senior political leaders of the two countries—with disastrous consequences. Perhaps the most significant contribution NGOs are making to correct this weakness is their work at the grassroots level to engage the support of village and neighborhood elites.

Faith-based NGOs in Europe and the United States have increasingly integrated reconciliation and conflict-resolution interventions into their programming during and immediately after civil conflicts. In separate initiatives, Catholic Relief Services and Norwegian Church Aid have begun these types of conflict-resolution programs using local religious institutions in Bosnia as the organizing mechanism. Mercy Corps International, a faith-based NGO headquartered in the United States, has initiated similar projects with religious leaders in Bosnia under the leadership of a preeminent Quaker educator and theologian, Landrum Bolling. World Vision is implementing conflict-resolution programs in Liberia, Burundi, and Rwanda using local church leaders to assist with the work.

CONCLUSION

NGO conflict-resolution work covers a broad and quite disparate range of activities that includes not only some of the more traditional methods described in this book, but also more programmatic activities intentionally designed to address some of the fundamental causes of conflict. This programmatic approach has been used by NGOs to conduct public education campaigns aimed at the larger society affected by the conflict; to hold seminars and workshops where people from opposing sides can confront each other with their stories of past suffering and their anxieties about the future; and to establish a history of what happened during the conflict that all sides can agree upon.

NGOs are not a panacea in a conflict-prone world. They have strengths and weaknesses, just like the other organizations that are part of the humanitarian response system. Assessing their strengths and weaknesses will help policymakers determine which NGOs should be encouraged to do which types of interventions, and under what circumstances. NGO activities in conflict resolution will surely grow, but it remains to be seen how these organizations will perform against the exaggerated expectations some enthusiasts have created for them.

REFERENCES

Anderson, Mary B. 1996. *Do No Harm: Supporting Local Capacities for Peace through Aid*. Cambridge, Mass.: Local Capacities for Peace Project/Collaborative for Development Action, Inc.

Johnston, Douglas, and Cynthia Sampson, eds. 1994. *Religion, The Missing Dimension of Statecraft*. New York: Oxford University Press.

Lederach, John Paul. Forthcoming. *Building Peace: Sustainable Reconciliation in Divided Societies*. Washington, D.C.: United States Institute of Peace Press.

Minear, Larry. 1991. *Humanitarianism under Siege: A Critical Review of Operation Lifeline Sudan*. Lawrenceville, N.J.: Red Sea Press and Bread for the World.

Montville, Joseph V. 1993. "The Healing Function in Political Conflict Resolution." In *Conflict Resolution: Theory and Practice*, ed. Dennis J. D. Sandole and Hugo van der Merwe. Manchester, U.K.: Manchester University Press.

Natsios, Andrew S. 1996. "Humanitarian Relief Interventions in Somalia: The Economics of Chaos." *International Peacekeeping* 3 (1): 69–91.

Steele, David A. 1995. Summary Report for "Conflict Resolution Training for Religious Representatives from Former Yugoslavia." Center for Strategic and International Studies, Washington, D.C., October 30, 1995.

Weiss, Thomas G., and Larry Minear, eds. 1993. *Humanitarianism across Borders: Sustaining Civilians in Times of War*. Boulder, Colo.: Lynne Rienner.

PART FOUR

TRAINING

11

CONTRIBUTIONS OF TRAINING TO INTERNATIONAL CONFLICT RESOLUTION

Eileen F. Babbitt

INTRODUCTION

As any conflict resolution trainer will tell you, when the participants in a conflict resolution training program are members of communities in conflict, the training becomes an intervention in that conflict. The trainer's intent is to change the protagonists' view of the conflict and introduce new ways of thinking and behaving that make resolution of the conflict more possible and likely. This is done in several ways.

Reframing the Parties' Conception of Their Conflict

Parties in conflict, especially protracted conflict, typically view their situation as out of control or hopeless. They see a bleak future, with little possibility of settling the conflict. Meanwhile, the conflict continues to claim lives and resources, and life cannot return to any state of normalcy. A training program can offer its participants accumulated knowledge about conflict dynamics and options for intervention to prevent or de-escalate a conflict. It can give participants the theoretical frameworks developed from research on actual conflicts, as well as case studies on the progression and resolution of conflicts from other regions.

The value of this type of training is twofold. First, it gives the participants some hope that there may be unexplored approaches to help them in their quest for a settlement. By themselves, of course, conflict resolution approaches are often not sufficient to settle or resolve a given conflict. But they can help make the parties aware of the experiences of other adversaries in similar conflicts, many of which have moved toward settlement and even resolution. It can be extremely useful for the protagonists to hear examples of other choices and options they may have to end their dispute.

The second contribution of training lies in presenting the antagonists/belligerents with entirely new ways of looking at conflict, not only in their specific situation but also in the often unconscious way individuals and groups view conflict overall. If the general view holds that conflict is resolved only by one party defeating another, or that conflict is always a prelude to violence, a training program can introduce alternative, more constructive ways of thinking about conflict. These alternatives can reveal options that not only address the short-term problems but also lay the groundwork for longer-term, sustainable outcomes.

Reframing the Parties' Conception of Their Own Side and the Other Side

Most conflict resolution training involves putting participants in the "shoes" of the other side, to try to encourage them to see the conflict not only from their own perspective but from that of their adversary. Effective negotiation usually requires such an understanding of the other side, not for altruistic purposes but out of the necessity to respond to the other party's concerns in order to get one's own needs met. Of course, for longer-term, sustainable relationships, adversaries must move beyond mere self-interest, but it is a sufficient initial incentive for getting them to look beyond their own point of view.

The outcome of such an exercise can be a more analytical view of the other side's interests, as well as a more objective view of the interests of one's own side and of the way the other side might perceive demands based on these interests. Parties in conflict rarely take the time for such analysis, and the opportunity to do so in a structured way can allow parties to begin to reframe the way they see their own and the other side's behavior.

Skills for Dialogue and Problem Solving

Training can assist participants in developing or improving communication, negotiation, and problem-solving skills that will be useful as they search for ways to resolve their conflict. Most people have developed their own approaches to negotiation and problem solving, but they may not have taken the time to step back and assess the effectiveness of these approaches. A training program offers the opportunity for such reflection, giving experienced participants the chance to evaluate and refine their skills and introducing less experienced participants to new skills and concepts.

In addition, the training format offers a relatively safe environment in which to learn and test new approaches and skills. Since the participants are not engaged in actual negotiation or problem solving, they are free to try out new behaviors and strategies without having to commit to outcomes publicly, especially when training programs are held with each party separately. The training may then become an effective prelude to bringing the parties together for further joint training, simulation, or actual negotiation. Joint training allows both parties to engage in a mutual learning process, with the crucial assumption that these new skills will form the basis for interaction between the parties when they do meet for dialogue or negotiation on the conflict.

ASSUMPTIONS INHERENT IN TRAINING

Conflict resolution training programs are based on several key assumptions. The first is that there are skills, both conceptual and behavioral, that make one better able to manage conflict constructively. Rather than viewing conflict as inherently bad, training assumes that conflict is a natural part of human dynamics, but that its management can be either destructive or constructive. Training seeks to enhance the capacity of participants to engage in constructive approaches.

A second assumption is that such skills, while seemingly "natural" only in particular individuals, can actually be taught and learned. It is often said that certain people are born negotiators or mediators, and indeed there are those who seem to intuitively know how to work with conflict constructively. Since the 1970s, such intuitive behavior has been studied extensively, resulting in the identification of mental and behavioral constructs that effective negotiators and problem solvers typically use. Moreover, these constructs have been translated into teaching tools that introduce them to participants in ways that are both enjoyable and productive.

A third assumption is that even the most effective "intuitive" conflict resolvers can benefit by making their approaches more conscious and transparent and reflecting on what works and what does not, based on their experience. Training can help them create a more analytic framework for their behavior and allow them to improve their effectiveness by knowing exactly what they do, and under what circumstances, that contributes to their success.

The final assumption relates to empowerment. If parties to a conflict are more aware of the conceptual and behavioral options they can employ, they are more likely to work out their differences nonviolently, whether on their own or with the assistance of a third party. They are also less likely to be manipulated by unscrupulous leaders or outsiders and instead can take charge of their own conflict resolution process. Trainings are not designed to solve a particular conflict; the parties themselves must be active in initiating conflict management and resolution activities in order to move toward peace. In short, the parties must desire change and be willing to work at it. Training can assist and supplement their work by giving them both the confidence and the skills to achieve varying degrees of success.

WHAT IS TRAINING?

Training differs from other types of conflict intervention in that its primary goal is educational; the structure and content of the program are expressly intended to impart new knowledge and skills to the participants. It is not intended as a negotiation, mediation, or problem-solving session. Rather, training is a skill-building exercise to prepare participants to be more effective as they work out their dispute.

Training also differs from more academically oriented educational programs in that it stresses the application of knowledge rather than the acquisition of knowledge for its own sake. Thus, the objective of a training program is increased competency or proficiency in a defined skill area. For example, training is often used to enhance job-related skills, as illustrated by the increased provision of conflict resolution training for diplomats and other official foreign policy actors. It has become important for nongovernmental actors as well, since the role of nongovernmental organizations (NGOs) and private individuals as conflict intervenors has increased in frequency and importance.

Because negotiation and conflict resolution require social interaction, effective training programs use interactive learning modes, such as discussion, simulation, and case study analysis, rather than merely didactic presentation. Simulations in particular put the participants into the roles of disputing parties, requiring them to work through a negotiation or problem-solving session and then discuss and analyze their experience with the trainer and the other participants (Winham 1991).

For example, one of the simulation exercises available through the Program on Negotiation's Clearinghouse at Harvard Law School involves a fictitious border dispute between two countries. Participants in the simulation are assigned roles as representatives of the two countries in conflict as well as representatives of international organizations and neighboring countries with interests in the dispute. The objective is to try to settle the dispute in a way that meets the most salient interests of all parties. Several groups play out the simulation in tandem, each coming up with its own outcome. In the debriefing, the group discusses why the outcomes differ and how the negotiating strategies of individuals in each role contributed to the various outcomes. This method allows participants in the training to grapple with the actual give-and-take of negotiation, rather than reflect on it from only a theoretical perspective.[*]

Another teaching mode is to draw upon participants' past experience and relate the new conflict resolution material to the skills and knowledge they already possess. This practice not only ensures the relevance of the subject matter, but also greatly increases the likelihood that the new skills will actually be adopted and used after the participants leave the training session. For example, in training sessions conducted by the United States Institute of Peace (USIP), representatives from political and military organizations and NGOs work together to develop understanding and strategies for collaboration in the context of complex emergencies or postconflict reconstruction. In these sessions, considerable time is devoted to learning from the participants what has and has not worked for them in the past and how that experience can be built on and enhanced by new knowledge and skills.

A third teaching mode involves designing a program so the participants learn from each other as well as from the trainers. Because participants in these training programs are often experienced professionals, their accumulated knowledge is relevant and useful. By incorporating the wide range of perspectives and expertise of as many as thirty people, a training program can cover broader material than if the course content were confined to only the trainers' perspective. Incorporating participants' perspectives is particularly important when conducting cross-cultural training, where the instructor is typically from a different cultural background than the participants.

---

[*] I have used examples throughout this chapter to illustrate various points. I recognize that these are but a sampling of the extensive work being done in international conflict resolution training, not only by other colleagues in the United States but also by many professionals in other countries. I relied on my firsthand knowledge of recent and current projects; therefore, many other examples that would have served equally well as excellent illustrations were left out.

In the USIP trainings mentioned above, participants work in several small-group exercises, in which the group's task is outlined by the trainers but group interaction is strictly among participants. As participants go through the various small-group activities, they have an opportunity to learn from different subsets of their colleagues. In their evaluations, many participants cite these exercises as one of the most enlightening elements of the training.

CONTRIBUTIONS OF TRAINING TO INTERNATIONAL CONFLICT RESOLUTION

Training contributes to conflict resolution in two ways: educationally and politically. Conflict resolution training can expand the skills repertoire of parties in conflict, introducing them to new ways of thinking and acting that will enhance their abilities to end their dispute. It can also address some of the political issues causing and perpetuating the conflict itself.

Educational Contributions

Conflict resolution training provides both analytical and behavioral instruction, enabling participants to expand their range of both assessments of the conflict and actions aimed at resolving or transforming it. The instruction is provided not only by the content of the program but by the format as well. Participants leave the program with new skills, or with existing skills honed, to work more effectively toward resolving their conflict.

Content. The content of training will vary depending on the needs of the participants and the philosophy and background of the trainers. For example, trainers who build on their experience as therapists or psychologists focus their training on interpersonal or intergroup dynamics. Trainers who have a legal background are more inclined to stress the cognitive components of conflict and teach negotiation or mediation skills. Trainers with a background in public policy or public participation tend to concentrate on consensus building or shared decision making. (The more sophisticated trainers, while still focusing on their own strengths, now incorporate elements of several of these dimensions into their programs.)

Similarly, participants come from both the official governmental and the nongovernmental sectors and from many parts of the world, making their needs and interests quite different from one program to the next. For example, officials are usually quite keen on learning more effective

negotiation techniques, but they are increasingly drawn to learning the conflict resolution activities and approaches typically embraced by nongovernmental actors. Participants dealing with a "hot" conflict (one in which
the level of violence is rising) need skills that differ from those geared to
participants whose conflict is latent or de-escalating. It is therefore crucial
for the conflict resolution trainer to conduct a thorough assessment of the
potential audience for the training to determine which skills and approaches
will be most relevant.

The content of trainings is drawn from several general categories. First,
trainings can include discussion of theoretical frameworks, where participants learn about conflict dynamics (i.e., the phases and sources of conflict
and conflict escalation). Second, participants can work together on skill
building in communication, negotiation, mediation, facilitation, consensus building, and/or problem solving. Third, trainings can incorporate issues of healing and reconciliation, including exercises to identify and
delegitimize stereotypes and acknowledge mutual injustices, historic grievances, and responsibility. Training modules in all three categories could
also include a discussion of what is being done in other parts of the world
to address similar problems.

Formats. Trainers use a number of different formats to impart the essential
aspects of conflict resolution theory and practice to participants. The most
commonly used is the experiential learning (i.e., learning by doing) model.
Briefly, this model involves a process in which information is processed
through four steps. Learners have *concrete experiences*, make *reflective observations* about the experiences, engage in *abstract conceptualization* by making generalizations from their experiences and observations, and use these
generalizations as a basis for further action, or *active experimentation* (Kolb
1984). In conflict resolution training, the use of simulations and roleplaying
exemplifies the application of this model. Participants share the concrete
experience of taking on a role and working through the enactment of an
actual negotiation or consensus-building process. They then reflect on this
experience during the exercise's debriefing. In subsequent simulations, they
extrapolate from their earlier experience and apply their learning in situations of increasing complexity. The participants conclude by actively working through the dynamics of their own conflict, using their newly acquired
concepts and skills.

In applying the experiential learning approach, trainers usually fall somewhere along a continuum, from more prescriptive to more elicitive styles of

teaching (Lederach 1995). At the prescriptive end of the continuum, the fundamental assumptions are that necessary skills can be imparted by a trainer to a participant and that a core set of such skills is universally applicable. The trainer is viewed as the expert who knows and has the skills that participants want and need. Training is viewed not only as a way to impart knowledge, but as a way to demonstrate how the knowledge is applied.

Among this format's advantages is that participants learn specific models and strategies that have proven effective for other disputants and are provided the opportunity to practice and eventually master the techniques. A disadvantage is that the trainer may define the needs of participants according to predetermined criteria for success that may not transfer appropriately into action for the disputants. The most notable example of this training style is the use of the tenets of principled negotiation as the basis for negotiation training.

The elicitive style is at the other end of the continuum. While the prescriptive style of training is based on the transfer of knowledge from trainer to trainee, the elicitive style "is an opportunity aimed primarily at discovery, creation, and solidification of models that emerge from the resources present in a particular setting and respond to needs in that context" (Lederach 1995, 55). Trainers in the elicitive style do not assume that they know what participants need and do not consider themselves experts the way prescriptive trainers do. Instead, they take the role of facilitators or catalysts. The participants themselves are seen as the experts, since they have the most knowledge of the conflict in which they are involved, its setting and context, and how different conflict management techniques might work in their particular setting. In the elicitive approach, the knowledge flows among participants and between participants and trainer.

In reality, most conflict resolution training falls somewhere along the continuum between prescriptive and elicitive; at its best, it combines the strengths of both.

Political Contributions

Training programs can contribute to the eventual political settlement of a conflict, not only by educating the participants in skills, but by changing or reinforcing particular aspects of the social or political system in which the conflict is situated. The contributions are made in three ways: the choice of goals set for the training; the format of the program; and the substantive content introduced to the participants.

Goals for the Training. The goals of any training session are the overarching impacts the convenors of the session hope to produce. These goals guide the trainer in putting together both the format and content of the program. The training session's goals reflect the intended outcomes of the program in terms of possible effects in the larger political and social system in which the conflict is occurring. Examples of such goals include the following:

1. *To validate or augment conflict resolution processes already operating in the conflict system.*

A conflict system comprises the parties to a given conflict (which may include external parties as well as the disputants themselves) and the political, social, and economic forces that act to perpetuate, escalate, or resolve the conflict. Within any given conflict system, processes are usually under way—initiated by members of the conflicting groups even as the conflict rages—to move the parties toward some kind of resolution of their differences. These processes may take the form of informal meetings convened by community leaders, media projects that involve discussions between journalists from the opposing sides, or educational efforts with children or with social and political elites. A training program can identify these types of initiatives and provide project leaders additional skills that can make their efforts more effective.

For example, John Paul Lederach of Eastern Mennonite University and Hizkias Assefa of the Nairobi Peace Initiative in Kenya have teamed up to provide training to grassroots conflict resolution projects in East and West Africa. Their goal is to identify indigenous efforts at peacebuilding and provide additional skills and other support needed to enhance these local initiatives.

2. *To introduce analytical concepts and behavioral skills that can prepare parties to transform the relationship that initiated and/or perpetuates the conflict.*

A conflict system is usually characterized by unconscious patterns of thought and behavior that keep the parties locked into an adversarial relationship in which no movement is possible and no settlement is acceptable. Notter and Diamond (1996) refer to these as conflict-habituated systems, in which the norms of behavior and thought within the system act to perpetuate the conflict. Volkan (1988) also speaks of the inherent need for enemies, in which the identity of each party in a conflict is defined in part by perpetuating an image of the other party as a hated enemy. Ironically, if the conflict moves toward resolution, the identity of one or both parties is threatened because they do not know how to define themselves if they do not have the "other" as the adversary.

A training program introduces and uses these concepts, allowing members of the conflicting groups to step outside their particular conflict system for a brief period and reflect on how the internal dynamic of that system may be creating obstacles to settlement. They can also begin to explore ways in which their relationship might be reorganized or transformed so the self-perpetuating cycle of conflict is broken and the system can realign itself toward more tolerance and coexistence. Such training programs may be conducted with parties either separately or together, depending on the volatility of the conflict and the adversaries' willingness to meet with each other.

It is true, of course, that the transformation of a conflict relationship often requires structural as well as psychological and behavioral change. Putting in place political, judicial, and social mechanisms that protect and reassure each party is essential to a stable settlement. A training program might also introduce information about how other countries have initiated such structural changes and what has worked under different circumstances.

A notable example of this kind of training is the Cyprus Consortium Project conducted by the Institute for Multi-Track Diplomacy in Washington, D.C., and the Conflict Management Group of Cambridge, Massachusetts. These two organizations have teamed up to train mixed groups of Greek and Turkish Cypriots at all levels, from young people to political party leaders. Building on initiatives begun by local peace activists, these training sessions have taken place over a three-year period, in Cyprus and in locations in the United States and western Europe. To date, more than four hundred people from the island have received training. Many of the participants have become trainers themselves, passing on the concepts of conflict transformation to an ever-widening audience.

3. *To empower local individuals and organizations to take constructive action, and to engender hope that such action will have an impact.*

In many countries experiencing protracted or violent conflict, there is a lack of hope that anything can be done to stem the violence or move the sides toward resolving their conflict. Training programs can introduce new ideas and skills for the members of each conflicting group to consider, opening up the possibilities for previously unfamiliar courses of action. By sharing information about successes (and failures) from other conflict situations, training programs can shore up the resolve to move forward, yet stay realistic about what can be done.

Organizations such as Partners for Democratic Change of San Francisco and CDR Associates of Boulder, Colorado, have undertaken extensive training efforts in central and eastern Europe. Working on issues such as legal reform and environmental planning, they have trained local leaders in negotiation and consensus-building skills so that new collaborative initiatives might be created and implemented, often across ethnic and racial lines.

4. *To foster the development of individual agency or group initiative in the wake of political systems that suppressed such initiative.*

Under repressive regimes, the notion of understanding and working from one's own interests is not a concept that has much meaning. Individuals and groups in such political systems are typically inculcated and socialized with a strong ideology that discourages independent thought and action, and thus fosters dependency on the state.

Most Western conflict resolution theory and teaching rests on the presumption that individuals and groups have their own interests and fundamental needs, and that the resolution of conflict depends on some understanding and acknowledgment of these needs. First, the individuals or groups in the conflict must be able to articulate those interests and needs to their counterparts or, at least, to an intermediary (Burton 1990; Kelman 1993). Then, they must take action, ideally together, to meet the fundamental needs of both sides.

Training programs can begin the process of identifying and thinking through these interests and needs and introducing ways of communicating them that are not completely offensive to the other side. Training can help participants consider the value of listening to the interests and needs of the other side, with a desire to understand rather than to discount or debate. It can also provide opportunities for participants to think through possible courses of action that would meet the interests of all sides and not just their own.

One example of such training was a series of programs run by the Balkans Peace Project of Cambridge, Massachusetts, in 1993 and 1994. These sessions took place in Macedonia (or the Former Yugoslav Republic of Macedonia, as it is officially known). Participants were from all the country's ethnic groups. As a member of the training team, I worked with my colleagues to introduce the concepts of conflict analysis and the skills of conflict resolution first to a group of political party officials and university faculty and then to a group of secondary school educators from the ethnic Slav Macedonian and Albanian communities. The outgrowth of these sessions was the establishment of two separate nongovernmental programs for conflict resolution education and training, headed by local professionals and reaching out into the wider community. These programs have been a great achievement for Macedonia, as it begins for the first time to build an active civil society separate from the state. Three years later, these organizations are still operating and flourishing.

5. *To build a network and support system for people within a conflict who are looking for nonviolent ways to work together.*

There are usually strong norms operating within a conflict system that serve to perpetuate the conflict. Such norms often revolve around stereotypes of both the enemy and one's own group (e.g., "they" are all demons; "we" are all righteous and possess the moral high ground). In-group mentality places a high premium on the perceived need for internal cohesiveness and prescribes severe penalties for defection from the "party line" of one's own group. Under these circumstances, those who do not advocate violence or seek some accommodation with the adversary may, at best, be marginalized or, at worst, be labeled traitors.

In a conflict resolution training program, participants can begin to identify others from within their own community or region, or even from other parts of the world, who are exploring options for moving the conflict resolution process forward. These like-minded individuals can then become part of an invaluable network, providing opportunities for joint projects or just moral support when people return home and attempt to disseminate these new ideas throughout their communities (sometimes against great odds).

One such project is currently being conducted in Bosnia under the leadership of David Steele and the Center for Strategic and International Studies in Washington, D.C. Steele is working in several communities with individuals of different religious faiths, bringing them together to share their stories and pain of the war and, based on their common desire to move beyond the current hatreds, create possibilities for common projects that will rebuild their trust in each other.

6. *To support the moderate "middle" in a conflict system that might otherwise be diminished or invalidated by extremists.*

This goal is a variation of the preceding one and speaks to the crucial political role that individuals trained in conflict resolution can play within their own societies. Sometimes, those who gravitate toward participation in conflict resolution training are society's "doves," whose proclivity is toward nonviolence under any circumstances. In protracted conflicts, however, people who occupy the middle of the political spectrum are also drawn to conflict resolution. This group is important to reach, because its members are often more politically influential than the doves, and their opinions and actions therefore carry more weight in their community's political debates.

Training programs can support these political moderates by exposing them to concepts and skills they can employ in tangible ways to demonstrate constructive conflict resolution processes in their own communities. If joint training programs are held with all conflicting parties present (as discussed below), the programs can begin to build coalitions of moderate voices across the dividing lines of the conflict (Kelman 1993). If nourished through ongoing contact, these coalitions can be powerful counterforces to the extremists within each community, especially in times of crisis or escalation of violence.

The work of many groups in the Middle East over the past fifteen years has sought to create such coalitions. For example, over several years, organizations such as the School for Peace at Neve Shalom/Wahat al Salaam in Israel, and more recently Search for Common Ground of Washington, D.C., have provided the forums and psychological safety to bring members of the adversarial groups together for training in conflict resolution, even when the respective political leaders would not meet directly with each other and when cycles of violence were on the upswing.

Format of the Training

The format the trainer chooses, often in consultation with prospective participants, can greatly enhance the political impact of the workshop. Three such formats are joint training sessions, training of trainers, and integration of training modules into dialogue or problem-solving workshops.

Joint Training. Joint training involves bringing the parties to a conflict together in a workshop, rather than working with them separately. This format was pioneered in labor-management relations in the United States to introduce frames of reference and techniques into contract negotiations that would diminish the likelihood of crippling strikes and would soften the sometimes brutal adversarial exchanges that severely damaged relationships between union members and companies. These training sessions were convened months before actual negotiations began, so that participants did not have to contend with the pressure of real-time negotiation while learning new approaches. It also gave the negotiating teams on each side time to think about the new techniques and discuss them with their constituencies, so that the adoption of any new behaviors in the contract negotiations would not catch the rank and file off guard.

Joint training in the context of protracted or violent conflict is not necessarily intended to prepare participants for a specific anticipated negotiation. When the training has been done under such circumstances, it is more likely that no negotiation is under way or even on the horizon. As such, the training program is a preliminary step in exploring whether negotiation is even possible. Its purpose in this context is to suggest common frames of reference, constructive problem-solving processes and language, and less adversarial and escalatory negotiation tactics, using hypothetical cases or examples from other similar conflicts. No actual negotiation of the disputants' conflict is planned or expected within such sessions; in fact, it is often a precondition for adversaries to agree to attend the same training session. However, informal contact during social time can often be quite productive in allowing parties to begin exploratory discussions. If these informal talks are found to be useful, the participants might even suggest to the trainers that the issues of the conflict become part of the discussion within the training sessions themselves. The Cypriot training mentioned above is a prime example of a joint training effort.

Alternatively, a training program can be used as a preventive strategy. If a political relationship between two communities is potentially problematic, a joint training session can provide skills and suggestions for processes that would allow tensions to be diffused before they become open conflicts. Training that the Balkans Peace Project conducted in Macedonia with ethnic Slav Macedonian and Albanian participants is an example of such preventive work. Search for Common Ground in Macedonia has continued this conflict resolution training work in the same communities.

Training the Trainers. This is another format that can have a significant political impact. This format's purpose is to impart conflict resolution concepts and skills to a professional and highly motivated group of participants, who will, in turn, set up training programs within their communities to pass the information along to others. Among the advantages of this format are that it enhances local capacity for conflict resolution skill building, provides a vehicle for reinforcing conflict resolution mechanisms that exist within the culture because of adaptations that local trainers will make to materials introduced externally, and transfers ownership of the training process to those residing within the conflict's venue, enhancing the goals of building indigenous initiative and agency. Partners for Democratic Change, whose headquarters is in San Francisco, California, is the most notable American organization to adopt this format. This organization has set up conflict resolution centers in several countries of central and eastern Europe and has trained scores of local trainers, who now provide further training and conflict resolution services within their own countries and elsewhere in the region.

Integration. A third format integrates training into a problem-solving process. Difficult moments inevitably arise in an ongoing discussion aimed at identifying and resolving problems between communities in conflict. Verbal attacks may ensue, stereotypes may be invoked, or old patterns of rhetorical exchange and recrimination may occur. At such moments, the facilitators may stop the action and insert a brief instructive module that addresses the problem the participants have just encountered. The advantage of this format is that it uses problems as they occur in real time as the basis for learning. For such a format to be effective, however, the participants must agree to it beforehand, so that the suggestion to break from the dialogue and move to a more instructive format is not seen as inappropriate or as an intrusion by the facilitator.

Such a format has been used by the Kettering Foundation team in its work in Tajikistan. Dr. Harold Saunders and Dr. Randa Slim, working with Russian counterparts, have been convening discussions with the factions in the Tajik conflict since 1993 (Slim and Saunders 1996). Instead of providing training as a prerequisite for discussion, they have integrated teaching modules into the dialogue itself, finding the participants more receptive to these pedagogical segments because they relate directly to a problem just encountered in the discussions.

Theme of the Workshop

Finally, the workshop's theme can be used to affect the conflict itself. The overarching theme frames the application of the skills to be presented. Four such themes are most relevant to today's conflict situations: preventive diplomacy or preventive action; managing complex humanitarian emergencies; postconflict reconstruction; and interagency/interinstitutional collaboration.

A training workshop that focuses on conflict prevention will be most useful in conflict areas where violence has not yet begun, but where there is concern that violence is possible in the near future. Macedonia is a good example of such a situation, where the potential for violent clashes between the ethnic Slav Macedonian majority and the ethnic Albanian minority exists, but so far has been kept from escalating. Such a training workshop would highlight the ways in which conflict resolution concepts and skills could be employed to prevent conflict escalation and would explore the roles of different actors (governmental, military, nongovernmental) in a coordinated prevention effort. Lessons from both successful and unsuccessful cases would be used as teaching tools. For example, the United States Institute of Peace (USIP), working with the U.S. Agency for International Development and the Department of State, is designing such a workshop for organizations working in the Horn of Africa.

Similar programs can also be designed that focus on managing complex humanitarian emergencies or on postconflict reconstruction and reconciliation. Again, the training emphasizes conflict resolution skills and concepts most relevant for those kinds of situations. USIP, in collaboration with the U.S. Army Peacekeeping Institute in Carlisle, Pennsylvania, has conducted several of these training programs on complex humanitarian emergencies and jointly hosted another such program in fall 1996 on postconflict peacebuilding, using Bosnia as the case study. Participants in these programs come from U.S. political agencies, the U.S. military, international organizations such as the United Nations and International Committee of the Red Cross, and the major international humanitarian NGOs.

The last theme, interagency and interinstitutional collaboration, is of increasing importance, because the complexity of current international conflicts brings in many actors other than national governments, and the coordination of myriad players on the ground can present daunting challenges. The cases of Somalia and Rwanda, for example, are being scrupulously studied to glean lessons for future complex emergencies. Similarly, the Carnegie Commission on Preventing Deadly Conflict is assembling case study data on successful prevention efforts; several analyses of Bosnia and Rwanda are providing valuable information about managing postconflict reconstruction. Thus, training programs either can deal separately with the issues of collaboration and coordination or can integrate them into programs focusing on each conflict phase.

ETHICAL CONCERNS AND OTHER CRITICISMS

Trainers who work directly with parties in conflict carry a large responsibility. By simply entering a conflict system, they change it. Like other intervenors, trainers need to think through the impact their presence will have on the workshop participants they are training and on the conflict system as a whole. Many practitioners suggest that the guiding principle for all trainers should be "do no harm." At a minimum, trainers should leave a situation no worse than when they arrived. Depending on the format, trainings can raise deep-seated emotions and painful issues. Trainers must have not only the skills but also the commitment to help participants address these issues in a way that does not leave trainees feeling worse than when they arrived.

Exporting Models That Are Not Culturally Relevant

The cultural relevance of training material developed in North America and used abroad is the subject of a growing debate in the conflict resolution community. Many believe that such conflict resolution materials can be adapted or adjusted for other cultures. Others consider these materials "acultural" or "culturally neutral," failing to see how their own cultural lenses have shaped the material (Fisher 1995; Lederach 1995). Such myopia may cause trainers to miss crucial cultural dynamics of the parties that may be contributing to the conflict (Fisher 1995).

Material developed in North America also simply may not make sense to people in other cultures. John Paul Lederach speaks of an experience of inadvertently turning two Guatemalans into "gringos" because he did not consider the subtle nuances of his training material. The Guatemalans were quick to point out that the way a roleplaying session had been set up reflected North American, not Guatemalan, attitudes (Lederach 1995). Thus, by failing to recognize cultural differences, trainers can substantially limit the impact of a training session and its material.

Perpetuating Dependence on Outsiders

Another ethical concern is that outside trainers who present themselves as experts with a tremendous amount of knowledge to dispense may fail to empower participants to take the initiative and work on their own. Participants may feel the need to validate their action with the expert before proceeding. Additionally, trainers, like other professionals, need to make a living. By creating a need for continual training, trainers may be guaranteeing themselves work but may not be acting in the participants' best interest.

Creating Dramatic Change in Individuals But Not Structures

A final ethical concern is how to prepare participants in training programs for reentering their communities. For example, in joint training programs, the simple act of bringing together individuals involved in a conflict can have a substantial personal impact on participants. People have been dramatically changed by these meetings. But while they themselves have changed, their society may remain the same, including the structural inequalities that continue to fuel hostilities. Participants may emerge from a training session to encounter suspicion or even hostility from family and friends, find that their jobs are in jeopardy, and in very polarized situations may even be in physical danger.

It is therefore imperative that trainers fully understand the system they are entering. They must not "parachute in" to provide one-time programs or be ignorant of the social, political, and cultural context of the conflict. Like other intervenors, they must prepare carefully for each training program, working whenever possible with local partners who can guide them and provide insight and awareness of what is happening on the ground. Only then will the training program be useful to the participants, not be naive or overly infused with North American values, and reflect awareness of what needs to be done to protect participants from undue suspicion and danger when they return to their communities.

EVALUATION

Given the concerns raised in the previous section, what has been done to evaluate the impact of international conflict resolution training? Unfortunately, efforts along these lines have been sparse and inconsistent to date. Most trainers construct evaluation material for their own use, confining their inquiry to questionnaires administered to the participants immediately after the workshop concludes. Questions are usually constructed to give the trainer specific feedback on participants' satisfaction with each element of the program and with the program as a whole. Often there are questions about what the participants thought was most relevant or useful and how they anticipate using the skills in the future. Rarely is the postsession evaluation followed up to determine whether participants are still using the skills and concepts even six months later.

Some scholar-practitioners have attempted to apply more rigorous designs to evaluate the immediate impact of the training. Fisher (1996) has administered both pre- and posttraining questionnaires, intending to document specific changes in participants' knowledge, skills, and attitudes as a result of the training program. Rothman and Ross (forthcoming) are currently involved in a broad-ranging study of conflict resolution interventions (including training) that focuses on defining measures of success. Preliminary results have led Rothman to design a more narrative approach to evaluation. This approach includes having participants describe more fully at the outset what they expect and want from the training program, and then documenting their ongoing reactions throughout the training workshop in a journal format. The approach is still too new to have generated any conclusive data on its usefulness.

Evaluation needs not only to document the impact of training programs on participants, but also to assess the impacts on the dynamics of the conflict itself. Developing this type of evaluation is a much more difficult challenge, because any change in the conflict will be hard to trace back to any particular training effort (i.e., it will be hard to prove cause and effect). However, many professionals in the field would welcome an evaluation method that would, at the very least, document any correlation between training and participants' individual actions that have a broader political impact.

PROFESSIONAL EDUCATION: ANOTHER KIND OF TRAINING

Any discussion of international conflict resolution training would be incomplete without some attention to professional education for foreign affairs professionals at both the entry and midcareer levels. Currently, such training in the United States is primarily provided by graduate schools of international affairs. Students in these programs, while not explicitly chosen from communities in conflict, are often those who have or will have policy- or decision-making positions in the United States and abroad. Unlike participants in the directed training programs described previously in this chapter, these graduate students may not be currently involved as parties in conflict. But their countries may be harboring latent conflicts in which they could one day become involved, or they may be potential third parties in conflicts occurring in other countries.

Unlike training provided to professionals on the job, graduate school training gives would-be policymakers a more fundamental theoretical base they can then draw from when faced with real-world situations. Policymakers on the job do not have much reflective time, and therefore their frames of reference for decision making come less from knowledge acquired while in office and more from the accrued knowledge they bring to their jobs. Graduate professional education is therefore an excellent point for intervention, to develop the personal skills of current and future leaders.

An example of the content of such professional training is provided by a survey done for the Association of Professional Schools of International Affairs in Washington, D.C. (Goodman and Mandell 1994). The survey found three models for teaching conflict resolution concepts and skills in these professional schools.

In *dedicated programs*, international conflict resolution is a distinct area of study that students can elect as a field of concentration. Such programs usually include core required courses plus a broader array of related courses. Schools in this category include American University's School of International Service, the University of Denver's Graduate School of International Studies, the Johns Hopkins University's School for Advanced International Studies, and Tufts University's Fletcher School of Law and Diplomacy.

In *integrated programs*, particular courses highlight international conflict resolution as a key problem area, but not as a stand-alone course or area of study. Instead, conflict resolution is incorporated into courses dealing with trade, environment, international security, and international organizations. Nine schools feature such programs: Georgetown University's Edmund A. Walsh School of Foreign Service; George Washington University's Elliott School of International Affairs; the University of Pittsburgh's Graduate School of Public and International Affairs; Princeton University's Woodrow Wilson School of Public and International Affairs; the School of Public Affairs at the University of Maryland, College Park; the Graduate School of International Relations and Pacific Studies at the University of California, San Diego; the University of Southern California's School of International Relations; the University of Washington's Henry M. Jackson School of International Studies; and the Yale Center for International and Area Studies at Yale University.

In *course-designated programs*, specific courses in international conflict resolution are offered. Students can elect these courses as part of their concentration in more broadly defined substantive areas of study. Columbia University's School of International and Public Affairs and Harvard University's John F. Kennedy School of Government offer this type of program.

The authors of this survey recommend several innovations for these graduate schools. If followed, these changes would take some of the best elements of the on-the-job professional training models described in the body of this chapter and integrate them into graduate study: more case-based and discussion-based learning; more short, specialized modules; more interdisciplinary training of faculty; more emphasis on behavioral skill-building in addition to conceptual training; more integration of nonofficial approaches and policy-relevant material; and more attention to cross-cultural and ethical issues.

CONCLUSION

The end of the Cold War has led to a dramatic increase in international conflict resolution training efforts, especially those that could be categorized as interventions. Factors contributing to that increase include the intrastate nature of many current conflicts and the corresponding rise in the number of nonstate actors involved in such conflicts. Because international conflict is no longer confined to interstate channels, NGOs are increasingly assuming the role of intervenors. Training is often the entry point through which NGOs establish their credibility with disputants without presuming to take on mediation or other third-party roles.

This situation is a marked departure from the traditional diplomacy of the past, in which professional diplomats and foreign ministries were the only players involved in resolving conflicts. As stated above, no conclusive data document the impact of this new type of intervention. The post-training data that do exist show clearly that participants in many international conflict resolution training programs are finding the skills and concepts useful and provocative, at least at first exposure. Many are setting up their own local programs and centers, which indicates their view of the importance of conflict resolution work.

Although longer-term impacts have not been systematically measured, observation by those in the field indicates that the best format for long-term impact is the training of trainers and educators. If local individuals and organizations can learn (or relearn, in the case of indigenous practices) the basic premises of conflict resolution, adapt them to be culturally and politically relevant for their own society, and then pass them on to others, a transformation will have begun. The challenge is to provide enough support, both financial and conceptual, to give the new ideas a chance to take root.

Another challenge is to connect any impact at the community and nongovernmental levels to more far-reaching political and structural changes at the decision-making levels of states. Some training programs, like those offered by the United States Institute of Peace and others, are being requested by state officials, both here and abroad, and by international organizations such as the United Nations and the Organization for Security and Cooperation in Europe. Also, many trainers now bring together official and nonofficial actors from the same conflict area because of the growing recognition that nonstate actors can play important roles in both the escalation and de-escalation of conflict. In addition, many graduates of the professional schools that teach international conflict resolution are themselves becoming important political actors and bringing their knowledge of conflict resolution into office with them.

Many professionals involved in international conflict resolution training hope that the cumulative effect of such training will be to create a critical mass of individuals and organizations, official and unofficial, having the skills and confidence to apply nonviolent approaches as a first step in resolving conflicts. In doing so, they draw from both the traditional skills of negotiation and mediation, and the more unconventional faith-based and social-psychological approaches. While recognizing that the use of force is sometimes necessary, conflict resolution trainers hope to disseminate the worldwide experience and capacity of choosing alternatives to force.

REFERENCES

Burton, John. 1990. *Conflict Resolution and Provention*. New York: St. Martin's Press.

Diamond, Louise, and Ronald Fisher. 1995. "Integrating Conflict Resolution Training and Consultation: A Cyprus Example." *Negotiation Journal* 11 (July): 287–301.

Fisher, Roger et al. 1992. *Getting to Yes*. Enlarged rev. ed. Boston: Houghton Mifflin.

Fisher, Ronald. 1995. "Training as a Form of Interactive Conflict Resolution in Divided Societies." Paper presented at the annual scientific meeting of the International Society of Political Psychology, July 5–9, 1995, Washington, D.C.

———. 1996. *Interactive Conflict Resolution*. Syracuse, N.Y.: Syracuse University Press.

Friere, Paolo. 1970. *Pedagogy of the Oppressed*. New York: Herder and Herder.

Goodman, Louis W., and Brian S. Mandell. 1994. *International Conflict Resolution for the 21st Century: Preparing Tomorrow's Leaders*. Washington, D.C.: Association of Professional Schools of International Affairs.

Kegan, Robert. 1994. *In Over Our Heads: The Mental Demands of Modern Life*. Cambridge, Mass.: Harvard University Press.

Kelman, Herbert C. 1992. "Informal Mediation by the Scholar/Practitioner." In *Mediation in International Relations: Multiple Approaches to Conflict Management*, ed. Jacob Bercovitch and Jeffrey Z. Rubin. New York: St. Martin's Press.

———. 1993. "Coalitions Across Conflict Lines: The Interplay of Conflicts Within and Between the Israeli and Palestinian Communities." In *Conflict Between People* and Groups: Causes, Processes, and Resolutions, ed. Jeffry A. Simpson and Stephen Worchel. Chicago: Nelson Hall.

Kolb, David. 1984. *Experiential Learning: Experience as the Source of Learning and Development*. Englewood Cliffs, N.J.: Prentice-Hall.

Kremenyuk, Victor A., ed. 1991. *International Negotiation: Analysis, Approaches, Issues*. San Francisco: Jossey-Bass.

Lederach, John Paul. 1995. *Preparing for Peace: Conflict Transformation Across Cultures*. Syracuse, N.Y.: Syracuse University Press.

Lewin, Kurt. 1948. *Resolving Social Conflicts*. New York: Harper and Row.

Mezirow, Jack. 1981. "A Critical Theory of Adult Learning Education." *Adult Education Quarterly* 32 (Fall): 3–24.

Mitchell, Christopher R. 1995. "Some Thoughts on Training Intervenors in Ethnic Conflicts," in *Ethnic Studies Network Bulletin*, no. 8 (January).

Murrell, Patricia H., and Charles Claxton. 1987. "Experiential Learning Theory as a Guide for Effective Teaching." *Counselor Education and Supervision* 27 (September): 4–14.

Notter, James, and Louise Diamond. 1996. *Building Peace and Transforming Conflict: The Practice of the Institute for Multi-Track Diplomacy*. Occasional Paper no. 7. Washington, D.C.: Institute for Multi-Track Diplomacy.

Rothman, Jay, and Marc Ross. Forthcoming. *Theory and Practice in Ethnic Conflict Management: Conceptualizing Success and Failure*. New York: Macmillan.

Slim, Randa, and Harold Saunders. 1996. "Managing Conflict in Divided Societies: Lessons from Tajikistan." *Negotiation Journal* 12 (January): 31–46.

Volkan, Vamik. 1988. *The Need to Have Enemies and Allies: From Clinical Practice to International Relationships*. Northvale, N.J.: Jason Aronson, Inc.

Winham, Gilbert. 1991. "Simulation for Teaching and Analysis." In *International Negotiation: Analysis, Approaches, Issues*, ed. Victor A. Kremenyuk. San Francisco: Jossey-Bass.

CONTRIBUTORS

Eileen F. Babbitt is assistant professor of international politics at the Fletcher School of Law and Diplomacy at Tufts University and director of its International Negotiation and Conflict Resolution Program. Previously, she was director of Education and Training at the United States Institute of Peace and deputy director of the Program on International Conflict Analysis and Resolution at Harvard University's Center for International Affairs. Dr. Babbitt is also an associate at Harvard Law School's Program on Negotiation. Her practice as a facilitator and trainer has included work in the Middle East, the Balkans, and the Horn of Africa. She has authored or coauthored many articles and chapters on international mediation and conflict resolution in several collections, including *When Talk Works: Profiles of Master Mediators* and *Mediation in International Relations*.

Jacob Bercovitch is professor of international relations at the University of Canterbury in Christchurch, New Zealand. He received his doctorate from the London School of Economics and has taught at the University of London and Hebrew University in Jerusalem. His main interests are in the areas of mediation and international conflict resolution, and he has written or edited numerous articles and eight books on these subjects, most recently *Resolving International Conflicts* (Boulder, Colo.: Lynne Rienner, 1996) and *International Conflict Management, 1945–1995* (Washington, D.C.: Congressional Quarterly, forthcoming).

Richard B. Bilder is Burrus-Bascom Professor of Law at the University of Wisconsin-Madison. Educated at Williams College, Harvard University Law School, and Cambridge University, Professor Bilder served as an attorney in the Office of the Legal Adviser at the U.S. Department of State before entering teaching. Among other positions, Professor Bilder has served as vice-president of the American Society of International Law, on the Board of Editors of the *American Journal of International Law*, on the Executive Council of the Law of the Sea Institute, on U.S. delegations to international conferences, and as an arbitrator in international and domestic disputes. He is the author of *Managing the Risks of International Agreement* (Madison: University of Wisconsin Press, 1981) and a number of articles and other scholarly publications.

Daniel Druckman is principal study director at the National Research Council in Washington, D.C. and professor of conflict management at George Mason University. Previously, he was Mathtech scientist at Mathematica, Inc., senior program manager at Booz, Allen, and Hamilton, and a research scholar at the International Institute of Applied Systems Analysis in Laxenburg, Austria. He has been a consultant to the Foreign Service Institute, the U.S. Arms Control and Disarmament Agency, and the United States Institute of Peace. Professor Druckman's numerous publications cover such topics as conflict resolution and negotiation, nationalism, group processes, nonverbal communication, and modeling methodologies. He received the 1995 Otto Klineberg Intercultural and International Relations Award from the Society for the Psychological Study of Social Issues for his work on nationalism.

Ronald J. Fisher is professor of psychology and founding coordinator of the Applied Social Psychology Graduate Program at the University of Saskatchewan in Saskatoon. Professor Fisher received his Ph.D. in social psychology from the University of Michigan. His major works include *Social Psychology: An Applied Approach* (St. Martin's Press, 1982), *The Social Psychology of Intergroup and International Conflict Resolution* (Springer-Verlag, 1990), and *Interactive Conflict Resolution* (Syracuse University Press, 1996). In addition to numerous chapters and articles in psychology journals, he has published in many of the leading interdisciplinary journals, including *Journal of Conflict Resolution*, *Negotiation Journal*, *International Journal of Conflict Management*, *Journal of Social Issues*, *Journal of Peace Research*, *Peace and Change*, and *Political Psychology*. His primary interest is in third-party interventions directed toward protracted social conflicts at the intergroup and international levels.

Cameron R. Hume is Minister-Counselor for Political Affairs at the U.S. Mission to the United Nations. Previous assignments include Italy, Tunisia, Syria, Lebanon, the Holy See, desk officer for South Africa, and member of the U.S. Secretary of State's Policy Planning Staff. He has been a fellow at the Council on Foreign Relations and at Harvard's Center for International Affairs, and a guest scholar at the United States Institute of Peace. He is the author of numerous articles and two books, *The United Nations, Iran, and Iraq: How Peacekeeping Changed* (Indiana University Press) and *Ending Mozambique's War* (U.S. Institute of Peace Press).

Herbert C. Kelman is the Richard Clarke Cabot Professor of Social Ethics at Harvard University and director of the Program on International Conflict Analysis and Resolution at Harvard's Center for International Affairs. His major publications include *International Behavior: A Social-Psychological Analysis* (editor, 1965), *A Time to Speak: On Human Values and Social Research* (1968), and *Crimes of Obedience: Toward a Social Psychology of Authority and Responsibility* (with V. Lee Hamilton, 1989). He has been engaged for many years in an action research program focusing on the Arab-Israeli conflict, with special emphasis on its Israeli-Palestinian dimension.

Louis Kriesberg is professor of sociology and Maxwell Professor of Social Conflict Studies at Syracuse University, where he also served as the founding director of the Program on the Analysis and Resolution of Conflicts from 1986 to 1994. In addition to over eighty book chapters and articles, Professor Kriesberg's writings include *Social Processes in International Relations, Social Conflicts, Intractable Conflicts and Their Transformation, Timing the De-Escalation of International Conflicts,* and *International Conflict Resolution.* Professor Kriesberg has also provided consultation or training on various aspects of conflict resolution for numerous organizations.

Andrew S. Natsios is vice president of the nongovernmental organization (NGO) World Vision U.S. and executive director of its technical arm, World Vision Relief and Development, both headquartered in Washington, D.C. Natsios was assistant administrator for the U.S. Agency for International Development's Bureau of Food and Humanitarian Assistance during 1991–93. Previously, he was director of the agency's Office of Foreign Disaster Assistance, responsible for managing the U.S. government's response to humanitarian and natural disasters abroad. He is the author of numerous articles on NGOs and international humanitarian-relief efforts.

J. Lewis Rasmussen is a program officer in the Education and Training Program at the United States Institute of Peace and played a principal role in developing the Institute's International Conflict Resolution Skills Training (ICREST) program for representatives of the U.S. and foreign governments and international governmental and nongovernmental organizations. He is also responsible for a variety of activities related to the interaction of political, military, and humanitarian actors in the prevention, management, and resolution of violent conflict. Among his publications is *Simulating a Diplomatic Negotiation: Conflict Resolution in the Middle East,* co-written with Ambassador Robert Oakley.

Cynthia Sampson is an associate of the Institute for Peacebuilding at Eastern Mennonite University in Harrisonburg, Virginia. She is an author and coeditor of two volumes of case studies on religiously motivated peacebuilding, *Religion, The Missing Dimension of Statecraft* (Oxford University Press) and *From the Ground Up: Mennonite Contributions to International Peacebuilding* (forthcoming). Ms. Sampson has worked with the conflict transformation program of the World Conference on Religion and Peace, as research coordinator of the Religion and Conflict Resolution Project at the Center for Strategic and International Studies, and as an international affairs editor at the *Christian Science Monitor.*

I. William Zartman is the Jacob Blaustein Professor of International Organization and Conflict Resolution and director of the African Studies and Conflict Management programs at the Johns Hopkins University's Paul H. Nitze School of

Advanced International Studies in Washington, D.C. Professor Zartman serves on the editorial boards for many professional journals on conflict studies and has written or edited numerous articles and books on the theory and practice of international conflict management, including his most recent edited works, *Governance as Conflict Management: Politics and Violence in West Africa* and *Sovereignty as Responsibility: Conflict Management in Africa* (Brookings Institution, 1996), and (with Victor A. Kremenyuk) *Cooperative Security: Reducing Third World Wars* (Syracuse University Press, 1995).

INDEX

PEACEMAKING IN INTERNATIONAL CONFLICT
METHODS & TECHNIQUES

This book is set in Goudy; the display type is Twentieth Century. Hasten Design Studio, Inc. designed the book's cover, and Joan Engelhardt and Day W. Dosch designed the interior. Day Dosch also did page makeup. Unless otherwise noted, the figures in this book were done by Kenneth P. Allen.